Adventures on America's Public Lands

Edited by Mary E. Tisdale and Bibi Booth

United States Department of the Interior
Bureau of Land Management

SMITHSONIAN BOOKS

Washington and London

© 2003 by the Smithsonian Institution
All rights reserved

Library of Congress Cataloging-in-Publication Data

Adventures on America's public lands / edited by Mary E. Tisdale and Bibi Booth.
       p.   cm.
    Expanded, updated ed. of: Beyond the national parks. 1998
    Includes index.
    ISBN 1-58834-081-3 (pbk.: alk. paper)
    1. Outdoor recreation —West (U.S.) Guidebooks.   2. Public lands —West (U.S.)—Guidebooks.   3. Wilderness areas—West (U.S.)—Guidebooks.   4. West (U.S.)—Guidebooks.   I. Tisdale, Mary E.   II. Booth, Bibi.   III. Beyond the national parks.

GV191.42.W47B49   2003
917.804 ' 34—dc21

                             2003041448

British Library Cataloguing-in-Publication Data available

Manufactured in the United States of America
10 09 08 07 06 05 04 03   5 4 3 2 1

(∞) The paper used in this publication meets the minimum requirements of the American National Standard for Information Sciences— Permanence of Paper for Printed Library Materials ANSI Z39.48-1984.

For permission to reproduce illustrations appearing in this book, please correspond directly with the Bureau of Land Management. Smithsonian Books does not retain reproduction rights for these illustrations individually, or maintain a file of addresses for photo sources.

PUBLISHER'S NOTE: Every attempt has been made to verify the accuracy of the information contained in this guidebook. If you discover errors, please write to Editor, *Adventures on America's Public Lands*, Bureau of Land Management, Office of Environmental Education and Volunteers, 1849 C Street, N.W. (LS-406), Washington, D.C. 20240.

DESIGN: Brian Barth
GRAPHICS AND LAYOUT: Jennifer Kapus
PRODUCTION: Martha Sewall
SEPARATIONS AND PRINTING: World Color Press

Photographic sequence:
(cover photo) Visitors to Oregon's Cascade-Siskiyou National Monument are treated to a spectacular view of volcanic Mt. McLoughlin, at 9,495 feet southern Oregon's tallest peak. *(John Craig, BLM Oregon State Office)*

(page i) Stair-step waterfalls, lacy ferns, and emerald beds of moss greet visitors to Swiftwater Recreation Site, the starting point of Oregon's North Umpqua Wild and Scenic River Corridor. *(John Craig, BLM Oregon State Office)*

(pages ii-iii) A backpacker takes a moment to savor Utah's breathtaking San Rafael Swell from a vantage point on The Wedge Overlook *(Jerry Sintz, BLM Utah State Office (retired))*

(pages iv-v) "Off the beaten path" is not just an expression in Utah's Grand Staircase-Escalante National Monument: most of its 1.9 million acres are devoid of trails. Here, two hikers forge their own course across the tawny swirls and waves of lithified sand dunes. *(Jerry Sintz, BLM Utah State Office (retired))*

(page vi) Metate Arch and eerie sandstone "hoodoos" decorate the Devils Garden in Utah's Grand Staircase-Escalante National Monument. These unique landforms developed when water seeped into vertical cracks in sedimentary rocks, which were then subject to winter "freeze-and-thaw" weathering. Wind has further sculpted the rock into fantastic shapes. *(Jerry Sintz, BLM Utah State Office (retired))*

Attractions by State

Appendices

(page xi, Acknowledgments) **The frosty peaks and extensive glaciers of the rugged Alaska Range are visible from nearly every portion of the Denali Highway. Among the chain's snow-capped mountains is 20, 320-foot Mt. McKinley, the highest mountain in North America.** (Dennis R. Green, BLM volunteer, Alaska State Office)

(page 1, Introduction) **Colorful shales and sandstones form skirts around the buttes and spires of Castle Valley, near Moab, Utah. The fancifully named "Priests and Nuns" towers are silhouetted in the background.** (Jerry Sintz, BLM Utah State Office (retired))

(page 9, Doing Your Part) **A BLM-Arizona volunteer and his son use a formerly wild burro, "adopted" from BLM and now a companion animal, as an alternative to hauling equipment on their own backs. More and more families, boldly taking along babies and young children on back country wilderness trips, are embracing the concept of pack animals.** (BLM)

(page 13, Welcome to Our World) **Sixth graders visiting Alaska's Campbell Creek Science Center pan for gold at one of six learning stations set up for spring Outdoor Week classes, an annual event.** (Ed Bovy, BLM Alaska State Office)

CONTRIBUTING BLM WRITERS/EDITORS

Washington, DC, Headquarters: Bibi Booth, Carolyn Cohen, Shelly Fischman, Kevin Flynn, Elizabeth Rieben, Mary E. Tisdale, Betsy Wooster

Alaska: Ed Bovy, Marcia Butoroc, Gene Ervine, Jim Herriges, Craig McCaa, KJ Mushovic

Arizona: Don Applegate, Bruce Asbjorn, Tina Bonilla, Dave Boyd, Lorraine Buck, Lori Cook, Diane Drobka, Nancy Guerrero, Becky Hammond, Rich Hanson, Jim Mahoney, Francisco Mendoza, Tom Schnell, Karen Simms, Carol Telles, Carrie Templin, Diane Williams, Bonnie Winslow

California: Jeff Fontana, Larry Mercer, Doran Sanchez

Colorado: Arden Anderson, Greg Gnesios, Heather Goodroe, Glade Hadden, LouAnn Jacobson, Diana Kossnar, Tina McDonald, Barb Perkins

Eastern States: Charles Bush, Donna Jones, Sylvia Jordan, Martha Malik, Patricia Tyler, Geoffrey Walsh, Faye Winters

Idaho: Bill Boggs, Wade Brown, Jeff Christenson, Shelley Davis-Brunner, David Freiburg, Bill Hagdorn, Frank Jenks, Jennifer E. Jones, LuVerne Grussing, Antonia Hedrick, Terry Kincaid, Blaine Newman, Larry Ridenhour, Kay Schiepan, Pete Sozzi, Dennis Thompson, Monica Zimmerman, Judi Zuckert

Montana/Dakotas: Ann Boucher

Nevada: Anna Atkinson, Barb Keleher, Terry Knight, Chip Kramer, JoLynn Worley

New Mexico: John Bailey, Paul Happel, Theresa Herrera, John Roney, Peg Sorensen, Dwayne Sykes, Kathy Walter

Oregon/Washington: Liz Aleman, Mark Armstrong, Lori Baker, Becky Brown, Keith Brown, Priscila Franco, Maya Fuller, Laura Graves, Trish Hogervorst, Doug Huntington, Saundra

Miles, Gregg Morgan, Ken White, Margaret Wolf
Utah: Kim Bartel, Laurie Bryant, Cimarron Chacon, Robin Fehlau, Glenn Foreman, Suzanne Garcia, Tom Gnojek, Stew Jacobson, Tina King, Britta Laub, Mike Leschin, Chris McAlear, Chad Niehaus, Marilyn Peterson, Katie Stevens, Craig Trinkle, Dennis Willis

Wyoming: Mary Apple, Eve Bennett, Shirley Bye-Jech, Jude Carino, Krystal Clair, Lesley Collins, Mark Goldbach, Ray Hanson, Gayle Irwin, Gary Long, Stephanie Sironen, Andy Tenney, Janine Terry, Cindy Wertz

GRAPHICS AND LAYOUT
Jennifer Kapus, National Science and Technology Center, Denver, CO

MAP REVIEW
Shelly Fischman, Washington, DC, Headquarters

TECHNICAL SUPPORT
Kevin Flynn, Washington, DC, Headquarters

SPECIAL THANKS TO:
- BLM Director Kathleen Clarke
- BLM Management, including Bob Johns, Acting Assistant Director for Communications; Celia Boddington, Group Manager, Public Affairs Group; Rodger Schmitt, Group Manager, Recreation Group *(retired)*; Bob Ratcliffe, Deputy Group Manager, Recreation Group; and the members of the BLM Executive Leadership Team
- The staff of the BLM Washington Office Public Affairs Group
- The staff of the BLM Washington Office Recreation Group
- The staff of the BLM National Landscape Conservation System
- The staff of Smithsonian Books, particularly Science Editor Vincent Burke *(retired)*; Managing Editor Duke Johns *(retired)*; Assistant Editor Nicole Sloan; Designers Brian Barth and Janice Wheeler; and Marketing Manager Kiki Forsythe.

Equestrian tourists gain a unique view of Oregon public lands and are able to travel longer distances than most hikers. *(Frank Lang, BLM Medford District Office)*

With its tree-covered banks, blue waters, and abundant "Blue Ribbon" trout, the Lower Blackfoot River offers some of the best floating and fishing in Montana. *(BLM Montana State Office)*

RIGHT A father and son finish setting up tents for a family campout on public lands in Oregon. *(BLM)*

LEFT **The Ruby Canyon stretch of the Colorado River carries boaters along the northern boundary of the Black Ridge Canyons Wilderness, through beautiful red rock canyons and the 1.5 billion-year-old metamorphic "Black Rocks." Notable wildlife includes bald eagles, peregrine falcons, and the occasional desert bighorn sheep.** *(Greg Gnesios, BLM Grand Junction Field Office)*

LOWER LEFT **The public lands offer challenges in spectacular settings for bikers of all abilities.** *(BLM)*

LOWER RIGHT **Nurtured by perennial Aravaipa Creek, large sycamore, ash, cottonwood, and willow trees flourish in Arizona's Aravaipa Canyon, providing welcome shade for a solitary horseback rider.** *(Beth Perault, BLM Arizona State Office)*

Rafters float the Rio Chama Wild and Scenic River against a backdrop of towering cliffs and heavily wooded side canyons. A major tributary of the Rio Grande, the river's colorful canyon is 1,500 feet deep along some stretches. *(BLM New Mexico State Office)*

FOR STARTERS

They are the places you know about and the places you never imagined—cacti and canyons, arroyos and outcrops, glacial ice fields and frozen tundra, wide-open vistas and solitary hideaways. They are your public lands, and they comprise a whopping 260 million acres of the United States—fully one-eighth of our nation's land area. Managed for multiple uses, our resource-rich public lands provide our nation with vital commodities as well as increasingly rare open space and critical wildlife habitat.

This book offers you a tantalizing glimpse of lands that are as intriguing and diverse as America itself. Public lands host a wide variety of outstanding, yet relatively unknown, places to hike, camp, fish, hunt, mountain bike, watch wildlife, pursue adventure sports, or just kick back and relax.

The Bureau of Land Management (BLM), a Federal agency within the U.S. Department of the Interior, manages these vast lands, and BLM employees from across the country serve as their proud, dedicated, and ardent custodians. In fact, our employees are so eager to share their enthusiasm for the public lands that they have carefully selected their personal "best bets" for inclusion here—favorite places on the public lands that offer exceptional (and, often, one-of-a-kind) opportunities for outdoor recreation. This book highlights these special places in hopes of sparking your interest in exploring, enjoying, and preserving your spectacular public lands.

WHAT ARE BLM PUBLIC LANDS?

Today's public lands are the remnants of the vast, Federally-owned tracts that were once known as the public domain, located mostly west of the Mississippi River and in Florida. During the 18th and 19th centuries, national policy provided for the eventual transfer of many of these lands to private ownership in order to build an economic foundation, encourage settlement of the West, and unite the boundless expanses of American territory into one nation. Of the original 1.8 billion acres of public domain, almost two-thirds ultimately went to citizens, corporations, and U.S. states during this period. Many of the remaining lands eventually were set aside as national forests, wildlife refuges, and national parks and monuments.

A large portion of the lands not devoted to these other purposes were designated simply as "public lands," the lands that would eventually come under the administration of BLM. (It is important to note that as used in this guide, the term "public lands" refers solely to those lands managed by the Bureau of Land Management, and generally, information is included for BLM-managed sites only.) In conjunction with lands managed by other Federal land management agencies, such as the National Park Service, the U.S. Forest Service, and the U.S. Fish & Wildlife Service, BLM public lands constitute a significant part of the network of superb Federal recreational opportunities offered to all Americans.

BLM: DECADES IN THE MAKING

In 1812, Congress established the General Land Office (GLO) to dispose of public domain lands. By 1870, however, a change in attitude about the potential national value of the re-maining unsettled lands led Congress to make the first moves toward public land preservation. The next several decades saw retention of essentially all of the Federal lands that are in existence today in the lower 48 states.

In 1934, the Taylor Grazing Act established the U.S. Grazing Service to manage grazing districts on 170 million acres of the public domain that were designated as public rangelands. Finally, on July 16, 1946, in an effort toward more efficient administration of the nation's natural resources, President Harry Truman officiated over a "marriage" of sorts, merging the GLO and the Grazing Service to create the Bureau of Land Management.

The new agency had a daunting task: to enforce thousands of laws — many mutually conflicting — while managing the resources on what was then more than 400 million acres of public lands spread mostly throughout 12 western states and Alaska. Ultimately, more than a third of those 400 million acres would be transferred to the control of other administrative entities in furtherance of national and Alaska Native interests.

By 1976, Congress had sorted out conflicting authorities and gave BLM a clear set of marching orders (termed a

Overnight trekkers in Aravaipa Canyon hike through a thriving Arizona desert streamside area that sustains javelinas, coatimundis, and more than 200 species of birds. *(Diane Drobka, BLM Safford Field Office)*

"mandate") with passage of the Federal Land Policy and Management Act (FLPMA) of 1976. This was welcome news: BLM now had the flexibility and discretion to manage the public lands for the benefit of all Americans—present and future with an innovative management policy of "multiple use and sustained yield." A 2001 reexamination of FLPMA in connection with the 25th anniversary of its passage decisively affirmed that the law still provided "the right mission for our time."

PUBLIC REWARDS FROM OUR PUBLIC LANDS

Public lands generate over $1 billion in revenue for the nation each year, while providing Americans with such necessities as coal, oil and gas, forest products, and livestock forage. At the local level, rural western communities benefit greatly from the economic fruits of such "working landscapes" through increases in employment and tax payments.

While commodity production and revenue are, of course, important, the public lands also host some of the nation's most remarkable landscapes and ecosystems. These areas are prized for their recreational, aesthetic, and scientific values, and often play a critical role in habitat and resource conservation efforts.

The public lands are home to over 3,000 species of wildlife and a wide array of plants, some of which are threatened or endangered. BLM also protects an estimated 4 million archaeological and historic sites — from the campsites of America's earliest human inhabitants to the historic ghost towns of the Old West. You can access additional information about these wonders via BLM's national Environmental Education Program website at *www.blm.gov/education*.

The challenges facing BLM in the 21st century are those associated with managing public lands in a fast-growing and ever-changing American West, where once-remote places are now within a short drive of population centers. The public lands have become some of the last remaining destinations for seekers of open space and outdoor pursuits. In fact, some of these places are so unique that they have been

Steele Creek Roadhouse, in Alaska's Fortymile region, is a picturesque reminder of the state's many 19th-century gold rushes. (BLM)

afforded special status and are managed almost exclusively to conserve their scientific, cultural, educational, ecological, and other values.

BLM's NATIONAL LANDSCAPE CONSERVATION SYSTEM

Many of BLM's prime conservation and recreation lands are now included in the agency's National Landscape Conservation System (NLCS). This system, created in June 2000, is an organized network of special places managed to ensure that their outstanding resources are preserved, protected, and enhanced for future generations.

All units included in the NLCS have been designated by Congressional act or by Presidential proclamation, and comprise: National Monuments (lands featuring historic landmarks, historic or pre-historic artifacts, unique geology, and/or other resources of cultural or scientific interest); National Conservation Areas (lands with exceptional natural, recreational, cultural, wildlife, aquatic, archaeological, paleontological, historical, educational, and/or scientific resources); Wilderness and Wilderness Study Areas; National Scenic and Historic Trails; and Wild and Scenic Rivers.

The NLCS provides BLM with the framework to both raise awareness of and protect these lands in order to ensure that the public will be able to experience their solitude and splendor, both now and in the future. Several of these special places are highlighted in the State chapters of this book; look for the NLCS icon. (Please see below for more about our activity icons.)

TIME TO EXPLORE YOUR 262-MILLION-ACRE BACKYARD!

Public lands really do belong to you and to all Americans. As with any backyard, big or small, the best way to learn about and enjoy it is firsthand. Why not get out there and walk across it, smell the air, hear the sounds, touch the earth? Get to know your public lands and you're bound to develop a personal connection and commitment to these special places.

During your visit, please be a good steward. Follow rules that call for packing out trash and avoiding disturbance of plants, wildlife, artifacts, and natural features. And while BLM invites you to make recreational use of the public lands, please remember that many of these places are wild and undeveloped —which often means that no amenities or creature comforts are available. This book will help you to understand what to expect, and prepare you for a safe, enjoyable, and memorable recreation experience.

WHAT'S NEW AND IMPROVED IN THIS GUIDE

Adventures on the Public Lands is an expanded, updated rendition of *Beyond the National Parks*, the highly popular, first-of-its-kind BLM recreation guide published in 1998. So what's new for the *Adventures* reader? Plenty. To begin with, there's a fresh, improved design that makes the book easier to use and navigate: among other enhancements, we've added new fonts, headers, and color coding of State chapters.

Each site profile now also provides a web address and contains a new category, "Special Features," which describes especially compelling or unique natural or cultural resources you'll find at the site. And RVers will be pleased to note that RV facilities are addressed in the "Camping and Lodging" section of each profile.

The guide now includes 178 sites, of which 49 are new selections; and many of the site profiles retained from *Beyond the National Parks* have been enhanced with expanded descriptions and new photos. Several new NLCS units are included, in part or in their entirety, in site profiles. And we've included even more activity icons, easy-to-recognize pictographs that tell visitors at a glance what types of recreation are in store at a particular site. There are 26 icons now, including one denoting NLCS units; that's nearly double the number in the previous edition, providing a lot more detail. (Please see the end of this introduction for a complete chart of icons and their meanings.)

HOW THIS GUIDE IS ORGANIZED

In the first portion of *Adventures*, we take a thematic approach to public lands recreation. In a series of two-page presentations, 18 groupings of recreational activities on the public lands are described. Included with each activity overview is a list of "favorites," prime recreation spots recommended by BLM employees. Several of the overviews also provide ethics sidebars on how to be a safe and responsible recreationist while enjoying the activities in that category.

Later in the book, we take a geographic approach that showcases sites in state groupings; each section opens with a state map that displays site vicinities. If you're seeking several sites that are close to one another, here's where to look. Information presented in site profiles includes location maps; directions; required fees; contact information; locations of nearest camping, lodging,

Nicknamed "Singing Mountain" by dune enthusiasts and playing a central role in several Pauite myths, Nevada's Sand Mountain features shifting quartz sands that often produce a low-frequency booming sound—best appreciated during a hair-raising slide down the gigantic dune's steep face. (*Bob Goodman*)

and supplies; and wheelchair accessibility. (Please note that we are continually striving to improve the accessibility of our developed recreation sites to persons of all abilities. Visitors should contact BLM office(s) to inquire about enhancements made at sites of interest since publication of this guide.) Since many sites offer more than one type of recreation, the activity icons at the end of each site profile are valuable as a quick-reference tool for those seeking either diverse or related activities.

Because the vicinity and location maps in this guide are not drawn to

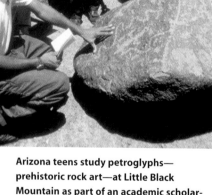

Arizona teens study petroglyphs— prehistoric rock art—at Little Black Mountain as part of an academic scholarship competition hosted by BLM.
(John Beckett, Beckett & Beckett Photography)

scale and may not display some smaller routes, we encourage visitors to carry detailed state maps or road atlases, and to refer to the text directions provided in each site write-up.

PLAN AHEAD AND BE PREPARED

The public lands offer unparalleled opportunities to recreate "off the beaten path"—but with these adventures come responsibilities. Whatever your choice of activities, please take steps to minimize your impact. (Please see the next section for "Leave No Trace," "Tread Lightly!," and other outdoor ethics guidelines.)

Many of the sites in this guide are located in wonderfully remote areas, so campsites are often undeveloped. In some instances, the nearest help and supplies may be hundreds of miles away. Many roads require four-wheel-drive vehicles and may be treacherous in certain types of weather.

To ensure a safe and enjoyable trip, please take sensible precautions. Prepare for weather extremes, and educate yourself about the hazards posed by poisonous plants and animals. Realize that at some point you will become hungry and thirsty, and possibly cold or hot, and pack accordingly. Pay attention to the advisories included in some of our site profiles. If you are planning to venture into a back country area, become familiar with back country rules and carry first aid supplies and other necessities. And always let someone know your itinerary.

In the course of planning your visit, contact the BLM office closest to your destination (see the "Contact Information" section of site profiles) to obtain detailed maps. Topographic maps are available from the U.S. Geological Survey; please telephone 1-800-HELPMAP, or visit *mcmcweb.er.usgs.gov/topomaps/ ordering_maps.html* for online map searches and orders.

A little careful planning will help make your outings both enjoyable and safe!

WANT MORE INFORMATION?

This guide is a tribute to the diversity of the public lands and the recreational activities they offer. But the profiles included here convey just a fraction of the fun and adventures that can be had out there in your 262-million-acre backyard. If you'd like more information, Appendices A and B will certainly point you in the right direction.

BLM PARTNERS, VOLUNTEERS, AND "FRIENDS"

Each year, partner organizations, "Friends" groups, cooperating associations, and more than 17,000 volunteers contribute to the care of our public lands by performing work that supports BLM programs. From the very young to the very old, they take part as individuals, families, groups, and organizations. These special helpers conduct scientific and restorative work at far-flung sites, serve as long-term campground hosts, provide administrative support in some of BLM's busiest offices, present interpretive and educational programs, operate bookstores, host information and visitor centers at remote locations, and frequently serve as BLM's sole "ambassadors" to local communities.

Many prominent success stories attest to the undeniable effectiveness of BLM's "second workforce." A few of the many shining examples of cooperative achievements profiled in this book alone are: Red Rock Canyon National Conservation Area, a desert showcase site just outside of Las Vegas; the Anasazi Heritage Center, a preeminent archaeology museum within Colorado's Canyons of the Ancients National Monument; and Oregon's National Historic Oregon Trail Interpretive Center, a noted educational resource for students of early American westward expansion and pioneer settlement.

A Florida Girl Scout plants mangrove seedlings as part of a volunteer wetlands restoration project at Jupiter Inlet Natural Area. *(Faye Winters, BLM Jackson Field Office)*

WE CAN ALWAYS USE MORE HELP . . .

BLM volunteers consistently report a sense of great satisfaction at "giving something back" to the public lands they love so dearly. If you are interested in learning about BLM volunteer opportunities, there are several avenues available to you:

- Write to, call, or fax individual BLM offices. (Please see Appendix A for contact information.)
- Visit the national BLM Volunteer Program website at *www.blm.gov/volunteer*, which provides web links to BLM State volunteer opportunities and e-mail links to BLM State Volunteer Coordinators.
- Visit Volunteer.gov, the national Federal interagency volunteer opportunity website located at *www/volunteer.gov/gov*, which enables prospective volunteers to search Federal volunteer opportunities using a variety of parameters and apply for positions online.
- Contact a national or local conservation group or organization to inquire about volunteer projects being conducted on public lands. BLM partner organizations are noted in some of our site profiles.

A FEW ABBREVIATIONS AND OUR 26 ACTIVITY ICONS

Three abbreviations that are frequently used in this book are:

RV = recreational vehicle
OHV = off-highway vehicle
ATV = all-terrain vehicle

For your convenience, here is a guide to the 26 activity icons used in the site profiles in the second half of this book:

ACTIVITY ICONS

All-terrain Vehicle Trail

Archaeological Site

Biking

Birdwatching

BLM Back Country Byway

Dirt Bike Trail

Fishing

Fossil Viewing

Four-wheel-drive Trail

Geologic Sightseeing

Hiking

Historic Site

Horseback Riding

Hunting

Interpreted Site

Motor Boating

National Landscape Conservation System

Non-motorized Boating

Picnic Area

Plant Viewing

Rafting

Sailing

Swimming

Wildlife Viewing

Wild Horse or Burro Viewing

Winter Sports

America's diverse and beautiful public lands are a wonder to experience, but they can also be fragile and highly sensitive to human visitation. It is important for outdoor recreationists, adventurers, and other visitors to do their part in safeguarding the public lands' irreplaceable natural and cultural resources. Following a few basic guidelines (and, of course, using a little common sense) will ensure that you fully enjoy your favorite outdoor activities, while also gaining the satisfaction of helping to preserve the lands that offer them.

NON-MOTORIZED ACTIVITY ETHICS: LEAVE NO TRACE

The Leave No Trace Center for Outdoor Ethics, a national, non-profit organization, offers these guidelines to help you to both stay safe and minimize your impacts while enjoying the outdoors:

Plan Ahead and Prepare— Know Before You Go!

- Know the regulations and special concerns for the area you are visiting.
- Prepare for extreme weather, hazards, and emergencies.
- Obtain and use a map of the area.
- Visit in small groups.
- Schedule your visit to avoid periods of high use.

Camp and Travel on Durable Surfaces— Choose the Right Path

- Durable surfaces include established trails and campsites, rock, gravel, dry grasses, and snow.
- Set up camp at least 200 feet from lakes and streams to protect sensitive areas.
- Remember: good campsites are found, not made.

Dispose of Waste Properly— Pack It In, Pack It Out!

- Take all trash, leftover food, and litter out with you.
- Properly dispose of what you can't pack out.

- Dig "catholes," the most widely accepted method of outdoor solid human waste disposal, when established latrines are not available. (Holes should be a few inches deep, 4–6 inches across, and at least 200 feet from obvious water channels.)

Leave What You Find
- Leave rocks, plants, archaeological and historic artifacts, fossils, and other objects of interest for others to discover.
- Preserve the past: examine, but do not touch, cultural or historic artifacts and structures.

Minimize Campfire Impacts
- Carry a cookstove, an essential piece of equipment for minimum-impact camping.
- Leave no evidence of your campfire.
- When possible, build your fire within an existing fire ring.
- Keep campfires small, and don't burn any longer than necessary.
- Allow wood to burn completely to ash.
- Put out fires with water, not dirt.

Respect Wildlife
- Remember: you are a visitor in their outdoor home.
- Learn about wildlife through quiet observation, and observe from afar.
- Don't feed wild animals; eating human food can upset their feeding cycles and habits and might encourage them to approach humans.

Be Considerate of Other Visitors
- Be courteous: Yield to other users on the trail and elsewhere.

- Listen to nature and avoid loud noises.

For more information on Leave No Trace principles, activity-specific ethics guidelines, and educational programs, please visit the Leave No Trace Center for Outdoor Ethics website at *www.lnt.org* or telephone (303) 442-8222.

MOTORIZED VEHICLE ACTIVITY ETHICS: TREAD LIGHTLY!

Tread Lightly! is a national, non-profit outdoor ethics organization that emphasizes low-impact principles. The organization's sole purpose is to educate motorized-vehicle riders and other recreationists to exercise responsible outdoor practices so that the great outdoors will be accessible, open, and well preserved for years to come. The organization's guidelines for responsible outdoor recreation, following the letters in "**T-R-E-A-D**," are:

Travel and recreate with minimum impact:
- Stay on designated trails and routes; resist the urge to create new trails and routes.
- Travel only on land and water surfaces that are open to your type of recreation.

Respect the environment and the rights of others:
- Respect designated wilderness areas by traveling only on foot or horseback.
- Be courteous to other users of the lands and waters by minimizing noise.

Educate yourself and plan and prepare before you go:

- Obtain information, maps, and proper equipment to make your trip safe.
- Know the local laws and regulations.
- Ask owners' permission to cross private property.
- Comply with all signs and barriers, and leave gates as you found them.

Allow for future use of the outdoors—leave it in better condition than you found it:

- Avoid sensitive areas, such as riparian (streamside) areas, lakeshores, and meadows, at all times.
- Cross streams only at fords where the road or trail intersects the streams; do not travel in stream channels.

- Climb hills only in designated areas to avoid new hillside scarring.
- Avoid disturbances to wildlife and livestock.

Discover the rewards of responsible recreation:

- Help preserve the beauty and resources of our public lands and waters for current and future generations by recreating responsibly.

For more information on Tread Lightly! principles, activity-specific ethics guidelines, and educational programs, please visit the Tread Lightly! website at *www.treadlightly.org* or telephone 1-800-966-9900.

In four-wheel-drive vehicles, modern-day pioneers explore one of the California desert's less-traveled historic roads. Well versed in "Tread Lightly!" ethics, these drivers are careful to stay on designated routes. *(Doran Sanchez, California Desert District)*

Backpackers establish a primitive camp below the layered cliffs of Utah's Grand Staircase-Escalante National Monument. *(Jerry Sintz, BLM Utah State Office (retired))*

BLM employees take pride in being the stewards of America's vast public lands. As the agency's on-the-ground caretakers, we've developed a special, intimate relationship with the spectacular resources in our charge. Working in cooperation with dedicated private partner organizations, we stand by our commitment to preserve our public lands' irreplaceable natural and cultural legacies, while also inviting the public to enjoy the exceptional variety of recreational opportunities these lands present. After all, the best way to gain an appreciation for—and under-standing of—these treasures is to get out and experience their splendor for yourself.

Lush wilderness areas, pristine trout streams, challenging off-highway-vehicle trails, intriguing petroglyphs, wild whitewater, world-class rock-climbing —if it's out there on the public lands, you can bet you'll find it represented in the following pages. Employees from every BLM State have chosen places that truly shine in their eyes, as well as those of the public. Tried and true, these sites promise to refresh, exhilarate, restore, educate, and inspire.

And while BLMers join visitors in relishing the recreational opportunities offered by the outstanding lands within our care, we are also dedicated to the serious business of focusing public attention on our mutual responsibility for their conservation. The selections presented in this guidebook have been determined to be suitable for recreational visitation at this time. Nevertheless, in all cases, we ask that you visit these wonderful places gently, in order to safeguard their treasures for the generations to come.

We are confident that the information in this guide will enhance your enjoyment of America's bountiful public lands, and we hope that your visits to these special spots will inspire your commitment to preserving their health and productivity. Here's wishing you many seasons of happy recreation and a lifetime of outdoor learning!

Mountain bikers pause to take in the spectacular alpine scenery surrounding Utah's challenging Slickrock Bike Trail. *(Frank Jensen)*

SOME FAVORITES

Arizona Trail–Northern Trailhead (AZ)

Vulture Peak Trail (AZ)

Alabama Hills (CA)

Bizz Johnson National Recreation Trail (CA)

Kokopelli's Trail (CO)

Oregon Trail Historic Reserve and Bonneville Point (ID)

North Wildhorse Recreation Area (NV)

Red Rock Canyon National Conservation Area (NV)

Water Canyon Recreation Area (NV)

Glade Run Recreation Area (NM)

Molalla River Recreation Site (OR)

Row River Trail (OR)

Slickrock Bike Trail, Sand Flats Recreation Area (UT)

Continental Divide National Scenic Trail (WY)

Hang on to Your Handlebars
Bike Trails and Tours

The term "bike trail" takes on an entirely new meaning on western public lands. So make sure your helmet is buckled tightly, because you can be sure that rocks will be close at hand—whether you're tackling the slickrock mountain biking trails in Utah or rocky, single-track routes through Colorado's San Juan Mountains.

The steep, smooth rocks and dramatic views of Utah's Slickrock Bike Trail in the Sand Flats Recreation Area have become legendary for mountain bikers from around the world. Numerous other trails criss-cross the area, challenging riders of all abilities. Kokopelli's Trail, for instance, connects to the Slickrock Trail and runs for 140 miles from Moab, Utah, to Loma, Colorado, near Grand Junction. Each spring, thousands of mountain bikers converge on Fruita, Colorado, for a 4-day mountain biking festival that features BLM trails such as the Kokopelli.

If you're trying to get away from the mountain biking traffic jams, consider one of BLM's Back Country Byways or mountain roads. These areas are lightly traveled and have stunning scenery that rewards the extra effort. California's Alabama Hills, for example, has dramatic rock formations of weathered granite—somewhat gentler in slope than the nearby Sierra Nevada Mountains. Northeastern Nevada has become a popular mountain biking destination, even though there are few established trails. Here, you can ride through badlands, river canyons, mountain forests, or vast high-desert basins. Looking for a serious adventure? Try the "Bloody Shins" Trail, accessible from the Water Canyon Recreation Area near Winnemucca, Nevada. BLM has developed a comprehensive management plan for mountain biking to ensure that this popular sport will continue to be managed properly. Over the next few years, thousands of miles of new trails—on all types of terrain—are likely to be developed.

REMEMBER
- Wear a helmet, eye protection, and other safety gear.
- Ride only where permitted. Stay on the trail or road.
- Control your bike.
- Always yield the trail to those passing or traveling uphill.
- Cross streams at a 90° angle; better yet, dismount and walk your bike through moving water.
- Respect wildlife; avoid sensitive species and habitat.

FOR MORE INFORMATION
BLM Mountain Biking Strategic Action Plan: *www.blm.gov/mountain_ biking*

"Responsible Mountain Bike Riding," Tread Lightly!: *www.treadlightly.org/edu.mv*; click on "Recreation Tips"

"Mountain Bicycling," Leave No Trace: *www.lnt.org*.

A family savors the refreshing waters of a spring-fed pool, the natural centerpiece of a veritable oasis in the Nevada desert. *(Elvis Wall, BLM Ely District Office)*

SOME FAVORITES

Gila Box Riparian National Conservation Area (AZ)

Lake Havasu (AZ)

Parker Dam Road Back Country Byway (AZ)

San Simon Valley (AZ)

Sharkey Hot Springs, Lewis and Clark Back Country Byway and Adventure Road (ID)

Chain-of-Lakes Complex (MT)

Shotgun Creek (OR)

Yakima River Canyon (WA)

RIGHT **Oregon recreation sites offer swimming opportunities for visitors of all ages. Here, two friends enjoy a peaceful float on a deep lake created 1,400 years ago when a landslide's house-size boulders dammed a local creek.** *(Jim Brende, BLM Coos Bay Field Office)*

Go with the Flow
Paddling and Floating Adventures

So, you're primed to get your feet wet, as it were, and try some canoeing, kayaking, or river rafting? The public lands can offer you just the ticket, whether your fancy is a calm, relaxing float through spectacular scenery or a hair-raising canyon trip down some of the wildest torrents imaginable.

Idaho's Lower Salmon River, for example, is a 112-mile stretch of whitewater fury that hurtles through the second-deepest canyon in the nation. Closed to vehicle access for much of its length, the river provides a supremely invigorating wilderness experience — and Class II–V whitewater runs — for the bold water-lover. And what can one say about a Rio Grande section, just south of BLM's Orilla Verde Recreation Area in New Mexico, featuring challenges locally known as the "rock garden" and "BLM Racecourse"? Sheer heaven!

Or consider the 60 Class II and III rapids along Utah's Green River, which flows through rugged Desolation and Gray Canyons, the deepest in the state. An Oregon standout is the Rogue National Wild and Scenic River, a true adventurers' river so popular that BLM had to institute an annual lottery for rafting permits there. And the famous 14-mile "Giant Gap" run on the North Fork American River is one of California's top whitewater challenges, a roller-coaster ride through a historic gold-mining area overhung by 2,000-foot cliffs.

Calmer moments might inspire "river rats" to try a flatwater canoe trip through the Upper Missouri River Breaks. Here, a journey through beautiful scenery is enhanced by a healthy dose of history, as boaters lazily drift downriver on one of the routes used by explorers Lewis and Clark — to go *upstream*. Also in Montana is the aptly-named Chain-of-Lakes, a string of four manmade lakes along the Missouri River that are interspersed with segments of free-flowing water. And if just the thought of maneuvering a boat overwhelms you, one lake in that "chain" even provides guided boat tours.

The public lands offer non-motorized aquatic excursions for every taste, every skill level — and every degree of courage. A little advance browsing through the site descriptions in this guide will help you to design the wet-and-wild vacation of a lifetime.

REMEMBER

- Always wear an approved personal flotation device.
- Know your boat's limits and know the river or lake.
- Travel only in areas that are open to your type of watercraft.
- Gather information about river or lake ecology.
- Obtain a river or lake map.
- If traveling a whitewater river, make sure your skills are up to the rapids' ratings.
- File a trip plan or permit if required.
- Dress appropriately for the weather and length of trip.

FOR MORE INFORMATION

BLM National Wild & Scenic Rivers: *www.blm.gov/nlcs/rivers.htm*

"Western River Corridors," Leave No Trace: *www.lnt.org*

A fisherman helps his daughter reel in a big one at Arizona's Lake Pleasant, near Agua Fria National Monument. *(John Beckett, Beckett & Beckett Photography)*

SOME FAVORITES

Dalton Highway (AK)

Gulkana National Wild River (AK)

Steese National Conservation Area (AK)

Betty's Kitchen National Recreation
    Trail (AZ)

Lake Havasu (AZ)

Sacramento River–Bend Area (CA)

Gunnison Gorge National Conservation
    Area (CO)

Lower Salmon River (ID)

Lake Vermilion Public Islands (MN)

Chain-of-Lakes Complex (MT)

Lower Blackfoot River (MT)

North Wildhorse Recreation Area (NV)

Pine Forest Recreation Area (NV)

Black River (NM)

Orilla Verde Recreation Area (NM)

North Umpqua Wild and Scenic River
    Corridor (OR)

Whittaker Creek (OR)

Gone Fishin'
Terrific Angling Spots

Fishing is more than the fish you catch. It's a quiet source of delight in an often chaotic world. The anticipation, the sound of lapping water, the sight of insects in the sunlight: the rivers and streams on America's public lands offer a watershed of opportunities to indulge in these simple pleasures.

The swift waters of Oregon's North Umpqua Wild and Scenic River are famous for their seasonal runs of steelhead and salmon as they migrate upriver to spawn. The river's forested corridor provides breathtaking scenery, world-class fly fishing, and the company of diving ospreys. If you prefer to watch eagles soar while you fish, and appreciate seasonal flexibility, Nevada's Wildhorse Reservoir might be the right bait for you. It offers year-round opportunities, including winter fishing through foot-thick ice, and is a high-desert home to channel catfish, rainbow trout, German brown trout, and other trout species.

If merging some popular movie culture with your fishing fits the bill, venture to the Lower Blackfoot River in Montana, of "A River Runs Through It" fame. You won't glimpse Robert Redford or Brad Pitt—they're long gone from "the set." But the Lower Blackfoot's "Blue Ribbon" bull trout and west slope cutthroat trout should be enough to lure you there.

Dead set on "getting away from it all"? Try Alaska's Gulkana National Wild River for some excellent sport fishing, best done in late June and early July. Plan on doing battle with Chinook and sockeye salmon, grayling, and rainbow and steelhead trout. Or if you prefer amenities to the call of the wild, head over to Arizona's Lake Havasu. Black and striped bass, crappie, bluegill, catfish, and trout abound in Havasu's coves and inlets, while lineside bass can be found around the Parker Strip. On shore, there are docks, RV hookups, hotels, and all manner of modern conveniences.

Whether you land "The Big One" or return home empty-handed save for memories and a good fish story, the public lands offer opportunities to cast a line any time of the year.

REMEMBER
- Respect the environment.
- Know the catch limits and legal length of the fish you intend to catch.
- Practice "catch and release."
- Take only what you need.
- Dispose of fish viscera properly; do not dump in stream or lake.
- Dispose of unwanted and tangled fishing lines properly.

FOR MORE INFORMATION
"Responsible Fishing," Tread Lightly!: *www.treadlightly.org/edu.mv*; click on "Recreation Tips."

A flower-strewn meadow near home offers a visitor a prime opportunity to introduce his daughter to the wonders of the wild. *(BLM)*

Right in Your Own Backyard
Getaways Close to Home

If you yearn for a quick getaway from urban crowding and noise, just pack your gear and head out to one of the many sites on America's public lands that are a quick hop from major city centers. In an hour or less, you can be enjoying your pick of recreational activities.

Red Rock Canyon, just 20 miles from the lights and action of Las Vegas, offers enticements of a quieter kind. Lithified sand dunes, frozen in time, offer the visitor a close-up perspective of geologic features that have been millions of years in the making. Unexpected waterfalls cascading into the canyons exemplify the mysteries and hidden dangers of the Mojave Desert.

Only minutes away from Sacramento, California, the Cosumnes River Preserve is one of the few protected wetland habitat areas in the state, sheltering some of the last remnants of the magnificent oak groves that once proliferated in the Central Valley. Visitors here can take a hike along a designated trail, participate in one of the preserve's special excursions, or spend a weekend on a guided kayak trip. And just 17 miles southwest of Yuma, Arizona, Betty's Kitchen National Recreation Trail welcomes day visitors to a lush, shady spot along the Lower Colorado River. The area is perfect for a picnic lunch, fishing from the pier, or a stroll along the 0.5-mile interpretive trail.

Whether you're looking for adventure, solitude, or a little of each, you might just find it on public lands minutes from your own backyard. Check out the following list, or simply browse this guide to discover the perfect place to enjoy those few precious hours.

SOME FAVORITES
Betty's Kitchen National Recreation
    Trail (AZ)
Big Morongo Canyon (CA)
Cosumnes River Preserve (CA)
San Miguel River Corridor (CO)
Jupiter Inlet Natural Area (FL)
Oregon Trail Historic Reserve and
    Bonneville Point (ID)
Chain-of-Lakes Complex (MT)
Red Rock Canyon National
    Conservation Area (NV)
Cascade Streamwatch at Wildwood
    Recreation Site (OR)
North Umpqua Wild and Scenic River
    Corridor (OR)
Row River Trail (OR)
Meadowood (VA)

REMEMBER
- Respect other visitors and protect the quality of their outdoor experience.
- Let nature's sounds prevail; avoid loud voices and noises.
- Be courteous; yield to other users of trails and other recreation areas.

Colorado's Canyons of the Ancients National Monument contains the nation's greatest known concentration of archaeological sites, in some locations reaching a density of more than 100 sites per square mile. Cliff pueblos such as this one were used by the Ancestral Northern Puebloan People, who occupied the area from AD 450–1300. (*Robert Jensen*)

SOME FAVORITES

Agua Fria National Monument (AZ)
Murray Springs Clovis Site, San Pedro Riparian National Conservation Area (AZ)
Sears Point (AZ)
Fish Slough (CA)
Canyon Pintado National Historic District (CO)
Lowry Pueblo National Historic Landmark (CO)

Lower Salmon River (ID)
Grimes Point/Hidden Cave Archaeological Area (NV)
Red Rock Canyon National Conservation Area (NV)
Casamero Chacoan Outlier (NM)
Three Rivers Petroglyph Site (NM)

Echoes From the Past
Intriguing Archaeological Sites

Renowned archaeological sites — remnants of prehistoric human lives and lifestyles — have been discovered on public lands throughout the American West. At these special spots, visitors can study the remains of early New World civilizations, mostly in the form of ruins and artwork, or simply pay their respects to times and peoples gone by.

In AD 1060, for example, as the Normans were settling into England, the Lowry Pueblo was home to a community of farmers on what is now public land in Colorado. The people hunted small game, crafted pottery, wove cotton, and lived in masonry structures 3 stories high. In about AD 1300, these ancients, the Ancestral Puebloans, abandoned their homes. Why? We are left only with the ruins of their buildings and kivas to help us formulate answers.

Some 60 miles east of the bright lights of Reno, Nevada, the public lands at Grimes Point host an ancient art gallery. Adjacent to what was once Lake Lahontan, a large body of water that long ago succumbed to the desert, are some 1,000 basalt boulders adorned with four styles of petroglyphs. The rock art ranges from the abstract (patterns of holes and lines dating back some 3,500 years) to the representative (depictions of lizards and other animals that date back about 1,000 years). One

wonders if the designs were intended as pure art; whether or not the images had ceremonial, instructive, or religious significance; or if they were simply Stone Age graffiti. Sears Point, along the Gila River about 75 miles east of Yuma, Arizona, is close by the historic Butterfield Overland Mail Route and the Juan Bautista de Anza National Historic Trail. But earlier people also once followed these routes and dwelled nearby. The precise prehistory of Sears Point, dating back thousands of years, is left for us to read in the form of petroglyphs, sleeping circles, lithic scatters, astrological sites, rock shelters, shrines, and cairns.

Beautiful artwork, evocative ruins, and tantalizing prehistory: quite a potent enticement to those interested in our nation's distant past — before America *was* America. The premier archaeological sites featured in this guide invite you to weave some culture into your vacation with some leisurely time-traveling.

REMEMBER

- Preserve the past; leave cultural objects undisturbed.
- Let photos and drawings be your souvenirs.
- Avoid touching rock art panels — skin oils accelerate their deterioration.

The three-story Cook Bank building, the tallest structure in Rhyolite, Nevada, cost $90,000 to construct and furnish with imported marble floors, electric lights, and indoor plumbing. Now skeletal ruins, the Cook Bank is the most photographed ghost-town building in the West. *(Suzy McCoy, BLM volunteer, Tonopah Field Station)*

SOME FAVORITES

Route 66 Historic Back Country
  Byway (AZ)
Punta Gorda Lighthouse (CA)
Garnet Range Back Country
  Byway (MT)
Rhyolite Historic Area (NV)
Lake Valley Historic Site (NM)
Cape Blanco Lighthouse (OR)

National Historic Oregon Trail
  Interpretive Center (OR)
Rogue River Ranch (OR)
Yaquina Head Outstanding Natural
  Area (OR)
Fort Meade Recreation Area (SD)
National Historic Trails Interpretive
  Center (WY)

Travels Through Time
Outstanding Historic Sites

In all their astonishing variety, human endeavors and events of the past few centuries have left their imprints scattered across our public lands. Such remnants chronicle early Americans' efforts to explore and settle, develop and defend. If we but listen, our nation's past can reach across the years to speak of westward expansion, sudden prosperity, pioneer hardships, and episodes of conflict.

At Oregon's National Historic Oregon Trail Interpretive Center, for example, living-history programs incorporate monologues, events, and insights from actual emigrant diaries in order to capture the heartening—and heartbreaking—details of pioneer life. Rhyolite, Nevada, was a 19th-century, desert Gold Rush boomtown whose population grew to over 8,000 within only 4 years. Abandoned in 1911 and now often described as "the best ghost town in Nevada," the townsite is studded with old-timey buildings, including Nevada's best-preserved beer-bottle house. Montana's Fort Meade, the late 19th-century home of the U.S. Army's famed 7th Cavalry and the 10th Cavalry's "Buffalo Soldiers," welcomes visitors to several significant places, including its Cavalry Post, Cavalry Museum, and Post Cemetery. And the Roaring Twenties–vintage Route 66 was a decided improvement over the hodge-podge of rutted tracks and trails that had been serving travelers before its construction. A descendant of the early 1900s "National Old Trails Road," the two-lane route connected the Midwest to California, and became "the Main Street of America" in the process. Now long supplanted by interstates and other highways, the twisting, historic highway charms motor tourists, who retrace authentic sections of it to get a glimpse of the past.

Historic locations such as these help us to understand the saga of America and to delve into very different lives in very different times. If you're ready for a trip into the past, pick yourself a perfect period and setting, and get a move on: there's no time like the present!

REMEMBER
- Preserve the past: leave historic objects, structures, and traces undisturbed.

World famous for its highly challenging Slickrock Bike Trail, Utah's Sand Flats Recreation Area also provides motor tourists with spectacular views of the Moab area's unique sandstone cliffs, canyons, and towers. *(BLM)*

SOME FAVORITES

Dalton Highway (AK)
Denali Highway (AK)
Black Hills Back Country Byway (AZ)
Bradshaw Trail (CA)
Alpine Loop (CO)
Gold Belt Tour National Scenic
    Byway (CO)
Lewis and Clark Back Country Byway
    and Adventure Road (ID)
Garnet Range Back Country
    Byway (MT)
Lunar Crater Back Country Byway (NV)
Red Rock Canyon National Conservation
    Area (NV)

Guadalupe Back Country Byway (NM)
Galice-Hellgate Back Country
    Byway (OR)
North Umpqua Wild and Scenic River
    Corridor (OR)
Colorado Riverway (UT)
Pony Express National Historic Trail (UT)
Oregon, Mormon Pioneer, California, and
    Pony Express National Historic Trail
    Auto Tour (WY)

Picture This
Scenic Drives

Whether you're seeking an afternoon car trip or an extended motor tour, be sure to pack your camera, because the public lands offer motorists a stunning variety of scenic drives, interpretive loops, and charming back country byways. Depending on the area you choose, you may see diverse wildlife, unique geologic features, wild horses or burros, ancient petroglyphs, fossil areas, historic mining remnants, ghost towns, or traces of American explorers and pioneers. Many of these public lands routes have been formally designated as back country byways, BLM's system of roads and trails through picturesque lands with high public interest. Byways vary from narrow, graded roads, passable only during a few months of the year, to two-lane, paved highways providing year-round access. Some byways follow national trails, routes designated by Congress for their historic or scenic significance.

Colorado's Gold Belt Tour National Scenic Byway leads visitors through mountainous terrain along historic miners' routes connecting Cripple Creek and the Victor Mining District, site of the largest Gold Rush in history. Lunar Crater Back Country Byway near Tonopah, Nevada, follows a 24-mile unpaved loop road through the ghostly Lunar Crater Volcanic Field, a veritable moonscape of unique geologic features. And the Lewis and Clark Back Country Byway and Adventure Road takes travelers from river bottoms to forested mountains as it winds its way from Idaho's Bitterroot Range to the Continental Divide, crossing it at Lemhi Pass as explorers Lewis and Clark once did.

History, geology, archaeology, wildlife — so many choices! But thankfully, there's no need to select only one pursuit. With some judicious route planning, motor recreationists can design public lands excursions to keep the whole crew happy, or, for longer trips, drivers can cruise from one route to another as they meander from state to state.

REMEMBER

- Obey all signs.
- Minimize impacts — stay on legally designated roads and trails.
- Bring along a map of the area — know where you are!

FOR MORE INFORMATION

Green, S.M. 2001. *Scenic Driving: Back Country Byways* (Second Edition). Helena, MT: Falcon Publishing Co. 296 pp.

Green, S.M. 1995. *Bureau of Land Management Back Country Byways: Your Complete Guide to the West's Most Scenic Back Roads* (Second Edition). Helena, MT: Falcon Publishing Co. 176 pp.

Near Moab, Utah, a climber grips a shallow crack to negotiate a sandstone wall at Indian Creek, known among diehards as "the crack-climbing capital of the world." Though the cracks and crags come in all sizes here, experience and good technique are crucial, since the walls are usually devoid of other handholds. *(BLM)*

Maximum High
Adventure Sports

A walk in the woods is nice, but let's face it—maybe you're after something, well, a little more "on the edge." If riding huge waves off the northern California coast appeals to you, try the surfing at King Range National Conservation Area. Those who prefer to stay dry might want to "sand surf" at Utah's Little Sahara Recreation Area. If you envy a hawk riding the air currents, perhaps hang gliding will be your calling. Hang gliding is popular at many remote BLM locations, such as Lake Abert and Abert Rim in Oregon. Or, if you prefer to stay on the ground while the wind carries you, check out the land sailing at Nevada's famous Black Rock Desert-High Rock Canyon Emigrant Trails National Conservation Area. For a real challenge, consider scaling a sheer rock face. BLM offers numerous outstanding rock climbing sites. Red Rock Canyon in Nevada, for example, is world-class.

All we ask is that you prepare and train yourself for these maximum adventures, and never venture out alone. You provide the equipment, safety gear, and the know-how to use it. The thrill is on us.

SOME FAVORITES

King Range National Conservation Area (CA): surfing

Thousand Springs Valley (ID): hang gliding

Black Rock Desert-High Rock Canyon Emigrant Trails National Conservation Area (NV): land sailing

Red Rock Canyon National Conservation Area (NV): rock climbing

Sand Mountain Recreation Area (NV): sand surfing

Organ Mountains (NM): rock climbing

Lake Abert and Abert Rim (OR): hang gliding

Little Sahara Recreation Area (UT): sand surfing

REMEMBER

- Check with land managers for advice, regulations, and maps.
- Obtain permits when necessary.
- Respect boundary markers; do not trespass on private land.
- Learn and follow standard safety practices for the sport and equipment.

Holter Lake, considered by many to be the most beautiful of west-central Montana's Chain-of-Lakes, welcomes pleasure-boaters to a setting bounded by the Beartooth Wildlife Management Area to the east and the Sleeping Giant Wilderness Study Area to the west. *(BLM Montana State Office)*

Full Throttle
Motor Boating Excursions

When the designers of western Arizona's Parker Dam completed their project in 1938, little did they realize that the resultant reservoir would become a recreational boating mecca. About 20 years later, however, enterprising developers purchased thousands of acres of land upstream of the dam and created a city. Finally, once the famous London Bridge was moved from England to its current lakeshore home, Lake Havasu achieved worldwide fame. Today, thousands of boats use Lake Havasu, which extends for hundreds of miles behind the dam, for motorized aquatic activities of all types, making it BLM's most popular motorized-boating recreation site. BLM maintains more than 100 campsites, accessible only by boat, on the shoreline of the lake.

For more placid trips, BLM manages 70 small islands in Lake Vermilion, one of the largest lakes in Minnesota and considered one of the most scenic in the U.S. The lake itself is a 40,000-acre boating paradise, with hundreds of islands and 1,200 miles of shoreline, located just south of the Boundary Waters Canoe Area Wilderness.

One of the West's most scenic natural water bodies is Coeur d'Alene Lake in northwestern Idaho. Boats using this large lake include small motorboats, powerful speedboats, houseboats, and even paddle-wheel steamboats. Each summer, the city of Coeur d'Alene celebrates antique wooden steam craft during its wooden boat festival. And even if you don't have a boat, you can still enjoy the lake by taking a day-long, 115-mile scenic drive along its perimeter.

SOME FAVORITES

Lake Havasu (AZ)
Parker Dam Road Back Country Byway (AZ)
Sacramento River–Bend Area (CA)
Coeur d'Alene Lake (ID)
Lake Vermilion Public Islands (MN)

REMEMBER

- Gather information about the river or lake's ecology.
- Obtain a river map or lake chart before your trip.
- Always tell others of your plans.
- Always wear an approved personal flotation device and carry appropriate safety equipment.
- Make sure you have enough fuel and oil for your trip. A good rule is to plan 1/3 of your fuel for the outbound trip, 1/3 for the return, and 1/3 in reserve.
- Know the regulations and environmental issues pertaining to the lake or river.
- Travel only in areas that are open to your type of watercraft.

A dirt bike rider in full racing gear soars over the sandbanks of California's Imperial Sand Dunes Recreation Area. *(Doran Sanchez, BLM California Desert District Office)*

SOME FAVORITES

Dalton Highway (AK)

Denali Highway (AK)

Black Hills Back Country Byway (AZ)

Gila Box Riparian National Conservation
   Area (AZ)

Dumont Dunes Off-Highway-Vehicle
   Area (CA)

Imperial Sand Dunes Recreation
   Area (CA)

Alpine Loop (CO)

Gold Belt Tour National Scenic
   Byway (CO)

St. Anthony Sand Dunes (ID)

Lewis and Clark Back Country Byway
   and Adventure Road (ID)

Glade Run Recreation Area (NM)

Black Rock Desert-High Rock Canyon
   Emigrant Trails National Conservation
   Area (NV)

Lunar Crater Back Country Byway (NV)

Sand Mountain Recreation Area (NV)

Little Sahara Recreation Area (UT)

The Roads Less Traveled
Off-Highway Adventures

There's nothing quite like the thrill of cruising over a sand dune. That's why thousands of off-highway-vehicle enthusiasts gather each year at California's Imperial Sand Dunes, which features dunes up to 300 feet high. Here, OHV drivers breeze through the sand in vehicles of many sizes and styles, from dune buggies to sand rails. Similar sandbanks can be found within the Saint Anthony Sand Dunes near Idaho Falls. Located far from the ocean, this vast dune complex covers 175,000 acres, with individual dunes ranging upwards of 600 feet high. And the Little Sahara dune complex in Utah measures 13 miles long and 3 miles wide. Want still higher — and more — sand? Try Sand Mountain, a unique Nevada locale that provides an almost vertical 700-foot sand face for thrill-seekers.

Sand vehicles, dirt bikes, all-terrain vehicles — pick your ride, and you'll find that there's a perfect spot designated on public lands managed by BLM. Public lands also offer great recreational opportunities for vehicles that stay on the road. BLM manages a variety of back country byways that take visitors to mountaintops and beyond, from the Idaho range where explorers Lewis and Clark crossed the Continental Divide to Colorado's Alpine and Gold Belt Loops, where gold miners once combed the mountains in search of fortune. Many of these roads can be traveled by passenger car. But four-wheel drivers will be particularly pleased with the more rugged, unpaved stretches.

BLM public lands even welcome a unique vehicle that shines only on very flat surfaces. At Nevada's remote Black Rock Desert Playa, sail-equipped "land yachts" harness the wind to race across an ancient lake bed. This is also the site of the world land-speed record of 763 miles per hour, set in 1997 by a British team with a rocket-powered vehicle.

With the popularity of sport-utility vehicles at an all-time high, millions of recreationists are eager to try their luck on back country roads, rocky OHV trails, and sandy hills. Since there's great potential for spills as well as thrills, however, drivers need to be careful and travel only where motorized vehicles are permitted.

REMEMBER
- Tread Lightly!: Drive responsibly to both protect the environment and preserve your opportunities to ride.
- Travel straight up or down a hill.
- In order to avoid collisions, always use a whip flag when riding sand dunes.
- Cross obstacles at an angle.
- Cross streams slowly and only at established fording points.
- Carry proper equipment for the trip.
- Bring enough spare clothing, water, and food for each traveler.
- Check your vehicle's tires and fluids.

FOR MORE INFORMATION
Tread Lightly!: *www.treadlightly.org*

Recreational dog-mushers use one of a network of BLM cabins as "home base" in the pristine White Mountains Recreation Area northeast of Fairbanks, Alaska. *(Susan Steinacher, BLM Northern District Office)*

SOME FAVORITES

Campbell Tract (AK): dog mushing, skijoring, cross-country skiing

White Mountains National Recreation Area (AK): dog mushing, snowmobiling, cross-country skiing

Bizz Johnson National Recreation Trail (CA): cross-country skiing

Alpine Loop (CO): cross-country skiing, snowshoeing, snowmobiling

Lewis and Clark Back Country Byway and Adventure Road (ID): snowmobiling, cross-country skiing

Garnet Range Back Country Byway (MT): snowmobiling, cross-country skiing

North Wildhorse Recreation Area (NV): snowmobiling, cross-country skiing, ice fishing

Pacific Crest National Scenic Trail, Cascade-Siskiyou National Monument (OR): cross-country skiing, snowshoeing, snowmobiling

Let It Snow
Winter Recreation

When most people think of winter recreation in the West, their thoughts probably turn first to the premier ski resorts that proliferate throughout the Rocky Mountains. While downhill skiing is certainly a popular pursuit, public lands in many parts of the West offer myriad other opportunities to enjoy everything that winter has to offer. And you don't need to spend a fortune on equipment and lift tickets, either. You can strap on a pair of cross-country skis or snowshoes and take off on a winter wilderness adventure.

Many trails that are perfect for hiking or mountain biking in other seasons become transformed when the snow falls. Take California's Bizz Johnson Trail, for instance, where snowflakes add spice to the pine and cedar scents of the forest. If you want to venture a little farther into the back country and don't mind a little more noise, there are plenty of opportunities for snowmobiling as well. Garnet Ghost Town in Montana's Garnet Range serves as a hub for snowmobilers from January through April. BLM maintains more than 50 miles of trails here, as well as warming shelters along the way. Snowmobilers in Nevada's North Wildhorse Recreation Area can make their way to the reservoir for some excellent ice fishing, too.

Head north to Alaska for still longer winters and more chances to play in the snow. Trails in Anchorage's Campbell Tract are set aside for a variety of uses, including dog mushing and skijoring. North of Fairbanks, in the White Mountains National Recreation Area, cross-country skiers, dog-sledders, and snowmobilers can make their way along more than 200 miles of trails — stopping overnight at rentable cabins or just spending a day in snowy solitude. No matter where you choose to "chill out," make sure you heed storm and avalanche warnings and let someone know where you're headed.

REMEMBER

- Stay on designated trails.
- Check the weather and plan accordingly. Be prepared for the worst conditions. (The website *www.recreation.gov* has links to weather information.)
- Sunlight burns even in the winter — use sun protection.
- Inquire about area regulations.
- If snowmobiling:
  - Travel at reasonable speeds and only on designated snowmobile trails or in areas where you're certain snowmobiling is permitted.
  - Wear protective equipment.
  - Ride with a partner, and if possible, carry a mobile phone for emergencies.
  - Show consideration for other recreationists and for wildlife.

Critical habitat for the Florida scrub jay is the rapidly vanishing Florida scrub ecosystem, scrub communities that are dependent on periodic wildland fires for ecosystem health. South Florida's Jupiter Inlet Natural Area has provided a safe haven for this Federally-listed threatened species. *(Jerry Sintz, BLM Utah State Office (retired))*

Winging It
Birdwatching Forays

Whether you have a weakness for webbed feet or your interests tend toward talons, the public lands present an array of birdwatching opportunities that once made Audubon himself smile. Located throughout the western United States and Alaska, these birdwatching sites can be found in a variety of latitudes, altitudes, and climates.

You can explore coastal wetlands along Oregon's New River, where you might spy colorful, green-winged teals or a rare snowy plover. Perhaps you're on the lookout for that elusive neotropical songbird to add to your checklist. Check out the San Pedro Riparian National Conservation Area (NCA) in Arizona, where the perennial river attracts more than 350 species—both year-round residents and migrants. Bring your binoculars and prepare to be awed by the hawks and eagles at Idaho's Snake River Birds of Prey NCA. The cliffs and canyons there are home to the greatest concentration of nesting birds of prey in North America. And if you've longed to observe "rush hour" on a migratory flyway, the public lands offer up several promising destinations—from New Mexico's Black River to the Cosumnes River Preserve near Sacramento, California, to central Oregon's Lake Abert.

Pack parkas, or desert boots, or waders, if you prefer—jackets and ties are most assuredly optional! Site access ranges from the exotic to the commonplace. You may need to fly in on a seaplane or float in on a raft.

Sometimes, it's as easy as stepping out of your vehicle. Birdwatching sites on public lands offer unique and diverse opportunities to watch gaggles, flocks, and pairs as they nest, migrate, breed, or just hang out.

SOME FAVORITES
Gulkana National Wild River (AK)
Aravaipa Canyon Wilderness (AZ)
San Pedro Riparian National
    Conservation Area (AZ)
Vermilion Cliffs National
    Monument (AZ)
Big Morongo Canyon (CA)
Cosumnes River Preserve (CA)
Snake River Birds of Prey National
    Conservation Area (ID)
Black River (NM)
Organ Mountains (NM)
Lake Abert and Abert Rim (OR)
New River Area (OR)

REMEMBER
- Respect nesting areas and birds—don't get too close.
- Do not overuse audio tapes to call birds.
- Don't leave any trash or leftover food behind. Human food can kill.
- Don't forget your binoculars and camera; a zoom lens is ideal for photography from afar.

For More Information
Partners in Flight:
www.partnersinflight.org

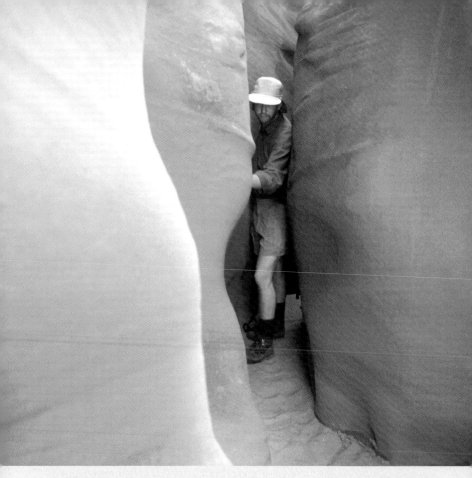

Some Utah "slot canyons" are so narrow that hikers can touch both curved walls at once, the sky appears only as a narrow strip of blue, and sunshine is reduced to occasional shafts of light. *(Jerry Sintz, BLM Utah State Office (retired))*

SOME FAVORITES

Vermilion Cliffs National Monument (AZ)

Trona Pinnacles (CA)

Garden Park Fossil Area (CO)

Craters of the Moon National Monument (ID)

Lunar Crater Back Country Byway (NV)

Red Rock Canyon National Conservation Area (NV)

El Malpais National Conservation Area (NM)

Kasha-Katuwe Tent Rocks National Monument (NM)

Diamond Craters Outstanding Natural Area (OR)

Cleveland-Lloyd Dinosaur Quarry (UT)

Grand Staircase-Escalante National Monument (UT)

Channeled Scablands (WA)

Red Gulch/Alkali National Back Country Byway and Red Gulch Dinosaur Tracksite (WY)

Rockin' Good Times
Geologic Sightseeing

Scablands and badlands, craters and critters (fossilized, that is). Whether you're an aspiring geologist or amateur paleontologist, the diverse landscapes of the public lands showcase features ranging from the delightfully bizarre to the simply breathtaking.

If gravity-defying arches and ghostly hoodoos are what you seek, wander among the water-carved, wind-polished sculptures that grace the remote expanses of the Grand Staircase-Escalante National Monument. Or perhaps your interests run to dinosaurs. If so, catch a guided tour of the fossil-rich, Jurassic bone beds of Cleveland-Lloyd Dinosaur Quarry, home of the fearsome (and, thankfully, extinct) allosaur. And finding your way backwards in time is an enticing proposition at colorful Vermilion Cliffs, where a lithified " layer cake" of seven stacked geologic formations is exposed to view.

The public lands also offer splendid opportunities for rockhounds and fossil fans alike: at some BLM sites, recreational collectors may gather small numbers of rocks, semi-precious gemstones, and certain plant and invertebrate — but not vertebrate — fossils. (Be sure to check out the ethics provided here, consult individual site descriptions for collecting guidelines, and contact BLM before rockhounding or fossil collecting.)

Eons of geologic processes and terrestrial upheavals have left their signatures across the public lands to awe, inspire, and educate visitors. The deep canyons beckon you, the peaks and pinnacles await. Just pack your binoculars, grab your compass, and choose the geologic journey that's right for you.

REMEMBER
- Respect and preserve the past — leave geologic features undisturbed.
- Contact BLM for rules about amateur collecting of rocks and plant and invertebrate fossil specimens.

FOR MORE INFORMATION
"Fossils on America's Public Lands," BLM brochure available from BLM offices (see Appendix A).

Indian paintbrush, a showy spring wildflower native to many western deserts, grows at elevations of 2,000–8,000 feet. Often found in large patches near semi-desert plants such as Mormon tea and sagebrush, Indian paintbrush is partially parasitic, growing on its own until its roots meet those of other plants and then penetrating those roots for nourishment. *(Doran Sanchez, BLM California Desert District Office)*

SOME FAVORITES

Dalton Highway (AK)
Denali Highway (AK)
Black Hills Back Country Byway (AZ)
Gila Box Riparian National Conservation
    Area (AZ)
Dumont Dunes Off-Highway-Vehicle
    Area (CA)
Fort Ord (CA)
Imperial Sand Dunes Recreation
    Area (CA)
Alpine Loop (CO)
Gold Belt Tour National Scenic
    Byway (CO)

Craters of the Moon National
    Monument (ID)
Lewis and Clark Back Country Byway
    and Adventure Road (ID)
Glade Run Recreation Area (NM)
Black Rock Desert-High Rock Canyon
    Emigrant Trails National Conservation
    Area (NV)
Lunar Crater Back Country Byway (NV)
Sand Mountain Recreation Area (NV)
Little Sahara Recreation Area (UT)

Stop and Smell the Sagebrush
Plant Viewing Areas

Take some time to walk among the sagebrush or roam a redwood forest, to explore unique plants of the desert or wetlands, or to enjoy a magnificent display of wildflowers in bloom. You may see butterflies or hummingbirds busily pollinating or small animals feeding amidst the gently swaying vegetation. In their many varieties, from trees and shrubs to wildflowers and grasses, native plants on American's public lands offer visitors stunning visual displays that will refresh the spirit.

Weaving through the San Juan Mountains of the Colorado Plateau, for instance, the Alpine Loop leads visitors through some of the most spectacular mountain vegetation in the United States. In the summer months, the meadows erupt with colorful alpine wildflowers, while September is the best time to appreciate the aspens as their leaves change to fall colors. Arizona's hot deserts (the Mojave, Sonoran, and Chihuahuan) are home to hundreds of species of plants, and a visit to the Sonoran Desert National Monument provides access to many of the most unusual. Towering saguaro cacti, for example, which are found nowhere else in the world, are renowned for their variety of fanciful shapes.   North

Dakota's Schnell Recreation Area hosts scarce native prairie, riparian (stream-side) areas, ponds, and hardwood draws, where centuries-old bur oaks thrive. Fort Ord, on the Monterey Peninsula, features some of the most pristine remaining tracts of maritime chaparral in California. Wildflowers, oak woodlands, wide-open grasslands, and freshwater marshes also thrive there, along with 46 different species of rare plants.

So keep a plant guide at the ready, load your camera, and strike out in search of your favorite flora. What better time than now, to stop and smell the sagebrush . . .

REMEMBER
- Avoid introducing or transporting the seeds of non-native plants and weeds by cleaning all gear, clothing, and shoes before leaving an area.
- Leave plants and other natural objects undisturbed so others may enjoy them.

FOR MORE INFORMATION
To find out about wildflower events on the Nation's public lands, contact: Celebrating Wildflowers, "Wild" Hotline, 1-800-345-4595 (April–July) or *www.nps.gov/plants/cw*.

Early American explorers gave the name "elk" to this second-largest member of the deer family (only the moose is larger) because the animals outwardly resembled the elk of Europe. Since American elk are really not closely related to European elk, the Native American term "wapiti" is sometimes used instead to distinguish the American animal. *(Jerry Sintz, BLM Utah State Office (retired))*

SOME FAVORITES

Aravaipa Canyon Wilderness (AZ)

Grand Canyon-Parashant National Monument (AZ)

Big Morongo Canyon (CA)

East Fork Salmon River (ID)

Pauls Valley Wild Horse and Burro Adoption Center (OK)

Axolotl Lakes (MT)

Ely Elk Viewing Area (NV)

Black River (NM)

El Malpais National Conservation Area (NM)

Dean Creek Elk Viewing Area (OR)

Yaquina Head Outstanding Natural Area (OR)

Book Cliffs Area (UT)

National Bighorn Sheep Interpretive Center and Whiskey Mountain Bighorn Sheep Area (WY)

Roaming Free
Wildlife Watching

Perhaps your idea of a dream vacation is leaving humans behind, and getting out to where the *really* wild things are. In settings ranging from scorching deserts to snowy alpine forests, the public lands shelter a huge variety of magnificent animal species.

Autumn visitors to the Ely Elk Viewing Area won't soon forget the sight (or sounds!) of Nevada's largest native animals during their annual rutting season, when mature bulls bugle their mating songs to court the assembled females. North America's biggest wintering herd of Rocky Mountain bighorn sheep caper effortlessly from cliff to crag at Wyoming's Whiskey Mountain Bighorn Sheep Area, the clatter of their hooves echoing against the rock faces. In fact, many public lands sites have been designated as "Watchable Wildlife Sites," locations so rich in unique viewing opportunities that they have been formally recognized by the Watchable Wildlife Program, a nationwide network of designated wildlife viewing sites dedicated to promoting wildlife-related recreation, education, and conservation. Distinctive white-on-brown "binoculars" signs on interstate highways and other roads help to identify routes to these preferred wildlife viewing sites.

And if you're after a glimpse of more familiar faces, keep an eye out for the bands of rugged wild horses and burros that roam freely over the western rangelands, particularly in Utah, Nevada, Wyoming, and Oregon. Under Federal law, some of these feral descendants of once-domestic livestock may be offered for "adoption" each year. Visitors to Oklahoma's Pauls Valley Wild Horse and Burro Adoption Center may see as many as 500 animals galloping across 200 lush acres of fenced pasturelands as these "living symbols of the American West" await new homes.

REMEMBER
- Respect wildlife. "Do not disturb" is the rule, especially at sensitive times and in fragile habitats.
- Learn through quiet observation, from afar. Back away if animals react to your presence.
- Never feed wild animals.

FOR MORE INFORMATION
Watchable Wildlife, Inc.: *www.watchablewildlife.org*
BLM Wild Horse and Burro Program: *www.wildhorseandburro.blm.gov*

Bering Glacier, southeast of Cordova, Alaska, at the edge of Vitus Lake, is the largest glacier in North America, and is considered a "surging glacier," a type that periodically moves very quickly. BLM sponsors a research base camp near Vitus Lake during the summer. *(Dennis R. Green, BLM volunteer, Alaska State Office)*

The name "Alaska" is derived from "Alyeska," the Aleut word for "Great Land." It's an apt descriptor: the state's tremendous size, more than twice that of Texas, is difficult to fully grasp. BLM administers about 24 percent of the state's area, 86 million acres that are vast and dramatic, featuring pristine vistas at every turn. Sparkling waters, alive with salmon and trout, entice floaters and fisherfolk alike. From wild white-water and scenic driving to snowmobiling and mountain climbing, public lands in Alaska offer a kaleidoscope of recreational opportunities in spectacular settings.

The Alaska Highway system has opened some formerly unapproachable landscapes to access by passenger car, truck, or RV. Steese Highway, for example, leads to the remote Steese National Conservation Area, where visitors may find themselves in the company of wolves and caribou. Road-weary travelers may even wish to unwind at the recreational hot springs scattered along the highway's 162-mile length. Denali Highway parallels the raw Alaska Range, while Taylor Highway leads to Fortymile River country, where 19th-century miners panned for gold. And Dalton Highway is the road for seekers of the "Land of the Midnight Sun" and the Arctic coastal plain beyond.

Visitors who prefer more civilized excursions can still taste the wild at Anchorage's Campbell Tract. There, urban adventurers may pursue both summer and winter activities under the watchful eyes of bears, moose, and other denizens of the tract's native ecosystems.

From the sweep of the Yukon River to the Arctic rainbows that redefine "stormy skies," Alaska has a wealth of natural and cultural resources to offer. A sense of adventure is a necessity; wild weather can occur on any day, and help is often far away. But that's all part of the thrill of exploring this Great Land.

Alaska

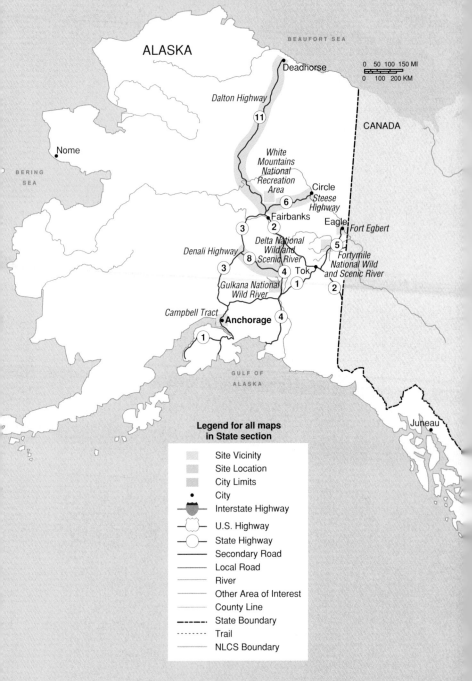

ALASKA

BEAUFORT SEA

Deadhorse

0 50 100 150 MI
0 100 200 KM

CANADA

Dalton Highway

⑪

Nome

BERING
SEA

White
Mountains
National
Recreation
Area

Circle

⑥

Steese
Highway

Fairbanks

③

②

Eagle

Fort Egbert

⑤

Denali Highway

Delta National
Wild and
Scenic River

⑧

③

④

Tok

Fortymile
National Wild
and Scenic River

Gulkana National
Wild River

①

②

Campbell Tract

④

•Anchorage

④

①

GULF OF
ALASKA

Juneau

**Legend for all maps
in State section**

	Site Vicinity
	Site Location
	City Limits
•	City
	Interstate Highway
	U.S. Highway
	State Highway
	Secondary Road
	Local Road
	River
	Other Area of Interest
	County Line
	State Boundary
	Trail
	NLCS Boundary

Campbell Tract

Location
In east Anchorage, Alaska.

Description
The Campbell Tract is a 730-acre natural area used mostly by urban recreationists seeking a piece of Alaska wilderness in the heart of the city. The tract is comprised of forested lands that provide a home for moose, black bears, wolves, and brown bears. Other animals that visitors may encounter include lynx, coyotes, foxes, porcupines, and squirrels. Campbell Creek meanders through the property and provides spawning and rearing habitat for rainbow trout, Dolly Varden, and king and silver salmon. The tract has 12 miles of trails that are used for non-motorized recreational activities year-round. BLM trails connect to other trails in the adjacent lands managed by the Municipality of Anchorage. The Campbell Creek Science Center is an outdoor science education center for persons of all ages that encourages interest and participation in the balanced management of natural resources. The tract is also a BLM administrative site with office buildings and a restricted-use airstrip.

Directions
In Anchorage, go east on East 68th Avenue for 1 mile until it ends at Abbott Loop Road. Turn right (south) on Abbott Loop Road for 100 feet. The entrance to the facility is on your left; the Campbell Tract facility sign will direct you. Another popular access point is reached by traveling on Tudor Road to Campbell Airstrip Road. Turn south and drive 1.1 miles to a small parking area. Campbell Creek is just a 2-minute walk away.

The Campbell Creek Science Center's Backyard Discoveries Program offers guided walks, nature inventories, and other hands-on science experiences geared to teaching visitors how to monitor ecosystem health. *(Dennis R. Green, BLM volunteer, Alaska State Office)*

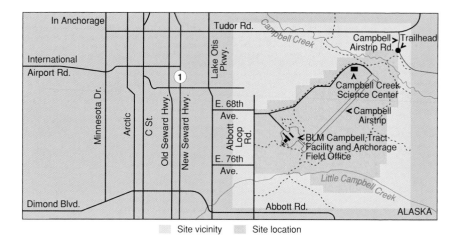

In Anchorage | Tudor Rd. | Campbell Airstrip Rd. | Trailhead
International Airport Rd.
Minnesota Dr. | Arctic | C St. | Old Seward Hwy. | New Seward Hwy. | Lake Otis Pkwy. | Abbott Loop Rd.
① | E. 68th Ave. | Campbell Creek Science Center | Campbell Airstrip | BLM Campbell Tract Facility and Anchorage Field Office
E. 76th Ave.
Dimond Blvd. | Abbott Rd. | Little Campbell Creek | ALASKA

Site vicinity   Site location

Visitor Activities
Hiking, wildlife viewing, biking, bird-watching, horseback riding, skiing, dog mushing, skijoring, and interpretation.

Special Features
Several different ecosystems are found on the Campbell Tract: streamside, mixed forests of spruce/birch, spruce/alder, and spruce/willow, wet shrubby meadows, and black spruce bottomland. Spawning salmon are often seen in Campbell Creek in July. Visitors should watch for bears along the waterways at this time of year.

Permits, Fees, Limitations
No fees. The area is restricted to non-motorized recreational use.

Accessibility
Accessible parking and pathways are found at the Campbell Creek Science Center in the northeastern quadrant of the tract.

Camping and Lodging
Camping is generally not allowed; however, non-profit organizations may obtain special BLM recreation use permits for overnight use.

Food and Supplies
Food and supplies are available in Anchorage.

First Aid
Hospitals and clinics are nearby. Providence Hospital, located at 3200 Providence Drive, is 2.5 miles north of the tract entrance on Abbott Loop Road.

Additional Information
The Campbell Tract is BLM's most visited and accessible site in Alaska. Because of its location, it is a favorite getaway for urban dwellers seeking year-round recreational opportunities.

The Campbell Creek Science Center is open 7:30 a.m.–4:30 p.m., Monday–Friday. Special programs and activities are offered on evenings and weekends. For additional information, contact the Center.

Contact Information
BLM - Anchorage Field Office
6881 Abbott Loop Road
Anchorage, AK 99507
Tel: (907) 267-1246
Fax: (907) 267-1267
www.anchorage.ak.blm.gov

Campbell Creek Science Center
Tel: (907) 267-1247
www.sciencecenter.ak.blm.gov

Activity Codes

(skiing, dog mushing, skijoring)

Dalton Highway

Location
Interior and Arctic Alaska, beginning
2 miles west of Livengood (north of
Fairbanks) and continuing north for 417
miles to the Deadhorse Airport, a few
miles from Prudhoe Bay.

Description
The Dalton Highway, built to haul
supplies to the Trans Alaska Pipeline
System and the Prudhoe Bay oil fields,
provides access to the scenic Arctic.
Traversing tundra and mountaintops,
the highway cuts a transect north across
Alaska, crossing the Yukon River, the
Arctic Circle, and the Brooks Range,
before almost reaching the Arctic
Ocean. Along this route, visitors can
observe caribou herds migrating across
the tundra, butterflies massing in the
chilly air, and grizzlies at rest in the
sun. Musk oxen browse sunlit slopes, a
tableau little changed in thousands of
years. Wildflower enthusiasts will
appreciate the tiny, profuse flowers on the
tundra, some easily recognized as dwarf
versions of familiar species. Even on the
summer solstice—when the sun literally
never sets—snowfalls are frequent in the
rugged environment served by the Dalton
Highway.

Directions
From Fairbanks, drive north about
10 miles on the Steese Highway (State
Highway 6) to Fox, then drive north
about 73 miles on the Elliott Highway
(State Highway 2) to its intersection
with the Dalton Highway, 2 miles west
of the turnoff to Livengood. From

**The Dalton Highway traverses Alaska's
northern boreal forest on its way to the
Brooks Range and the Arctic Coastal Plain.**
*(Dennis R. Green, BLM volunteer, Alaska State
Office)*

there, it is 56 miles northwest on the Dalton Highway to Yukon Crossing, an additional 119 miles north to Coldfoot, and 295 miles further to the Deadhorse Airport near Prudhoe Bay.

Visitor Activities

Birdwatching, picnicking, hiking, scenic drives, big-game hunting, fishing, rafting, canoeing, wildlife viewing, plant viewing, biking, and geologic sightseeing.

Special Features

One of the best places to see Dall sheep is on the rocky slopes of Atigun Pass (Mile 240, elevation 4,739 feet). This is the highest point within the Alaskan road system. The sheep may also be seen between Atigun Pass and Galbraith Lake (Mile 275), as well as on Slope Mountain (Miles 297–301). Canoeing is possible on Jim River, which crosses the highway in several locations.

Permits, Fees, Limitations

No fees are required for non-commercial visits. Much of the land within the

Musk oxen, once hunted to extinction in Alaska, have been reintroduced and can now be seen from the Dalton Highway north of the Brooks Range. *(Dennis R. Green, BLM volunteer, Alaska State Office)*

Dalton Highway corridor is tundra or permafrost and, as such, is highly vulnerable to damage, and is closed to recreational off-highway driving. Scars such as tire tracks and even footprints can last for decades; visitors should "tread lightly."

Accessibility

Some facilities are accessible.

Camping and Lodging

Lodging is available along the Dalton Highway at Yukon River Crossing (Mile 56), Coldfoot (Mile 175), and Deadhorse (Mile 414). The entire Dalton Highway corridor is open to camping. A privately-managed campground is at Coldfoot. There is a public campground (managed by BLM, with no hookups) at Marion Creek, 5 miles north of Coldfoot.

Food and Supplies

Supplies are available in Fairbanks; limited supplies are available in Coldfoot and Deadhorse.

First Aid

The highway corridor is extremely isolated, and visitors must be self-sufficient. There are no public or emergency medical facilities along the Dalton Highway. The nearest hospital is in Fairbanks.

Additional Information

The best time to drive the highway is late May–mid-September. Visitors should travel with safety in mind in this remote region; travelers are on their own. Highway services are limited to Yukon Crossing, Coldfoot, and Deadhorse, so vehicles should be in good working order before being used

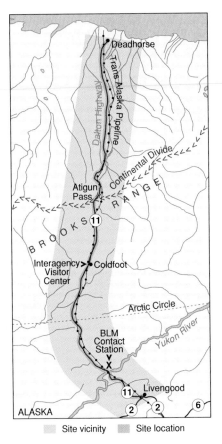

Site vicinity   Site location

no services from Coldfoot until the end of the highway at Deadhorse, a distance of 242 miles, travelers should check their gas and other supplies before proceeding north. Because of oil-company security measures, private vehicles may not access the Arctic Ocean but van tours may be arranged through hotels in Deadhorse.

An excellent opportunity to learn about the plants and animals of the Alpine Tundra is available at the Finger Mountain Interpretive Trail (Mile 98). The BLM visitor contact station at Yukon Crossing (Mile 56) and the Arctic Interagency Visitor Center at Coldfoot (Mile 175) are open every day throughout the summer. Staff are available to answer questions and provide information on road conditions and wildlife sightings.

Travelers may obtain additional information at the BLM visitor information stations at Yukon Crossing and Coldfoot and obtain a copy of *Birds Along the Dalton Highway* or *Riches from the Earth: A Geologic Tour Along the Dalton Highway.*

on this trip. Visitors are advised to carry two regular spare tires, emergency flares, extra gas and windshield wiper fluid, bug repellent, rain gear, a first aid kit, emergency food and water, and camping gear. Travelers should turn on their lights and slow down when other vehicles are approaching and avoid stopping on the road.

The Dalton Highway is primarily a gravel-surfaced, industrial highway; drivers should slow down and pull over to allow high-speed trucks to pass and to minimize the chances of windshield damage from flying rocks. As there are

Contact Information

BLM - Northern Field Office
1150 University Avenue
Fairbanks, AK 99709
Tel: (907) 474-2302
Fax: (907) 474-2280
aurora.ak.blm.gov/arcticinfo/travel-1.htm
Arctic Interagency Visitor Center
(June–August only)
Tel: (907) 678-5209

Activity Codes

Delta National Wild and Scenic River

Location

Approximately 90 miles north of Glennallen, Alaska, from Mile 22 (Tangle Lakes Campground) on the Denali Highway (State Highway 8) to Mile 212.5 on the Richardson Highway (State Highway 4).

Description

The Delta National Wild and Scenic River is a network of 160 miles of streams and 21 lakes nestled among rolling, hilly tundra hosting eskers, moraines, kettles, and other glacial features. Ptarmigans, bald eagles, and waterfowl mingle with Dall sheep, moose, bears, and caribou among the tundra flora and spruce-poplar forests. The streams and lakes offer anglers graylings, round whitefish, burbots, longnose suckers, and, in late winter and early spring, lake trout.

Boating trips of varying lengths, both with and without portages, are another popular recreational pursuit. One popular route takes boaters north toward the Lower Tangle Lakes to the Delta National Wild and Scenic River, and then continues through tundra-covered rolling hills to Richardson Highway. On this trip, visitors can see the falls of the Delta River, 10 miles north of Tangle Lakes Campground. The falls are a major scenic highlight, and must be portaged at all times. A longer trip involves traveling south through the Upper Tangle Lakes through a series of portages to Dickey Lake (on the other side of a drainage divide) and then continuing down the Middle Fork of the Gulkana National Wild River to Sourdough Campground. (See the site entry for the Gulkana National Wild River.)

Directions

From Glennallen, drive north approximately 90 miles on State

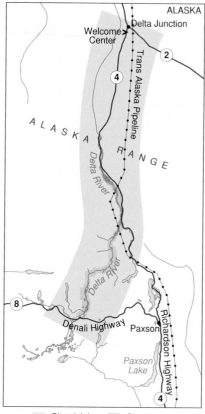

Site vicinity   Site location

Highway 4 (Richardson Highway) to
State Highway 8 (Denali Highway) to
Paxson. Then travel about 21 miles west
of Paxson on State Highway 8 to the
Delta National Wild and Scenic River
Wayside and Trailhead at Tangle Lakes,
the headwaters of the Delta River.

Visitor Activities
Fishing, canoeing, rafting, wildlife viewing, birdwatching, hunting (big-game,
bird, and waterfowl), hiking, seasonal
berry picking, and archaeological site.

Special Features
The portion of the Delta National
Wild and Scenic corridor adjacent to
Highway 8 intersects the Tangle Lakes
Archaeological District, listed on the
National Register of Historic Places for
the presence of numerous sites dating to
some of North America's earliest and
most-continuous human occupation.
This section of the corridor also offers
spectacular views of the Alaska Range.

Permits, Fees, Limitations
No user fees or permits are required for
non-commercial travel on the river.
Commercial outfitters should contact
BLM for fee and permit information.

Accessibility
Toilets at the Delta National Wild and
Scenic River Wayside and Trailhead are
wheelchair-accessible.

Camping and Lodging
Developed campsites near the put-in are
available at Tangle Lakes Campground,
21 miles west on State Highway 8, on a
first-come, first-served basis; there are
no fees for camping. Camping is limited
to 14 days at any site in a 60-day period. Lodging is available at roadhouses

**The falls of the Delta River are
impassable and must be portaged by all
river travelers.** *(Dennis R. Green, BLM
volunteer, Alaska State Office)*

at Miles 20 and 22 on State Highway 8;
reservations are suggested. There are
many undeveloped campsites for boaters
among the Tangle Lakes and along the
Delta National Wild and Scenic River.

Food and Supplies
A limited selection of food and supplies
can be obtained in the Paxson area, at
the junction of Richardson and Denali
Highways, and various roadhouses along
both highways.

First Aid

No first aid is available anywhere within the Delta National Wild and Scenic River corridor. Limited medical facilities are available at clinics along the Richardson Highway in Glennallen (82 miles south of Paxson) and Delta Junction (81 miles north of Paxson).

Additional Information

A popular launch site is located at Tangle Lakes. The take-out point is 62 miles downstream at approximately Mile 212 of State Highway 4. Travelers should allow 2–3 days and be prepared for Class I, II, and III rapids, and one portage. They should also be prepared for any kind of weather, as it can rain or snow at any time during the summer. Restroom facilities on the river are limited to a pit toilet at the portage. Users are asked to bury human waste or bring along a portable toilet to pack it out. Primary river use takes place in late May–early June and late September–early October. Tangle Lakes, at an elevation of 2,800 feet, can be ice-covered through mid-June. Contact BLM for local conditions.

Contact Information

BLM - Glennallen Field Office
P.O. Box 147
Glennallen, AK 99588
Tel: (907) 822-3217
Fax: (907) 822-3120
www.glennallen.ak.blm.gov
www.glennallen.ak.blm.gov/delta1.html

Activity Codes

other – seasonal berry-picking

Denali Highway

Location

A 135-mile, mostly gravel road between Cantwell and Paxson, Alaska.

Description

The Denali Highway parallels the south side of the Alaska Range for its entire 135-mile length between Paxson and Cantwell. Although it was once the original travel route to Denali National Park, today it is often overlooked by many motorists. Nevertheless, this highway rewards the leisurely traveler with outstanding scenery, good opportunities to view wildlife, and best of all, wilderness in all directions. The highway also provides access to the Gulkana and Delta Rivers at Tangle Lakes, which straddle the highway 22 miles west of Paxson.

Directions

Begin your trip at either end of the highway at Cantwell or Paxson.

Visitor Activities

Wildlife viewing, hiking, rafting, canoeing, floating, fishing, archaeological site, all-terrain driving, snowmobiling, mountain biking, berry picking, picnicking, geologic sightseeing, and scenic drives.

Special Features

Dramatic views of the Alaska Range, with some peaks exceeding 13,000 feet in elevation, provide a constant backdrop to the north. Many geologic features that are reminders of the last major ice age can also be observed.

Permits, Fees, Limitations

The Denali Highway is open for travel generally from mid-May–early October. Visitors should not attempt travel during any other time, as snowdrifts can block the road.

Accessibility

None.

Camping and Lodging

BLM maintains campgrounds at Brushkana Creek (Mile 105) and Tangle Lakes (Mile 21.5). Campgrounds are on a first-come, first-served basis. Fees are charged at Brushkana Creek. Camping is limited to 14 days in a 60-day period. Lodging is available at Paxson, Cantwell, and at roadhouses located at Miles 20, 22, 42, and 82.5, respectively (reservations suggested).

Food and Supplies

A limited selection of food and supplies can be obtained in the Paxson area, the Cantwell area, and roadhouses located at Miles 20, 22, 42, and 82.5, respectively.

First Aid

Limited medical services are available at clinics in Delta Junction, 81 miles north of the eastern terminus of Denali Highway along the Richardson Highway (State Highway 4); Cantwell, at the western terminus of the Denali Highway; and Glennallen, 82 miles south of the eastern terminus of Denali Highway along Richardson Highway (State Highway 4). The nearest hospital is located in Fairbanks. Alaska State Troopers maintain posts in Delta Junction, Cantwell, and

Many ponds along the Denali Highway were created by blocks of ice left behind by melting glaciers; these now provide important habitat for both migrating and nesting waterfowl. *(Dennis R. Green, BLM volunteer, Alaska State Office)*

Glennallen, but they can take a considerable amount of time to respond to an emergency call along the highway.

Additional Information

The Denali Highway is open for travel generally from mid-May–early October, except for snowmobilers. Other travelers should not attempt to drive the highway during any other time, as snowdrifts can block the road. The first 21 miles west of Paxson are paved; thereafter, the highway is gravel until the last 3 miles east of Cantwell. The maximum recommended speed for travel when no other vehicles are in sight is 30 miles per hour. Drivers are cautioned to avoid windshield damage from flying gravel by slowing down when passing oncoming vehicles.

A loop trip from Fairbanks is 436 miles and a loop trip from Anchorage is 600 miles, so travelers should allow several days for these trips. Limited

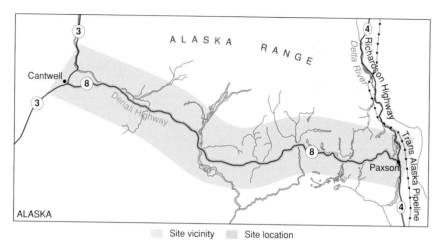

Site vicinity ▦ Site location

services are available, so drivers should make sure their vehicles are in proper working condition and that they have adequate fuel before beginning their trip. They should also be prepared for all types of weather; it can be hot and sunny one day and cold and rainy the very next. It can snow in any month of the year.

Contact Information
BLM - Glennallen Field Office
P. O. Box 147
Glennallen, AK 99588

Tel: (907) 822-3217
Fax: (907) 822-3120
www.ak.blm.gov
www.glennallen.ak.blm.gov/DenaliHwy/denali.html
www.glennallen.ak.blm.gov/DenaliHwy/denhigrmn.html (auf Deutsch)

Activity Codes

other - seasonal berry-picking

Fort Egbert

Location
In the town of Eagle, Alaska.

Description
The fort is a former Yukon River U.S. Army post that was established in 1899 to bring law and order to the Fortymile country during the Klondike Gold Rush. After the boom, the Army Signal Corps operated a telegraphy and wireless station until about 1925. Currently BLM manages five restored structures in cooperation with the local Eagle Historical Society. Exhibits and tours are available in the summer. An interpretive trail on the fort grounds provides access to the ruins of other structures. Fort Egbert National Historic Landmark

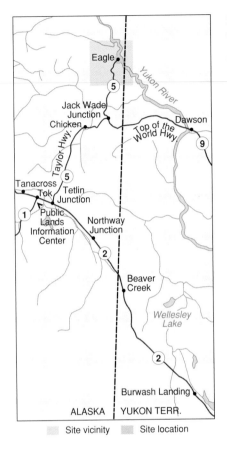

Site vicinity Site location

includes the fort as well as structures in the adjacent community of Eagle.

Directions

From Tok, travel east 12 miles on State Highway 2 to the Taylor Highway (State Highway 5). Take the Taylor Highway 160 miles northeast to its end in the settlement of Eagle. Visitors coming from Dawson City, Yukon Territory (Canada), can connect with the Taylor Highway at Jack Wade Junction by way of the Top of the World Highway and then travel about 45 miles north to Eagle/Fort Egbert.

Visitor Activities

Hiking, historic site, and interpretation.

Special Features

Once a Federal presence on the Yukon River during the Alaska Gold Rush, Fort Egbert remains as the only standing frontier-era fort of its kind in Alaska. It became a key communications center for Alaska when the 1,506-mile-long Washington-Alaska Military Cable and

Fort Egbert and the adjacent town of Eagle offer glimpses into Alaska's historic Gold Rush era. *(Ann Jeffery, BLM)*

Telegraph System (WAMCATS) was completed in 1903 under the direction of a 21-year-old Army lieutenant named Billy Mitchell, who made his headquarters at the fort between 1901 and 1903. This all-American route was Alaska's first communications link with the rest of the United States. Exhibits and historical tours, which begin at 9:00 a.m., are conducted from Memorial Day to Labor Day. The daily guided walking tours provided by the Eagle Historical Society take 2–3 hours and go to 4–6 museums. A highlight of the tour is Fort Egbert with its granary and mule barn full of relics.

Permits, Fees, Limitations

No permits required for non-commercial travel. There is a fee for historical tours; children under 12 years of age are free. Tour information is available from the Eagle Historical Society, (907) 547-2325.

Accessibility

Several historical buildings can be entered and toured on the lower levels by wheelchair. Upper floors of the old buildings are not wheelchair-accessible.

Camping and Lodging

BLM manages a 16-site campground near the fort. A fee is charged for campsites, which are available on a first-come, first-served basis. A motel and cabins are available in the adjacent town of Eagle, within walking distance of the fort.

Food and Supplies

Eagle has both a general store and a cafe.

First Aid

This area is extremely isolated. Limited first aid is available in Eagle from volunteer emergency medical technicians and a local nurse. The nearest hospital is more than an 8-hour drive away in Fairbanks. Weather permitting, evacuation by plane may be available from an airstrip near Eagle.

Additional Information

Summer access is via the Taylor Highway; for the last 60 miles, it is a narrow, winding road unsuitable for large motor homes or trailers. Plan to visit between May and mid-September, as this road is not accessible during the winter months.

Contact Information

BLM - Tok Field Station
Fortymile Management Area
P. O. Box 309
Tok, AK 99780
Tel: (907) 883-5121
Fax: (907) 883-5123
aurora.ak.blm.gov/fortymile/FMwelcome.html

Activity Codes

Fortymile National Wild and Scenic River

Location
60 miles northeast of Tok, Alaska.

Description
Fortymile River is an extensive network of creeks and rivers in east-central Alaska, nearly 400 miles of which have been designated a National Wild and Scenic River. Boaters have many choices for recreational trips through deep, winding canyons lined with forests of birch, spruce, and aspen. Remnants of past mining operations dot the river banks as mementos of the area's rich mining history.

Directions
From Tok, proceed east 12 miles on State Highway 2 to Taylor Highway and then to a drop-off point, such as the South Fork Bridge Wayside or Fortymile Bridge at distances of 75 and 112 miles, respectively, along Taylor Highway. Air taxi shuttles to remote drop-off and take-out points can also be arranged in Tok or Fairbanks.

Visitor Activities
Canoeing, rafting, birdwatching, wildlife viewing, geologic sightseeing, historic site, and fishing.

Special Features
The Kink, a river feature created in 1898 when prospectors blasted a 100-foot rock ridge to drain a meander on the North Fork, about 25 miles upstream from the confluence with the Fortymile River, is on the National Register of Historic Places.

Permits, Fees, Limitations
No fees for non-commercial use.

Accessibility
None.

Camping and Lodging
Camping is available at Walker Fork (Mile 82, Taylor Highway) and West Fork (Mile 49, Taylor Highway). Lodging is available in both Tok, 12 miles west along State Highway 2 (Alaska Highway) from its intersection with the Taylor Highway, and Eagle (Mile 160, Taylor Highway).

Food and Supplies
Groceries and other supplies can be obtained in Tok and in Delta Junction

Near eastern Alaska's border with Canada, Gold Rush-era mine remnants dot the banks of the Fortymile River, which boasts challenging rapids with such colorful names as "The Kink" and "Deadman's Riffle." *(Craig McCaa, BLM Northern Field Office)*

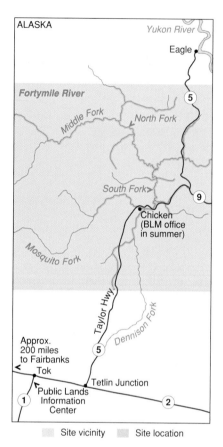

ALASKA
Yukon River
Eagle
Fortymile River
Middle Fork
North Fork
⑤
South Fork
⑨
Chicken
(BLM office
in summer)
Mosquito Fork
Taylor Hwy
Dennison Fork
Approx.
200 miles
to Fairbanks
⑤
Tok
Tetlin Junction
Public Lands
Information
Center
① ②

▨ Site vicinity ▨ Site location

and in Tok at the Tok Clinic, Mile 124, Tok Cutoff Road, (907) 883-5855.

Additional Information
At the BLM office in Tok (on East First Street, currently behind the State Trooper office), visitors can obtain the latest information on river conditions and advice on trip options. There are many levels of difficulty, depending on the segment of river selected. Visitors are encouraged to obtain U.S. Geological Survey topographic maps, to advise someone of their travel itinerary, and to bring clothes suitable for all types of weather. River travel is through remote areas where rescue would be both difficult and time-consuming.

There are active mining operations (suction dredging) along several portions of the river. Visitors should respect private property. River trips take 3–10 days, depending on the trip option selected. Rapids vary from Class II–V. River travelers must be capable of dealing with difficult river conditions in a wilderness setting.

Contact Information
BLM - Tok Field Station
Fortymile Management Area
P. O. Box 309
Tok, AK 99780
Tel: (907) 883-5121
Fax: (907) 883-5123
aurora.ak.blm.gov/fortymile/FMwelcome.html

Activity Codes

and Fairbanks, 108 miles and 212 miles, respectively, northwest of Tok along State Highway 2.

First Aid
Travelers must be prepared to be self-sufficient; the nearest hospital is in Fairbanks, which could be up to a day's travel from Taylor Highway. Limited first aid is available in Eagle at the Eagle Village Health Clinic, (907) 547-2243,

Gulkana National Wild River

Location
60 miles north of Glennallen, Alaska.

Description
The Gulkana is one of the five most used rivers in Alaska, primarily because of its easy access at put-in and take-out points. The river is known for its excellent sport fishing, particularly for Chinook (king) salmon during late June and early July. The Gulkana also contains sockeye salmon, grayling, and rainbow trout, as well as the northernmost population of steelhead trout in North America.

Directions
From Glennallen, drive northeast about 15 miles on State Highway 1 (Glenn Highway) to State Highway 4 (Richardson Highway). Travel about 20 miles north on Highway 4 to the put-in at Sourdough Campground. Continue north for an additional 25 miles to the put-in at Paxson Lake Campground. The take-out for Paxson Lake is at the Sourdough Campground; the take-out for Sourdough Creek is at the Gulkana Bridge.

Visitor Activities
Fishing, canoeing, rafting, hiking, wildlife viewing, hunting (waterfowl, spruce grouse, ptarmigan), and bird-watching.

Paxson Lake is the most popular put-in location for beginning a 3-day trip down the main stem of the Gulkana River. *(Dennis R. Green, BLM volunteer, Alaska State Office)*

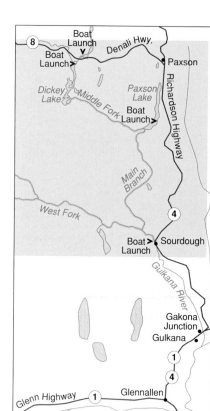

Site vicinity   Site location

Accessibility

Toilets at both Paxson Lake Campground boat launch and Sourdough Creek Campground are wheelchair-accessible. Sourdough Creek Campground features accessible trails and fishing ramps.

Camping and Lodging

Overnight stays anywhere within the National Wild River corridor are limited to 2 weeks at any site. Campgrounds located at the beginning and end of the National Wild River corridor charge fees. Paxson Lake Campground (Mile 175, Richardson Highway) offers 20 pull-in, 20 tent, and 10 walk-in sites; has water and a dump station; and is open from mid-May–early October. Sourdough Creek Campground (Mile 147.5, Richardson Highway) has 42 campsites and is open from mid-May–early October. Fees are charged at both campgrounds. There are numerous undeveloped campsites for boaters along the Gulkana National Wild River. Several roadhouses and lodges may also be found along Richardson Highway.

Food and Supplies

Limited food and supplies are available at roadhouses and lodges along Richardson Highway. A larger selection of food and supplies may be found in Glennallen and in Delta Junction (Mile 266, Richardson Highway, about 151 miles north).

First Aid

No first aid is available anywhere along the Gulkana National Wild River. Limited medical facilities are available at the Cross Roads Medical Center in Glennallen.

Special Features

Visitors can expect to view nesting bald eagles and harlequin ducks along the Gulkana streamside corridor. There are numerous small lakes and wetlands surrounding the Gulkana, which provide important habitat for numerous species of waterfowl, such as trumpeter swans, mallards, and pintails.

Permits, Fees, Limitations

No user fees or permits for non-commercial travel on the river.

Additional Information

The Gulkana is suitable for rafting and experienced canoeists. Floating the 50 miles from Paxson Lake to Sourdough Creek Campground takes 3–4 days, traverses Class I, II, III, and IV rapids, and includes one portage. Canyon Rapids should be scouted before attempting passage by raft. Canoeists should take the 0.25-mile portage. The main stem of the river (between Paxson and Sourdough) receives the heaviest use in July and August, particularly on weekends. Other more remote areas (Middle Fork and West Fork) receive less use; wilderness trips of up to 14 days are possible and visitors see few, if any, people.

Visitors should call BLM to learn the water conditions before beginning a trip, and should be prepared for any kind of weather; it can rain or snow at any time during the summer. Restroom facilities on the river are limited to a few pit toilets. Users are asked to bury human waste or bring along a portable toilet to pack it out. Most river use takes place between ice break-up in late May or early June and ice freeze-up in late September or early October. Tangle Lakes, 15 miles west of Paxson, just beyond the headwaters of the Gulkana/Tangle River system, can remain frozen until mid-June.

Contact Information

BLM – Glennallen District Office
P.O. Box 147
Glennallen, AK 99588
Tel: (907) 822-3217
Fax: (907) 822-3120
www.glennallen.ak.blm.gov

Activity Codes

Steese Highway

Location

162 miles from Fairbanks east to Circle, Alaska.

Description

Northeast of Fairbanks, the Steese Highway follows century-old Gold Rush trails. The Steese Highway provides access to the southern edge of the White Mountains National Recreation Area and the Steese National Conservation Area (NCA).

The Steese NCA, which straddles the Steese Highway, is still remote and offers a broad vista of the land inhabited

Steese Highway travelers glimpse the summer "midnight sun" from Eagle Summit. *(Dennis R. Green, BLM volunteer, Alaska State Office)*

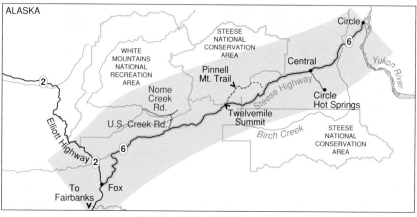

ALASKA

Circle

STEESE NATIONAL CONSERVATION AREA

WHITE MOUNTAINS NATIONAL RECREATION AREA

Central

Yukon River

Pinnell Mt. Trail

Nome Creek Rd.

Steese Highway

Circle Hot Springs

U.S. Creek Rd.

Twelvemile Summit

STEESE NATIONAL CONSERVATION AREA

Birch Creek

Elliott Highway

Fox

To Fairbanks

■ Site vicinity   ■ Site location

mainly by wolves and caribou. Primitive camping and hiking opportunities in pristine surroundings are some of the great attractions of this area. In the summer, BLM's Cripple Creek Campground is a peaceful place to unwind, try some fishing, or pan for gold along the Chatanika River.

At Twelvemile Summit, Mile 85.5 (Fairbanks is Mile 0), and Eagle Summit, Mile 108, wildflowers bloom in June and early July. Later in the year, berries ripen during the long, sunny days. Surfbirds (small, short-legged shore birds) nest on the rocky ridges, and wimbrels nest among the clumps of grasses and sedges on the tundra. Eagle Summit provides a rare location below the Arctic Circle where visitors can view the famous "Midnight Sun" for a few days around June 21, the summer solstice. In winter, the Yukon Quest Sled Dog Race follows Birch Creek National Wild and Scenic River (south of the Highway at Miles 94, 139, and 147) before going over Eagle Summit.

The Steese NCA also has two major destinations for back country summer

travel. The Pinnell Mountain National Recreation Trail is a 27-mile hike along stark, scenic ridgelines. This trail is recognized internationally as one of the premier trails of Alaska. Birch Creek National Wild and Scenic River is a Class I–III float with good road access at both ends of the trip.

Directions

From Fairbanks, travel north along State Highway 2 (Steese Expressway) to Fox, where you pick up Steese Highway (State Highway 6). Steese Highway ends 162 miles east at the Yukon River in the town of Circle.

Visitor Activities

Hiking, big-game and bird hunting, birdwatching, wildlife viewing, plant viewing, canoeing, rafting, fishing, historic site, mountain climbing, gold panning, dog mushing, snowmobiling, and cross-country skiing.

Special Features

Travelers should make a point to visit the tiny communities of Circle Hot Springs and Circle on the Yukon River

The Pinnell Mountain National Recreation Trail is known for its wildflower displays in June and July, and provides an opportunity to view the "midnight sun," even though the site is well south of the Arctic Circle. *(Dennis R. Green, BLM volunteer, Alaska State Office)*

(Miles 127.8 and 162, respectively) to see examples of mining towns that have matured over the course of the last century. Other reminders of gold mining include the Davidson Ditch (Mile 57.3), a system of pipes and irrigation ditches that supplied water to the gold dredges north of Fairbanks.

Permits, Fees, Limitations

No fees. No motorized vehicles are allowed in portions of the Steese NCA designated as Research Natural Areas. Areas designated as primitive allow motorized access only in winter. Other restrictions may apply. Contact BLM for maps and specific information.

Accessibility

Waysides have wheelchair-accessible vault toilets. Eagle Summit Wayside, at Mile 108, has a wheelchair-accessible trail.

Camping and Lodging

Only back country camping is available. Lodging is available in Central (Mile 127.8). No camping is allowed in Research Natural Areas within the Steese NCA.

Food and Supplies

Food and supplies are available in Fairbanks, Central, and Circle.

First Aid

Visitors need to carry their own first aid supplies as no help is available in this remote back country. Central has emergency services. The nearest hospital is in Fairbanks.

Additional Information

The Pinnell Mountain National Recreation Trail is 27 miles long, traversing from ridgeline to ridgeline. It is a primitive trail that can be considered difficult, with elevation changes of more than 500 feet over 0.5 mile. Severe weather systems often affect high ridge-line areas. The area is remote and U.S. Geological Survey quadrangle maps (at 1:63,360 scale) are recommended.

The Birch Creek National Wild and Scenic River is 110 miles from Upper Birch Creek Wayside (Mile 94) to Lower Birch Creek Wayside (Mile 147), with an additional 16 miles from Lower Birch Creek Wayside to the 147 Mile Bridge on Steese Highway. Visitors will encounter some Class III rapids above the confluence with Wolf Creek. Just downstream from the confluence with Clums Fork, there are some Class II rapids. Rapids should be scouted before running.

Contact Information

BLM - Northern Field Office
1150 University Avenue
Fairbanks, AK 99709-3844
Tel: (907) 474-2200
Fax: (907) 474-2282
aurora.ak.blm.gov/Steese

Alaska Public Lands Information Center
250 Cushman Street, Suite 102A
Fairbanks, AK 99701
Tel: (907) 456-0527
Fax: (907) 456-0514
www.nps.gov/aplic/about_us/faplic.html

Activity Codes

other – rock climbing, mountain climbing, gold panning

White Mountains National Recreation Area

Location
60 miles northwest of Fairbanks, Alaska.

Description
This 1-million-acre area is used primarily from February–April, when dog mushers, snowmobilers, and skiers come to take advantage of the winter solitude and northern lights. BLM maintains 11 winter cabins, which are connected by a network of more than 300 miles of groomed winter trails.

Much of the area is too wet to hike through in the summer, but Beaver Creek National Wild and Scenic River and several short trails offer other opportunities for back country adventures.

Directions
Begin your trip at the BLM office in Fairbanks or the Alaska Public Lands Information Center (an interagency office) in Fairbanks, where you can

Caribou Bluff Cabin offers cozy shelter to intrepid travelers in BLM's White Mountains National Recreation Area. *(Craig McCaa, BLM Northern Field Office)*

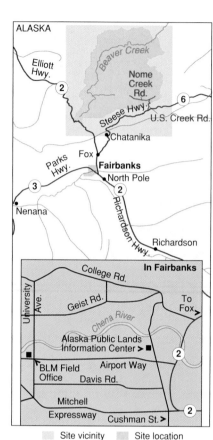

ALASKA

Elliott Hwy.
2
Beaver Creek
Nome Creek Rd.
Steese Hwy.
6
U.S. Creek Rd.
Chatanika
Parks Hwy.
Fox
Fairbanks
North Pole
3
Nenana
Richardson Hwy.
Richardson

In Fairbanks
College Rd.
University Ave.
Geist Rd.
Chena River
To Fox
Alaska Public Lands Information Center
2
BLM Field Office
Airport Way
Davis Rd.
Mitchell Expressway
Cushman St.
2

Site vicinity   Site location

obtain detailed directions, as well as the latest information on trail and weather conditions.

To get to the White Mountains National Recreation Area: From Fairbanks, travel north on Elliott Highway (State Highway 2). Most summer hiking occurs along the Summit Trail at Mile 28, Elliott Highway. Winter access is at Mile 28 as well as Mile 57, Elliott Highway. Primary summer access is via the U.S. Creek Road at mile 57 of the Steese Highway (State Highway 6).

Visitor Activities

Hiking, wildlife viewing, floating, fishing, dog mushing, snowmobiling, and cross-country skiing.

Special Features

The White Mountains are known for their unusual and distinctive limestone peaks, which weather into a mixture of white and gray rocks. Ecosystems vary considerably with elevation, and include alpine tundra, upland coniferous forests of black and white spruces, mixed forests of paper birch, aspen, and spruce, and lowland forests of spruce with willows dominating the streamside zones along creeks and other waterways. A number of small tributary streams run fast and clear, uniting to form Beaver Creek, which drains the area as it flows into the Yukon River. The White Mountains National Recreation Area (NRA) is home to a variety of animals, including Dall sheep, grizzly bears, wolves, wolverines, and caribou.

Permits, Fees, Limitations

Summer use of off-highway vehicles is limited to certain areas and certain vehicle weights. Visitors should contact BLM for further information and maps.

Accessibility

None.

Camping and Lodging

BLM maintains the Mount Prindle and Ophir Creek Campgrounds in the Nome Creek Valley; these can be reached via U.S. Creek Road at Mile 57, Steese Highway, and are closed in winter. Eleven BLM public recreation cabins are available by reservation only; there is a use fee charged per group per night. Visitors should contact BLM for reservations well in advance of any trip: (907) 474-2251 (local), 1-800-437-7021 (toll-free). Weekend dates in March and April are the first to fill up. Cripple Creek Campground is located at Mile 60, Steese Highway. Lodging is available in Fairbanks.

Food and Supplies

Food and supplies are available in Fairbanks.

First Aid

Visitors should carry their own first aid kits, as no help is available in this wilderness setting. The nearest hospital is in Fairbanks.

Additional Information

Winter use is most popular on weekends, February–April, when moderate temperatures and longer days make travel easier. Visitation is not encouraged from October–January, when temperatures occasionally reach -65°F and there are less than 5 hours of sunlight per day. Winter trails are maintained on an infrequent basis, so U.S. Geological Survey topographic maps and good route-finding abilities are necessities. Visitors should also have at least a basic knowledge of winter survival skills.

Contact Information

BLM - Northern Field Office
1150 University Avenue
Fairbanks, AK 99709
Tel: (907) 474-2302
Fax: (907) 474-2282
aurora.ak.blm.gov

Alaska Public Lands Information Center
250 Cushman Street, Suite 102A
Fairbanks, AK 99701
Tel: (907) 456-0527
Fax: (907) 456-0514
www.nps.gov/aplic/center

Activity Codes

The Borealis-LeFevre Cabin near the Beaver Creek National Wild and Scenic River is just one of 11 rustic cabins available for rent in the White Mountains Recreation Area. Most people visit the recreation area in the winter, when frozen ground allows for easier travel.
(Dennis R. Green, BLM volunteer, Alaska State Office)

Massive sandstone formations within the Tinajas Altas Mountains dwarf a hiker in this remote Sonoran Desert area east of Yuma, Arizona. *(Diane Drobka, BLM Safford Field Office)*

Stretching across 11.6 million acres, Arizona's public lands are located mostly in the northwestern and central western portions of the state. Rugged canyons, sprawling rangelands, lakes, forests, and mountains are all part of the landscape, which also encompasses four spectacular deserts: the Chihuahuan, Sonoran, Mojave, and Great Basin. Arizona's public lands also host pinyon-juniper and ponderosa pine forests in many upland elevations, as well as wetlands and riparian (streamside) habitats in places like the Gila Box and along the San Pedro River.

Whether a visitor seeks a challenging back country bike ride or a scenic tour in the comfort of an air-conditioned recreational vehicle, Arizona's public lands provide a wide range of recreational activities. Hiking, biking, rockhounding, off-highway driving, hunting, nature study, and even water sports are just some of the offerings. Many developed campgrounds, long term visitor areas, and commercial recreational facilities are easily accessible to visitors of all ages and abilities. For those desiring solitude, Arizona's public lands provide plenty of room to pack it in, pitch a tent, and pack it out.

Some of the nation's oldest and best-preserved pre-historic and historic sites are found on Arizona's public lands. These include rock art dating to 6,000 years ago, remnants of a Spanish military fort, a historic working cattle ranch and schoolhouse, and Indian dwellings that are more than 1,000 years old.

Adventure seekers can explore 47 wilderness areas, 5 national monuments, 3 national conservation areas, national historic and recreation trails, numerous recreational facilities, and natural and cultural resources too diverse and abundant to imagine.

From river rafting in the Gila Box Riparian National Conservation Area to bird and wildlife watching in the San Pedro Riparian National Conservation Area, from braving the hairpin curves of the Route 66 Historic Back Country Byway to boating on Lake Havasu, Arizona's public lands offer a wealth of recreational choices.

Arizona

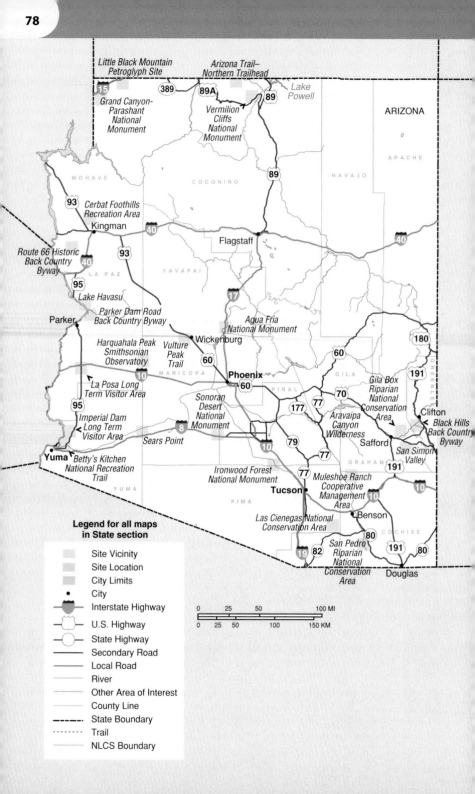

Agua Fria National Monument

Location
40 miles north of Phoenix, Arizona.

Description
The Agua Fria National Monument was among the first BLM areas to be designated a national monument. The 71,000-acre region contains one of the most significant systems of prehistoric sites in the Southwest. At least 450 prehistoric sites and 4 major settlements have been discovered. Stone masonry pueblos are typically situated at the edges of steep canyons, while petroglyphs—images carved into the surfaces of boulders and cliff faces—offer clues about the people who once lived here.

Directions
From Phoenix, take Interstate 17 north about 40 miles to the Badger Springs Exit (Exit #256) or 3 miles further north to the Bloody Basin Road Exit (Exit #259). These two roads provide the major access points to the monument area.

Visitor Activities
Hiking, archaeological site, wildlife viewing, birdwatching, hunting (big-game and upland game-bird), scenic drives, and four-wheel driving (but no off-road travel is allowed).

Special Features
Within the monument, a desert grassland extends across an extensive mesa cut by canyon walls and the Agua Fria River. The area is the home to coyotes, bobcats, antelope, mule deer, javelinas, a variety of small mammals, and songbirds. Eagles and other raptors may also be spotted. Native fish, such as the longfin dace, Gila mountain sucker, Gila chub, and speckled dace, live in the Agua Fria River and its tributaries.

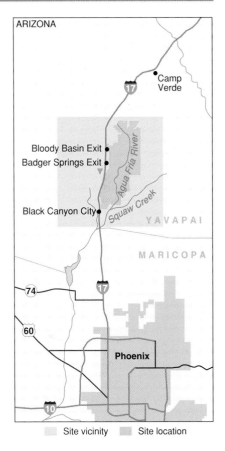

Site vicinity   Site location

The monument's prehistoric ruins offer insights into the lives of the people who inhabited this area from AD 1250–1450. Archaeologists believe that as many as several thousand people once lived in the area's pueblo communities. They also believe that many more prehistoric sites remain to be discovered within this remote and rugged monument.

Permits, Fees, Limitations
None.

Accessibility
None.

Camping and Lodging
There are no developed facilities within the national monument. Primitive camping is permitted, with a 14-day limit. Campgrounds and motels are located in the nearby communities of Black Canyon City (45 miles north of Phoenix on Interstate 17) and Cordes Lakes (about 90 miles north of Phoenix on U.S. Highway 93).

Food and Supplies
Food and supplies are available in the adjacent communities of Black Canyon City and Cordes Lakes.

First Aid
There is no first aid station on-site. The nearest hospital is located in north Phoenix.

Additional Information
The elevation of the monument ranges from 2,000–4,000 feet. Summer visitors must take extra precaution to drink plenty of water, as temperatures may exceed 110°F. Sunscreen, sunglasses, and hats are recommended. Visitors are reminded to have a full tank of gas and carry plenty of water. Vehicles should be in good condition to travel the rocky terrain. The hot desert sun stirs rattlesnakes and other reptiles as early as February. Flash floods caused by

Agua Fria National Monument's petroglyphs showcase a wide variety of images, including clearly-recognizable animals.
(Diane Drobka, BLM Safford Field Office)

sudden storms can also be hazardous in washes.

Pueblo la Plata showcases a major settlement of stone masonry pueblos. To get there, travel 8.3 miles on Bloody Basin Road from the entrance of the national monument. Turn north (left) and follow the dirt road for approximately 1 mile. Limited parking is available. Walk to the site by following the rocky and uneven trail.

Contact Information

BLM - Phoenix Field Office
21605 North 7th Avenue
Phoenix, AZ 85027
Tel: (623) 580–5500
Fax: (623) 580–5580
phoenix.az.blm.gov

Activity Codes

Aravaipa Canyon Wilderness

Location

22 miles southeast of Winkelman, Arizona (west entrance).
53 miles west of Safford, Arizona (east entrance).

Description

The cooling perennial waters of Aravaipa ("Ar-ah-vie-pah") Creek have carved a scenic canyon through the Sonoran Desert at the northern end of the Galiuro Mountains in southeastern Arizona. Saguaro cacti dot the canyon slopes, and a mixed-broadleaf riparian forest lines the canyon along the creek. The canyon, up to 1,000 feet deep in places, is home to desert bighorn sheep, javelinas, coatimundis, ringtail cats, and other wildlife. The creek is home to several native fish species, and over 200 species of birds live among the cottonwoods, sycamores, willows, ash, and other riparian areas in the canyon. Aravaipa Canyon Wilderness is 11 miles long, and elevations range from 3,060 feet at the eastern trailhead to 2,630 feet at the western trailhead. Nine major side canyons feed into Aravaipa and,

along with caves, outcrops, and chimneys, entice visitors to explore. Strong hikers can traverse from end to end in 8–10 hours, while photographers, nature watchers, and those wanting to explore side canyons may take one or two overnights and still never see it all.

Directions

From Phoenix to the west trailhead (120 miles), take U.S. Highway 60 to Superior. At Superior, take State Highway 177 to Winkelman, then take State Highway 77 south for 11 miles to Aravaipa Road (at Central Arizona College). Turn left and go 12 miles to the west trailhead along a paved and graded dirt road. From the trailhead, it is a 1.5-mile hike through Nature Conservancy lands to the west wilderness boundary. Driving directions to both the east and west trailheads from Phoenix, Tucson, and Safford are available on the BLM Aravaipa Canyon website (see Contact Information).

Visitor Activities

Hiking, wildlife viewing, plant viewing, birdwatching, horseback riding, geologic sightseeing, and big-game and small-game hunting.

Special Features

Aravaipa Creek flows year-round, an unusual phenomenon in the Arizona desert. Nurtured by this abundant water source, large sycamore, ash, cottonwood, and willow trees flourish along the stream, flanked by other riparian vegetation. In the fall, a kaleidoscope of brilliant red and golden leaves contrasts dramatically with the surrounding tans of the Sonoran Desert landscape.

Permits, Fees, Limitations

An entry permit is required and may be reserved up to 13 weeks in advance of entry date. Use is limited to 50 people per day: 30 entering from the west trailhead, and 20 entering from the east trailhead. This system helps to reduce the potential impacts to the environment caused by human use and allows visitors to enjoy the canyon's solitude. A fee is charged. Permits can be booked on BLM's online reservation system (*www.az.blm.gov*); this requires advance payment via credit card.

Accessibility

None within the wilderness. The information kiosk and restroom at the east entrance, and ranger station at the west end, are wheelchair-accessible.

Camping and Lodging

Fourmile Canyon Campground is a year-round area located in Klondyke, just 0.75 mile southwest of the site on Fourmile Canyon Road. This is a 10-unit campground with tables, grills, toilets, water, and trash cans, but no hookups. Daily fees are charged. Camping also is permitted on adjacent public lands with no facilities. Lodging is available in small towns near each end of the wilderness.

Food and Supplies

Food and supplies are available in Klondyke (10 miles south), Safford (53 miles east) and Winkelman (22 miles northwest).

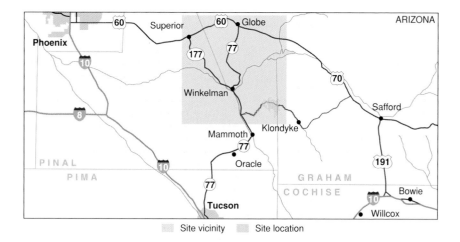

Site vicinity   Site location

Horseback tours through 11 miles of Aravaipa Canyon Wilderness allow visitors to experience the scenic wonders of this desert riparian (streamside) canyon without getting their feet wet. *(Diane Drobka, BLM Safford Field Office)*

First Aid

No first aid is available on-site. The hospital nearest to the east trailhead is located in Safford. The nearest medical facilities closest to the west trailhead are in Kearny, 33 miles northwest on State Highway 177, and San Manuel, 30 miles southwest on State Highway 77.

Additional Information

Hiking in the canyon is considered to be moderately difficult, and numerous calf- and knee-deep stream crossings are required. The wilderness is open year-round, but spring and fall are the best times to hike. Summer can be quite hot, and winter is chilly. The avenues of access to both ends of the wilderness cross lands owned by The Nature Conservancy; this private property should be respected. The BLM Aravaipa Canyon website also provides detailed information about hiking, camping, and natural history. Visitors should call BLM to obtain an entry permit.

Contact Information

BLM - Safford Field Office
711 14th Avenue
Safford, AZ 85546
Tel: (928) 348-4400
Fax: (928) 348-4450
www.az.blm.gov/sfo/index.htm
Aravaipa Canyon website
www.az.blm.gov/sfo/aravaipa/permits.htm

Activity Codes

Arizona Trail– Northern Trailhead

Location

28 miles east of Kanab, Utah.

Description

The 12.5-mile northern trailhead stretch of the Arizona Trail makes its way south through the steep and rugged eastern flank of Buckskin Mountain, where it treats visitors to sweeping views of the Vermilion Cliffs, Coyote Buttes, Kaibab Plateau, and southern Utah. The trail continues to the Grand Canyon and beyond, eventually traversing some 800 miles to Mexico.

Directions

From Kanab, take U.S. Highway 89 east about 35 miles to House Rock Valley Road. Turn south on House Rock Valley Road and travel 9 miles to the Stateline Campground and the Arizona Trail Trailhead. Continue south on House Rock Valley Road (into Arizona, where the road is numbered BLM 1065) for 7 additional miles to BLM 1025 (also called Winter Road), and turn west. Continue about 5 miles to the Arizona Trail. Hikers can head north from here across Buckskin Mountain to the Utah border, or head south to the Kaibab Plateau within the Kaibab National Forest.

Visitor Activities

Hiking, mountain biking, big-game hunting, geologic sightseeing, and wildlife viewing.

Special Features

This section of the trail offers spectacular panoramas of northern Arizona and southern Utah. The North Rim of the Grand Canyon lies another 50 miles down the Arizona Trail. Buckskin Mountain is a famous deer wintering area.

Permits, Fees, Limitations

No permits or fees are required to use the trail. Hunting is allowed under Arizona Game and Fish Department regulations.

Accessibility

The trail is not wheelchair-accessible. The restroom at the Stateline Campground, at the northern trailhead, is accessible.

Camping and Lodging

The Stateline Campground is located at the northern trailhead. The nearest lodging is in Kanab, Utah, and Page, Arizona, 74 miles east of Kanab on U.S. Highway 89.

Gambel's quail are frequent sights along the Arizona Trail. Males, such as the one perched on a thicket here, are somewhat larger than females, and may also be distinguished by their brown "caps," black throats, and sinuous white head stripes. *(Lynn Chamberlain, BLM)*

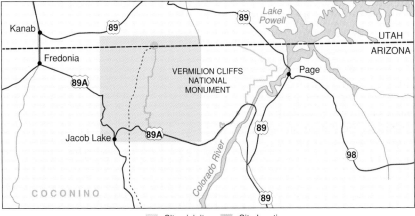

Site vicinity   Site location

Food and Supplies
There are no sources of food or supplies on-site. The nearest stores are in Kanab and Page.

First Aid
There are no first aid facilities on-site. First aid is available in Kanab and Page. The nearest hospital is in Flagstaff, Arizona, approximately 125 miles south on U.S. Highway 89.

Additional Information
Hiking in foothills may be hazardous because of loose rock, steep slopes, and extreme summer temperatures. Fall, winter, and spring are the best times to visit. For access to the trailhead, high-clearance vehicles are recommended. Parts of the trail are steep.

Contact Information
BLM - Arizona Strip Field Office
345 E. Riverside Drive
St. George, UT 84770
Tel: (435) 688-3246
Fax: (435) 688-3258
www.az.blm.gov/asfo/index.htm

Activity Codes

Betty's Kitchen National Recreation Trail

Location
17 miles southwest of Yuma, Arizona.

Description
The Betty's Kitchen trail and interpretive area offer a lush, shady environment along the Lower Colorado River. Visitors can kick off their shoes while casting a line and fishing from the pier, pack a lunch or barbecue in the picnic area, or take a stroll along the 0.5-mile interpretive trail. No matter what the time of year, Betty's Kitchen promises visitors a peek at some of Arizona's wildlife.

Directions
From Yuma, take State Highway 95 (16th Street) east 5 miles to Avenue 7E. Turn north on Avenue 7E, following it 9 miles to a point just past Laguna Dam. Turn left at the sign for Betty's Kitchen Wildlife and Interpretive Area.

Visitor Activities
Fishing, picnicking, wildlife viewing, plant viewing, birdwatching, hiking, and interpretive tours.

Special Features
Betty's Kitchen is named after a café that stood at this site in the 1930s. This oasis in the desert boasts a variety of flora (palo verde, buccaris, quailbush, mesquite, cattails, cottonwoods, and willows) and fauna (diamondback rattlesnakes, desert cottontails, common king snakes, raccoons, tree lizards, great horned owls, egrets, and numerous migrating songbirds) which may be sighted along the interpretive trail.

A BLM employee, "armed" with a scaly partner, talks with a group of local students about wildlife in the Betty's Kitchen area. *(Lori Cook, BLM Yuma Field Office)*

Permits, Fees, Limitations
There is a per-vehicle day-use fee.

Accessibility
None.

Camping and Lodging
Free primitive camping is available at nearby Mittry Lake Wildlife Area. Camping for a nightly fee is available at BLM's Imperial Dam Recreation Area, approximately 15 miles north on State Highway 95. Motels and hotels are available in Yuma.

Food and Supplies
No food or supplies are available on-site. Restaurants and food stores are located in Yuma.

First Aid
There is no first aid available on-site. The nearest hospital is located in Yuma. There is also a medical facility at the Yuma Proving Ground, 9 miles up the gravel road past the Mittry Lake Wildlife Area.

Additional Information
Betty's Kitchen is best visited during the spring, winter, and fall. Daily summer temperature highs are 100°-118°F. Although mosquitoes are generally not present, they occur periodically, so

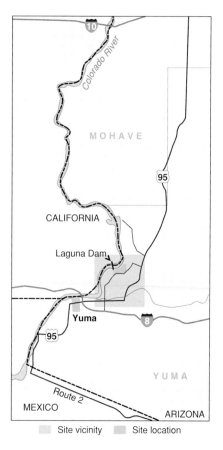

Site vicinity   Site location

insect repellent is recommended. Most anglers fish for bluegill, channel catfish, and flathead catfish, although large-mouth bass can also be caught at Betty's Kitchen. The best time of year for birdwatching is during the spring migration in April and May. The Betty's Kitchen Protective Association assists BLM with management of the site.

Contact Information
BLM - Yuma Field Office
2555 E. Gila Ridge Road
Yuma, AZ 85365
Tel: (928) 317-3200
Fax: (928) 317-3250
www.az.blm.gov/yfo/index.htm

Activity Codes

Black Hills Back Country Byway

Location
18 miles east of Safford, Arizona (south end).
4 miles south of Clifton, Arizona (north end).

Description
The Black Hills Back Country Byway offers 21 miles of scenic driving adventure through the northern end of

the Peloncillo Mountains in southeastern Arizona. Along the byway are sweeping views of the Black Hills, Gila Mountains, Mount Graham, and Gila River Valley. Major attractions visible from the byway include the Gila Box Riparian National Conservation Area along the Gila River, the Phelps Dodge Copper Mine at Morenci, a Civilian Conservation Corps work camp, over

100 erosion-control structures, and a historic prison labor camp. Side trips off the byway provide four-wheel-drive and mountain bike access to the Gila River and spectacular overlooks of the Gila River canyon.

Directions

To reach the south end from Safford, travel 10 miles east on U.S. Highway 70 to its junction with U.S. Highway 191. Turn left onto U.S. Highway 191 and continue 8 miles to the southern end of the byway (Milepost 139). The northern end of the byway is accessed from U.S. Highway 191 by turning west at Milepost 160, 4 miles south of Clifton.

Visitor Activities

Scenic drives, picnicking, hiking, environmental education, mountain biking, all-terrain driving, wildlife and wildflower viewing, birdwatching, historic site, horseback riding, big- and small-game hunting, fishing, canoeing, kayaking, archaeological site, geologic sightseeing, and interpreted site.

Special Features

Many primitive side roads beckon off-highway-vehicle enthusiasts and provide challenging rides for experienced mountain bicyclists. There are intensely-colored fire agates for rock collectors at the nearby Black Hills Rockhound Area, while volcanic rock formations of multicolored lava flows intermixed with ash falls along the road can be studied and photographed. Hiking along roads and trails or cross-country rewards visitors with scenic vistas of the Gila Box and views of the area's plentiful wildlife, which includes whip-tailed lizards, roadrunners, and coyotes. The historic Old Safford Bridge is a popular launch site for those floating through

Owl Creek Campground along the back country byway provides a scenic view of the route as it traverses the Gila Box Riparian National Conservation Area via the Old Safford Bridge. *(Diane Drobka, BLM Safford Field Office)*

the Gila Box Riparian National Conservation Area. Boating is popular along the Gila River near the historic Old Safford Bridge (between Mileposts 16 and 17). This is a popular launch site for trips through the Gila Box Riparian National Conservation Area.

Permits, Fees, Limitations
No fees are charged for driving the byway.

Accessibility
The following areas are wheelchair-accessible: Owl Creek Campground (10 miles south of Safford on U.S. Highway 191), Canyon Overlook Picnic Area (midway along the byway, about 10 miles in from either entrance), and the Phelps Dodge interpretive exhibit (13.1 miles in from the south end).

Camping and Lodging
Owl Creek, perched on a cliff over-looking the historic Old Safford Bridge, is a developed campground with seven units that include tables, grills, and a restroom. Camping fees are charged. Potable water is not available. Primitive camping is permitted on adjacent public lands except in riparian areas such as the picnic sites below the bridge. Camping is limited to 14 consecutive days in any one location. Lodging is available in Clifton and Morenci, 4 miles north of the north end, and Safford, 18 miles west of the south end.

Food and Supplies
Food and supplies are available in Clifton, Morenci, and Safford.

First Aid
No first aid is available on-site. The nearest hospitals are in Morenci and Safford.

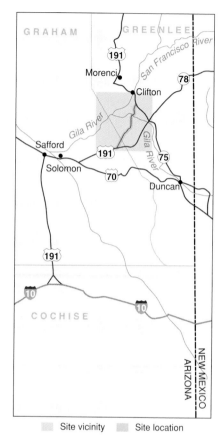

Site vicinity   Site location

Additional Information
The byway is narrow and winding, with occasional steep grades and tight turns. Much of the road is maintained, but a high-clearance or four-wheel-drive vehicle is recommended. A 1-mile section near the middle of the byway can be rough and impassable following heavy rains or snow. A brochure (free) and an interpretive travel tape (for sale) are available from BLM's Safford Field Office. Numerous interpretive signs and kiosks are located along the byway. Elevation ranges from 3,800–5,500 feet.

Contact Information
BLM – Safford Field Office
711 14th Avenue
Safford, AZ 85546
Tel: (928) 348-4400
Fax: (928) 348-4450
www.az.blm.gov/sfo/index.htm

Activity Codes

other - environmental
education

Cerbat Foothills Recreation Area

Location
1 mile north and west of downtown
Kingman, Arizona.

Description
The Cerbat Foothills Recreation Area
rises above the Kingman city limits to
the north and west, providing a dramatic backdrop to the city. Eleven miles
of trails for hikers, mountain bikers, and
horseback riders await visitors, and another 30 miles of trails are in various
stages of planning. Trail users cross a
landscape that hosts drought-resistant
desert plants and hardy animals, and
features haunting silhouettes of weather-
carved rock outcrops and mesas. The
higher elevations along the trails offer
stunning, panoramic views of neighboring valleys and mountain ranges.

Directions
Badger Trail can be accessed by driving
north on U.S. Highway 93 out of
Kingman. The trailhead is located
5 miles beyond the city limits, on the
right side of the highway, about
0.25 mile north of the junction with
State Highway 68. Camp Beale Springs
Loop Trail is located on Fort Beale
Road, about 0.25-mile west of its intersection with Clack Canyon Road.

Visitor Activities
Hiking, mountain biking, horseback
riding, wildlife viewing, plant viewing,
picnicking, and geologic sightseeing.

Special Features
Abundant, weather-carved landforms
are scattered throughout the area. The
recreation area has been locally referred
to as Kingman's "Little Monument
Valley." With abundant winter rain,
wildflower viewing can be excellent.

**The large flowers of the saguaro
cactus color the Sonoran Desert from
late April–June. Each blossom opens
a few hours after sunset and lasts until the
next afternoon. The spectacle repeats itself
nightly for about 4 weeks, until as many as
100 flowers have bloomed and wilted on
each saguaro.** *(BLM Yuma Field Office)*

Good examples of local flora in the form of ocotillo, Mojave yucca, cholla, and catclaw cactus can be observed. Local wildlife includes red-tailed hawks, coyotes, and a variety of lizards and snakes.

Permits, Fees, Limitations
None.

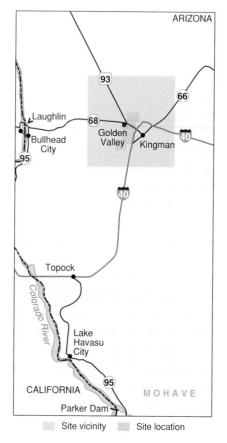

Site vicinity   Site location

Accessibility
None.

Camping and Lodging
Camping is not permitted at trailheads, but is permissible in the back country. Lodging is available in Kingman.

Food and Supplies
There are no services available on-site. Food and supplies are available in Kingman.

First Aid
There are no first aid services on-site. The Kingman Regional Medical Center in Kingman provides full-service emergency care.

Additional Information
The best time to visit this area is October–April. Summertime use is discouraged because of excessive heat and dangerous lightning storms, along with a lack of available water and shade. Rattlesnakes are common in the area.

Contact Information
BLM - Kingman Field Office
2475 Beverly Avenue
Kingman, AZ 86401
Tel: (928) 692-4400
Fax: (928) 692-4414
www.az.blm.gov/kfo/index.htm

Activity Codes

Gila Box Riparian National Conservation Area

Location

20 miles northeast of Safford, Arizona (west end).
5 miles south of Clifton, Arizona (east end).

Description

Rivers and creeks may seem out of place in the Arizona desert, but 23 miles of the Gila River and 15 miles of Bonita Creek are included in this special Riparian National Conservation Area (NCA), designated by Congress in 1990. The Gila River canyon section, known as the Gila Box, features patchy mesquite woodlands, mature cottonwoods, sandy beaches, and grand, buff-colored cliffs. Bonita Creek, popular for birdwatching, hiking, and picnicking, is lined with large cottonwoods, sycamores, and willows. Canoeing, kayaking, and rafting enthusiasts take advantage of the spring runoff to enjoy an easy to moderately difficult floating adventure down the Gila. Many people also float the river in inflatable kayaks during the low water of the summer. Lower water also affords hikers the opportunity to safely enjoy the scenic canyon. The perennial creek and riparian vegetation make this a cool, year-round desert oasis. Prehistoric structures, historic homesteads, Rocky Mountain bighorn sheep, and over 200 species of birds are found within the NCA. A network of primitive roads provides hours of back country adventure for four-wheel-drive and mountain bike trekkers.

Directions

To reach the west side from Safford, travel 5 miles east on U.S. Highway 70 to Solomon. At Solomon, turn left on Sanchez Road and follow the road to the end of the pavement. From there, follow the signs to Bonita Creek and the lower end of the Gila Box.

To reach the east side from Safford, take U.S. Highway 70 east 10 miles to its junction with U.S. Highway 191. Turn left and follow Highway 191 about 29 miles to Milepost 160, which is 4 miles south of Clifton. Turn left onto the signed Black Hills Back Country Byway, and follow the road 4 miles to the conservation area.

Thousand-foot cliffs lining the Gila River near Safford give the Gila Box Riparian National Conservation Area its name. The canyon is best explored by raft or kayak, and views along the river often include herds of Rocky Mountain bighorn sheep.
(Diane Drobka, BLM Safford Field Office)

Visitor Activities
Rafting, canoeing, kayaking, picnicking, birdwatching, scenic drives, fishing, wildlife viewing, hiking, biking, historic site, archaeological site, horseback riding, swimming, wildflower viewing, four-wheel driving, geologic sightseeing, and hunting (big-game and bird).

Special Features
The Gila Box Riparian National Conservation Area includes four perennial waterways, the Gila and San Francisco Rivers and Bonita and Eagle Creeks. This region is a very special riparian ecosystem abounding with plant and animal diversity. The impressive Gila Conglomerate cliffs tower more than 1,000 feet above the Gila River, and bighorn sheep are commonly spotted. Cliff dwellings, rock art, and a homestead cabin are evidence of earlier occupation along this important perennial stream. The Bonita Creek Watchable Wildlife Viewing Area provides a bird's-eye view of the riparian canyon below, with over 100 species of birds recorded here, including raptors such as zone-tailed hawks, bald and golden eagles, and peregrine falcons, as well as colorful migrating birds.

Permits, Fees, Limitations
Use of the Flying W Group Day Use Picnic Area is free of charge, but the area can be reserved for a fee. Those floating the river also pay a use fee.

Accessibility
Both campgrounds, the Bonita Creek Wildlife Viewing Area, the Flying W Group Day Use Site, and all picnic areas are wheelchair-accessible.

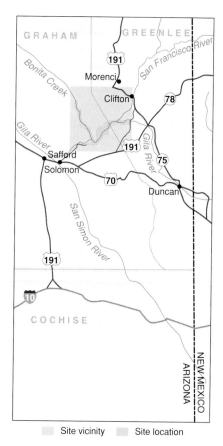

Site vicinity   Site location

Camping and Lodging
Developed campgrounds include the 13-unit Riverview Campground and the 7-unit Owl Creek Campground. Each has tables, shade structures, grills, restrooms, and trash cans. Riverview also has potable water. Fees are charged at both. Camping is also permitted on adjacent public lands, but no facilities are available. Camping is not permitted in riparian areas or designated picnic sites. Camping at developed sites, and primitive camping elsewhere, is limited to 14 consecutive days. There are no

permits or fees for primitive camping. Lodging is available in Clifton (5 miles north of the eastern entrance on U.S. Highway 191) and Safford.

Food and Supplies
Food and supplies are available in Clifton, Morenci (7 miles north of Clifton on U.S. Highway 191), Safford, and Thatcher (23 miles west of the eastern entrance on U.S. Highway 70, just past Safford).

First Aid
No first aid is available on-site. The nearest hospitals are in Morenci and Safford.

Additional Information
A color brochure with a map is available free from BLM. Major access points are generally reachable by passenger car, but other roads may be rough at times because of infrequent maintenance. Four-wheel-drive vehicles are required

on many roads. Check with BLM for up-to-date road conditions. Elevations range from 3,100–4,400 feet. The conservation area is open year-round. Summer temperatures can be extremely hot, and some winter days quite cold. Flooding may occur during winter and summer rainy seasons, as well as during spring runoff.

Contact Information
BLM - Safford Field Office
711 14th Avenue
Safford, AZ 85546
Tel: (928) 348-4400
Fax: (928) 348-4450
www.az.blm.gov/sfo/index.htm

Activity Codes

Grand Canyon-Parashant National Monument

Location
30 miles southwest of St. George, Utah.

Description
The Grand Canyon-Parashant National Monument covers more than 1 million acres of remote canyons, mountains, and buttes. Extremely rugged and isolated, this monument is suitable for the hearty outdoor adventurer only. Grand Canyon National Park forms the monument's southern border. The monument is home to countless biological, historical, and

The Grand Canyon-Parashant National Monument affords visitors miles of unspoiled desert vistas. *(BLM)*

archaeological treasures. It is managed jointly by the BLM and the National Park Service.

Directions

From St. George, take River Road south approximately 6 miles to the Arizona/Utah border. BLM Road 1069 will then lead you to several access points.

Visitor Activities

Four-wheel driving, hiking, wildlife viewing, plant viewing, birdwatching, big-game hunting, archaeological site, historic site, horseback riding, and geologic sightseeing

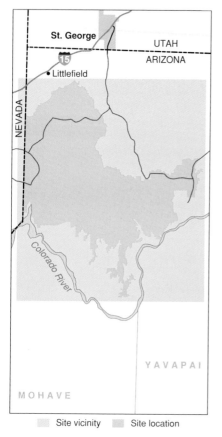

Site vicinity　　Site location

Special Features

For those people willing to make the long, remote drive, this monument offers spectacular vistas and abundant natural and cultural resources. Vegetation ranges from Mojave Desert flora to ponderosa pine forest. A variety of wildlife lives in the monument, including mule deer, bighorn sheep, wild turkeys, and four species of rattlesnakes. This is one of the premier areas for mule deer hunting in the country.

Within the monument, Paleozoic and Mesozoic sedimentary rock layers are relatively undeformed and unobscured by vegetation, offering visitors the opportunity to learn about the geologic history of the Colorado Plateau. The monument encompasses the lower portion of the Shivwits Plateau, an important watershed for the Colorado River and the Grand Canyon. The monument also contains countless biological, archaeological, and historical resources. Fossils are abundant throughout the monument. Among these are large numbers of invertebrate fossils, including bryozoans and brachiopods.

Prehistoric use is documented by irreplaceable rock art images, quarries, villages, watchtowers, farms, burial sites, caves, rock shelters, trails and camps. Historic ranch structures and corrals, fences, water tanks, and the ruins of sawmills are scattered across the monument, evidence of the remote family ranches and the lifestyles of early homesteaders.

Permits, Fees, Limitations

Hunting permits are extremely limited and regulated through the Arizona Game and Fish Department (*www.azgfd.com*).

Ponderosa pines root on steep, storm-battered cliffs within the Grand Canyon-Parashant National Monument. *(BLM)*

Accessibility
None.

Camping and Lodging
There are no developed campgrounds. The nearest lodging is in St. George, Utah.

Food and Supplies
There are no services on-site. The nearest food and supplies are in St. George.

First Aid
There is no first aid station on-site. The nearest hospital is in St. George.

Additional Information
Road conditions vary based on weather conditions. Visitors should call BLM before venturing to this monument. This remote area is not easily accessed. Before attempting to visit the Grand Canyon-Parashant National Monument, visitors should obtain a map at the Interagency Information Center, 345 E. Riverside Drive, St. George, Utah. Visits to this monument require special planning and awareness of potential hazards such as unmarked, rugged roads, venomous animals, extreme heat, and flash floods. Visitors should bring plenty of water, food, extra gasoline, and at least two spare tires. High-clearance vehicles are recommended.

Contact Information
BLM - Grand Canyon-Parashant
    National Monument
345 E. Riverside Drive
St. George, UT 84770
Tel: (435) 688-3246
Fax: (435) 688-3358
www.az.blm.gov/asfo/index.htm or www.nps.gov/para

Activity Codes

Harquahala Peak Smithsonian Observatory

Location
100 miles northwest of Phoenix, Arizona.

Description
The Harquahala Peak Observatory, now deserted, was built in 1920 by the Smithsonian Astrophysical Observatory to measure and record solar activity. From 1920–1925, a group of dedicated scientists lived and worked atop the highest mountain in southwestern Arizona, struggling against both extreme isolation and frequently inclement weather. Built of adobe bricks made at the mountain, with wood frame walls upon a stone and concrete foundation, the Harquahala Observatory was later covered and roofed with corrugated sheet metal for protection. This building was an observatory without telescopes; rather, a series of instruments designed to measure the amount of solar energy reaching the earth was used to aid in weather forecasting.

In 1975, the Harquahala Peak Observatory was listed on the National Register of Historic Places. In 1979, and again in 2002, emergency stabilization was undertaken on the deteriorated building. The abandoned observatory, perched nearly 6,000 feet above the desert, offers incredible views, historic ruins, and a great place for a picnic lunch. The road to the peak, the Harquahala Mountain Back Country Byway, provides an exciting ride for four-wheel-drive enthusiasts. This is a fully interpreted site.

Directions
From Phoenix, drive west on U.S. Highway 60 approximately 75 miles, and turn left in Aquila at Eagle Eye Road. Drive south for 17.6 miles, and then turn right at the Harquahala Mountain Back Country Byway road sign, where there is a staging area for off-loading jeeps or quads. The 10.5-mile drive to the observatory is on a rugged, four-wheel-drive road.

Visitor Activities
Four-wheel and all-terrain driving, historic site, interpretive display, deer hunting, hiking, biking, picnicking, horseback riding, plant viewing, wildlife viewing, and scenic drives.

Special Features
From the summit of the peak, the view is a panorama of surrounding desert and mountains 100 miles distant. Visitors will see relict "islands" of chaparral and desert grasslands, high peaks and foothills, and deep, rocky canyons and valleys. The area sustains the largest mule deer herd in western Arizona, a major raptor population, and one of the few desert bighorn sheep herds that is increasing in size.

The story of the Harquahala Smithsonian Observatory is told through an interpretive display that features period photographs and excerpts from letters written by Smithsonian staff. *(David Scarbrough, BLM Phoenix Field Office)*

Permits, Fees, Limitations
None.

Accessibility
Facilities at the Harquahala Mountain Back Country Byway staging area and observatory are wheelchair-accessible.

Camping and Lodging
On-site camping is primitive. There are no developed campsites. Five campsites, with tables and fire rings, are located at the byway staging area and along the byway. No other facilities or services, including potable water and garbage

collection, are provided. Camping is permissible with a 14-day camping limit.

Food and Supplies

There are no services on-site. Food and supplies are available in Aquila (17 miles north on Eagle Eye Road), and 43 miles west on U.S. Highway 60 in Wickenburg.

First Aid

There is no first aid station on-site. The nearest hospital is in Wickenburg.

Additional Information

High-clearance and four-wheel-drive vehicles are needed to travel to the observatory. Vehicles must be in good condition. Travel during rain or snowfall is not advised. Open mine shafts, as well as rattlesnakes and other poisonous creatures, are present.

The Harquahala Back Country Byway staging area has parking for up to 15 vehicles, an off-highway-vehicle of-floading ramp, single vault toilet, shaded ramada, and interpretive display. Hikers can trek 4 miles to the summit via the Harquahala Peak Pack Trail. Created in 1920, the trail was once used by mules to haul supplies and materials to the then-active observatory. The trailhead is accessible off U.S. Highway 60 between Aquila and Wenden.

The inside of the observatory building is not accessible because of hazardous conditions. The area is open all year, but summer daytime temperatures are extremely high, usually exceeding 100°F. The best time to visit is October–April. Visitors are advised to bring plenty of water and to pack out all refuse.

Contact Information

BLM - Phoenix Field Office
21605 North 7th Avenue
Phoenix, AZ 85027
Tel: (623) 580-5500
Fax: (623) 580-5580
www.az.blm.gov/pfo/index.htm

Activity Code

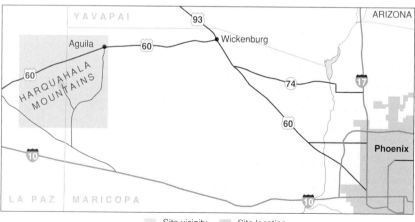

Site vicinity   Site location

Ironwood Forest National Monument

Location
25 miles northwest of Tucson, Arizona.

Description
Taking its name from one of the longest-living trees in the Arizona desert, the 129,000-acre Ironwood Forest National Monument is a true Sonoran Desert showcase. Sharing the habitat with the ironwood trees are mesquite, palo verde, creosote bush, and saguaro cactus, which blanket the monument floor in the shadow of rugged mountain ranges.

Directions
From Tucson, take Interstate 10 west 25 miles to Trico Road (Exit #236). Travel west approximately 6 miles. Turn right on Silverbell Road; continue 2 miles to the monument boundary. Visitors can continue 8 more miles to the Ragged Top Mountain area.

Visitor Activities
Hiking, mountain biking, wildlife viewing, plant viewing, horseback riding, wildflower viewing (in spring), hunting (javelina, deer, and quail), bird-watching, geologic sightseeing, historic site, and archaeological site.

Special Features
Ragged Top Mountain is the biological and geological crown jewel of the national monument. Several endangered and threatened species live within the monument, including the Nichol's Turk's head cactus and the lesser long-nosed bat. The

Within the Ironwood Forest National Monument, 3,907-foot-high Ragged Top Mountain harbors a profusion of Sonoran Desert species. *(Chris Tincher, BLM Oklahoma Field Office)*

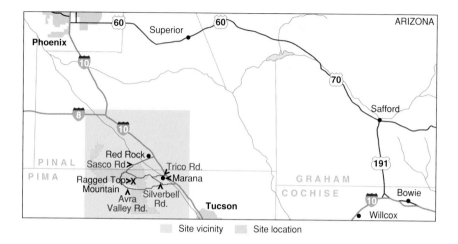

Site vicinity   Site location

national monument also contains habitat for cactus ferruginous pygmy owls. The desert bighorn sheep dwelling in the region are the last viable population indigenous to the Tucson basin. The area features abundant rock art sites and other archaeological objects of scientific interest. Humans have inhabited the area for more than 5,000 years. More than 200 sites from the prehistoric Hohokam period (AD 600–1440) have been recorded in the area. In more modern times, the area was a source of minerals and continues to support active mining operations today.

Permits, Fees, Limitations
No permits are required to visit the national monument. Vehicles must stay on existing routes.

Accessibility
None.

Camping and Lodging
Primitive camping is available.

Food and Supplies
The nearest stores are in Tucson.

First Aid
There is no first aid available on-site. The nearest hospitals are in Tucson.

Additional Information
The monument is a travel corridor for illegal immigrants traveling from Mexico. All suspected illegal activities should be reported to BLM or local law enforcement authorities. Visitors should avoid contact with persons exhibiting suspicious behavior or engaged in dangerous activities. Visitors should drive with caution and look for fast-moving vehicles and pedestrians on back roads. Some roads are rugged; high-clearance or four-wheel-drive vehicles are recommended in those areas. Hazards include poisonous snakes, Africanized bees, and potential encounters with illegal users of public lands. Hunting is permitted through the Arizona Game and Fish Department. The national monument contains State trust lands and private lands. Recreation on State trust lands requires a permit from the State of Arizona. Visitors should not trespass on private lands.

Contact Information

BLM – Tucson Field Office
12661 E. Broadway
Tucson, AZ 85748
Tel: (520) 258-7200
Fax: (520) 258-7238
www.az.blm.gov/tfo/index.htm

Activity Codes

Lake Havasu

Location

Along the Arizona-California border near Lake Havasu City, Arizona (approximately 15 miles south of Interstate 40).

Description

Havasu, a Native American word for "blue waters," is a 30-mile-long lake created by the 1938 construction of Parker Dam across the Colorado River. Enclosing more than 25,000 acres of water, the rugged shoreline includes numerous bays and coves. The area around this popular desert lake is home to Lake Havasu City, the Chemehuevi Tribe, two national wildlife refuges, and the famed London Bridge. Visitors enjoy the area's warm climate, mountains, and wide variety of recreational offerings on the water and across the rugged back country. Shoreline camping on the lake and watercraft recreation are favorites of visitors. There are numerous back country trails and four-wheeling areas, as well as hiking and biking opportunities.

Historic London Bridge, which was purchased at auction from the city of London, England, in 1968, was reconstructed over a channel on the lake and now serves as a major tourist attraction in Lake Havasu City. English

Village, a Tudor-style area of shops and restaurants nestled under the bridge, also attracts many tourists. Cruising across the lake to the Chemehuevi Tribe's Resort and Casino is another popular activity.

In the Mohave Mountains east of Lake Havasu City, four-wheel-drive enthusiasts negotiate the boulder-strewn trail to Crossman Peak *(Diane Williams, BLM Lake Havasu Field Office)*

Lake Havasu's
Mesquite Bay Fishing
Pier is a perfect spot
from which to enjoy
a desert sunset.
*(Greg Harris, BLM Lake
Havasu Field Office)*

Directions

From Interstate 40, take Arizona State Highway 95 (the exit is about 9 miles east of the California border) south about 15 miles to Lake Havasu City, Arizona. Or, from Interstate 10, take Arizona State Highway 95 north (Quartzsite exit) about 75 miles through Parker to Lake Havasu City, which borders the lake.

Visitor Activities

Motor and sail boating, picnicking, swimming, fishing, wildlife viewing, plant viewing, hiking, shoreline exploration, all-terrain and four-wheel driving, dirt biking, scenic drives, archaeological site, historic site, birdwatching, wild burro viewing, geologic sightseeing, and interpreted site.

Special Features

The Lake Havasu Fisheries Improvement Program, a BLM-led cooperative partnership that has been in operation since the early 1990s, is improving access for shoreline anglers and increasing sport fishing opportunities by enhancing fish habitat in the lake. The program is also improving the outlook for the endangered razorback sucker and bonytail chub.

Permits, Fees, Limitations

There are many commercial boat launching sites on Lake Havasu, most of which charge fees.

Accessibility

Several shoreline fishing access sites and piers have been constructed along the lake; each of the following is wheelchair-accessible: Site Six (on McCulloch Boulevard on the island), Mesquite Bay (two sites with the Havasu National Wildlife Refuge on London Bridge Road, just north of Industrial Boulevard), Havasu Springs (off Arizona State Highway 95 on the south end of Lake Havasu), Take Off Point (at Parker Dam off Arizona State Highway 95), and at the Bill Williams National Wildlife Refuge (about 23 miles south of Lake Havasu City on Arizona State Highway 95).

Camping and Lodging

BLM maintains over 100 shoreline campsites, accessible only by boat, on Lake Havasu. These are located on the Arizona side of the lake between Parker Dam and

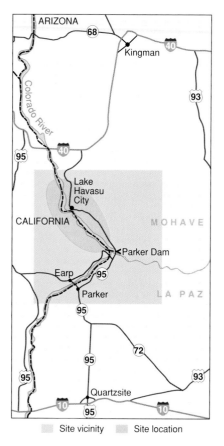

Site vicinity   Site location

Lake Havasu City. Amenities at each site include picnic tables, shade ramadas, grills, and restrooms. BLM-leased concessions (Havasu Springs and Black Meadow Landing, which is 15 miles south of Lake Havasu City on the California shore) provide campsites for RVs as well as overnight lodging. Arizona State Parks offers campgrounds at Windsor Beach, just north of the London Bridge in Lake Havasu City, and at Cattail Cove, 9 miles south of the city on Arizona Highway 95. In addition, Lake Havasu City has many hotels, motels, and restaurants.

Food and Supplies

Numerous major grocery stores, gas stations, and restaurants are located in Lake Havasu City, Arizona. In addition, most commercial launch sites, including Black Meadow Landing, Havasu Springs, and Havasu Landing (directly across from Lake Havasu City on the California shore), offer limited groceries and fuel.

First Aid

Emergency services may be accessed by calling 911 both on the lake and in the city. Havasu Regional Medical Center is located in Lake Havasu City.

Additional Information

Visitation is very high throughout the summer and on weekends and holidays.

Contact Information

BLM - Lake Havasu Field Office
2610 Sweetwater Avenue
Lake Havasu City, AZ 86406
Tel: (928) 505-1200
Fax: (928) 505-1208
Toll Free: 1-888-213-2582
www.az.blm.gov/lhfo/index.htm

Activity Codes

La Posa and Imperial Dam Long Term Visitor Areas

Location

The La Posa Long Term Visitor Area (LTVA) is located approximately 2 miles south of Quartzsite, Arizona. The Imperial Dam LTVA is located approximately 25 miles north of Yuma, Arizona, on the California side of the Colorado River.

Description

Each autumn, as fall's brightly-colored leaves twist in the mild air, birds of numerous species migrate to the warmer

BLM long term visitor areas along the Colorado River offer RVers chances for solitude as well as socializing. *(BLM)*

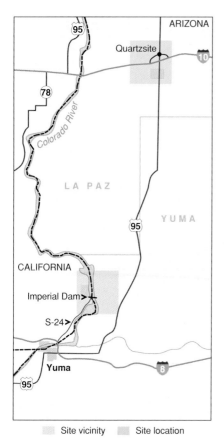

Site vicinity ▢ Site location

over-use of, the fragile desert ecosystem. The La Posa campground encompasses approximately 11,400 acres, and Imperial Dam is approximately 3,500 acres in area. Both campgrounds are located in flat topography and are sparsely vegetated with plants such as creosote bush, palo verde, ironwood, mesquite, and various species of cactus. The Colorado River offers visitors a variety of water sports ranging from fishing to speedboat racing.

Directions

La Posa LTVA: From Interstate 10, exit at the town of Quartzsite, Arizona. Take State Highway 95 south 2 miles to the four campgrounds within the LTVA. Imperial Dam LTVA: Take Interstate 8 to Yuma, Arizona. Take the 4th Avenue exit to County Road S-24. Go north approximately 22 miles to Senator Wash Road. Turn left onto Senator Wash Road and follow it for approximately 3 miles to the campgrounds, located north of Yuma on the California side of the Colorado River.

Visitor Activities

Picnicking, rockhounding, plant viewing, wildlife viewing, biking, all-terrain and dirt bike driving, horseback riding, wild horse and burro viewing, and hiking. The Imperial Dam LTVA offers fishing, boating, and swimming.

Special Features

In early February, hints of new life begin to appear in the seemingly desolate desert. Colors reach full bloom from mid-March–mid-April; most trees flower from April–May. Visitors to Yuma may see the following common flowers: desert lilies, desert sand verbena, beavertail cactus, and desert mallow.

temperatures. Joining these feathered creatures, thousands of "snowbirds" (seasonal human residents, who travel to warmer climates for the winter) come from the nation's East Coast, Pacific Northwest, Canada, and even Europe each fall and winter to meet up with old friends and enjoy peace and quiet away from big-city living. To meet their needs, BLM created the La Posa and Imperial Dam LTVAs in 1983. These large, designated camping areas offer a unique haven for winter vacationers, and their establishment guards against encroachment upon, and

A rockhunter's paradise surrounds Quartzsite. Agate, limonite cubes, gold, and quartz are especially good "finds." Wild horses and burros, deer, bighorn sheep, and coyotes roam the area.

Permits, Fees, Limitations
An LTVA permit is required from September 15–April 15 each season and is valid for up to 7 months. A short-term permit can be purchased for a 14-day stay. From April 16– September 14, there is a per-vehicle day-use fee.

Accessibility
Vault toilets and restroom facilities throughout the campgrounds are wheelchair-accessible.

Camping and Lodging
Primitive camping in the LTVAs is available from September 15–April 15 on a continuous basis. From April 16– September 14, the maximum stay is 14 days in any 28-day period.

Food and Supplies
No food or supplies are available on-site. Restaurants and groceries are located in Yuma and Quartzsite, Arizona.

First Aid
There is no first aid available on-site. The closest hospital to the La Posa LTVA is approximately 45 miles north in Parker, Arizona. There is also a medical facility in Quartzsite. The closest hospital to the Imperial Dam LTVA is approximately 25 miles south in Yuma. There is also a medical facility at the Yuma Proving Ground, 25 miles north on State Highway 95.

Additional Information
These areas are open year-round; however, summer daytime temperature highs are 100°–118°F. The best time to visit is during the mild winter months.

Contact Information
BLM - Yuma Field Office
2555 E. Gila Ridge Road
Yuma, AZ 85365
Tel: (928) 317-3200
Fax: (928) 317-3250
www.az.blm.gov/yfo/index.htm

Activity Codes

other - rockhounding

Las Cienegas National Conservation Area

Location
45 miles southeast of Tucson, Arizona.

Description
Las Cienegas National Conservation Area (NCA) is nationally recognized for its more than 200 species of birds. This 45,000-acre area offers rolling grasslands, oak-studded hills connecting several "sky island" mountain ranges, and lush riparian corridors. Pronghorn antelope also find the area quite appealing and live here year-round. Cienega Creek, with its perennial flow and lush riparian

corridor, forms the lifeblood of the NCA and supports a diverse plant and animal community.

Directions

From Tucson, drive south on Interstate 10 for 25 miles to exit 281. Head south for 20 miles on State Highway 83. Near Milepost 40, turn east into the Empire Ranch entrance.

Storm clouds gather over the grasslands of Las Cienegas National Conservation Area. Dramatic afternoon monsoons are typical of southern Arizona in late summer. *(BLM)*

Visitor Activities

Wildlife viewing, plant viewing, birdwatching, horseback riding, hiking, mountain biking, historic site, hunting, and scenic drives.

Special Features

The conservation area embraces unique and rare vegetative communities, including five of the rarest habitat types in the American Southwest: cienegas (marshlands), cottonwood-willow riparian forests, salt-tolerant sacaton grasslands, mesquite bosques, and semi-desert grasslands. The fact that many of Hollywood's classic, big-budget "westerns" were filmed at the Empire Ranch underscores its scenic attributes. The historic Empire Ranch remains a working cattle ranch, complete with enchanting old headquarters. It now operates under an innovative rangeland management style unique to the area.

Permits, Fees, Limitations

Permits are not required to visit the conservation area. However, commercial, competitive, and large organized group events require a special recreation permit. Vehicles must remain on designated routes. A valid hunting permit issued by the Arizona Game and Fish Department is required. Recreational activities on State trust land require a permit from the State of Arizona.

Accessibility

None.

Camping and Lodging

Primitive camping is allowed in existing sites only. Camping may not exceed 14 consecutive days. Visitors must camp at least 0.25 mile from cattle and wildlife

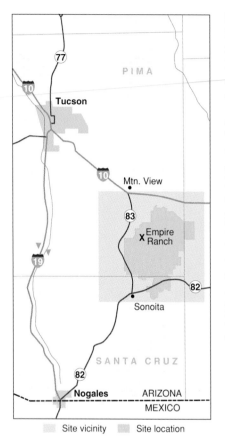

Site vicinity   Site location

First Aid

First aid is available at the Santa Cruz Sheriff's office in Sonoita. The nearest hospitals are located in Sierra Vista, about 40 miles southeast, and Tucson, approximately 50 miles northwest.

Additional Information

The Empire Cienega Ranch located within the conservation area is a working cattle ranch. Visitors are asked to leave all gates as they are found. There is no trash pick-up, so visitors need to pack out all trash. A BLM Land Use Plan completed in 2002 calls for an interpretive trail and program at the historic ranch. The area is a travel corridor for illegal immigrants traveling from Mexico. Visitors should report all suspected illegal activities to BLM or local law enforcement authorities and stay safe by avoiding contact with persons exhibiting suspicious behavior or engaged in dangerous activities. Hazards include poisonous snakes and Africanized bees.

Contact Information

BLM – Tucson Field Office
12661 E. Broadway
Tucson, AZ 85748
Tel: (520) 258-7200
Fax: (520) 258-7238
www.az.blm.gov/tfo/index.htm

Activity Codes

water holes. Campers need to bring water and firewood. The nearest lodging is available in Sonoita, 5 miles south on State Highway 83, and in Patagonia, 17.5 miles south on State Highway 82. Campfires are allowed in existing fire rings, except during periods of extreme fire danger. Only dead and downed wood may be used as fuel.

Food and Supplies

A gas station and a variety of restaurants and services are located in the town of Sonoita.

Little Black Mountain Petroglyph Site

Location
10 miles southeast of St. George, Utah.

Description
More than 6,000 years of human history have been recorded as rock art drawings scattered across the Little Black Mountain Petroglyph Site. More than 500 individual rock art designs and elements on the cliffs and boulders surround the base of a 500-foot mesa. The designs are associated with the cultures of the Great Basin, Western Anasazi, and Lower Colorado River. It is thought that representations of turtles, lizards, and bear paws may be symbols with social or religious meanings.

Directions
From St. George, travel south on River Road for 5 miles to the Arizona State Line. Continue for 0.3 mile then turn left (east) and drive 4.5 miles to the site.

In the spring, bold, orangey blooms appear atop the spiny pads of the prickly pear cactus. Once the bloom is over, the plant produces succulent, pear-shaped fruits.
(BLM)

Portions of this road are rough and a high-clearance vehicle is recommended.

Visitor Activities
Archaeological site, plant viewing, wildlife viewing, picnicking, biking, birdwatching, and geologic sightseeing.

Special Features
Various rock art images are displayed on large boulders that fell from the cliffs long ago. Creosote and other species of Mojave Desert vegetation provide habitat for a variety of desert birds (Gambel's quail, red-tailed hawks), mammals (coyotes, antelope, ground squirrels), and reptiles (collared and whip-tailed lizards, Great Basin rattlesnakes). April and May are the best months to see desert plants in bloom. Cryptogamic soil, a very delicate crust of fungus and lichens on the soil surface, exists throughout the area.

Permits, Fees, Limitations
There are no fees or permits required to visit the area.

Accessibility
None.

Camping and Lodging
No camping or lodging facilities are available on-site. Lodging is available in St. George.

Food and Supplies
No food or supplies are available on-site. Food and supplies are available in St. George.

First Aid
No first aid is available on-site. The nearest hospital is in St. George.

Additional Information
The area is very hot in the summer. A high-clearance vehicle is recommended. Touching or climbing on rock art boulders and walking on the fragile cryptogamic soil are prohibited. Rattlesnakes and scorpions inhabit this area, so visitors are asked to use caution and common sense. A restroom and picnic table are available on-site. The 9-mile Dutchman Loop mountain bike trail connects to this site from the Sunshine Trail Road 10 miles south of St. George.

Contact Information
BLM – Arizona Strip Field Office
345 E. Riverside Drive
St. George, UT 84790
Tel: (435) 688-3246
Fax: (435) 688-3258
www.az.blm.gov/azfo/index.htm

Activity Codes

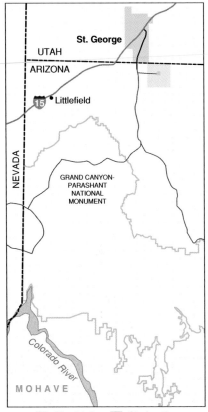

Site vicinity   Site location

Muleshoe Ranch Cooperative Management Area

Location
20 miles northwest of Willcox, Arizona.

Description
Rugged mountains, canyon streams, saguaro cacti, and mesquite bosques greet visitors to the Muleshoe Ranch Cooperative Management Area. Local desert dwellers include coatimundis, javelinas, and a wide variety of neo-tropical migratory birds and native fish. The mosaic of public and private lands, which includes BLM's Redfield Canyon Wilderness, the U.S. Forest Service's Galiuro Wilderness, and The Nature

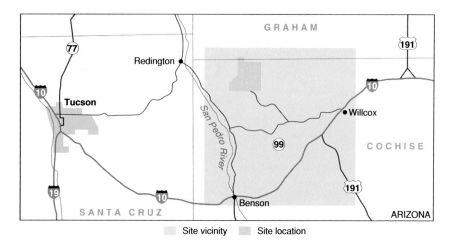

Site vicinity   Site location

Conservancy's Muleshoe Ranch Preserve, offers a diversity of remote recreational opportunities.

Directions
In Willcox, take Interstate 10 to exit 340 and go south. After about 0.25 mile, turn right on Bisbee Avenue, go 4 miles, and then turn right on Airport Road. After 15 miles, bear right at a fork in the road. Drive 14 more miles on Jackson Cabin road to The Nature Conservancy's Muleshoe Ranch Preserve Headquarters. An information kiosk is located along the main road immediately after the headquarters. The headquarters also includes a visitor center.

Visitor Activities
Wildlife viewing, plant viewing, biking, birdwatching, hiking, hunting (big-game and bird), horseback riding, interpretation, four-wheel driving (on roads only), historic site, and scenic drives.

Special Features
The 49,000-acre Muleshoe Ranch includes seven perennial streams representing some of the best remaining aquatic and riparian habitat in Arizona, a haven for rare native fish (including the speckled dace and Gila chub). Wildlife is diverse and plentiful. Nesting gray and zone-tailed hawks and common black hawks can be found here. Old homesteads dot the landscape, showcasing the area's 150 years of pioneer history.

Permits, Fees, Limitations
No fees are required to travel the Muleshoe Ranch. Visitors must sign the guest register at the information kiosk just past the Muleshoe Ranch Headquarters. All wilderness areas prohibit the use of motorized vehicles, and additional specific use rules apply in some areas. Hunting is allowed on BLM and Forest Service lands, but is not allowed on The Nature Conservancy's properties. Be sure of your location if you hunt. Collecting flora, fauna, minerals, firewood, or artifacts is prohibited. All vehicles must remain on designated roads.

Accessibility

The information kiosk at the entrance to Jackson Cabin Road is wheelchair-accessible.

Camping and Lodging

The Nature Conservancy's Muleshoe Ranch Preserve offers *casitas* ("little houses") for guests. Minimum-impact backpack camping is also allowed. Car and RV camping is not permitted. Back country facilities include Pride Ranch, managed by The Nature Conservancy, and Jackson Cabin and Hooker Cabin, managed by the Forest Service. Use of these rustic facilities is on a first-come, first served basis, free of charge. Lodging and RV parks are available in Willcox, 30 miles southeast of the Muleshoe Preserve.

Food and Supplies

Food and supplies are available in Willcox.

First Aid

First aid is available through The Nature Conservancy's headquarters. The nearest hospital is in Willcox.

Additional Information

Visitors should bring a good map, water, and food. Spring, fall, and winter are the best times to visit. Travelers are asked to educate themselves about heat, poisonous wildlife, prickly plants, and thunderstorms, all of which pose potential hazards. All roads are dirt and rugged, so plenty of travel time should be allowed. The Jackson Cabin Road provides access to the Galiuro and Redfield Canyon Wilderness Areas. Additional information is available at The Nature Conservancy's Visitor Center.

Contact Information

BLM - Safford Field Office
711 14th Avenue
Safford, AZ 85546
Tel: (928) 348-4400
Fax: (928) 348-4450
www.az.blm.gov/sfo/index.htm
Muleshoe Ranch Headquarters
Tel: (520) 212-4295

Activity Codes

A lone saguaro perches like a sentinel on an escarpment at Muleshoe Ranch, a rugged desert area that is home to such unique wildlife as coatimundis and javelinas. *(Diane Drobka, BLM Safford Field Office)*

Parker Dam Road
Back Country Byway

Location
Along the Colorado River between Parker, Arizona, and Parker Dam, California (about 35 miles south of Lake Havasu City, Arizona).

Description
The Lower Colorado River's warm desert environment features accessible shorelines for boating, fishing, and swimming, as well as campgrounds, day-use recreation areas, boat launch facilities, scenic highways, and designated off-highway-vehicle areas. The Parker Dam Road Back Country Byway features interpretive areas as well as BLM's largest concession-leased RV parks. BLM shoreline fishing piers and a boat launch are located directly on the north side of Parker Dam at Take Off Point on Lake Havasu.

Directions
From Interstate 10, travel California State Highway 95 or Arizona State Highway 95 north about 40 miles to Parker. From Parker, travel Arizona State Highway 95 north along the Colorado River toward Lake Havasu, or cross the bridge into California to Parker Dam Road.

Or, from Interstate 40, travel Arizona State Highway 95 south about 35 miles, through Lake Havasu City, Arizona, into Parker. At Parker Dam, take Arizona State Highway 95S, which becomes Parker Dam Road after crossing the dam. For the Parker Strip Area in

The Colorado River meets the Mojave Desert near the Empire Landing Campground.
(Mike Wilson, BLM Lake Havasu Field Office)

Arizona, remain on Arizona State Highway 95 and Business Route 95 for facilities.

Visitor Activities

Motor boating, fishing, plant viewing, wildlife viewing, hiking, swimming, off-highway driving (on the California side, between Parker Dam and the Colorado River Indian Tribes Reservation surrounding Parker), four-wheel driving, picnicking, archaeological site, historic site, birdwatching, wild burro viewing, geologic sightseeing, rockhounding, and scenic drives.

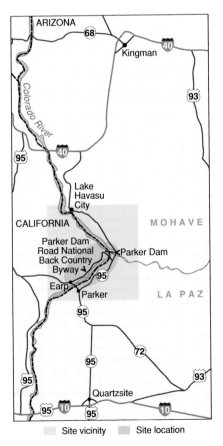

Site vicinity   Site location

Special Features

The Colorado River in this desert area has long attracted people, wildlife, and vegetation along the river canyon, creating what is called the "Thread of Life." The back country byway offers many scenic river views and a chance to see wild burro herds.

The principal cultural resources identified within Parker Strip are prehistoric artifacts associated with the indigenous peoples of the region (San Dieguito, Armagosa, Patayan, and Yuman cultures). These include campsites, stone tool flakes and ceramic shards, cobble quarries, trails, rock rings, sleeping circles, and various rock alignments and cairns. A limited number of historic mining and dam construction sites from the 1930s are also located within the area.

Permits, Fees, Limitations

Buses and RVs are not permitted to cross Parker Dam because of security considerations. Day-use areas charge fees.

Accessibility

All facilities are wheelchair-accessible, and include accessible trails and/or ramps to facilities.

Camping and Lodging

BLM-leased concessions offer lodging along Parker Strip on the California side of the river. Motels, RV parks, and primitive dispersed camping are available on the Arizona side. Fees are charged for developed campgrounds, including Empire Landing and Crossroads campgrounds, located approximately 7 and 8 miles south of Parker Dam, respectively, on the California side of the river. Along the Arizona side of Lake Havasu between Lake Havasu City and Parker Dam, there are about 125 BLM boat-in shoreline campsites, some with facilities including restrooms, shade armadas, and cooking grills. These can be accessed only by water from any of several boat launch ramps, including Take Off Point at Parker Dam.

Food and Supplies

Major grocery stores and gas stations are available in Parker and Lake Havasu City, Arizona (about 38 miles north of Parker on Arizona State Highway 95). Small general stores for food, gas, and supplies are available along Parker Dam Road in California.

First Aid

Emergency services along the river are provided by San Bernardino County (California side) and LaPaz County (Arizona side). Hospitals are located in Parker and Lake Havasu City, Arizona.

Additional Information

This area is extremely popular with all ages throughout the year, hosting northern "snowbirds" (seasonal human residents, who travel to warmer climates in the winter), as well as regional and nationwide visitors year-round.

Contact Information

BLM – Lake Havasu Field Office
2610 Sweetwater Avenue
Lake Havasu City, AZ 86406
Tel: (928) 505-1200
Fax: (928) 505-1208
Toll Free: 1-888-213-2582
www.az.blm.gov/lhfo/index.htm

Activity Codes

other – rockhounding

Route 66 Historic Back Country Byway

Location

6 miles west of Kingman, Arizona.

Description

Historic Route 66 is endeared as one of America's first transcontinental highways, and this 42-mile stretch of two-lane blacktop is one of its last and best-preserved segments. This portion of the highway includes what was once considered one of the most fearsome obstacles for "flatland" travelers in the 1930s: the hairpin curves and steep grades of Sitgreaves Pass, which define Route 66 as it makes its way over the Black Mountains of western Arizona.

Directions

From Kingman, travel west on Interstate 40 about 5 miles to Exit 44 (McConnico/Oatman). Follow Oatman Road west for about 0.5 mile to a left turn on Historic Route 66. The back country byway begins here, and ends 42 miles to the southwest at the community of Golden Shores.

Visitor Activities

Scenic drives, historic site, wild burro viewing, wildlife viewing, plant viewing (primarily desert vegetation, such as creosote bush, rabbitbrush, mesquite, and Joshua tree), interpreted site.

Special Features

The rugged landscape of the Black Mountains provides favored habitat for desert bighorn sheep and wild burros. The mountain range also historically produced significant amounts of precious metals, primarily gold. Travelers along this stretch of Route 66 will see evidence of historic mining activity, including Gold Road Mine and the mining town of Oatman. Oatman now serves more tourists than miners, and visitors can experience the flavor of the Old West here through staged gunfights, strolls on old wooden sidewalks, and a refreshing sarsaparilla in the local saloon.

Permits, Fees, Limitations

No permits or fees are required to travel along Route 66. Private tourist attractions may involve fees. The nature of the highway imposes some limitations. Vehicles over 40 feet in length are legally not permitted on the portion of Route 66 passing through the Black Mountains. Drivers intimidated by the narrowness of the road, hairpin turns, steep drop-offs, or the lack of guardrails on the sides of the highway may not wish to attempt this drive. Wide vehicles such as RVs are also not advised.

Accessibility

The back country byway can be driven in any type of vehicle less than 40 feet in length, subject to the limitations above. Information kiosks at both ends of the byway are wheelchair-accessible.

Camping and Lodging

Primitive camping without fees is available on public lands year-round. Motel lodging is abundant in Kingman and limited in Oatman, which is situated midway along the byway.

Food and Supplies

Food and supplies are available in Kingman, along Route 66 in Oatman, and at the end of the byway in Golden Shores.

First Aid

The nearest hospitals are in Kingman, and in Bullhead City (28 miles north of Golden Shores on Highway 95). First aid is available from the Oatman Volunteer Fire Department and the Golden Shores Fire Department along Route 66.

Offering panoramic views of the Black Mountains, Oatman Road meanders toward its intersection with Historic Route 66 outside Kingman. (Gordon Warren, BLM Arizona State Office)

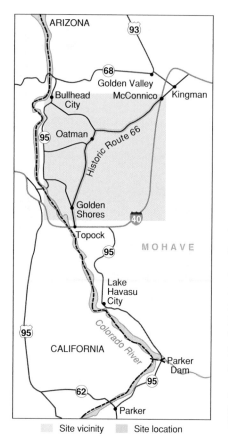

Site vicinity   Site location

Additional Information

The extreme heat of the summer months can limit activity levels outside vehicles. Cars must be in good operating condition. Visitors are reminded to bring plenty of water for drinking and in case of radiator overheating. Many plants and animals in the desert can be hazardous. The back country byway can be traveled any time of year. Most of the road is in the open desert, with no facilities other than those in Oatman. The Federally designated Warm Springs and Mount Nutt Wilderness Areas are adjacent to the back country byway. Visitors may hand-feed wild burros in Oatman.

Contact Information

BLM - Kingman Field Office
2475 Beverly Avenue
Kingman, AZ 86401
Tel: (928) 692-4400
Fax: (928) 692-4414
www.az.blm.gov/kfo/index.htm

Activity Codes

San Pedro Riparian National Conservation Area

Location
6 miles east of Sierra Vista, Arizona.

Description
The San Pedro Riparian National Conservation Area (NCA) was designated by Congress in 1988. Some 40 miles of the upper San Pedro River meander through the conservation area. The primary purpose for the special designation was to protect and enhance the desert riparian ecosystem, a rare remnant of what was once an extensive network of similar riparian systems throughout the American Southwest. One of the most important riparian areas

Willows typical of the San Pedro Riparian National Conservation Area are reflected softly in the San Pedro River after a storm. *(James Mahoney, BLM San Pedro Riparian National Conservation Office)*

in the United States, the San Pedro Area runs through the Chihuahuan and Sonoran Deserts in southeastern Arizona along the San Pedro River. The river corridor is home to 84 species of mammals, 14 species of fish, 41 species of reptiles and amphibians, and 100 species of breeding birds. It also provides invaluable habitat for 250 species of migratory and wintering birds, and contains archaeological sites with evidence of human occupation from 11,200 years ago.

Directions
From Tucson, take Interstate 10 east 40 miles to State Highway 90. Follow the highway south approximately 30 miles through Huachuca City to Fry Boulevard in Sierra Vista. Follow this street for 6 miles east until you reach the San Pedro House, which serves as a visitor center and bookstore.

Visitor Activities
Birdwatching, picnicking, plant viewing, wildlife viewing, archaeological site, historic site, hunting, hiking, fishing, biking, horseback riding, guided hikes, interpretive site, and weekend children's programs.

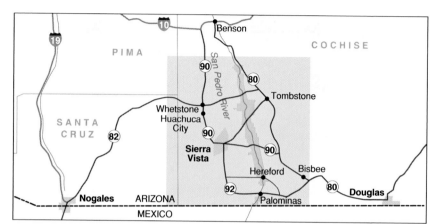

Site vicinity   Site location

Special Features

The conservation area features the intact remains of the Spanish Presidio Santa Cruz de Terranate, a Spanish fortress marking the northern extension of New Spain into the New World. The presidio was built in 1775 to help bar nomadic raiders from the frontier. The Murray Springs Clovis Site is a significant archaeological resource that dates back 11,000 years and has yielded evidence, mostly in the form of distinctive spear points, of some of the earliest known people to inhabit North America. An interpretive trail leads visitors to the site. The area also features the ruins of the old mining town of Fairbank, including the San Pedro House, a 1930s-era converted ranch house.

Goodding willows and Fremont cottonwoods line the river banks, providing habitat for white-tailed deer, mule deer, and javelinas. Over 250 species of migratory and breeding birds —including more than 30 kinds of raptors—make the NCA a primary destination for birdwatchers. Longfin dace and desert sucker are the only native species of fish found in the river.

Permits, Fees, Limitations

Firearm use is permitted only for regulated hunting, and only in certain areas; a permit from the Arizona Game and Fish is required. Contact BLM for specific information on hunting.

Accessibility

Wheelchair-accessible restrooms are available at the San Pedro House, and accessible trails are under construction.

Camping and Lodging

Only back country camping is available, and a permit is required. Campfires are permitted only in designated areas. Contact BLM for information on camping fees and permits.

Food and Supplies

Food and supplies are available in Sierra Vista (6 miles west of the NCA), Whetstone (28 miles north of Sierra Vista), Bisbee (approximately 10 miles east of the NCA), as well as in the towns of Hereford and Palominas, which are within the NCA.

First Aid

There is no first aid on-site. The nearest hospital is in Sierra Vista.

Additional Information

The San Pedro River is subject to seasonal flooding, and summer monsoons are common. Birdwatching is best in the spring and fall. Picnic facilities are available at Fairbank (within the San Pedro Riparian NCA) and at the San Pedro House. Visitors should call ahead for a schedule of guided walks, hikes, and children's programs. The San Pedro gift shop/bookstore is open from 9:30 a.m.–4:30 p.m. daily. The region is a travel corridor for illegal immigrants traveling from Mexico. Visitors are asked to please report all suspected illegal activities to BLM or local law enforcement authorities and to stay safe by avoiding contact with persons exhibiting suspicious behavior or engaged in dangerous activities.

Contact Information

BLM - San Pedro Riparian National Conservation Office
1763 Paseo San Luis
Sierra Vista, AZ 85635
Tel.: (520) 439-6400
Fax: (520) 439-6422
tucson.az.blm.gov

Activity Codes

other – weekend children's programs, guided hikes

San Simon Valley

Location

7 miles southeast of Safford, Arizona.

Description

Approximately 500,000 acres of public land in the San Simon Valley provide unlimited recreational opportunities amongst the creosote and mesquite. The valley, framed by jagged mountain ranges, is part of the Chihuahuan Desert ecosystem and home to a wide range of wildlife, including quail, doves, deer, and javelinas. The Hot Well Dunes Recreation Area is located in the heart of the valley. This Special Recreation Management Area provides unique opportunities for off-highway driving

Hot Well Dunes Recreation Area in the San Simon Valley of southeastern Arizona provides a 2,000-acre "play area" for off-highway vehicles. *(Diane Drobka, BLM Safford Field Office)*

and hot-water bathing. The 2,000-acre Hot Well Dunes Recreation Area is a designated off-highway-vehicle play area. It includes 10 developed campsites, a restroom, and an information kiosk. At the entrance, a pond has been developed as a wildlife viewing area. Near the campsites, two hot tubs provide soaking opportunities in 106°F artesian water.

Directions

The San Simon Valley can be accessed by three primary routes:

Haekel Road (chip-sealed): From Safford, travel 7 miles east on U.S. Highway 70. Turn right on BLM's Haekel Road. This road takes visitors through approximately 33 miles of the San Simon Valley.

Fan Road (maintained dirt): From Bowie, turn right (north) on Central Avenue and proceed 2 miles to Fan Road. Continue north on Fan Road for 8 miles, and then turn left on Haekel Road.

Tanque Road (maintained dirt): From U.S. Highway 191, turn onto Tanque Road near Milepost 105. Tanque Road runs for 12 miles before meeting Haekel Road.

Visitor Activities

Scenic drives, wildlife viewing, birdwatching, picnicking, horseback riding, biking, hunting (for quail, doves, javelinas, and mule deer), interpretation (on the wildlife and geologic history of the Hot Well Dunes area), hot-water bathing, and off-highway driving (all-terrain, four-wheel-drive, dirt-bike within the Hot Well Dunes).

Special Features

Once an ancient lakebed, the valley was home to prehistoric mammoths, horses,

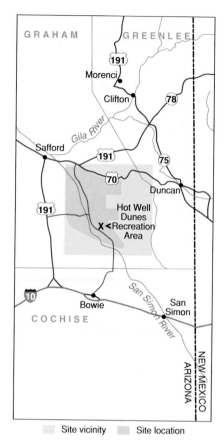

Site vicinity   Site location

and other creatures. Today, the grassland valley attracts mule deer, javelinas, quail, and doves, and also serves as a haven for wintering raptors.

Permits, Fees, Limitations

Fees are charged for all uses in the Hot Well Dunes Recreation Area.

Accessibility

Most of the San Simon Valley is accessible by standard passenger vehicle, making activities such as sightseeing, off-highway driving, and wildlife viewing available to individuals with disabilities. The restrooms and hot tubs at Hot Well Dunes Recreation Area are wheelchair-accessible.

Camping and Lodging

Hot Well Dunes Recreation Area, in the center of the San Simon Valley, contains 10 campsites with tables, grills, restrooms, and trash cans. No hookups are available. The campground is open year-round. Primitive camping is permitted on all public lands in the San Simon Valley, but there are no facilities in these areas. Camping is limited to 14 days. Lodging is available in Safford and Willcox, Arizona (on Interstate 10, about 12 miles west of U.S. Highway 191).

Food and Supplies

Food and supplies are available in Safford, Willcox, and Bowie (26 miles east of Willcox on Interstate 10).

First Aid

There is no first aid available on-site. The nearest hospital is located in Safford.

Additional Information

Public lands in the San Simon Valley are open year-round, but it is best to visit in the spring, fall, and winter. Summer can be quite hot. The roads through the San Simon Valley are not regularly maintained. At certain times of the year, some roads can be very rough and may be impassable after heavy rains.

Contact Information

BLM - Safford Field Office
711 14th Avenue
Safford, AZ 85546
Tel: (928) 348-4400
Fax: (928) 348-4450
www.az.blm.gov/sfo/index.htm

Activity Codes

other - hot-tub soaking

Sears Point

Location

75 miles east of Yuma, Arizona, or 40 miles west of Gila Bend, Arizona.

Description

Dozens of petroglyph panels carved by ancient and modern travelers make up the core of this fascinating archaeological site located on a basalt mesa. These petroglyphs attest to the importance of the Gila River as a vital prehistoric and historic travel route through Arizona. Traces of the historic trails can be seen in the floodplain. The Juan Bautista de Anza National Historic Trail and Butterfield Overland Mail route follow the course of the Gila River as it winds its way past Sears Point. Sears Point also hosts a sizable mesquite bosque containing significant wildlife habitat.

Directions

Take Interstate 8 east from Yuma, Arizona, for 75 miles, or 40 miles west from Gila Bend, to the Spot Road exit. Travel east on the north frontage road for about 1 mile to Avenue 76-1/2 East. Turn north and drive along the dirt

Isolated boulders provided an ideal canvas for prehistoric and historic artists, whose petroglyphs mark their passage across Sears Point. *(Tom Zale, BLM Yuma Field Office)*

road for approximately 7 miles. The volcanic basalt mesas will come into view to the west. Parking is provided in the cleared area in front of the ridge.

Visitor Activities

Archaeological site, historic site, bird-watching, hiking, plant viewing, geologic sightseeing, and stargazing.

Special Features

At Sears Point, people have etched images from their lives into the rock for thousands of years. The most abundant of these date from AD 500 to the 1800s. The long period of human migration through Sears Point is evident not only from the petroglyphs, but also in other features at the site, including sleeping circles, lithic scatters, astrological constructions, rock shelters, shrines/cairns, and a historic canal.

Permits, Fees, Limitations

No fees or permits are required. Four-wheel-drive vehicles are needed to cross

soft potholes in the road during dry seasons, and roads are slippery and muddy during wet seasons. Trails are unstable and not maintained.

Accessibility

Some petroglyphs are visible from the parking area.

Camping and Lodging

Primitive camping is permitted on public lands with a 14-day maximum per calendar year. No camping is permitted within the Area of Critical Environmental Concern. Lodging is available in Yuma and Gila Bend.

Food and Supplies

There are no services on-site. Some supplies are available in Dateland, located 20 miles west of Spot Road.

First Aid

There is no first aid station on-site. The nearest hospital is located in Yuma.

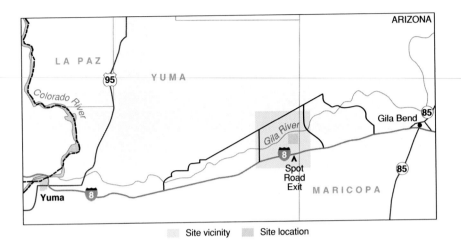

Site vicinity   Site location

Additional Information

The site is open all year. The best time to visit is during the cooler months, since summer temperature highs average over 100°F. Bees are common. Hiking is difficult on loose gravel and boulders. Paths are visible, but not maintained. Archaeological resources are protected under the Antiquities Act of 1906 and Archaeological Resources Protection Act of 1979.

Contact Information

BLM - Yuma Field Office
2555 E. Gila Ridge Road
Yuma, Arizona 85365
Tel: (928) 317-3200
Fax: (928) 317-3250
www.az.blm.gov/yfo/index.htm

Activity Codes

other - stargazing

Sonoran Desert National Monument

Location

60 miles southwest of Phoenix, Arizona.

Description

This 486,000-acre national monument is the classic western landscape, the place where one can imagine horsemen riding across the desert, spying outlaws behind the rocks, watching the shadows of giant saguaro cacti move across the desert floor. The monument's rugged mountain ranges are separated by wide valleys that contain a spectacular diversity of plant and animal species, including several large saguaro cactus forests. The monument also encompasses significant archaeological and historic sites including several important historic trails. The wilderness areas offer excellent opportunities for solitude and unconfined recreation. The North Maricopa Mountains Wilderness has two hiking and equestrian trails, the 9-mile Margie's Cove Trail and the 6-mile Brittlebush Trail. The Table Top Wilderness also has two hiking and equestrian trails, the 7-mile Lava Flow Trail and the 3-mile Table Top Trail. A four-wheel-drive route follows the trail corridor for approximately 10 miles through the national monument.

Directions

From Phoenix, take Interstate 10 south approximately 50 miles to Interstate 8 west. Access to the southern part of the monument is available at the Vekol Road interchange (Exit 144). For information about other access routes, contact BLM.

Visitor Activities

Picnicking, hiking, historic site, hunting, scenic drives, plant viewing, birdwatching, biking, wildlife viewing, four-wheel driving, archaeological site.

Special Features

The most striking of the monument's plant communities are its saguaro cactus forests. The saguaro is a signature plant of the Sonoran Desert. Individual saguaro plants are indeed magnificent, but a crowd of these huge plants, together with the wide variety of trees, shrubs, and herbaceous plants that make up the forest community, is an impressive sight to behold.

Significant archaeological and historic sites include rock art sites, lithic quarries, and scattered artifacts. Vekol Wash is believed to have been an important prehistoric travel and trade corridor between the Hohokam people

Winter clouds drift over the South Maricopa Mountains within the Sonoran Desert National Monument. *(Rich Hanson, BLM Phoenix Field Office)*

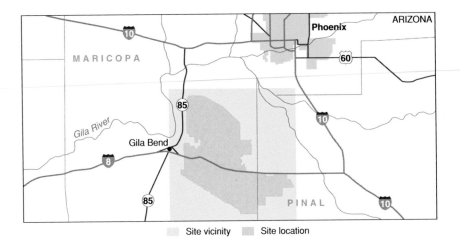

Site vicinity ■ Site location

and tribes located in what is now Mexico. Evidence of large villages and permanent habitation sites exists throughout the area, and particularly along the bajadas of the Table Top Mountains. The Lava Flow Trail meanders through the lowlands of the wilderness area. Desert bighorn sheep, coyotes, quail, javelinas, giant spotted whip-tail lizards, Ajo Mountain whip-snakes, and numerous birds, reptiles, and raptors abound. Important natural water holes, known as tinajas, exist throughout the monument. The endangered acuna pineapple cactus is also found in the monument.

A section of the Juan Bautista de Anza National Historic Trail crosses the national monument. This Congressionally designated trail parallels the Butterfield Overland Stage Route, the Mormon Battalion Trail, and the Gila Trail.

Permits, Fees, Limitations

Access to the Sand Tank Mountains, located south of Interstate 8, requires a permit. Call BLM for information on acquiring a permit. Motorized and mechanized vehicles, including bicycles, must remain on existing routes and are not permitted in the wilderness areas. Collection, removal, or damage to natural and cultural resources, including artifacts, plants (living or dead), and rocks, is prohibited.

Accessibility

None.

Camping and Lodging

The national monument has no developed camping facilities. BLM's Painted Rock Campground is located approximately 26 miles west of Gila Bend. Lodging is available in Gila Bend, approximately 25 miles west of the Vekol Road interchange on Interstate 8.

Food and Supplies

There are no services in the national monument. Stores and gas stations are available in nearby Gila Bend.

First Aid

There is no first aid station on-site. The nearest hospital is located in Casa

Grande, approximately 30 miles east of the Vekol Road interchange on Interstate 8.

Additional Information
Because of extreme summer temperatures, activities are best pursued from late October–mid-April. Drinking water is not available, so visitors are reminded to bring an adequate supply. Vehicles should be in good working order, and should have a full tank of gas and full-size spare tire. Cellular phones do not work in many areas of the national monument. The main access routes and washes are prone to heavy seasonal rains and flash floods. Check with BLM for current conditions. This is a remote area; recreational opportunities are primitive and access roads are not maintained. No water or trash collection is provided.

The desert sun stirs rattlesnakes and other reptiles as early as February.

Recreationists must drink plenty of water. Flash floods caused by sudden storms can be dangerous in washes, so visitors should have a survival plan to prevent emergency situations. Visitors are encouraged to contact BLM for a map of the monument.

Contact Information
BLM - Phoenix Field Office
21605 North 7th Avenue
Phoenix, AZ 85027
Tel: (623) 580-5500
Fax: (623) 580-5580
www.az.blm.gov/pfo/index.html

Activity Codes

other - stargazing

Vermilion Cliffs National Monument

Location
10 miles southwest of Page, Arizona.

Description
The 3,000-foot escarpment of the Vermilion Cliffs reveals seven major geologic formations in layer-cake fashion. This remote, unspoiled, 294,000-acre national monument is a geologic treasure of towering cliffs, deep canyons, and spectacular sandstone formations. Paria Canyon, located within the Paria Canyon-Vermilion Cliffs Wilderness,

offers an outstanding 4- to 5-day wilderness backpacking experience. For a shorter—but still spectacular—experience, many visitors hike through the nearby Coyote Buttes area.

Directions
There are no paved roads within the monument. From Page, Arizona, take U.S. Highway 89 south for approximately 25 miles, then turn west on U.S. Highway Alternate 89 (89A) for approximately 30 miles to the cliffs. From

The Paria River rises in the spring, often necessitating travel through ankle- to knee-deep water that is home to sensitive native fish, including the flannelmouth sucker and the speckled dace. *(BLM)*

Kanab, Utah, take U.S. Highway Alternate 89 (89A) south for 37 miles to Jacob Lake, Utah. From there, continue east on Alternate 89 approximately 25 miles to the cliffs. The Paria Contact Station is located in Utah on U.S. Highway 89, 44 miles east of Kanab.

Visitor Activities
Scenic drives, geologic sightseeing, hiking, four-wheel driving, birdwatching, wildlife viewing, and plant viewing.

Special Features
The Paria Canyon-Vermilion Cliffs Wilderness is located mostly within the national monument and was designated in 1984. The national monument is home to desert bighorn sheep, mule deer, a variety of raptors, and California condors, which have been reintroduced into the region after successful captive breeding.

Permits, Fees, Limitations
Permits required for hikes in Paria Canyon and the Coyote Buttes area are available online at *www.az.blm.gov/paria/index2.html.*

Accessibility
None.

Camping and Lodging
Three lodges are located along U.S. Highway 89A west of the Navajo Bridge over the Colorado River (about 15 miles north of the intersection of U.S. Highway 89 and 89A). Lodging is also available in Jacob Lake, Arizona (on U.S. Highway 89A, 37 miles south of Kanab, Utah), and Fredonia, Arizona (7 miles south of Kanab on U.S. Highway 89A), as well as in Page and Kanab.

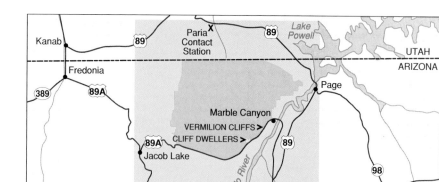

Site vicinity ▪ Site location

Food and Supplies
Limited food and supplies are available at the 3 lodges. The nearest sources of food and supplies are Page and Kanab.

First Aid
No first aid is available within the national monument. The nearest reliable first aid is at Lee's Ferry (managed by the National Park Service), approximately 30 miles west of Page on U.S. Highway 89A. The nearest hospital is in Flagstaff, Arizona, 125 miles south on U.S. Highway 89 at the intersection with Interstate 40.

Additional Information
Visits to the area require special planning and awareness of potential hazards such as rugged and unmarked roads, venomous reptiles and invertebrates, extreme heat, deep sand, and flash floods. Hiking in foothills may be hazardous because of loose rock, steep slopes, and extreme summer temperatures. Fall, winter, and spring are the best times to visit.

There are several trailheads for Paria Canyon, but the most convenient is the White House trailhead, located 2 miles south of U.S. Highway 89 near the Paria Contact Station in Utah. The Coyote Buttes area also has several access points. Wire Pass, the main trailhead, is 8.3 miles south of U.S. Highway 89. The dirt access road is located between Miles 25 and 26 on U.S. Highway 89 between Page and Kanab.

Restroom facilities are located at the Paria Contact Station, and at several trailheads including Lee's Ferry, Wire Pass, and White House.

Contact Information
BLM – Vermilion Cliffs
   National Monument
430 South Main
Fredonia, AZ 86022
Tel: (435) 688-3200
Fax: (435) 688-3258
azstrip.az.blm.gov

Activity Codes

Within Vermilion Cliffs National Monument, Paria Canyon presents a challenging and enjoyable 38-mile trek for the experienced, well-prepared hiker. *(BLM)*

Vulture Peak Trail

Location
10 miles southwest of Wickenburg, Arizona.

Description
Vulture Peak Trail is a short, but steep, trail that takes hikers 2 miles from the base of Vulture Peak, elevation 2,480 feet, to a saddle at 3,420 feet, just below the summit. The trail is located in the Sonoran Desert and treats visitors to a larger-than-life garden including saguaro cactus, palo verde, mesquite, bursage, creosote, jojoba, ocotillo, ironwood, and numerous cactus species, including prickly pear, teddybear cholla, barrel cactus, hedgehog cactus, and various shrubs and grasses. Years with abundant winter rains can result in springtimes with hillsides awash in thick blankets of wildflowers. Hikers can expect to see globe mallows, mariposa lilies, blackfoot daisies, lupine, red penstemon, desert poppies, and brittlebushes. The area provides habitat for a number of mammals, birds, reptiles, and amphibians.

Directions
From Wickenburg, drive west on U.S. Highway 60 for 2.5 miles, turn left at the Vulture Mine Road, and drive south for 7 miles, then turn left at the Vulture Peak Trail sign to the parking lot.

The beavertail cactus, which thrives on dry, rocky slopes, is one of the many varieties of desert plants that greet hikers on the Vulture Peak Trail. The large, brilliant blooms appear in springtime. *(Doran Sanchez, BLM California Desert District Office)*

Visitor Activities
Hiking, picnicking, horseback riding, mountain biking, all-terrain and four-wheel driving, plant viewing, wildlife viewing, and geologic sightseeing.

Special Features
Vulture Peak Trail meanders through classic Sonoran Desert landscapes, including dense stands of saguaro, cholla, and other cactus varieties. The trail crosses wide desert washes and offers dramatic, scenic vistas of rugged desert mountain ranges and valleys in all directions.

Permits, Fees, Limitations
None.

Accessibility
Vulture Peak Trail is not wheelchair-accessible. The primary trailhead is suitable for passenger cars and may be reached via the paved Vulture Mine Road from Wickenburg. An upper trailhead, suitable only for four-wheel-drive vehicles, is near the base of Vulture Peak. Four-wheel-driving visitors should follow the posted primitive dirt road from the primary trailhead.

Camping and Lodging
On-site camping is primitive. There are no developed campsites.

Food and Supplies
There are no services on-site. Food and supplies are available in Wickenburg.

First Aid

There is no first aid station on-site. The nearest hospital is located in Wickenburg.

Additional Information

From May–September, afternoon temperatures range from 100°–112°F. Average annual precipitation ranges from 8–10 inches a year, most of which occurs during the summer monsoon season. Lightning and flash floods are hazards to expect in July, August, and September. The best time to visit is October–April. Visitors are advised to bring plenty of water and to pack out all refuse. Rattlesnakes and other poisonous creatures may be encountered, so visitors should watch for them and be careful where placing hands and feet. Hikers need to be in good physical condition to ascend the final section to the top of the peak. From the saddle (4,320 feet), experienced hikers can scramble up an extremely steep, narrow chute to the summit of Vulture Peak, which tops out at 3,660 feet. The final ascent is not maintained and should be attempted only by experienced and well-conditioned hikers. The primary trailhead offers a picnic table and parking for 15 vehicles. The four wheel-drive trailhead offers parking for four vehicles. No other facilities or services, including water and trash collection, are provided.

Contact Information

BLM - Phoenix Field Office
21605 North 7th Avenue
Phoenix, AZ 85027
Tel: (623) 580-5500
Fax: (623) 580-5580
www.az.blm.gov/pfo/index.html

Activity Codes

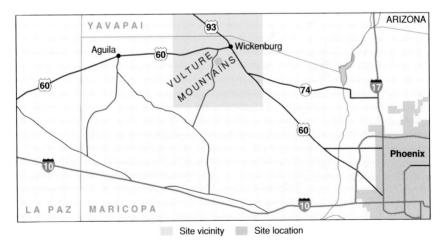

Site vicinity   Site location

Magnificent vistas lure hikers to California's King Range National Conservation Area, one of the last pristine stretches of California coastline. *(Bob Wick, BLM Arcata Field Office)*

From the subtle to the sublime, vivid and exciting recreation opportunities abound in California. Its 14 million acres of BLM public lands offer remoteness and majesty ranging from the desolation of the Great Basin to the grandeur of the Pacific Ocean. Most of California's public lands are located in the southern California Desert, with smaller, but still significant, concentrations throughout the state. The terrain of these public lands is extremely diverse, encompassing sagebrush plains and old-growth forests, rolling sand dunes and the rugged Pacific coastline, lush streamside areas and austere high desert.

No matter what your experience level, you will find myriad adventures to challenge and enlighten. Hike or bike through historic railroad tunnels along the Bizz Johnson National Recreation Trail or careen down one of California's exceptional whitewater runs. Other not-to-be-missed sites include the wonderfully remote King Range National Conservation Area along California's "Lost Coast," and the Imperial Sand Dunes, an off-highway enthusiasts' paradise in southern California. The public lands provide recreation opportunities for thousands of visitors seeking superb hiking trails, rivers, off-highway vehicle areas, campgrounds, and wilderness experiences.

The best time to visit California is year-round! California's diverse climate offers everything from desert heat to alpine snow. In the desert, scorching summers give way to sunny and mild autumns for off-highway vehicle play—or solitude. Primeval, old-growth forests provide shaded trails away from the desert in the hot months. For winter fun, a blanket of snow and cross-country skiing await on your favorite trail.

Most of California's public lands are accessible from major roadways, but by getting off the highway and exploring a few back roads, you can also escape to some of the more remote regions of the state.

California

Alabama Hills

Location

About 2 miles west of Lone Pine, California.

Description

This 30,000-acre area received its name from a Confederate warship responsible for wreaking havoc on northern shipping during the Civil War. Prospectors sympathetic to the Confederate cause named their mining claims after the C.S.S. Alabama, and eventually the name stuck to these unique hills.

The rounded, weathered contours of the Alabamas form a sharp contrast with the crisply-sculpted ridges of the nearby Sierra Nevada Mountains. Unlike the Sierra peaks, the Alabama Hills' granite rock has been etched by wind and water, creating rounded and soft-looking boulders and leaving desert varnish — a mottled black coating of iron and manganese compounds — on many of the rocks. The scenic rock formations have been the setting for many commercials and movies, including "The Shadow" and "How the West Was Won." These geologic features also lure rock climbers, hikers, and mountain bikers, and several streams in the area attract anglers.

The Alabama Hills attract campers, hikers, mountain bikers, and rock climbers, as well as filmmakers, who have used the scenic rock formations as the setting for numerous movies and commercials. *(James Pickering, BLM California State Office)*

Directions

From Lone Pine, proceed west on Whitney Portal Road for about 2.5 miles and turn right (north) on Movie Road. Continue for about 1 mile to Movie Flat, where many films have been shot. Whitney Portal and Movie Roads also intersect with numerous other dirt roads and trails that provide access to the hills.

Visitor Activities

Mountain biking, hiking, movie location sightseeing, technical rock climbing, horseback riding, fishing, and scenic drives.

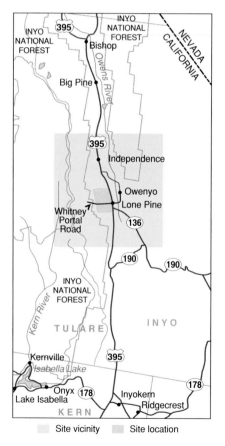

Site vicinity ▮ Site location

Special Features

Both the Alabamas and the Sierras resulted from a cataclysmic uplifting of the earth's crust about 100 million years ago. Millennia of wind, snow, and wind-blown sand have shaped the unusual rounded formations seen in the Alabamas. In contrast, the Sierras were weathered by the continual freezing and thawing typical of higher altitudes.

Wildflowers bloom earlier in the Alabama Hills than in the nearby Sierras. Desert paintbrush, prairie smokes, and lowly penstemons are likely to be spotted in May and June along the arid hillsides. Lucky spring-time visitors may also encounter male sage grouse gathering in open areas and "strutting" as part of their mating ritual.

Permits, Fees, Limitations

No fees, although donations are encouraged to maintain the area.

Accessibility

This site is wheelchair-accessible.

Camping and Lodging

The nearest BLM campground is Tuttle Creek Campground, with 85 sites but no potable water. To reach the campground, travel 3.5 miles west of Lone Pine on Whitney Portal Road. Turn left (south) on Horseshoe Meadows Road and travel about 1.5 miles to the signs for the campground on the right. Lone Pine Campground, an Inyo National Forest campground, is located about 6 miles west of Lone Pine on Whitney Portal Road. County campgrounds are also available in the area. Contact the Inyo County Parks and Recreation Department, (760) 878-2411, for additional information. Lone Pine has several motels.

Food and Supplies
No supplies or facilities are located on-site. The nearest sources are in Lone Pine.

First Aid
No first aid is available on-site. The nearest hospital is located in Lone Pine.

Additional Information
The Alabama Hills are very hot in the summer and snow is possible in the winter. However, at any time of the year, visitors can find inclement weather in the area. The best times to visit the Alabamas are fall, winter, and spring. No matter what time of year, visitors should remember to bring water. Most of the Alabamas are accessible only by dirt roads. Some of the softer roads require four-wheel-drive capability. The main county road, Movie Road (located off Whitney Portal Road, about 2.5 miles west of Lone Pine), is maintained for passenger vehicles. Vehicle and mountain bike use is restricted to existing routes

The Lone Pine Chamber of Commerce on Main Street in Lone Pine and the Interagency Visitor Center, located 2 miles south of Lone Pine on U.S. Highway 395, provide additional information on the area. The Lone Pine Chamber also has information about annual events such as the Lone Pine Film Festival and the Wild Wild West Race for runners.

Contact Information
BLM - Bishop Field Office
785 North Main Street, Suite E
Bishop, CA 93514
Tel: (760) 872-4881
Fax: (760) 872-5050
www.ca.blm.gov/bishop/alabamas.html

Activity Codes

other - movie location sightseeing, technical rock climbing

American River Recreation Areas

Location
North Fork: about 30 miles northeast of Auburn, California.
South Fork: about 20 miles southeast of Auburn, California.

Description
North Fork: The famous Giant Gap 14–mile run of the North Fork of the American River is one of California's top whitewater challenges, for experts only. Cliffs tower 2,000 feet above the river, a nationally designated wild and scenic river. Heaps of mine tailings and old cabin ruins border this roller-coaster ride through the historic "Mother Lode."
South Fork: Nicknamed the "Gold Rush River," the South Fork of the American River is treasured as the most popular whitewater run in California. Even before

Tranquil here, the South Fork of the American River still provides an exciting trip for rafters —though nothing like the wild, "experts-only" ride on the river's North Fork. *(BLM)*

James Marshall's fortuitous 1848 gold find at Sutter's Mill, the "Rio de los Americanos" had a local reputation as a wild and capricious mountain stream. Today, tempered by upstream dams, the South Fork still lurches and bucks through cataracts of boulders, drops, and chutes. The 21-mile run can be negotiated in one full day, but most rafters prefer to camp overnight on the river between two exciting half-day runs. Along the Dave Moore Nature Trail (on California Highway 49 about 16 miles southeast of Auburn), visitors can still see evidence of the intense mining activity that took place during the great Gold Rush.

Directions

North Fork: To get to the rafting put-in at Euchre Bar, take Interstate 80 northeast from Auburn for about 30 miles to the Alta Exit. Turn right on Morton Road, and then left on Casa Loma Road. After about 1 mile, turn right at the sign for the Euchre Bar trail. The trailhead is about 2 miles down a mostly dirt road. The put-in is a steep, 2-mile hike down from the trailhead. To get to the rafting take-out, take Interstate 80 northeast from Auburn for about 15 miles to Colfax. Take the State Highway 174 exit south and follow the signs to Iowa Hill Road, which descends for about 3 miles to the

river. The take-out point is a camp-
ground on the far side of the bridge.
South Fork: To get to the put-in from
Auburn, take State Highway 49 south
about 25 miles toward Placerville. Make
a sharp left onto State Highway 193
and descend slowly to the Chili Bar
Reservoir, with access to the river.
(Note: State Highway 193 intersects
twice with State Highway 49. The Chili
Bar Reservoir is near Placerville.)
Another put-in point is at Marshall Gold
Discovery State Park on State Highway
49 at Coloma (18 miles south of
Auburn). The take-out point is at Folsom
Lake State Recreation Area, which can
be reached by taking State Highway 49
north for about 7.5 miles past Coloma to
Salmon Falls Road. Turn left on Salmon
Falls Road and follow it approximately
5 miles to the Salmon Falls Bridge.

Visitor Activities

Whitewater rafting, hiking, historic site,
birdwatching, wildlife viewing, fishing,
kayaking, swimming, and picnicking.

Special Features

Rafters encounter more than 75 rapids
on their way through the North Fork's
Giant Gap. About 5 miles downstream
from the put-in at Euchre Bar, Canyon
Creek enters the North Fork after passing over several 25–30-foot waterfalls.
Old mining trails lead from the riverbank up to the top of the falls.

Marshall Gold Discovery State Historic Park is located on the South Fork
of the American River at Coloma along
Highway 49. This park is the location of
Sutter's Sawmill, one of the most significant historic sites in the United States.
The discovery of gold there changed
the course of California history.

Permits, Fees, Limitations

A free county tag is required for private
rafting trips and is available through the
El Dorado County Parks and Recreation
office in Placerville, (530) 621-5330.

Accessibility

North Fork: The terrain is very rugged
and not wheelchair-accessible.

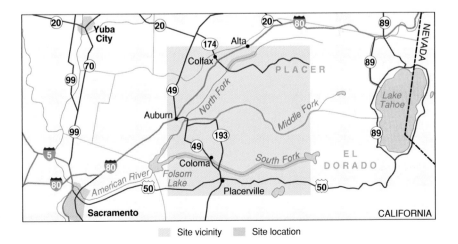

Site vicinity   Site location

South Fork: The Dave Moore Nature Area has a wheelchair-accessible trail.

Camping and Lodging

Along the North Fork, there is a state park campground at the Iowa Hill Bridge, on Iowa Hill Road off State Highway 174. Along the South Fork, camping is abundant in private, county, and state campgrounds. The American River Recreation Area covers a large geographic area and is located near Sacramento, which is only 50 miles west on Interstate 80. Visitors are encouraged to contact BLM for recommendations on campgrounds for specific areas. The nearest lodging is available in Auburn, Colfax (about 15 miles northeast of Auburn on Interstate 80), and Placerville (26 miles southeast of Auburn at the intersection of State Highway 49 and U.S. Highway 50).

Food and Supplies

Food and supplies can be obtained in Auburn, Colfax, Placerville, and Sacramento.

First Aid

First aid is available from commercial outfitters and state park rangers. The nearest hospitals are located in Auburn and Placerville.

Additional Information

There are many tourist-oriented services available on-site. The best times to float the river are spring and summer. The river offers Class IV–V rapids on the North Fork, and Class III rapids on the South Fork. Visitors planning to go river rafting should go with a professional guide who will prepare them with proper gear and safety information. Visitors should contact BLM for a list of permitted outfitters.

Contact Information

BLM - Folsom Field Office
63 Natoma Street
Folsom, CA 95630
Tel: (916) 985-4474
Fax: (916) 985-3259
North Fork:
www.ca.blm.gov/folsom/nfamerican.html
South Fork:
www.ca.blm.gov/folsom/sfamerican.html

Activity Codes

Big Morongo Canyon

Location

15 miles north of Palm Springs, California.

Description

Big Morongo Creek rises to the surface for just 3 miles between the Mojave and Colorado Deserts before it disappears underground again. The resulting desert canyon oasis was used for centuries by nomadic Native Americans, who found water and game plentiful here. More than 235 bird species have been observed in the Big Morongo Canyon

Preserve, including several rare species. Many additional transient species are present during the spring and fall migration seasons. Water also attracts desert bighorn sheep, raccoons, bobcats, coyotes, and other mammals. The preserve is listed as a Watchable Wildlife site.

Directions

From Palm Springs, travel about 3 miles west on Interstate 10 to State Highway 62. Travel north on State Highway 62 for 11.5 miles to Morongo Valley. Turn right on East Drive and go about 200 yards to the preserve entrance on the left.

Visitor Activities

Birdwatching, plant viewing, wildlife viewing, hiking, horseback riding, picnicking, and guided tours.

Special Features

One of the 10 largest cottonwood and willow riparian habitats in California, the stream here is a lifeline for migrating and breeding birds, such as indigo buntings and yellow-breasted chats. Threatened yellow-billed cuckoos and endangered least Bell's vireos have also been spotted in Big Morongo Canyon. Dawn and dusk are the best times to watch for raccoons, bobcats, and foxes; bighorn sheep are most likely to be seen in summer.

Permits, Fees, Limitations

No fees. No unauthorized vehicles or bicycles are permitted beyond the parking lot. No dogs or other pets are allowed in the preserve. Firearms and hunting are restricted. Smoking is not allowed. Hiking and horseback riding are permitted on designated trails only.

Accessibility

Some portions of the trails are wheelchair-accessible. Contact BLM for details.

Camping and Lodging

Primitive camping is available at Morongo Valley Park, 5 miles north of Big Morongo Canyon on State Highway 62. Camping is free. Developed camping is available at the Black Rock Campground in Joshua Tree National Park, about 10 miles north of Morongo Valley on State Highway 62. Lodging is available in Palm Springs, Desert Hot Springs (about 11 miles southeast), and Yucca Valley (about 10 miles northeast on State Highway 62).

Food and Supplies

Food and supplies are available in Morongo Valley.

Big Morongo Canyon's boardwalk offers visitors the opportunity to explore the abundant plant and animal life at this unique desert oasis. (Doran Sanchez, BLM California Desert District Office)

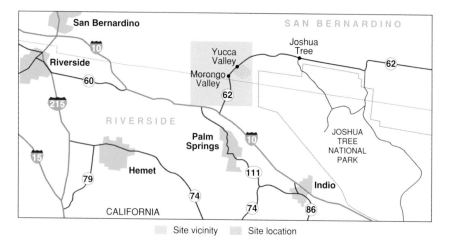

Site vicinity   Site location

First Aid
No first aid is available on-site. The Avalon Urgent Care Center is in Yucca Valley, and the nearest hospital is located in Palm Springs.

Additional Information
The preserve is open daily from 7:30 a.m.–sunset. Picnic facilities, restrooms, and detailed trail maps are available at the preserve. Winter, fall, and spring are the best times of the year to visit this area. The preserve has a desert climate with hot, dry summers and moderate winters. Rainfall is scarce, and winter and spring nighttime temperatures can be cool.

Contact Information
BLM - Big Morongo Canyon Preserve
Attn: Preserve Manager
P.O. Box 780
Morongo Valley, CA 92256
Tel: (760) 363-7190
Fax: (760) 363-1180
pub4.caso.ca.blm.gov/palmsprings/wf-morongo.html

Activity Codes

Bizz Johnson
National Recreation Trail

Location
Located within the city limits of Susanville, California.

Description
In 1978, Southern Pacific Railroad abandoned most of the old Fernley and Lassen Railroad branch line, which had carried lumber and passengers from 1914 until operations ended in 1956. BLM spearheaded the "rails-to-trails" conversion of the old railroad grade with the support of former Congressman Harold T. "Bizz" Johnson, who

served in the U.S. House of Representatives from 1958-1980. Today, the 30-mile trail is used by hikers, mountain bikers, equestrians, and cross-country skiers. For the first 16 miles, the trail follows the Susan River. As it winds through the rugged Susan River Canyon, the trail crosses the river 12 times on bridges and trestles and passes through two tunnels. The landscape is a combination of semi-arid canyon and upland forests of pine and firs. The trail has four distinct seasons because of the high altitude.

Directions

In Susanville, follow State Highway 36 (Main Street) to Weatherlow Street.

Turn south on Weatherlow, which becomes Richmond Road, and continue 0.5 mile to Susanville Railroad Depot Trailhead Visitor Center. The trail begins at the depot (601 Richmond Road).

Visitor Activities

Hiking, mountain biking, horseback riding, cross-country skiing, fishing, wildflower viewing, wildlife viewing, birdwatching, historic site, and interpretive programs.

Special Features

The trail winds through three bioregions —the Great Basin, the Sierra Nevada, and the Cascade Range—featuring

A trail for all seasons, the **Bizz Johnson National Recreation Trail** follows the route of an old railroad through river canyons and upland forests, offering dramatic scenery to bikers, hikers, equestrians, and cross-country skiers. *(BLM)*

landscapes ranging from high desert to grasslands to oak woodlands, as well as dense cedar and pine forests. Many birds are attracted to the river, including belted kingfishers, hooded orioles, canyon wrens, and several types of birds of prey.

Permits, Fees, Limitations
None.

Accessibility
The 6-mile segment from Devil's Corral trailhead (7 miles west of Susanville on State Highway 36) to Hobo Camp, off Richmond Road in Susanville, is wheel-chair-accessible. This is the most scenic part of the trail and includes two tunnels and eight bridges.

Camping and Lodging
Primitive camping is permitted along the trail on BLM and U.S. Forest Service lands. There is a 7-day camping limit between trailheads unless otherwise posted. The undeveloped, drive-in Goumaz Campground, with five sites, is on U.S. Forest Service land between the trail and the Susan River. (Take State Highway 44 approximately 10 miles northwest of Susanville. Turn south on Forest Road 30N03 and follow this dirt road 3 miles to the campground. The road is not suitable for passenger cars.) No camping is allowed at or within 1 mile of the Hobo Camp picnic area or the Devil's Corral trailhead, unless authorized. Camping is prohibited along South Side Road within the Susan River Canyon west of Hobo Camp.

Lodging is available in Susanville, Westwood (22 miles west of Susanville on State Highway 36), and the surrounding area. For a list of area lodging, call the Lassen County Chamber of Commerce, (530) 257-4323.

Food and Supplies
No food or supplies are available on-site. Water sources along the trail are not safe to drink. Restaurants, groceries, and supplies are available in Susanville and Chester, about 35 miles west on State Highway 36.

First Aid
No first aid is available on-site. The nearest hospitals are located in Susanville and Chester.

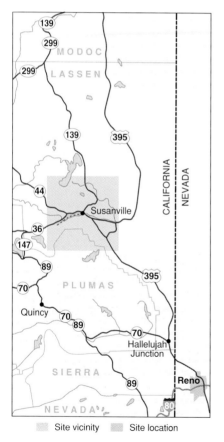

Site vicinity   Site location

Additional Information

The remarkable autumn colors and scenery along the Bizz Johnson Trail earned it 1 of 12 feature spots on the Rails-To-Trails Conservancy's 2002 "Fall Foliage on the Web" rail-trails guide. Each year in early fall, visitors and residents flock to the Susanville Depot for the Rails to Trails Festival. Featured events at the depot and along the trail include railroad handcar rides and races, mountain bike rides, walks, barbecues, chili cook-offs, live music, and children's activities.

Contact Information

BLM - Eagle Lake Field Office
2950 Riverside Drive
Susanville, CA 96130
Tel: (530) 257-0456
Fax: (530) 257-4831
www.ca.blm.gov/eaglelake/bizztrail.html

Activity Codes

Bradshaw Trail

Location

The western end of this 65-mile BLM back country byway begins about 35 miles southeast of Indio, California. The trail's eastern end is about 15 miles southwest of Blythe, California.

Description

The first road through Riverside County was blazed by William Bradshaw in 1862, as an overland stage route beginning in San Bernardino, California, and ending in La Paz (now Ehrenberg), Arizona. The trail was used extensively between 1862 and 1877 to transport miners and other passengers to the gold fields at La Paz. The trail is now a graded dirt road that traverses mostly public land between the Chuckwalla Mountains and the Chocolate Mountain Aerial Gunnery Range.

Directions

From Indio, take Interstate 10 east to the State Highway 86 Expressway and

Observant travelers might be lucky enough to spot a bighorn sheep in the rocky terrain along the historic Bradshaw Trail. *(Doran Sanchez, BLM California Desert District)*

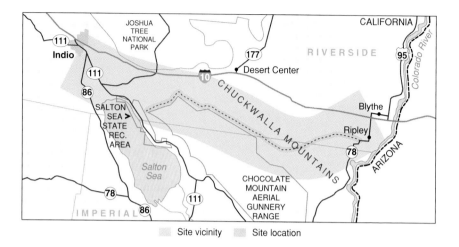

Site vicinity   Site location

travel about 10 miles to Avenue 66. Turn left and proceed for about 0.5 mile, and then turn right onto State Highway 111. Then proceed about 18 miles south on State Highway 111 to the Salton Sea State Recreation Area. (Or follow State Highway 111 from downtown Indio directly to the recreation area.) Across from park headquarters is Parkview Drive. Go east on Parkview Drive for about 1.7 miles, then left on Desert Aire for about 0.5 mile to Canal Road. Follow Canal Road east for about 10 miles to Drop 24 and the beginning of the Bradshaw Trail.

Or, from Blythe, take Interstate 10 west for about 3 miles to the State Highway 78 exit. Go south on State Highway 78 for about 12 miles to the eastern end of the trail. Look for the Bradshaw Trail sign on the right about 5 miles past the community of Ripley.

Visitor Activities

Four-wheel driving, wildlife viewing, plant viewing, birdwatching, scenic drives, rockhounding, and hiking.

Special Features

The trail offers spectacular views of the Chuckwalla Bench, Orocopia Mountains, Chuckwalla Mountains, and the Palo Verde Valley. The Salton Sea, near the trail's western end, is one of the largest salt lakes on earth. Wildlife in the area includes wild burros, mule deer, bighorn sheep, coyotes, kit foxes, other small mammals, and birds.

Permits, Fees, Limitations

All commercial and competitive activities require a land-use or special recreation permit from BLM. The Bradshaw Trail is within a "limited use area," which means vehicles are restricted to approved routes. Wilderness areas adjacent to the trail are posted as closed to all motorized vehicles.

Accessibility

Wheelchair-accessible restrooms are available at Wiley's Well and Coon Hollow Campgrounds within the Mule Mountains Long-Term Visitor Area.

Camping and Lodging

The Mule Mountain Long-Term Visitor Area (LTVA), located at the intersection of the Bradshaw Trail and Wiley's Well Road, is available for camping stays up to 7 months from mid-September–mid-April. Two developed campgrounds are part of the LTVA. Wiley's Well Campground is located at the intersection of Wiley's Well Road and the Bradshaw Trail; Coon Hollow Campground is located about 4 miles farther south on Wiley's Well Road. (From Blythe, take Interstate 10 west for about 17 miles to the Wiley's Well Road exit. Go south on Wiley's Well Road for about 8 miles to Wiley's Well Campground, or 12 miles to Coon Hollow Campground.) The campgrounds provide campsites with picnic tables, shade ramadas, and grills. Other campgrounds are available at Lake Cahuilla (4 miles southeast of La Quinta on Avenue 58), Joshua Tree National Park (about 25 miles east of Indio and north of Interstate 10), and Corn Springs (about 38 miles west of Blythe and 8 miles south of Interstate 10 on Corn Springs Road). Primitive vehicular camping is allowed within 100 feet of the trail except in designated wilderness areas. Use of previously disturbed areas is encouraged. Fourteen-day camping restrictions apply. The cities of Indio and Blythe offer complete accommodations.

Food and Supplies

Food, supplies, and gasoline are available in Indio, Blythe, Chiriaco Summit (about 30 miles east of Indio on Interstate 10), and Desert Center (48 miles west of Blythe on Interstate 10).

First Aid

There is no first aid available along the Bradshaw Trail. Hospitals are located in Indio and Blythe.

Additional Information

The trail is a dirt road periodically graded by the Riverside County Transportation Department. Four-wheel-drive vehicles are recommended because of stretches of soft sand and dry wash conditions. The Chocolate Mountain Aerial Gunnery Range is located immediately south of the trail. This is a live bombing range that is closed to all public entry. VISITORS SHOULD NOT ENTER THE BOMBING RANGE. Summers can be extremely hot. Visitors should carry plenty of water, always tell someone of their plans, and stick to their itinerary. GPS units and cell phones are highly recommended, although cell phones may not work in some locations along the trail.

Contact Information

BLM - Palm Springs Field Office
690 West Garnet Avenue
P.O. Box 581260
North Palm Springs, CA 92258
Tel: (760) 251-4800
Fax: (760) 251-4899
www.ca.blm.gov/palmsprings/bradshaw.html

Activity Codes

other - rockhounding

Cache Creek

Location
8 miles east of Clearlake Oaks, California.

Description
The 75,000-acre Cache Creek area is cooperatively managed by BLM and the California Department of Fish and Game to enhance wildlife habitat, protect cultural resources, and provide primitive recreational opportunities. Most of this secluded, hilly expanse of oak woodlands, grasslands, and chaparral is closed to motor vehicles, so access is limited to hikers and horseback riders. Rafters and kayakers can also take advantage of year-round water flow in the creek itself.

Directions
Redbud Trail: From Clearlake Oaks, travel east on State Highway 20 for 8 miles to the Redbud trailhead.
Blue Ridge Trail: From Clearlake Oaks, travel east approximately 25 miles on State Highway 20 to its junction with State Highway 16. Turn right and travel south on State Highway 16 for 10 miles. Turn right on County Road 40, proceed 0.25 mile, and cross Cache Creek on a low-water bridge. Turn onto the access road that parallels the creek, and proceed downstream to the parking area. If the road is closed by winter weather, park at the Cache Creek Regional Park, at the junction of State Highway 16 and County Road 40, and walk in. The trailhead is about 150 yards downstream from the low-water bridge on a trail paralleling the creek.

Or from Woodland, take State Highway 16 north to Cache Creek Regional Park, which is located at the junction with County Road 40, about 5 miles past the town of Rumsey. Follow directions above to the Blue Ridge Trailhead.

Visitor Activities
Hiking, hunting, horseback riding, wildflower viewing, birdwatching, wildlife viewing, rafting, kayaking, picnicking, guided tours, and guided wildflower-viewing walks.

Special Features
One of the few free-roaming tule elk herds in California wanders over the area's grasslands and chaparral. In summer, they seek out the creek's reliable water and shade. The Cache Creek area is also home to endangered bald eagles, wild turkeys, black bears, black-tail deer, and other upland species. In addition, the area holds pockets of rare adobe lilies as well as archaeological resources dating back 5,000 years. The Hill

Cache Creek provides hikers and horseback riders the opportunity to view spring wildflower displays and one of the largest populations of wintering bald eagles in California.
(James Pickering, BLM California State Office)

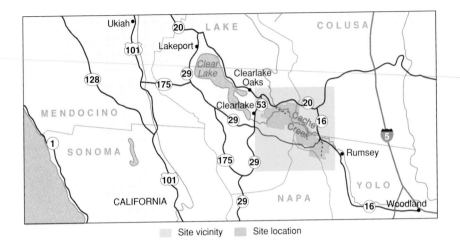

Site vicinity   Site location

Patwin Indians used the area as a refuge after their first contact with Europeans.

Permits, Fees, Limitations
No fees. The Wilson Valley portion of Cache Creek (approximately 6 miles up the trail from the Redbud trailhead) is closed for tule elk calving from April 15–June 30. Campfires may be prohibited during periods of extreme fire danger.

Accessibility
A wheelchair-accessible toilet and picnic tables are available at the Redbud Trail.

Camping and Lodging
Primitive camping is permitted; there are no developed camping areas. Lodging is available in Clearlake Oaks.

Food and Supplies
Food and supplies are available in Clearlake, about 3 miles south of State Highway 20 on State Highway 53.

First Aid
No first aid is available on-site. The nearest first aid is available at Redbud Hospital in Clearlake.

Additional Information
The best times to visit are fall, winter, and spring. Summer provides optimal conditions for rafting, though Cache Creek can be impassable at times of high water. Restroom facilities are available at the Redbud and Blue Ridge trailheads. No potable water is available on-site. Guided bald eagle tours are popular mid-January–mid-February. Guided wildflower-viewing hikes are popular on Saturdays in April. Call BLM for schedule information on guided bald eagle and wildflower tours.

Contact Information
BLM - Ukiah Field Office
2550 North State Street
Ukiah, CA 95482
Tel: (707) 468-4000
Fax: (707) 469-4027
www.ca.blm.gov/caso/wf-cachecrk.html

Activity Codes

Carrizo Plain National Monument

Location
80 miles west of Bakersfield, California.

Description
Located adjacent to the southwest edge of the San Joaquin Valley in eastern San Luis Obispo County, the Carrizo Plain is the largest remaining tract of the San Joaquin Valley biogeographic province, with only limited evidence of human alteration. The 250,000-acre area is a diverse complex of habitats for many endangered, threatened, and rare species of plants and animals. Seasonal recreational opportunities abound, many of them focused on the plain's abundant birds and wildflowers. Hikers can visit the glistening bed of white salt known as Soda Lake, ancient rock art sites, and Wallace Creek, made crooked by movement along the San Andreas Fault. Soda Lake, Elkhorn, and Seven Mile roads within the monument combine to offer a 70-mile scenic loop drive. Large areas of the Carrizo Plain are also open for hunting of doves, chukars, cottontail rabbits, deer, tule elk, and feral pigs.

Directions
North entrance: From Bakersfield, take State Highway 58 west for about 70 miles, then turn south onto Soda Lake Road to access the monument. (Soda Lake Road is about 40 miles east of Santa Margarita, off State Highway 58.) *South entrance:* From Bakersfield, take State Highway 99 south for about 22 miles to the exit for State Highway 166. Take State Highway 166 west for about 35 miles to Soda Lake Road (70 miles east of Santa Maria, or 9 miles west of Maricopa). Turn north on Soda Lake Road to access the monument.

The Guy L. Goodwin Education Center is located 0.5-mile west of the junction of Soda Lake Road and Painted Rock Road. From State Highway 58, turn south onto Soda Lake Road and continue for 13 miles, then turn right onto Painted Rock Road. Or from State Highway 166, turn north onto Soda Lake Road and continue for approximately 30 miles, and then turn left onto Painted Rock Road.

Several short trails in the Carrizo Plain National Monument lead visitors to an ancient rock art site, a creek bed disrupted by the San Andreas Fault, and Soda Lake, one of the largest remaining natural alkali wetlands in California. *(BLM)*

Visitor Activities
Hiking, big-game and bird hunting, horseback riding, mountain biking, archaeological site, plant viewing, bird-watching, and wildlife viewing.

Special Features

The Carrizo Plain contains habitat for California condors and is the first area in California to reintroduce both pronghorn antelope and tule elk, native ungulates that had been hunted to extinction in the region by the late 1800s. In winter, hundreds of sandhill cranes stop by on their migratory route to roost in muddy Soda Lake, located just east of Soda Lake Road. Many other species of birds also winter here. Among the endangered and threatened species that make their homes on the Carrizo Plain are San Joaquin kit foxes, blunt-nosed leopard lizards, San Joaquin antelope squirrels, and giant kangaroo rats, as well as plants such as California jewelflowers, Hoover's woolystars, and San Joaquin woolythreads.

Along the eastern edge of the Carrizo Plain, some of the most spectacular, corrugated topography associated with the San Andreas Fault is clearly visible. Ridges rise sharply from the plain to form the Panorama and Elkhorn Hills. Vernal pools and salt-encrusted sag ponds appear along the fault, trapping rainwater that harbors fairy and brine shrimps. Stream channels, such as Wallace Creek, course abruptly northward as they cross the fault line.

Painted Rock, a large, U-shaped rock outcrop just south of the Goodwin Education Center, features what was once an elaborate, multicolored pictograph site created by the Chumash people of the Santa Barbara Channel region. Both the interior and exterior sides have paintings, which include geometric images as well as human figures, snakes, and a variety of aquatic images. The pictographs were badly vandalized in the 1920s, but many of the paintings are still visible.

Permits, Fees, Limitations

No fees. At certain times of the year, special fire restrictions may be in effect and free campfire permits are required. Contact BLM for an update on current restrictions.

Accessibility

Wheelchair-accessible public restrooms are located at the Guy L. Goodwin Education Center and at the Painted

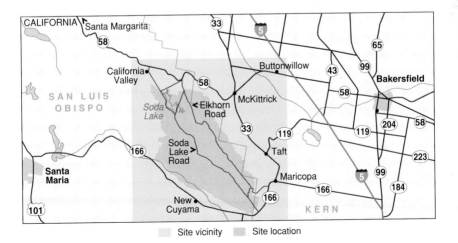

Site vicinity ☐ Site location

Rock Parking Area, both located off Soda Lake Road south of State Highway 58.

Camping and Lodging

The KCL campground (off Soda Lake Road, approximately 5 miles south of the education center) is equipped with eight picnic tables and eight fire pits. It has some of the few shade trees found in the national monument. The Selby Campground (south on Selby Road, just south of the education center) is equipped with five picnic tables and four fire pits. It is nestled at the base of the Caliente Mountains. There are no shade trees, but this campground is more secluded, and the camper is only steps away from unlimited hiking in the wilderness study area that lies outside the campground boundaries. Car camping is also allowed in certain areas of the monument. (Maps at information kiosks located at the north and south entrances to the monument indicate where car camping is permitted.) There is no fee for campfire permits, which may be obtained at the Goodwin Education Center, the Bakersfield BLM office, and from any BLM ranger in the area.

Food and Supplies

Restaurants and grocery stores closest to the south entrance of the monument are located in Maricopa (9 miles east at the intersection of State Highways 166 and 33). From the north entrance of the monument, the closest supplies are in Buttonwillow (45 miles east on State Highway 58) and Santa Margarita (about 40 miles west on State Highway 58).

First Aid

The nearest emergency services are in Maricopa and Buttonwillow.

Additional Information

Many roads within the monument are unpaved and may be impassable during wet weather; visitors should check on road conditions before leaving home. Several short hiking trails take visitors to some of the highlights of the monument. The 0.25-mile Soda Lake Trail begins on Soda Lake Road and leads to the shore of Soda Lake. The 0.2-mile Wallace Creek Trail, located off Elkhorn Road, offers visitors a view of the offset creek bed along the San Andreas Fault. The 0.7-mile-long Painted Rock Trail, located off Soda Lake Road south of the education center, leads to rock art created by the Chumash people, who inhabited the area before the arrival of the Spanish.

The Goodwin Education Center has interpretive exhibits and weekend guided tours, as well as up-to-date information on weather, road conditions, and special closures. The center is open from December–May, usually from Thursday–Sunday, 9 a.m.–5p.m. Visitors should contact BLM prior to visiting for specific operating hours of the center.

Contact Information

BLM - Bakersfield Field Office
3801 Pegasus Drive
Bakersfield, CA 93308
Tel: (661) 391-6000
Fax: (661) 391-6040
Guy L. Goodwin Education Center
Tel: (855) 475-2131
www.ca.blm.gov/bakersfield/carrizoplain.html

Activity Codes

Chappie/Shasta Off-Highway Vehicle Recreation Area

Location
10 miles north of Redding, California.

Description
Visitors to the rolling, brushy hills near Shasta Lake in northern California will find off-highway-vehicle (OHV) riding challenges for all abilities. More than 250 miles of roads and trails are open to motorcyclists, all-terrain-vehicle drivers, and four-wheelers. The area is near Shasta Dam and Shasta Lake, and there are overlooks of the Sacramento River below the dam. The area, named for former U.S. Congressman Eugene Chappie, is open year-round with some seasonal restrictions during the wet, winter months.

Directions
To the Shasta Dam staging area (with facilities): From Redding, take Interstate 5 north about 10 miles to the Shasta Dam exit. Follow Shasta Dam Boulevard to the dam. There are directional markings on the pavement. Continue on the road across the dam. Turn left past the dam and continue to a 3-way stop sign, and turn right. (Streets are not named.) The road leads to the OHV parking area, about 2.5 miles down.
To Matheson Road Access (no facilities): From Redding, take State Highway 299 west about 2 miles to Iron Mountain Road. Turn right on Iron Mountain Road and continue for about 5 miles to Matheson Road. Turn right on Matheson Road following the "Matheson

OHV Access" signs. Parking is allowed along the shoulder of the road and in pullouts in accordance with the existing signs.

Visitor Activities
Off-highway driving, four-wheel driving, competitive events, mountain biking, hiking, wildlife viewing, bird-watching, plant viewing, and fishing.

Special Features
Vegetation in the area ranges from Sacramento River riparian, manzanita chaparral, and knobcone pine at lower elevations to oak woodlands, ponderosa pine, and Douglas fir at higher elevations and on north slopes. Wildlife species in the area include ospreys, bald eagles, mule deer, and bears.

An off-highway driver maneuvers over a rocky section of the Chappie/Shasta Off-Highway Vehicle Area. *(Eric J. Lundquist, Esq., American Motorcyclist Association)*

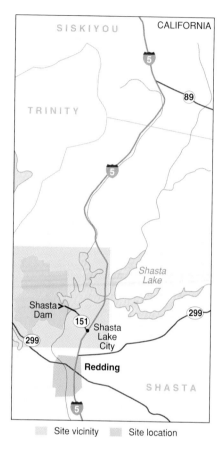

Site vicinity ▨ Site location

Permits, Fees, Limitations
A PERMIT IS NOW REQUIRED
TO CROSS SHASTA DAM TO THE
OHV AREA. Visitors must apply for
permits 72 hours in advance at the
Redding BLM Field Office, Shasta-
Trinity U.S. Forest Service office, or the
Bureau of Reclamation Shasta Dam
Visitors Center. No fees. RVs are not
permitted to cross the dam. A California off-highway-vehicle registration is
required for all motorized vehicles. Hel-
mets are required for riders of motorized off-highway vehicles. All engines
must be equipped with spark arresters
and must meet California noise emission
requirements.

Accessibility
The campground and two river overlooks are wheelchair-accessible. The
overlooks are on Shasta Dam Boulevard,
about 6 miles west of Interstate 5.

Camping and Lodging
Camping is available on-site in a
U.S. Forest Service campground
offering pit toilets, potable water, and
sites for RVs, but no hookups. There is
a daily campground fee. To reach the
campground, take Shasta Dam Boulevard across the dam. The campground is
located at the base of the dam. Motels
are available in Redding.

Food and Supplies
The nearest supplies are available in
Shasta Lake, 10 miles east on Shasta
Dam Boulevard (State Highway 151).

First Aid
There is no first aid available on-site;
however, camp hosts with phones are
on-site and can assist in emergencies.
The nearest hospital is located in
Redding.

Additional Information
The best times to visit are fall, winter,
and spring. Summertime temperatures
of over 100°F can make activities
very uncomfortable. Poison oak grows
at lower elevations. There is no potable
water in the area, except at the
campground. There are opportunities
for both non-competitive recreational
riding and participation in organized
competitions, such as the Shasta
National Hare Scramble. Information

about organized events is published in local newspapers and regional magazines. The OHV area consists of intermingled public lands and private lands. It is managed by BLM, the U.S. Forest Service, the Bureau of Reclamation, and the National Park Service. Some private lands, including an active mine, are closed to the public. Visitors should respect private property rights, and heed signs.

Contact Information

BLM - Redding Field Office
355 Hemsted Drive
Redding, CA 96002
Tel: (530) 224-2100
Fax: (530) 224-2172
www.ca.blm.gov/redding/chappie_ohv.html

Activity Codes

other - competitive OHV events

Cosumnes River Preserve

Location

20 miles south of Sacramento, California.

Description

The Cosumnes River Preserve is home to California's largest remaining valley oak riparian forest, and is one of the few protected wetland habitat areas in the state. The Cosumnes River is the only free-flowing river left in California's Central Valley. Only minutes from California's capital, this is a critical stop on the Pacific Flyway for migrating and wintering waterfowl. Over 200 species of birds have been sighted on or near the preserve, including state-listed threatened Swainson's hawks, greater and lesser sandhill cranes, Canada geese, and numerous ducks. The preserve includes 40,000 acres of current and potential wetlands and valley oak forests. BLM manages about 14,000 acres of the preserve.

Directions

From Sacramento, take Interstate 5 south 20 miles, and exit at Twin Cities Road. Head east 1 mile on Twin Cities Road to Franklin Boulevard, and then head south on Franklin for 2 miles to the preserve.

The Cosumnes River, the Central Valley's last remaining undammed river, is also a critical stop for migrating birds on the Pacific Flyway. *(Leah Ward, BLM California State Office)*

Visitor Activities
Hiking, canoeing, birdwatching, plant viewing, wildlife viewing, and interpretive programs.

Special Features
The preserve includes 40,000 acres of central valley grasslands, vernal pools, wetlands, and valley oak forests, making this an area rich in biodiversity. During winter, hundreds of thousands of waterbirds can be seen in the preserve, including tundra swans, snow geese, northern pintails, cinnamon teals, and least sandpipers.

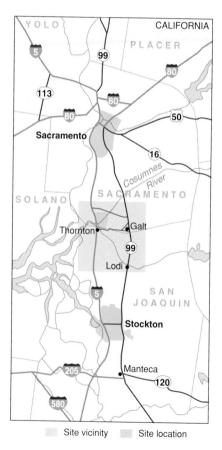

Site vicinity   Site location

Permits, Fees, Limitations
None.

Accessibility
The visitor center on Franklin Boulevard is wheelchair-accessible.

Camping and Lodging
No camping is available on-site or nearby. Commercial facilities offer lodging in Sacramento, Galt (5 miles south on State Highway 99), and Lodi (15 miles south on State Highway 99).

Food and Supplies
Food and supplies are not available on-site. The nearest sources are in Sacramento, Galt, and Lodi.

First Aid
No first aid is available on-site. The nearest hospitals are located in Galt and Lodi.

Additional Information
The best time to observe waterfowl is during the winter months. Waterfowl, cranes, wading birds, and shorebirds are seen from October–March; birds of prey are present from November–April. Songbirds are common in fall and spring. Visitors are asked to stay on the trails. Delta Meadows Park (west of Interstate 5 near the preserve) provides small-boat access to the Lost Slough Wetlands part of the preserve.

Contact Information
BLM - Folsom Field Office
63 Natoma Street
Folsom, CA 95630
Tel: (916) 985-4474
Fax: (916) 985-3259
www.ca.blm.gov/folsom/cosumnesriv.html

Activity Codes

Cow Mountain Recreation Area

Location
8 miles east of Ukiah, California.

Description
This 60,000-acre area offers a variety of recreational opportunities. The North Cow Mountain Recreation Area is set aside for non-motorized recreation, with over 17 miles of trails for hikers, mountain bikers, and equestrians. The South Cow Mountain Recreation Area offers 120 miles of interconnected trails over 23,000 acres for off-highway vehicles. The rugged terrain provides challenges for all abilities from beginner to advanced. A creek and a mountain ridge separate the two recreation areas, and the trail systems do not interconnect. With elevations ranging from 800–4,000 feet, the area offers beautiful views of Ukiah and Lake County.

Directions
From Ukiah, take State Highway 101 south about 0.5 mile to the Talmage exit. Go east on Talmage Road about 1.5 miles. Turn right at East Side Road. Travel less than 0.5 mile to Mill Creek Road, which is on the left. Continue on Mill Creek Road 3 miles to the turnoff for the North Cow Mountain area, or 5 miles to the entrance to South Cow Mountain.

Or, from the community of Lakeport (State Highway 29, west shore of Clear Lake), take 11th Street to Scotts Valley Road. To reach North Cow Mountain, continue on Scotts Valley Road 6 miles to the Glen Eden Trailhead on the right. Park in signed areas. To access South Cow Mountain from Lakeport, take 11th Street (becomes Riggs Road), turn right on Scotts Creek Road, and proceed 2 miles to the end.

Visitor Activities
Hiking, picnicking, wildlife viewing, birdwatching, plant viewing, sanctioned motorcycle events, black-powder shoots, and motorcycle and off-highway driving.

Special Features
Named for the longhorn cattle that once roamed wild in the region, the Cow Mountain Recreation Area consists mostly of steep, chaparral-covered slopes with scattered stands of fir, pine, and oak. The area features pockets of old-growth fir; several species of oak; willows; over 31 miles of streams; 13 reservoirs; and habitat for black-tail deer, bears, wild turkeys, and other upland species.

Permits, Fees, Limitations
There may be seasonal site closures to prevent damage to roads and trails. Off-highway-vehicle use is permitted only in the South Cow Mountain area.

Off-highway motorcyclists relish the dips and dust of one of South Cow Mountain's many motorized-recreation trails. *(James Pickering, BLM California State Office)*

Accessibility
None.

Camping and Lodging
There are two developed campgrounds with toilets, picnic tables, and barbecue grates, but no potable water:

Mayacmas Campground (nine sites): From Ukiah, exit U.S. Highway 101 south at Talmage Road, then go 1.5 miles east to Eastside Road. Turn right and proceed 0.3 mile to Mill Creek Road. Turn left, and proceed 3 miles to Mendo Rock Road, and follow it to the site, about 10 miles.

Red Mountain Campground (10 sites): From Ukiah, exit U.S. Highway 101 south at Talmage Road, then go 1.5 miles east to Eastside Road. Turn right and proceed 0.3 mile to Mill Creek Road. Follow Mill Creek Road 8 miles to the staging area, veer right where the road forks (there is a directional sign), and continue less than 1 mile to the campground.

Food and Supplies
The nearest location for supplies is in Ukiah.

First Aid
No first aid is available on-site. The nearest hospital is located in Ukiah. For emergencies, visitors should dial 911.

Additional Information
The best times to visit are fall, winter, and spring. The access from Scotts Creek Road to South Cow Mountain is a rugged, unimproved dirt road, which is impassable during the winter because of high water at a creek crossing. Before exploring the Cow Mountain Recreation Area, obtain a free map from BLM. All roads are steep and winding and not recommended for trailers or RVs.

Contact Information
BLM - Ukiah Field Office
2550 North State Street
Ukiah, CA 95482
Tel: (707) 468-4000
Fax: (707) 468-4027
www.ca.blm.gov/ukiah/cowmtn.html

Activity Codes

other - black-powder shoots

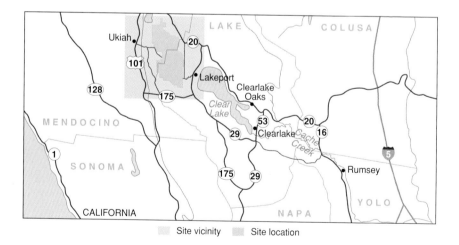

Site vicinity   Site location

Dumont Dunes
Off-Highway-Vehicle Area

Location

Approximately 31 miles north of Baker, California.

Description

The Dumont Dunes Off-Highway-Vehicle Area is an exciting and remote area for off-highway-vehicle recreation. Bordered by steep, volcanic hills and the slow-running Amargosa River, the region is easily recognized from a distance by its distinctive sand dunes. The elevation here varies from 700 feet at the river to 1,200 feet at the top of Competition Hill, the tallest of the dunes. The hills away from the dunes provide ample opportunities for wildlife watching and birdwatching, and the shores of the Amargosa are popular with rockhounders.

Directions

The riding area is south of the Amargosa River and east of State Highway 127, about 31 miles north of Baker, California. There are two ways of getting to the dunes. The Little Dunes staging and camping area is directly off State Highway 127, where immediate staging is possible. One mile north of Little Dunes, just off State Highway 127, is Dumont Road, a dirt road that follows the Amargosa River for approximately 4 miles before crossing it, leading to the main field of large dunes.

Visitor Activities

All-terrain driving, four-wheel driving, dune-buggy riding, dirt-bike riding, wildlife viewing, birdwatching, and rockhounding.

Rising as high as 1,200 feet, the Dumont Dunes Off-Highway-Vehicle Area provides riders with outstanding views of the surrounding California desert. *(James Pickering, BLM California State Office)*

Special Features

The historic Tonapah and Tidewater Railroad, to the east of the dunes, was in operation between 1905 and 1940. The vegetation here consists of creosote scrub, some annual grasses, and wildflowers in the spring. Early spring wildflower displays in this vicinity can be quite impressive.

Permits, Fees, Limitations

Currently, there are no fees for use of the area. However, fees are being considered to reinvest revenue in the area for additional services.

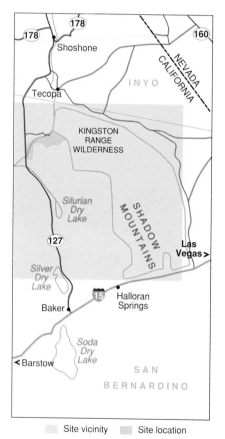

Site vicinity   Site location

Accessibility

The Dumont Dunes Off-Highway-Vehicle Area is accessible to people with disabilities only through the use of recreational vehicles.

Camping and Lodging

Camping is allowed anywhere within the riding area as long as it does not block travel on a road. Camping is limited to a 14-day stay. Private campgrounds are located in Baker, Tecopa (4.5 miles east of State Highway 127, about 20 miles north of the dunes), or Shoshone (on State Highway 127, approximately 27 miles north of the dunes).

Food and Supplies

Food and supplies are available in Shoshone and Baker.

First Aid

The nearest emergency response is located in Baker. The closest hospitals are in Barstow, California (almost 100 miles to the southwest on Interstate 15) and Las Vegas, Nevada (about 120 miles east on Interstate 15). Cellular reception is spotty at Dumont, at best. There are emergency call boxes on State Highway 127. Visitors should call 911 for emergency assistance.

Additional Information

The Kingston Range Wilderness borders the riding area to the north and east; this area is closed to motor vehicles. Travel outside the riding area to the south is permitted only on designated routes. The Salt Creek Area of Critical Environmental Concern is adjacent to Dumont Dunes to the west; this area is also closed to motor vehicles.

The low elevation in the area makes for warm to extremely hot conditions in spring and summer. Extremes of heat and cold are common in this area.

Contact Information
BLM – Barstow Field Office
2601 Barstow Road
Barstow, CA 92311

Tel: (760) 252-6000
Fax: (760) 252-6099
www.ca.blm.gov/barstow/dumont.html

Activity Codes

other – rockhounding

Fish Slough

Location
5 miles north of Bishop, California.

Description
The 36,000-acre Fish Slough is a place where geographic isolation, geology, climate, and hydrology have created a rare and irreplaceable ecosystem. Located in the transition zone between the Mojave Desert and Great Basin biomes, Fish Slough encompasses an array of plant communities, including wetlands, alkali meadows, and uplands. With 126 taxa described, Fish Slough represents one of the richest wetland floras in the Great Basin. Designated a BLM Area of Critical Environmental Concern, Fish Slough also provides habitat for rare endemic plants, such as Fish Slough milk-vetches and alkali Mariposa lilies.

The Sierra Mountain Range provides a stunning backdrop for the rich wetlands of Fish Slough. *(James Pickering, BLM California State Office)*

Directions

From Bishop, take U.S. Highway 6 north for 1.5 miles. Turn west on Five Bridges Road and proceed 2.5 miles to Fish Slough Road. Turn right. The entrance is 0.5 mile beyond.

Visitor Activities

Horseback riding, hiking, archaeological site, scenic drives, geologic sightseeing, wildlife viewing, plant viewing, bird-watching, and interpretation.

Special Features

Unusual geologic features have created an underground water basin for springs and a colorful surface landscape with abrupt cliffs and volcanic terraces. The warm hues and pastel tones of these features are striking in the early morning and evening hours. Ponds in the slough may host endangered Owens pupfish and Owens tui chubs. Marshy areas are often home to waterfowl and birds of prey. Raccoons and striped skunks also frequent the marshes.

A few dozen prehistoric rock carvings, or petroglyphs, feature geometric designs that were probably made within the last 1,000 years. To protect these sites, local Native Americans have requested that information on the petroglyphs' location only be made available to visitors in person at the BLM Bishop Field Office.

Permits, Fees, Limitations

None.

Accessibility

This site is wheelchair-accessible.

Camping and Lodging

The nearest BLM campground is Horton Creek, approximately 8.5 miles northwest of Bishop on U.S. Highway 395. Call BLM for more information on the camping season. Private and county campgrounds are also available in the area. Call the Bishop Visitor Center, (760) 873-8405, for more information on these. Bishop also has a variety of motels and restaurants.

Food and Supplies

No supplies or facilities are located on-site. The nearest sources are in Bishop.

First Aid

No first aid is available on-site. The nearest hospital is located in Bishop.

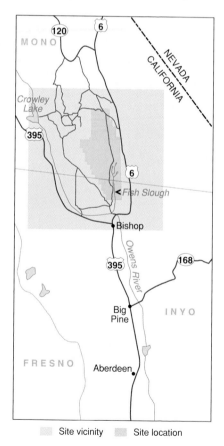

Site vicinity   Site location

Additional Information

Fish Slough is very hot in the summer and snow is possible in the winter. However, at any time of year, visitors may encounter inclement weather in the area. The best times to visit Fish Slough are fall, winter, and spring; no matter what time of year, visitors should be sure to bring along drinking water.

BLM and the Audubon Society offer a variety of interpretive activities in the slough throughout the year. Contact BLM for further information.

Much of the slough area is visible from roads, but vehicles should be suitable for dirt roads. The main dirt roads are very well-maintained, but secondary roads require high-clearance vehicles and possibly four-wheel-drive vehicles. Secondary roads may be impassable in winter or following episodes of heavy precipitation. Visitors, including hikers, are asked to stay on developed roads.

Contact Information

BLM - Bishop Field Office
785 North Main Street, Suite E
Bishop, CA 93514
Tel: (760) 872-4881
Fax: (760) 872-2894
www.ca.blm.gov/caso/wf-fishslough.html

Activity Codes

Fort Ord

Location

5 miles north of Monterey, California.

Description

This 7,200-acre portion of a former Army base features an elaborate system of trails that is well-suited to hiking, biking, and equestrian use. Fort Ord contains one of the largest maritime chaparral areas in all of California, as well as oak woodlands, rolling grassy hills, wetlands, and ponds. Forty-six different rare plants and animals thrive in the rugged hills, including coast wallflowers, Monterey manzanitas, tiger salamanders, fairy shrimp, and mountain lions.

Directions

From Monterey, travel 5 miles north on State Highway 1 to the Fort Ord/California State University Monterey Bay main entrance. Make a right onto North-South Road, travel 1 mile, and then make a right onto Parker Flats Cut-Off. Travel 4 miles and then make a left onto Parker Flats Road. Travel 5 miles to Eucalyptus Road and the BLM office.

More than 50 miles of trails through hilly grasslands and maritime chaparral lure bikers, equestrians, and hikers to Fort Ord.
(James Pickering, BLM California State Office)

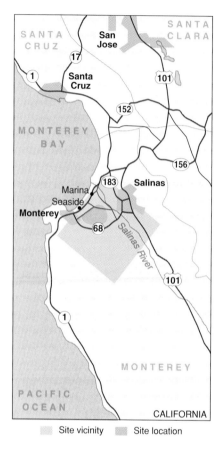

Site vicinity   Site location

Visitor Activities

Horseback riding, hiking, biking, interpretive exhibits and trails, environmental education programs, scenic drives, plant viewing, wildlife viewing, and birdwatching.

Special Features

Cool mornings are the best time to see black-tail deer, turkeys, bobcats, coyotes, gopher snakes, red tailed hawks, Canada geese, coast horned lizards, and California quail. It takes some luck to catch a glimpse of a badger, mountain lion, or golden eagle. For many of the

rare plants at Fort Ord, 50–90 percent of their worldwide habitat is located here.

Permits, Fees, Limitations

No fees. Most back country roads are closed to vehicle traffic. Prohibited activities include shooting, off-highway-vehicle use, and off-trail travel.

Accessibility

Special trail map descriptions are being prepared for people with physical limitations. Contact BLM for more information regarding these maps.

Camping and Lodging

No camping is permitted on-site. Camping is available in nearby Monterey County parks. Lodging can be found throughout the Monterey Peninsula and in Salinas, about 20 miles northeast of Monterey at the intersection of State Highway 68 and U.S. Highway 101.

Food and Supplies

Food and supplies are available in Marina and Seaside, which are immediately adjacent to Fort Ord on State Highway 1.

First Aid

First aid is available on-site through the Fort Ord Fire Department. The nearest hospitals are located in Monterey and Salinas.

Additional Information

Parking areas are available for access to hiking, bicycle, and equestrian trails. Several trails at Fort Ord connect with the Juan Bautista de Anza National Historic Trail, which runs from Nogales, Arizona, to San Francisco, California.

BLM sponsors an active environmental education program at Fort Ord.

More than 3,000 students from around the Monterey Peninsula visit Fort Ord public lands each year for science projects or for special field trips focusing on soil erosion, wetland ecology, or habitat restoration.

Weather can be cold at any time of the year. Spring is probably the best time of the year to visit. A trail map is available free of charge by calling the BLM Fort Ord Project Office or by downloading from the Hollister Field Office website.

Contact Information
BLM - Hollister Field Office
20 Hamilton Court
Hollister, CA 95023
Tel: (831) 630-5000
Fax: (831) 630-5055
BLM Fort Ord Project Office
Tel: (831) 394-8314
www.ca.blm.gov/hollister/fort_ord_home.html

Activity Codes

Imperial Sand Dunes Recreation Area

Location
40 miles east of El Centro, California.

Description
This 40-mile-long dune system is one of the largest in the United States. Formed by windblown beach sands of ancient Lake Cahuilla, some crests reach heights of over 300 feet. These expansive dune formations offer picturesque scenery, opportunities for solitude, a chance to view rare plants and animals, and a playground for off-highway vehicles. Remains of the historic Plank Road that once carried travelers across the sandy dunes can also be seen in the Buttercup Valley

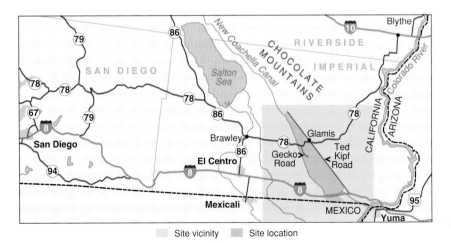

Site vicinity Site location

Southern California's Imperial Sand Dunes Recreation Area attracts OHV users by the thousands, particularly on holiday weekends from fall through spring. *(Doran Sanchez, BLM California Desert District Office)*

area (south of Interstate 8, about 20 miles west of Yuma, Arizona). BLM manages portions of the dune system for different uses. The portion of the dunes south of State Highway 78 is a popular OHV recreation area centered on the paved Gecko Road. Other portions of the Imperial Sand Dunes that are also popular with OHV users include Mammoth Wash (north of Algodones Dunes Wilderness) and Buttercup Valley.

Directions

Gecko Road: From Brawley, California (about 15 miles north of El Centro on California Highway 86), take State Highway 78 east for about 25 miles to the Gecko Road exit. This paved road, with campgrounds located alongside, provides access to the dunes area south of State Highway 78. Other access points east of Gecko Road include Osborne Overlook and the Glamis Flats.

Buttercup Valley: From El Centro, take Interstate 8 east for about 40 miles (or from Yuma, Arizona, take Interstate 8 west for

about 20 miles) to the Grays Well Road Dune Buggy Flats/Gordon Well exit. Turn left at the stop sign and follow the paved road to the end to reach the dunes. *Mammoth Wash:* Take State Highway 78 east from Brawley for about 27 miles to Ted Kipf Road. Turn left (north) on Ted Kipf Road, a dirt road that parallels the railroad tracks, and follow this road for about 13 miles past the Algodones Dunes Wilderness Area, the part of the dunes that is closed to off-highway vehicles. Signs indicate where the open OHV area begins.

Visitor Activities

Dune-buggy riding, dirt-bike riding, all-terrain driving, four-wheel driving, historic site, interpretation.

Special Features

The prevailing winds from the north and northwest continue to shape and move the dunes. Even though the sandy expanses appear lifeless, a surprising number of plants and animals have adapted to this harsh environment. Creosote bushes, sandpaper plants, and desert witchgrass are just a few of the dune plants with deep roots that tap underground water supplies and anchor the plants in the shifting sands. Few large mammals inhabit the dunes area, but coyotes and mule deer are occasionally seen crossing the dunes. Geckos do inhabit the area, but hibernate in winter and are active only at night during the rest of the year.

The North Algodones Dunes Wilderness, located north of State Highway 78, is also part of the Imperial Sand Dunes system. The wilderness is divided into two distinct zones. The largest and tallest dunes are located on the west side, while the east side contains smaller dunes and numerous washes. Several unique plant and animal species—including mesquites, smoke trees, ironwoods, and desert willow trees, as well as desert tortoises and Colorado desert fringe-toed lizards—make their homes in these dunes, which are closed to OHV use.

Permits, Fees, Limitations

Weekly and seasonal passes are available for purchase from automated self-pay stations at the dunes and from BLM. One pass is needed per primary vehicle, i.e., any vehicle being driven into the recreation area. Passes are not required for trailers or vehicles in tow. A seasonal pass is valid from October 1–September 30 of the following year. All California laws applicable to OHVs apply in the recreation area. For more information, contact BLM.

Accessibility

Restrooms and the visitor contact station at Gecko Road are wheelchair-accessible.

Camping and Lodging

Two BLM campgrounds along paved Gecko Road provide hard-surface parking, vault toilets, and trash facilities. The Cahuilla Ranger Station, located on Gecko Road at the intersection with State Highway 78, is open weekends from October–May.

Food and Supplies

On-site at the dunes, numerous vendors provide basic food and services. The Glamis store, located adjacent to the dunes, also provides basic food and services. The closest restaurants and grocery stores are in Brawley and Yuma.

First Aid

Only emergency first aid is available on-site. Medical and hospital services are available in Brawley, El Centro, and Yuma.

Additional Information

The area is open year-round. The best time to visit is fall–spring. Summer is very hot, with temperatures over 120°F during the day. Visitors should bring water.

Contact Information

BLM - El Centro Field Office
1661 South Fourth Street
El Centro CA 92243
Tel: 760) 337-4400
Fax: (760) 337-4490
www.ca.blm.gov/elcentro/sanddunes.html

Activity Codes

Johnson Valley Off-Highway Vehicle Recreation Area

Location
35 miles east of Victorville, California.

Description
The 189,000-acre Johnson Valley Off-Highway Vehicle (OHV) Recreation Area offers outstanding trails for competitive off-highway motorcycle racing, enduro and trial events, and day play-riding. Sloping bajadas, narrow canyons, flat dry lakes, sand dunes, and twisting trails through low, rocky mountains provide a variety of experiences for all levels of riders. The Johnson Valley Yucca Rings Area of Critical Environmental Concern (ACEC), Soggy Lake Creosote Rings ACEC, Cougar Buttes' huge rock slabs, ruins of historic mines, range cattle, and a wide variety of desert animal and plant life offer unique nature and touring experiences.

Directions
From Victorville, travel 25 miles east on State Highway 18 to Lucerne Valley. Take State Highway 247 east to Camp Rock Road (5 miles from Lucerne Valley), Bessemer Mine Road (13 miles), or Boone Road (24 miles). Travel north on any of these roads to reach access routes into the OHV area. Follow the signs.

Visitor Activities
"Hare and hound" competitions, European scrambles, car/truck races, enduros, trial events, OHV races, recreational OHV riding, scenic drives, land sailing, model-rocket

Site vicinity   Site location

flying, wildlife viewing, hiking, rockhounding, hunting (upland game birds), and rock climbing.

Special Features
The area is characterized by vegetation typical of the Mojave Desert, including creosote scrub, annual grasses, wildflowers, and Joshua trees. The desert tortoise,

In the Johnson Valley Off-Highway Vehicle Recreation Area, a motorcyclist threads his way through the arid, rocky terrain typical of many southern California deserts. *(Doran Sanchez, BLM California Desert District Office)*

a Federally protected species, lives in the area as well.

Permits, Fees, Limitations

California Department of Motor Vehicle "Green Sticker" OHV registration is mandatory for ALL vehicles that are not "street legal." Spark arresters are necessary and must satisfy U.S. Forest Service requirements. Vehicles must have legal headlights and taillights if they are used at night. All competitive events, such as dual sport rides, enduros, and "hare and hound" races, require a BLM permit. Contact BLM for more information.

Accessibility

None.

Camping and Lodging

Camping is permitted anywhere in the open area, but is limited to a maximum of 14 days. There are no designated campgrounds or designated sites. Lodging is available in Victorville, Apple Valley (8 miles east of Victorville on State Highway 18), Hesperia (8 miles south of Victorville on Hesperia Road), Lucerne Valley (10 miles southwest of the OHV area on State Highway 247), and Barstow (35 miles north at the intersection of State Highway 247 and Interstate 15).

Food and Supplies

Food and supplies are available in Victorville, Lucerne Valley, Barstow, Apple Valley, Hesperia, and Flamingo Heights (10 miles south of the OHV area on State Highway 247).

First Aid

There is no first aid available on-site. The nearest medical assistance is at the California Department of Forestry station on State Highway 247 in Lucerne Valley. The nearest hospitals are located in Victorville and Apple Valley.

Additional Information

The Twenty-Nine Palms Marine Air-Ground Combat Center is located on the eastern border of the OHV area. Riders should not enter this area. This site is open year-round. Rockhounds may keep what they find, within limits; contact BLM for more information.

Contact Information

BLM - Barstow Field Office
2601 Barstow Road
Barstow, CA 92311
Tel: (760) 252-6000
Fax: (760) 252-6099
www.ca.blm.gov/barstow/johnson.html

Activity Codes

other - rockhounding, rock climbing, land sailing, model-rocket flying

King Crest National Recreation Trail

Location
About 30 miles west of Garberville, California.

Description
This is a rugged, 10.5-mile hiking trail to the top of King Peak, elevation 4,087 feet, the highest point in the King Range National Conservation Area. The hike is challenging, but hikers find rewarding ocean views high above the fog. The trail is narrow and winding with many switchbacks, and is not recommended for horses.

Directions
From U.S. Highway 101 just north of Garberville, take the Redway exit. Go through Redway and turn west on Briceland Road. Continue on Briceland Road, which becomes Shelter Cove Road, for 22 miles. Then turn north on King Peak Road, and continue 6 miles to Saddle Mountain Road. Continue 2 miles to the trailhead.

Visitor Activities
Hiking, wildlife viewing, plant viewing, and birdwatching.

Special Features
The trail climbs through brush and Douglas fir forest, leading to dramatic views of the Lost Coast. Much of the trail corridor burned in 1990. This has added endless vistas of the Lost Coast, Mattole Valley, and inland mountain ranges. A 2.7-mile loop to Miller Camp involves an 800-foot descent and climb and passes a refreshing spring.

Permits, Fees, Limitations
Fees and permits are required for organized commercial groups.

Accessibility
None.

Hikers on the King Crest National Recreation Trail are rewarded with magnificent views of earth, sea, and sky. (Bob Wick, BLM Arcata Field Office)

Camping and Lodging

The nearest developed campground is the Horse Mountain Campground on King Peak Road, near the junction with the Saddle Mountain Road turnoff. Campfire permits are required year-round, including for use of portable stoves. All permits are available from BLM. The closest lodging is located in Shelter Cove, 12 miles from the trailhead via Saddle Mountain, King Peak, and Shelter Cove Roads.

Food and Supplies

The nearest supplies are located in Shelter Cove.

First Aid

The closest first aid is available in Shelter Cove. The nearest hospital is located in Garberville, about 30 miles east on U.S. Highway 101.

Additional Information

Hikers should carry plenty of water; there are no water sources along the trail. The trail is high-elevation and very hot in summer months. It is very windy along the summit. Hikers should also be watchful for poison oak, and be aware that they are hiking in mountain lion and bear habitat. Hikers should also watch for ticks and rattlesnakes. The trail is very steep and winding, gaining 2,300 feet in elevation between the south trailhead and the summit. Hikers should be in good physical shape. Hikers must negotiate heavy brush in some areas.

There is a serious bear problem developing in the King Range National Conservation Area. Bears are coming into camps and taking food. This is a dangerous situation for people and bears alike. Burying or hanging food and

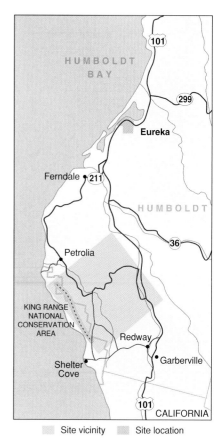

Site vicinity   Site location

other scented items is not effective. Back country hikers must use bear-resistant canisters to store these items.

Contact Information

BLM – Arcata Field Office
1695 Heindon Road
Arcata, CA 95521
Tel: (707) 825-2300
Fax: (707) 825-2301
www.ca.blm.gov/arcata/krncahike.html

Activity Codes

King Range National Conservation Area

Location
55 miles south of Eureka, California.

Description
One doesn't just stumble across the King Range National Conservation Area (NCA)—it takes some searching. But this dramatic meeting of land and sea will reward visitors for their efforts. The King Range, located along the northern California coast, rises from sea level to over 4,000 feet in less than 1 mile. Rugged topography and record rainfalls create over 60,000 acres of desolate grandeur. The mountains, streams, forests, and beaches are ideal for fishing, hunting, and sightseeing. Recreation opportunities are as diverse as the landscape. The Douglas-fir-clad peaks attract hikers, hunters, campers, and mushroom collectors, while the coast beckons surfers, anglers, beachcombers, and abalone divers, to name a few. The highlight of the King Range is the Lost Coast National Recreation Trail, which winds hikers along 26 miles of secluded coastline, including the remote Punta Gorda lighthouse.

Directions
From Eureka, travel 14 miles south on U.S. Highway 101 to the Ferndale exit. Proceed 5 miles southwest on County Road 211 to Main Street in Ferndale. Follow Main Street approximately 1 mile to its end. Turn right on Ocean Avenue, then immediately left on Wildcat Road. Continue 30 miles to Petrolia. Turn right on Lighthouse Road and travel 5 miles to Mattole Campground.

Or, from U.S. Highway 101 just north of Garberville, take the Redway exit. Go through Redway and turn west on Briceland Road. Continue on Briceland Road, which becomes Shelter Cove Road, for about 23 miles to the community of Shelter Cove, another access point for the King Range.

Visitor Activities
Hiking, hunting, fishing, wildflower viewing, horseback riding, scenic drives, birdwatching, wildlife viewing, tidepool viewing, surfing, interpretive activities, and picnicking.

Special Features
Offshore rocks, tidepools, and kelp beds are inhabited by seals, sea lions, and a variety of marine birds. California gray whales can be spotted offshore in winter

The search for the perfect wave takes some California surfers to the remote King Range National Conservation Area. (Bob Wick, BLM Arcata Field Office)

and spring. The mountains are a mix of Douglas fir forest, chaparral, and grassland, providing habitat for black-tail deer and black bears. Nearly 300 species of native and migratory birds have been spotted in the King Range. The old-growth forest is important habitat for northern spotted owls, bald eagles, and Cooper's hawks.

Permits, Fees, Limitations

Fees and permits are required for all organized commercial groups.

Accessibility

Near the community of Shelter Cove are two campgrounds, Wailaki and Nadelos, which are wheelchair-accessible (see directions below).

Camping and Lodging

There are several developed campgrounds with pit toilets, fire rings, and potable water. Fees are charged. Wailaki, Nadelos, Tolkan, and Horse Mountain campgrounds are all located in the southern part of the NCA, while the Mattole Campground is in the northern part.
Wailaki and Nadelos Campgrounds: From Shelter Cove, drive 5 miles east on Shelter Cove Road to Chemise Mountain Road. Turn right and continue 2 miles to Nadelos Campground, or 2.5 miles to Wailaki Campground.
Horse Mountain and Tolkan Campgrounds: From Shelter Cove, drive 4 miles on Shelter Cove Road to King Peak Road. Turn left on King Peak Road and continue 5 miles to Tolkan Campground, or 7 miles to Horse Mountain Campground.
Mattole Campground: From Petrolia, turn west on Lighthouse Road and travel 5 miles to the campground on the ocean.

Primitive camping is also allowed in the NCA, with some limitations along

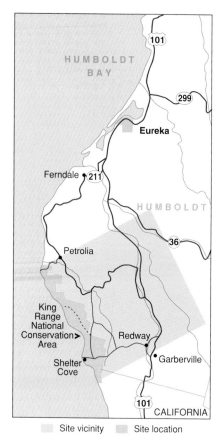

Site vicinity   Site location

King Peak Road and near developed campgrounds. Campfire permits are required year-round, including for use of portable stoves. All permits are available from BLM.

Lodging is available in Shelter Cove and in Garberville.

Food and Supplies

Food and supplies are available in Shelter Cover and Petrolia.

First Aid

First aid is available in Shelter Cove and Garberville. Neighboring fire departments provide full medical aid for various areas of the NCA. The nearest hospital is located in Garberville. For emergencies, visitors should dial 911.

Additional Information

Tide tables should be consulted when planning any hike along the beach. Some parts of the Lost Coast Trail are impassable at times of high tide. At any time, large "sleeper" waves can pose a serious danger to hikers along the beach. Hikers can also expect frequent and dense morning fog. The best times to visit are April, May, September, and October. This is one of the wettest spots along the Pacific Coast. But water sources are still scarce along the upland trails; hikers should carry drinking water. Several parcels of private property are located along the coastline; visitors should respect landowners' private property rights.

There is a serious bear problem developing in the King Range NCA, including along the beach. Bears are coming into camps and taking food. This is a dangerous situation for people and bears alike. Burying or hanging food and other scented items is not effective. Back country hikers must use bear-resistant canisters to store these items.

Contact Information

BLM - Arcata Field Office
1695 Heindon Road
Arcata, CA 95521-4573
Tel: (707) 825-2300
Fax: (707) 825-2301
www.ca.blm.gov/arcata/king_range.html

Activity Codes

other - tidepool viewing, surfing

Kingston Range Wilderness

Location

50 miles northeast of Baker, California.

Description

The Kingston Range encompasses more than 200,000 acres, including 17 miles of continuous ridgeline above 6,000 feet, capped by the 7,300-foot Kingston Peak. A small stand of white fir survives on Kingston Peak, and over 500 plant species make this a botanically diverse wilderness area. It is one of four areas in California where banded Gila monsters have been sighted. Year-round water and wetland habitat provide food and shelter for diverse birds, fish, mammals, and insects.

Desert flora thrive in the botanically diverse Kingston Range Wilderness. *(Doran Sanchez, BLM California Desert District Office)*

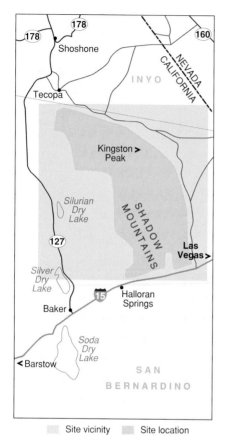

Site vicinity   Site location

Directions
Because it is a wilderness area, the Kingston Range has no defined entrances, campgrounds, or other facilities. Access to the area from the west is from State Highway 127 north of Baker in the vicinity of Silurian Dry Lake, or from the Old Spanish Highway in the vicinity of Tecopa (about 55 miles north of Baker, 1 mile east of State Highway 127). The eastern side of the wilderness area can be reached by taking Interstate 15 about 26 miles east of Baker. Take the Cima Road exit north

for about 14 miles to Excelsior Mine Road, which takes you north into the range.

Visitor Activities
Hiking, deer hunting, plant viewing, wildlife viewing, and birdwatching.

Special Features
The southern bajadas of the Kingston Range slope down into Kingston Wash, where year-round water provides habitat for wildlife such as pupfish, yellow-billed cuckoos, prairie falcons, desert tortoises, and bighorn sheep.

Permits, Fees, Limitations
No fees. No commercial uses are allowed. Motorized vehicles, bicycles, and hang gliders are not permitted.

Accessibility
None.

Camping and Lodging
Primitive camping is available. There are no developed campsites. Lodging is available in Baker and in Barstow (about 60 miles west of Baker on Interstate 15).

Food and Supplies
Food and supplies are available in Baker.

First Aid
Ambulance service is available in Baker. The nearest hospitals are located in Barstow and in Las Vegas, Nevada (160 miles east on Interstate 15).

Additional Information
The best times to visit are spring and fall; however, the area is open year-round. No facilities are available. Visitors should be aware of the hazards of desert travel, both in winter and summer.

They should plan their trips carefully, tell someone where they are going, and stick to their itinerary. They should always carry appropriate maps and know how to use them. Proper dress includes a hat, sunglasses, and sunscreen. Visitors should carry plenty of drinking water (at least 1 gallon per person per day). There are abandoned mine shafts in the area. Visitors should keep vehicles well-maintained and carry extra water for their vehicles.

Contact Information

BLM - Needles Field Office
101 West Spikes Road
Needles, CA 92363
Tel: (760) 326-3896
Fax: (760) 326-4079
www.ca.blm.gov/caso/kingst.html

Activity Codes

Lower Kern River

Location

42 miles east of Bakersfield, California.

Description

Located within BLM's Keyesville Special Management Area is an approximately 3.5-mile stretch of the Lower Kern River. This whitewater river attracts about 12,000 commercial and non-commercial rafters from all over the United States each year. In the 1850s, the area swarmed with miners, and today recreational gold panning still takes place along the river and its tributaries. The surrounding Keyesville Special Management Area — over 7,000 acres southwest of the Lake Isabella dam — also attracts mountain bikers and off-highway-vehicle users.

Directions

From Bakersfield, travel east 42 miles on State Highway 178 to State Highway 155. Turn left (north) and travel 1 mile to Keyesville.

From Ridgecrest, travel west 62 miles on State Highway 178 to State Highway 155. Turn right (north) and travel 1 mile to Keyesville.

Visitor Activities

Mountain biking, rafting, kayaking, canoeing, fishing, four-wheel driving, dirt-bike riding, and gold panning.

Special Features

The Lower Kern supports a rich riparian environment, providing habitat for neotropical songbirds and ospreys. Sycamores, cottonwoods, and blue oaks line the riverbanks. The river itself is home to trout and bass.

Permits, Fees, Limitations

A boating permit is required for the river. There is no charge for the permit, which can be obtained from the U.S. Forest Service office in Lake Isabella (at the intersection of State Highways 178 and 155) or Kernville (about 12 miles north of Lake Isabella — follow State Highway 155 north and then continue north on Burlando Road).

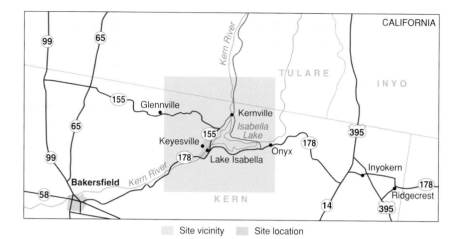

CALIFORNIA

TULARE

INYO

KERN

Glennville · Kernville · Isabella Lake · Keyesville · Onyx · Lake Isabella · Inyokern · Bakersfield · Kern River · Ridgecrest

⬛ Site vicinity   ⬛ Site location

Accessibility
The toilets located near the river are wheelchair-accessible, but the river itself is not.

Camping and Lodging
Primitive camping is available. A free interagency campfire permit is required and can be picked up at the offices of BLM, the U.S. Forest Service, or the California Department of Forestry. Fees are charged at other campgrounds in the area, including the Main Dam Campground, which is located across State Highway 155 from the entrance to the Keyesville Special Management Area. Motel lodging can be found in the town of Lake Isabella.

Food and Supplies
Restaurants, grocery stores, and supplies are available in Lake Isabella.

First Aid
Emergency services are available in Lake Isabella.

Additional Information
BLM maintains three launch sites for river rafting trips. BLM South and Slippery Rock are located southwest of the main dam on State Highway 155. Keyesville Bridge is on State Highway 178 southwest of the town of Lake Isabella. Hazards in the area include several unfenced mine shafts and rattlesnakes. Weather and other information is available from BLM. River flow is dependent on releases from the Isabella Dam; the release rate for the river may be obtained from the Southern California Energy Company's Kern River Flow Phone at 1-877-537-6356 or (760) 376-8821.

Contact Information
BLM – Bakersfield Field Office
3801 Pegasus Drive
Bakersfield, CA 93308
Tel: (805) 391-6000
Fax: (805) 391-6040
www.ca.blm.gov/bakersfield/keyesville.html#
RECREATION

Activity Codes

other – gold panning

Merced River Recreation Area

Location
55 miles northeast of Merced, California.

Description
Beginning in the high country of Yosemite National Park, the Merced River makes a headlong rush through glacially-carved canyons, rugged mountains, and foothills to the San Joaquin Valley. Rafters and kayakers can tackle the rapids from numerous access points along the river, or visitors can join a trip run by a commercial raft company. For those who prefer to stay along the shore, there's excellent trout fishing and the chance to watch an eagle dive for its dinner.

The 8-mile Merced River Trail, located within the recreation area, is an ungroomed, and for the most part un-shaded, trek for hikers, mountain bikers, and horseback riders. The trail follows the old Yosemite Railroad grade along the main branch of the river from the Briceburg Visitor Center to the confluence with the Merced's North Fork. Trail users will pass vestiges of a water diversion flume from the turn of the 20th century, or perhaps encounter a crew of contemporary '49-ers combing the shoals with a gold dredge.

Directions
From Merced, located on State Highway 99, travel 40 miles east on State Highway 140 to Mariposa. Then travel another 15 miles on State Highway 140 to the Briceburg Visitor Center, located where State Highway 140 meets the river.

Visitor Activities
Whitewater rafting (Class III–V), kayaking, fishing, wildlife viewing, birdwatching, wildflower viewing, hiking, mountain biking, picnicking, hobby gold prospecting, horseback riding, and swimming.

Special Features
During the spring runoff period, usually from April–June, the hillsides of the V-shaped canyon are often covered with colorful wildflowers.

Permits, Fees, Limitations
None.

Accessibility
Campgrounds are wheelchair-accessible.

Camping and Lodging
There are three BLM campgrounds along the Merced River between Briceburg and Bagby, which is located about 16 miles north of Mariposa, where State Highway 149 crosses the Merced. They are the

Besides attracting rafters and kayakers, the Merced River also lures hikers and cyclists along a trail that follows the route of the old Yosemite Railroad. *(James Pickering, BLM California State Office)*

McCabe Flat Campground, Railroad Flat Campground, and Willow Placer Campground. The campgrounds are only accessible by crossing the bridge at Briceburg and heading downriver on the Merced River Trail. Vehicles are allowed, but the bridge is not recommended for trailers and large RVs. The campgrounds are about 2.5 miles apart. A nightly camping fee is charged. Commercial lodging is available in Mariposa.

Food and Supplies:
Food and supplies are available in Mariposa.

First Aid
BLM crews with emergency medical technicians are on duty on weekends during the rafting season, which is generally from April–July, depending on weather and the amount of snowpack in the mountains. The Mariposa County Sheriff and Fire Department also provide first aid. The Mariposa County Sheriff can be reached at (209) 966-3614, and the Mariposa County Fire Department can be reached at (209) 966-3621.

Additional Information
The best times to visit are spring and summer. The Merced River Recreation Area is near the entrance to Yosemite National Park and provides overflow or alternative camping for park visitors, as well as a beautiful setting for river enthusiasts. Many commercial raft outfitters, licensed and supervised by BLM, offer trips on the Merced River. Contact BLM for a list of approved commercial raft operators and their schedules.

Contact Information
BLM - Folsom Field Office
63 Natoma Street
Folsom, CA 95630
Tel: (916) 985-4474
Fax: (916) 985-3259
www.ca.blm.gov/folsom/mercedriverrec.html

Activity Codes

other - gold prospecting

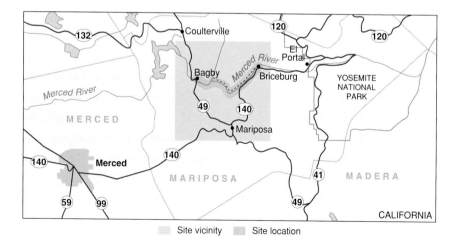

Site vicinity   Site location

Owens Peak Wilderness Area (Short Canyon)

Location
20 miles northwest of Ridgecrest, California.

Description
The majority of this wilderness area is composed of the rugged eastern face of the Sierra Nevada Mountains. Owens Peak, the highest point of the southern Sierra Nevadas, rises to more than 8,400 feet. The mountainous terrain has deep, winding, open, and expansive canyons, many of which contain springs with extensive riparian vegetation. This transition zone between the Great Basin, Mojave Desert, and Sierra Nevada ecoregions hosts a great variety of vegetation.

Directions
From Ridgecrest, travel west on State Highway 178 about 9 miles to U.S. Highway 395. Follow U.S. Highway 395 north, continuing 1 mile past its intersection with State Highway 14. Take the Leliter Road exit west and follow the signs to Short Canyon.

Visitor Activities
Hiking, horseback riding, upland game-bird hunting, wildlife viewing, plant viewing, and birdwatching.

Special Features
Vegetation varies considerably within the wilderness area, with a creosote desert scrub community on the bajadas; scattered yuccas, cacti, annuals, cottonwoods, and oak trees in the canyons and valleys; and a juniper-pinyon woodland with sagebrush and digger/gray pine on the upper elevations. After a wet winter, the canyons explode with colorful wildflower displays, including coreopsis, California poppies, buckwheats, and gilias. Spring is also a good time for birdwatching when neotropical migrant songbirds make their way north up the flanks of the Eastern Sierra. Other wildlife in the area includes mule deer, golden eagles, and prairie falcons.

Permits, Fees, Limitations
No fees. No commercial uses are allowed. No motorized vehicles, bicycles, or hang gliders are allowed.

Accessibility
None.

Camping and Lodging
Primitive camping is available, with a 14-day limit; there are no developed sites. No facilities are available. Lodging is available in Ridgecrest.

California poppies are just some of the many spring wildflowers that reward hikers in Short Canyon, part of the Owens Peak Wilderness Area. *(James Pickering, BLM California State Office)*

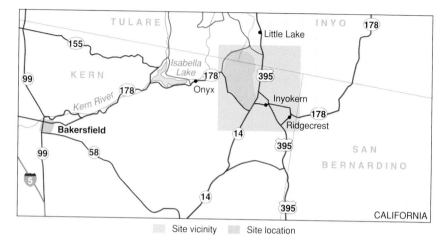

Site vicinity ◾ Site location

CALIFORNIA

Food and Supplies
Food and supplies are available in Ridgecrest.

First Aid
There is no first aid available on-site. The nearest hospital is located in Ridgecrest.

Additional Information
The site is open year-round. Good hiking shoes or walking shoes are recommended. Spring is the best time to view wildflowers in Short Canyon, which is an easy hike from the nearby parking area. Other canyons in the area, including Indian Wells Canyon and Sand Canyon, offer vehicle access to the wilderness boundary.

Indian Wells Canyon is west of State Highway 14, about 15 miles northwest of Ridgecrest. Sand Canyon is west of U.S. Highway 395 about 5 miles north of its intersection with State Highway 14.

Contact Information
BLM - Ridgecrest Field Office
300 South Richmond Road
Ridgecrest, CA 93555
Tel: (760) 384-5400
Fax: (760) 384-5499
www.ca.blm.gov/ridgecrest/owens.htm

Activity Codes

Pacific Crest National Scenic Trail–Owens Peak Segment

Location
75 miles east of Bakersfield, California.

Description
The Pacific Crest National Scenic Trail is a continuous hiking trail from the

Mexican border to the Canadian border. The Owens Peak segment begins at Walker Pass in Kern County (75 miles east of Bakersfield), and extends 41 miles north to the Sequoia National Forest at Rockhouse Basin, where the

Domelands Wilderness begins. Elevations range from 5,245 feet at Walker Pass to 7,600 feet on Bear Mountain. The trail offers spectacular views of the surrounding mountains and valleys.

Directions

From Bakersfield, take State Highway 178 east about 75 miles to Walker Pass. Or, from Ridgecrest, travel 25 miles west on State Highway 178 to Walker Pass.

Visitor Activities

Hiking, hunting (upland game-bird), horse packing, plant viewing, bird-watching, and wildlife viewing.

Special Features

The trail passes through the Owens Peak Wilderness Area, which is located in the rugged eastern face of the Sierra Nevada Mountains. Depending on the elevation of the trail segment, pinyon-juniper woodlands, creosote desert scrub, yuccas, and cacti may be seen. Wildflowers are also found along the trail in spring and summer.

Permits, Fees, Limitations

The trail is for hiking and equestrian use only; no bicycles or motorized vehicles are permitted.

Accessibility

None.

Camping and Lodging

Camping is available at the Walker Pass Trailhead Campground, just west of Walker Pass on State Highway 178. The campground has water (from April–October), toilets, parking, fire grates, and corrals. Chimney Creek Campground is a primitive campground with water that is not potable because of the area's naturally occurring uranium. The campground is located on Canebrake Road off State Highway 178 (about 35 miles west of Ridgecrest), but hikers can access it from the trail (0.25 mile off the trail and marked by a sign). A California campfire permit is required to have a campfire. Permits are available from BLM, U.S. Forest Service, and California Department of Forestry offices.

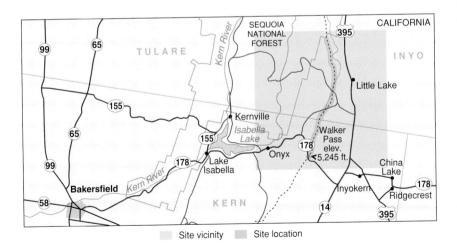

Site vicinity   Site location

Lodging is available in Lake Isabella (35 miles west of Walker Pass on State Highway 178), Kernville (22 miles west on State Highway 178, then 13 miles north on Sierra Way), and Ridgecrest.

Food and Supplies

Food and supplies are available in Onyx, 17 miles west of Walker Pass on State Highway 178, or Inyokern, 16 miles east on State Highway 178.

First Aid

First aid is available at the BLM South Fork Fire Station, (760) 378-3317, located on State Highway 178, 10 miles west of Walker Pass, or at the BLM Chimney Peak Fire Station, (760) 371-5326, located on Canebrake Road and accessible from the trail. The nearest hospital is located in Ridgecrest.

Additional Information

Visitors should be prepared for all weather conditions. Summer temperatures range from 32°F to over 100°F. The trail is usually free of snow by mid-May, but sudden and severe snowstorms can still occur at that time. Springtime means strong winds, and summer thunderstorms bring lightning and the possibility of fire and flash floods. In addition, frequent rock slides can make some sections of the trail particularly hazardous for equestrians. Extreme care is advised. There are small springs and streams in the Spanish Needles area (the trail passes through this back country area), but visitors should pack their own water.

Contact Information

BLM - Bakersfield Field Office
3801 Pegasus Drive
Bakersfield, CA 93308
Tel: (661) 391-6000
Fax: (661) 391-6040
*www.ca.blm.gov/bakersfield/
pctowenspeak.html*

Activity Codes

Punta Gorda Lighthouse

California's Punta Gorda Lighthouse, located within the King Range National Conservation Area, was once considered the "Alcatraz" of lighthouses because of its remote location. *(James Pickering, BLM California State Office)*

Location

58 miles south of Eureka, California.

Description

Located along the Lost Coast in the King Range National Conservation Area, the Punta Gorda fog station began operating on June 22, 1888, and the lighthouse on January 15, 1912. Isolated and remote, the lighthouse was widely thought of as the "Alcatraz" of lighthouses, a place where employees were stationed as a punishment for misconduct. Throughout its operation, the lighthouse remained a frontier settlement in the midst of a modernizing world. During good weather, a keeper would ride horseback into the village of Petrolia to carry back what fresh supplies he could. For much of the winter, flooded streams and fierce winds kept the area cut off from civilization. The lighthouse was in service for 39 years until it was taken over by the U.S. Coast Guard during World War II and finally closed in 1951. The property was transferred to BLM in 1963, and was placed on the National Register of Historic Places on October 5, 1976.

Directions

From Eureka, travel 14 miles south on U.S. Highway 101 to the Ferndale exit. Proceed 5 miles on County Road 211 to Main Street in Ferndale. Follow Main Street approximately 1 mile to its end. Turn right on Ocean Avenue, then immediately left on Wildcat Road. Continue 30 miles to Petrolia. Turn right on Lighthouse Road and travel 5 miles to Mattole Campground. The Lost Coast National Recreation Trail begins at the Mattole information kiosk, and leads south 3 miles to the lighthouse.

Visitor Activities

Hiking, wildlife viewing, birdwatching, wildflower viewing, picnicking, and historic site.

Special Features

Punta Gorda, Spanish for "substantial point," is one of the westernmost points on California's long coast. Several shipwrecks occurred along the coast before the lighthouse was built. Occasionally, some of the wrecks' remains can be seen in the surf off the point. Loons,

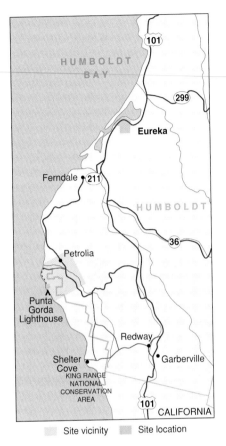

Site vicinity   Site location

grebes, gulls, kingfishers, and pelicans are among the many species of birds seen along the Lost Coast. Harbor seals are often seen where the Mattole River meets the Pacific.

Permits, Fees, Limitations

None.

Accessibility

None.

Camping and Lodging

Mattole Campground has no hookups or potable water, but offers pit toilets.

Lodging is available in Petrolia, Ferndale, Eureka, and Garberville, 67 miles south of Eureka on U.S. Highway 101.

Food and Supplies
Food and supplies are available in Petrolia.

First Aid
The Petrolia Fire Department provides full medical aid for this site. The emergency number is 911. The nearest hospital is in Garberville.

Additional Information
Frequent and dense morning fog should be expected. The best months to visit are April, May, September, and October. Punta Gorda is one of the wettest spots along the Lost Coast Trail. From the Mattole Campground to the lighthouse, visitors should allow at least 5 hours for the 6-mile round-trip hike, as the soft sand makes for slow going. Hikers should bring at least 2 quarts of water per person and plan to hike during low tide, since this short stretch of the Lost Coast Trail may be impassable at high tide. Tide tables are posted at the Mattole kiosk.

Contact Information
BLM - Arcata Field Office
1695 Heindon Road
Arcata, CA 95521-4573
Tel: (707) 825-2300
Fax: (707) 825-2301
www.ca.blm.gov/arcata/king_range.html

Activity Codes

Rademacher Hills Trail

Location
Within the city limits of Ridgecrest, California.

Description
The Rademacher Hills Trail is a 14-mile network of trails that extends through desert terrain on the south side of Ridgecrest. This trail is open to hiking, jogging, horseback riding, and mountain biking. Once a network of mining paths, segments of the Rademacher Hills Trail system provide differing degrees of trail difficulty, ranging from open, flat desert to steep, rocky ridges. The view from the ridges takes in the town of China Lake and Indian Wells Valley as well as the Panamint Mountains and Telescope Peak in Death Valley National Park.

Directions
The centrally located Sunland Trailhead is the primary trailhead for accessing the Rademacher Hills Trail system. The Sunland Trailhead is reached by driving south in Ridgecrest on China Lake Boulevard to College Heights Boulevard. Continue for 3.5 miles on College Heights Boulevard; then turn east on Belle Vista Road for 0.5 mile to the Sunland Trailhead. The turn east off College Heights Boulevard is marked by a BLM Sunland Trailhead directional sign.

Visitor Activities
Hiking, jogging, horseback riding, mountain biking, and interpretation.

Special Features

The large desert basin on the south side of Ridgecrest is located along the uplifted northern flank of the Rademacher Hills. This creates an 18,000-acre "viewshed," which is highly visible from Ridgecrest. The South Ridgecrest viewshed is an area where BLM, recreational users, and interest groups are actively working to protect and enhance scenic, ecological, and recreational resources. Desert plants, such as creosote bushes, are the most common form of vegetation in the area.

Permits, Fees, Limitations

There are no fees. Most of the trail is closed to vehicles to avoid conflicts with non-vehicular users and nearby residents. This area is within the Ridgecrest city limits, and is closed to all firearm use by city ordinance.

Accessibility

None.

Camping and Lodging

There is no camping on-site. Camping is available from private providers in the city of Ridgecrest.

Food and Supplies

Food and supplies are located in Ridgecrest.

First Aid

Emergency services are located in Ridgecrest.

Additional Information

There are 11 trailheads at various points along the trail. These trailheads have parking areas where users can access the trail system and consult kiosks with trail information.

The trail system is designed to offer the opportunity for both loop trips and point-to-point trips.

Contact Information

BLM - Ridgecrest Field Office
300 S. Richmond Road
Ridgecrest, CA 93555
Tel: (760) 384-5400
Fax: (760) 384-5499
www.ca.blm.gov/ridgecrest/rademacher.html

Activity Codes

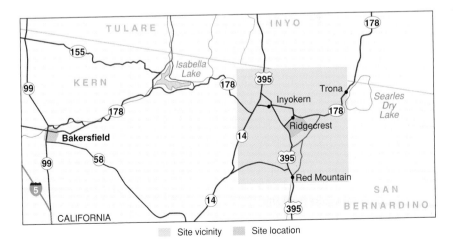

Site vicinity ▨ Site location

Sacramento River–Bend Area

Location
Between Red Bluff and Redding, California.

Description
The Sacramento River, California's longest, makes a splash with visitors thanks to easy access for fishing and boating. Kayaks, canoes, rafts, and powerboats all ply the deceptively tranquil waters that meander down the Sacramento Valley. Some 18,000 acres of public land provide exceptional recreation opportunities along the BLM-managed stretch of the river from Jelly's Ferry south to Sevenmile Creek. Visitors can choose among hiking, mountain biking, picnicking, camping, and wildlife watching, as well as great shoreline fishing for salmon, steelhead, and trout. BLM has designated this area an Area of Critical

Environmental Concern in order to protect streams and oak woodland habitats and the wildlife that depends on them.

Directions
From the town of Red Bluff, go 5 miles north on Interstate 5. Take the Jelly's Ferry Road exit north 3 miles to Bend Ferry Road. The Bend Boat Ramp is located at the east end of the bridge. Continuing 2 miles northeast brings visitors to the edge of the public lands.

Visitor Activities
Hiking, hunting (for quail, deer, waterfowl, doves, and turkeys), mountain biking, horseback riding, fishing, rafting, canoeing, kayaking, boating, swimming, birdwatching, and wildlife viewing.

Special Features
Ospreys, also known as fish eagles, earn their name along this stretch of the river. Other wildlife that frequents the area includes river otters, bald eagles, ringtail cats, black-tail deer, red-tailed hawks, and bobcats. Valley oak, live oak, gray pine, cottonwood, willow, and ash trees grow throughout the area. Blue oak woodlands festoon the uplands.

Permits, Fees, Limitations
No fees for casual use. Fees may apply to organized activities or events.

Accessibility
Paynes Creek Recreation Area, located 2.5 miles after the bridge on Bend Ferry Road, has a wheelchair-accessible fishing pier.

Wheelchair-accessible fishing piers—and good shoreline fishing—attract many anglers to the Paynes Creek Recreation Area along the Sacramento River. *(James Pickering, BLM California State Office)*

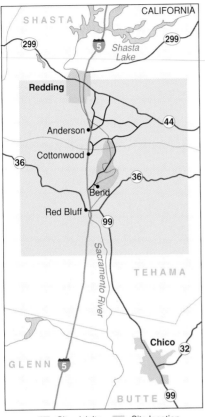

Site vicinity　　Site location

Camping and Lodging

There are no established campgrounds, but camping is allowed at some parking areas and back country camping is also permitted. Massacre Flat, a historic site along the riverbank, allows for primitive boat-in camping. Group camping is available at Reading Island for a fee. Groups must obtain a permit in advance. (Reading Island is 5 miles east of Cottonwood, California. Take the Balls Ferry Road exit off Interstate 5, then take Adobe Road east.) Free overnight camping at Reading Island is available for individuals (boat-in only camping). Lodging is available in Red Bluff and Redding.

Food and Supplies

The Bend Store is located near the Bend Boat Ramp. Red Bluff is a full-service community, approximately 7 miles south of Bend.

First Aid

The nearest hospital is in Red Bluff.

Easy access and tranquil waters interrupted by a few Class II rapids make the Sacramento River in the Bend area a popular and scenic canoe trip. *(BLM)*

Additional Information

Interesting places to visit in the area include the Coleman National Fish Hatchery (follow signs from the Anderson exit off Interstate 5, 20 miles north of Red Bluff), Battle Creek Wildlife Area (near where Battle Creek joins the Sacramento River), Ide Adobe State Historic Park (21659 Adobe Road, Red Bluff), and the Sacramento River Discovery Center, which is located within the Lake Red Bluff Recreation Area (off Interstate 5 in Red Bluff).

Contact Information

BLM - Redding Field Office
355 Hemsted Drive
Redding, CA 96002
Tel: (530) 224-2100
Fax: (530) 224-2172
www.ca.blm.gov/redding/sacramento.html

Activity Codes

South Yuba National Recreation Trail

Location

Approximately 10 miles north of Nevada City, California.

Description

This 12-mile trail leads hikers, mountain bikers, and horseback riders through steep, pine-choked canyons to gentler slopes and open wildflower meadows. Historic flumes and waterworks provide ample evidence of the 19th-century hydraulic mining that took place here. Visitors to the area can still try their luck by gold panning today. The trail also provides access to swimming holes and rainbow trout pools along the Yuba River's roaring South Fork. And when flows are favorable—in spring and early summer—Class IV–V rapids on the South Yuba attract serious kayakers.

Directions

From State Highway 49 in Nevada City, turn north on Coyote Street, which becomes North Bloomfield Road. Travel north on North Bloomfield Road for about 10 miles to the South Yuba Recreation Lands. A parking area is located at Edwards Crossing, where the road crosses the river.

Visitor Activities

Mountain biking, birdwatching, hiking, horseback riding, picnicking, swimming, fishing, rockhounding, kayaking, and gold panning.

Special Features

The scars of hydraulic mining operations remain along the Yuba River even though operations ceased over a century ago. Gold in this region was not typically found in the form of nuggets, but rather as fine particles that were more difficult to extract from the sediment. Gold miners literally washed away entire mountainsides of dirt in their quest for the precious metal. Hydraulic mining was eventually outlawed because of the mud and debris that washed downstream.

Permits, Fees, Limitations
None.

Accessibility
A limited number of campsites at the South Yuba Campground are wheelchair-accessible.

Camping and Lodging
The South Yuba Campground is located on North Bloomfield Road (a gravel road) about 1.5 miles past the one-lane bridge over the river. It has 16 campsites for tents or RVs, piped water, pit toilets, picnic tables, fire grills, and garbage collection. Fees are charged for camping and there is a 14-day limit. No reservations are taken for the camp-ground. Numerous private and public campgrounds are also located nearby. Lodging is available in Nevada City.

Food and Supplies
Food and supplies are located in Nevada City.

First Aid
Emergency services are located in Nevada City.

Additional Information
In 1999, a 39-mile stretch of the South Yuba River was designated a state wild and scenic river by the governor of California. The nearby Malakoff Diggins State Historic Park provides visitors with information about the colorful mining history of the region.

Contact Information
BLM – Folsom Field Office
63 Natoma Street
Folsom, CA 95630
Tel: (916) 985-4474
Fax: (916) 985-3259
www.ca.blm.gov/folsom/yubacampground.html

Activity Codes

other – rockhounding, gold panning

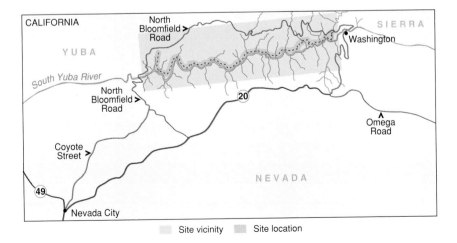

Site vicinity   Site location

Trona Pinnacles

Location
20 miles east of Ridgecrest, California.

Description
The Trona Pinnacles are some of the most unique geological features in the California Desert Conservation Area. The unusual landscape consists of more than 500 tufa spires, some as high as 140 feet, rising from the bed of the Searles Dry Lake basin. The pinnacles vary in size and shape from short and squat to tall and thin, and are composed primarily of spongy calcium carbonate (tufa). The Trona Pinnacles have been featured in many commercials, films, and still-photo shoots. A 0.5-mile hiking trail leads into the heart of the pinnacles for a close-up view of the spires and the surrounding desert.

Directions
From Ridgecrest, travel 20 miles east on State Highway 178 to its intersection with Trona-Red Mountain Road. Continue east on State Highway 178 for 7.7 more miles, and turn south on BLM Road RM 143. Take this dirt road for 5 miles to the site.

Visitor Activities
Geologic sightseeing, hiking, picnicking, and mountain biking (on existing routes only).

Special Features
The spires were formed underwater from 10,000–100,000 years ago when Searles Lake was one of a chain of interconnected Pleistocene lakes stretching from Mono Lake to Death Valley. Today, the pinnacles are about 2,000 feet above sea level in the western Mojave Desert.

Permits, Fees, Limitations
Motor vehicles and bikes are allowed only on designated routes or trails

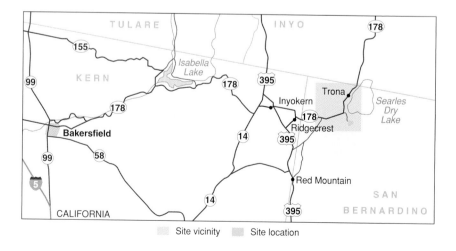

Site vicinity ▮ Site location

Ancient tufa spires create an eerie desert "moonscape" that attracts sightseers and filmmakers alike to the Trona Pinnacles. *(BLM)*

to protect the area's fragile natural resources.

Accessibility
None.

Camping and Lodging
Primitive camping is permitted; there are no developed sites. Lodging is available in Ridgecrest.

Food and Supplies
Food and supplies are available in Ridgecrest.

First Aid
The nearest hospital or source of assistance is Ridgecrest.

Additional Information
The site is open year-round; the best times to visit are fall, winter, and early spring. Early morning, early evening, and nights with a full moon provide the most dramatic views. Good hiking or walking shoes are recommended. The 5-mile-long dirt access road is usually accessible by passenger vehicle; following a rain, however, the road may be impassable to all vehicle, including those with four-wheel drive.

Contact Information
BLM – Ridgecrest Field Office
300 South Richmond Road
Ridgecrest, CA 93555
Tel: (760) 384-5400
Fax: (760) 384-5499
www.ca.blm.gov/ridgecrest/trona.html

Activity Codes

Brilliantly-colored wildflowers line the Alpine Loop as it winds through Colorado's snow-capped San Juan Mountains. *(BLM)*

Colorado's 8.4 million acres of public lands are located primarily in the western portion of the state, showcasing spectacular terrain, from alpine tundra to colorful canyons and mesas. The range of elevation from 4,000–14,000 feet provides for a variety of climates, vegetation, and wildlife communities.

Recreational opportunities are plentiful throughout the state, year-round. Winter sports include cross-country skiing, snowshoeing, and snowmobiling. Warmer seasons entice visitors to whitewater adventures, fishing, hiking, mountain biking, off-road vehicle activities, world-renowned rock climbing, wildlife viewing, and spectacular sightseeing.

Colorado public lands also provide important habitat for deer, elk, and antelope, as well as threatened and endangered species. The state hosts three National Landscape Conservation System areas. Canyons of the Ancients National Monument, near Cortez, contains the highest known density of archaeological sites anywhere in the United States. Gunnison Gorge National Conservation Area and Wilderness Area, near Montrose, features landscapes including adobe badlands, rugged pinyon/juniper-covered slopes, and the spectacular double canyon of Gunnison Gorge. And Colorado Canyons National Conservation Area contains sheer-sided, red-rock canyons; natural arches and alcoves; plant and animal fossils; and Native American rock art.

Many beautiful Colorado vistas can be experienced from the comfort of an automobile. Drivers can enjoy the historic Gold Belt Tour National Scenic Byway, or the spectacular scenery of the Alpine Loop National Back Country Byway. Escapes to remote areas are also abundant, though visitors should check with BLM before starting on such wilderness adventures. For example, a rafting trip on the rugged, 200-mile-long Dolores River brings visitors to isolated country, where self-reliance and advance information are key.

From the picturesque to the primitive, Colorado public lands have it all. Visitors in search of the unique need only browse the pages ahead.

Colorado

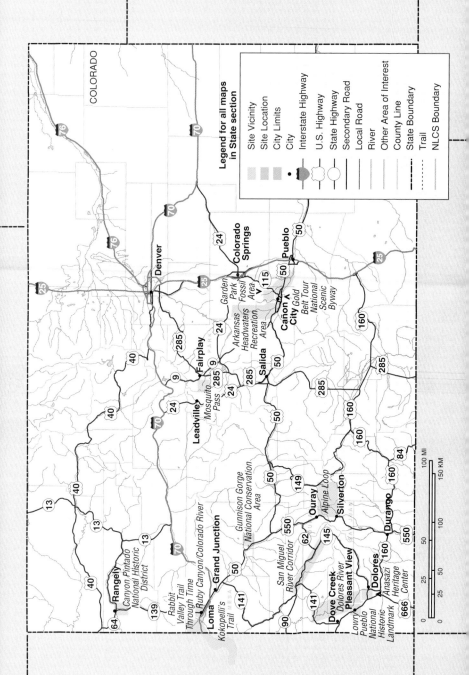

COLORADO

Legend for all maps in State section

- Site Vicinity
- Site Location
- City Limits
- City
- Interstate Highway
- U.S. Highway
- State Highway
- Secondary Road
- Local Road
- River
- Other Area of Interest
- County Line
- State Boundary
- Trail
- NLCS Boundary

Denver

Colorado Springs

Pueblo

Garden Park Fossil Area

Cañon City

Gold Belt Tour National Scenic Byway

Arkansas Headwaters Recreation Area

Fairplay

Mosquito Pass

Salida

Leadville

Gunnison Gorge National Conservation Area

Ouray

Alpine Loop

Silverton

San Miguel River Corridor

Durango

Dove Creek

Dolores River

Pleasant View

Dolores

Anasazi Heritage Center

Lowry Pueblo National Historic Landmark

Grand Junction

Loma

Ruby Canyon/Colorado River

Kokopelli's Trail

Rabbit Valley Trail Through Time

Canyon Pintado National Historic District

Rangely

100 MI
150 KM

Alpine Loop

Location
A network of jeep roads that weave through the San Juan Mountains and the towns of Lake City, Silverton, and Ouray in southwestern Colorado.

Description
This national back country byway takes visitors on a day-long, 65-mile loop through spectacular alpine scenery surrounded by 14,000-foot peaks. The byway roads were originally built by 19th-century miners, whose presence can be felt in the ghost towns and historic mining sites scattered through the area. Colorful displays of alpine wildflowers enhance the pristine mountain views.

Directions
The western entrances of the loop can be accessed via U.S. Highway 550 near Silverton (about 50 miles north of Durango) or near Ouray (about 35 miles south of Montrose). The eastern entrance to the loop is in Lake City, which is on State Highway 149, 55 miles southwest of Gunnison or 50 miles northwest of Creede.

Visitor Activities
Four-wheel driving, scenic drives, fishing, hiking, wildflower viewing, picnicking, mountain biking, cross-country skiing, snowshoeing, snowmobiling, ghost towns, and historic site.

Special Features
Five of Colorado's 14,000-foot peaks can be seen from points along the byway. Hiking trails lead to Redcloud Peak, Sunshine Peak, and Handies Peak. Alpine wildflowers generally bloom in late July–early August, and fall aspen colors peak in September.

Permits, Fees, Limitations
None.

Accessibility
The towns of Silverton, Ouray, and Lake City cater to tourists and have hotel rooms, restaurants, and restrooms that are fully accessible.

Camping and Lodging
Camping and lodging are available in Silverton, Ouray, and Lake City. There are three developed campgrounds on the Lake City side of the route. Primitive camping is allowed on public lands

Spectacular scenery, historic ghost towns, and four-wheel-drive roads make a tour of the Alpine Loop a high-country treat. *(Rick Athearn, BLM Colorado State Office (retired))*

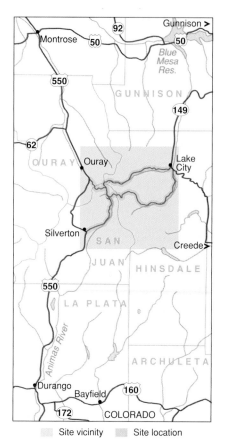

Site vicinity   Site location

along the byway. Fees are charged only
for overnight camping in developed
campgrounds.

Food and Supplies
Food and supplies are available in Lake
City, Silverton, and Ouray.

First Aid
Silverton, Ouray, and Lake City all have
emergency medical services. The closest
hospitals are located in Montrose (35
miles north of Ouray), Gunnison (55
miles northeast of Lake City), and
Durango (50 miles south of Silverton).

Additional Information
The visitor centers in Silverton, Ouray,
and Lake City provide information and
maps. There are 10 restrooms along the
loop. This area is in the high Colorado
Rockies and is subject to changing
weather. The route is usually open from
early June–mid-October, and is closed
during the winter. Short thundershow-
ers are common on summer afternoons.
While much of the loop is accessible
by ordinary passenger vehicle, a four-
wheel-drive vehicle is needed to
complete the loop over Engineer Pass
(18 miles west of Lake City) and
Cinnamon Pass (about 12 miles south
of Ouray). To protect this fragile
environment, vehicle use is limited
to designated roads. An informative,
20-page area visitor's guide, called *The
Alpine Explorer*, is available for purchase
from BLM. It includes a detailed map,
points of interest, history, safety tips, and
much more.

Contact Information
For southern parts of the loop:
BLM - Columbine Field Office
15 Burnett Court
Durango, CO 81301
Tel: (970) 247-4874
Fax: (970) 385-1375

For northern parts of the loop:
BLM - Gunnison Field Office
216 North Colorado Street
Gunnison, CO 81230
Tel: (970) 641-0471
Fax: (970) 642-4425
www.co.blm.gov/gra/gra-al.htm

Activity Codes

Anasazi Heritage Center

Location
3 miles west of Dolores, Colorado.

Description
The Anasazi Heritage Center is the headquarters and visitor center for Canyons of the Ancients National Monument. This unique archaeological museum features the history and culture of the Four Corners region. The center's films, hands-on discovery area, interactive computer programs, and exhibits explore archaeology, local history, and the lifeways of the Pueblo, Ute, and Navajo peoples. Visitors to the center are invited to "touch the past": grind corn, weave on a loom, use microscopes, and examine actual artifacts. Special exhibits are complemented by lectures, demonstrations, and visitor activities. A 0.5-mile interpretive trail leads to Escalante Pueblo, where there is a panoramic hilltop view. The center grounds also offer spectacular views of McPhee Lake, Four Corners mountain ranges, and the Great Sage Plain.

Directions
From Dolores, travel west on State Highway 145 about 2.5 miles, then turn west (right) on State Highway 184. Travel less than 1 mile to the center entrance.

Visitor Activities
Archaeological site, hands-on activities, interactive computer programs, exhibits, theater, traveling exhibits, hiking, picnicking.

Special Features
The Anasazi (or Ancestral Puebloan people), who are showcased in the heritage center, settled and farmed in the Four Corners region between about AD 1 and AD 1300, producing fine baskets, pottery, cloth, ornaments, and

At the Anasazi Heritage Center, visitors can view artifacts from native peoples. *(BLM)*

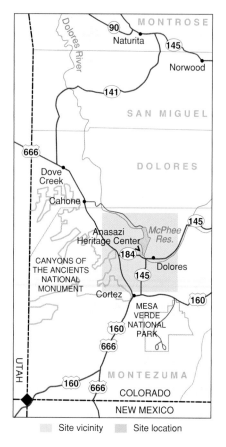

Site vicinity ▨ Site location

Golden Eagle, Golden Access, and Golden Age passes are honored.

Accessibility

This is a fully accessible site.

Camping and Lodging

No camping is allowed at the Anasazi Heritage Center. Lodging is available in Dolores and in Cortez (about 12 miles south of Dolores on U.S. Highway 160). McPhee Campground (U.S. Forest Service) is located 3 miles west of the center on State Highway 184. Commercial camping is available in Dolores and Cortez.

Food and Supplies

Food and supplies are available in Dolores and Cortez.

First Aid

There is limited first aid available on-site. The nearest hospital is in Cortez.

Additional Information

The Anasazi Heritage Center is a visitor-friendly museum and interpretive site that is open 7 days a week, year-round, except for Thanksgiving, Christmas, and New Year's Day. There are restrooms, as well as a theater and bookstore.

Contact Information

BLM - Anasazi Heritage Center
27501 Highway 184
Dolores, CO 81323
Tel: (970) 882-4811
Fax: (970) 882-7035
www.co.blm.gov/ahc/hmepge.htm

Activity Codes

tools. Their architectural achievements included cliff dwellings and pueblos. Right in front of the museum are the remains of the Dominguez Pueblo, a four-room structure that probably was home to one or two families. The nearby remains of Escalante Pueblo, a compact village of the mid-1100s, reflect the Chaco culture, which was concentrated in northwestern New Mexico.

Permits, Fees, Limitations

There is an admission fee. (For more information, see the BLM website.)

Arkansas Headwaters Recreation Area

Location
150-mile stretch of the Arkansas River from Leadville to Lake Pueblo, Colorado.

Description
This area is one of the most popular river-rafting spots in the United States and also provides some of the best fishing in Colorado. The spectacular scenery is highlighted by rocky canyons that provide excellent opportunities to view Rocky Mountain bighorn sheep. There are 28 developed river-access areas. Popular activities include rockhounding at Ruby Mountain, fishing for brown trout at Hecla Junction, and wildlife-watching at the Five Points Watchable Wildlife Area in Bighorn Sheep Canyon. The area is jointly managed by BLM and the Colorado Division of Parks and Outdoor Recreation.

Directions
The Arkansas Headwaters Recreation Area extends about 150 miles from Leadville to Lake Pueblo through the towns of Buena Vista (about 35 miles south of Leadville on U.S. Highway 24), Salida (about 100 miles west of Pueblo on U.S. Highway 50), Cañon City (43 miles west of Pueblo on U.S. Highway 50), and Florence (35 miles west of Pueblo at the intersection of State Highways 67 and 115).

Visitor Activities
Fishing, rafting, kayaking, wildlife viewing, rockhounding, picnicking, and interpretation.

Special Features
The 150-mile Arkansas River corridor within the Arkansas Headwaters Recreation Area is one of the most

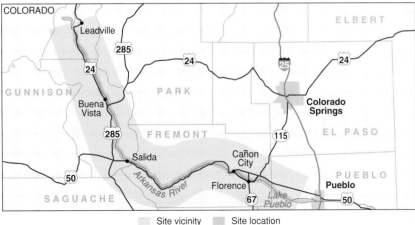

Site vicinity   Site location

diverse and attractive river corridors in Colorado. Descending from lofty mountain peaks near Leadville, the Arkansas flows through wide-open grasslands at altitudes of 10,000 feet and traverses a diverse range of ecosystems on its way downhill. The free-flowing part of the river ends at Lake Pueblo Reservoir, just west of the city of Pueblo. Visitors are likely to see wildlife that includes elk, mule deer, mountain goats, and bighorn sheep, as well as stellar jays, water ouzels, mallards, and common mergansers.

Permits, Fees, Limitations

Commercial rafting outfitters are required to have a commercial contract. Check with the Colorado Division of Wildlife for fishing license requirements, (719) 530-5520. A fee is charged for daily vehicle passes, which are required at all day-use sites. Annual passes and other special passes are also available; check the website for details.

Accessibility

Most facilities include universally-accessible restrooms, picnic areas, parking, and campsites.

Camping and Lodging

Camping is available at five sites along the river; fees are charged at all sites. From north to south, they are:
Railroad Bridge: From U.S. Highway 24 in Buena Vista, turn east at the only stoplight in town and then travel 2 blocks past the railroad tracks to N. Colorado Avenue and turn left. This will turn into County Road 371. Travel 6.2 miles to the campground.
Ruby Mountain: From Buena Vista, travel south on U.S. Highway 285 about 6 miles to County Road 301. Turn east toward the river on County Road 301. Go across the river to the end of the pavement and turn right onto County Road 300. Drive 2.4 miles to the campground.
Hecla Junction: From Salida, travel north on State Highway 291 for about 7 miles to the intersection with U.S.

Challenging rapids draw rafters to Colorado's Arkansas River, one of the most popular whitewater destinations in the country. *(BLM)*

Highway 285. Turn north on Highway 285, and travel about 1 mile to County Road 194. Turn east on County Road 194 and go 2.4 miles to the campground.

Rincon: Off U.S. Highway 50, about 8 miles east of Salida.

Five Points: Off U.S. Highway 50, about 22 miles west of Cañon City.

Lodging is available along U.S. Highway 24 in Leadville and Buena Vista; along U.S. Highway 50 in Salida and Cañon City; and in Pueblo, which is located at the intersection of U.S. Highway 50 and Interstate 25.

Food and Supplies

Food and supplies are available in Leadville, Buena Vista, Salida, Howard (12 miles southeast of Salida on U.S. Highway 50), Cotopaxi (25 miles southeast of Salida on U.S. Highway 50), Texas Creek (28 miles west of Cañon City on U.S. Highway 50), Cañon City, Florence (34 miles west of Pueblo on Colorado Highway 115), and Pueblo.

First Aid

There is no first aid available on-site. The nearest hospitals are in Leadville, Salida, Cañon City, and Pueblo.

Additional Information

This is a very well-developed recreation area, easily accessible from three major highways (U.S. Highways 50, 24, and 285). The sites are open year-round. The recreation area headquarters is in Salida. Chambers of Commerce are located in Buena Vista, Salida, Cañon City, and Florence.

Contact Information

BLM - Arkansas Headwaters Rec. Area
307 W. Sackett Ave
Salida, CO 81201
Tel: (719) 539-7289
Fax: (719) 539-3771
www.parks.state.co.us

Activity Codes

other - rockhounding

Canyon Pintado National Historic District

Location

3 miles south of Rangely, Colorado.

Description

Canyon Pintado National Historic District encompasses over 16,000 acres of public land along 15 miles of State Highway 139, part of the Dinosaur Diamond Scenic and Historical Byway. Canyon Pintado (Spanish for "Painted Canyon") received its name in 1776, when Fathers Dominguez and Escalante noted numerous examples of ancient Native American rock art as they traveled through the Douglas Creek Valley.

The prehistoric Fremont culture and the historic Ute Indians created much of the rock art that is visible in the canyon today. Eight rock art sites and three other historic and prehistoric sites

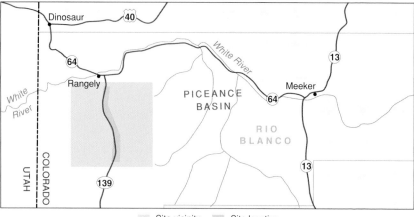

Site vicinity   Site location

are interpreted for the public within the historic district, right along the highway. Visitor orientation kiosks, including restrooms and picnic tables, are located at the south end of the historic district and at the north end, at the East Four-Mile Draw site. A brochure with map is available from the Rangely Chamber of Commerce (209 E. Main St., Rangely, (970) 675-5290) and at the BLM Dinosaur Welcome Center in Dinosaur, Colorado (18 miles northwest of Rangely on State Highway 64).

Starting out from this information kiosk, visitors can view the "Painted Canyon," which is decorated with 1,000-year-old rock art. *(Rick Athearn, BLM Colorado State Office (retired))*

Directions

From Rangely, Colorado (junction of State Highways 64 and 139), travel south on State Highway 139. The district begins about 3 miles south of Rangely and continues for 15 miles.

Visitor Activities

Picnicking, hiking, rock art viewing, archaeological site, historic site, mountain biking, and scenic drives.

Special Features

The area contains etched (petroglyphs) and painted (pictographs) panels, including zoomorph (animal), anthropomorph (human), and abstract figures.

Permits, Fees, Limitations

None.

Accessibility

Both of the visitor orientation kiosks and restrooms are accessible. Some assistance may be needed on the trails to State Bridge Draw (Mile 59.7 on State Highway 139), Cow Canyon (Mile 57.8), Kokopelli (Mile 56.0), and Waving Hands (Mile 53.5), while the East Four-Mile Draw Loop Trail

(Mile 61.3) and the Lookout Point Trail (Mile 67.6) are difficult, steep trails receiving little maintenance.

Camping and Lodging

No camping is permitted inside the fences at the developed sites. Primitive camping is allowed on public lands outside the developed sites. Lodging and a developed campground are available in Rangely.

Food and Supplies

Food and supplies are available in Rangely.

First Aid

There is no first aid available on-site. The nearest hospital is in Rangely.

Additional Information

Hundreds of additional rock art panels can be found within the historic district, many of which are easily accessed from the highways or from back country roads and trails. There are additional rock art sites open to the public in the Rangely and Dragon Trail (County Road 23 south of Rangely) areas.

Contact Information

BLM - White River Field Office
P.O. Box 928
73544 Highway 64
Meeker, CO 81641
Tel: (970) 878-3800
Fax: (970) 878-3805
www.co.blm.gov/wrra/index.htm

Activity Codes

Dolores River

Location

Access to this 200-mile-long river begins about 30 miles north of Cortez, Colorado.

Description

The Dolores River flows through western Colorado from the rugged La Plata Mountains north to its confluence with the Colorado River in Utah. Multi-day whitewater rafting trips along the river treat visitors to outstanding views of sandstone cliffs, alpine and desert plants and wildlife, and evidence of prehistoric inhabitants of this rugged area.

Directions

From Cortez, travel 30 miles north on U.S. Highway 666. The put-in is at the Bradfield Bridge Recreation Site, 6 miles east of Cahone, Colorado. There are several possible put-in and take-out points, depending on how many days you wish to spend on the river. Contact BLM for specific locations.

Visitor Activities

Fishing, whitewater rafting, canoeing, wildlife viewing, birdwatching, plant viewing, scenic drives, picnicking, and swimming.

Special Features

Ponderosa pine groves and red sandstone cliffs gradually give way to rolling, arid hills and desert vegetation, including pinyon-juniper forests, yuccas, and cacti. Bald eagles may occasionally be spotted,

Western Colorado's Dolores Rivers winds through brilliantly colored sandstone canyons, offering boaters whitewater thrills and spectacular views. *(BLM)*

along with deer, bears, foxes, skunks, turtles, lizards, and herons. Like the ever-changing landscape, the river alternates between challenging rapids and long stretches of calm water.

Permits, Fees, Limitations
A permit is required for commercial rafting, but not for private boaters. Boaters are required to register at launch sites. Check with the Colorado Division of Wildlife for fishing license requirements, (970) 247-0855.

Accessibility
None.

Camping and Lodging
There are 18 campsites at the Bradfield Bridge campground; a fee is charged.

Dispersed camping is also permitted along the river. Lodging is available in Cortez.

Food and Supplies
Food and supplies are available in Naturita (about 70 miles north of Cahone on State Highway 141), Dolores (about 25 miles southeast of Cahone on State Highway 145), and Norwood (about 80 miles northeast of Cahone on State Highway 145).

First Aid
First aid is not available on-site. The nearest hospital is in Cortez.

Additional Information
The Dolores River is a primitive recreation area with few visitor facilities.

Camping and Lodging

Primitive camping is allowed on public lands and there is a public campground located in Red Canyon Park (12 miles north of Cañon City on Shelf Road), as well as numerous private campgrounds located near towns along the route. Lodging is available in Cañon City (43 miles west of Pueblo on U.S. Highway 50), Florence (34 miles west of Pueblo on State Highway 115), Florissant (34 miles west of Colorado Springs on U.S. Highway 24), Cripple Creek (about 18 miles southeast of Florissant on Teller County Road 1), and Victor (5 miles southeast of Cripple Creek on State Highway 67).

Food and Supplies

Food and supplies are available in Cañon City, Florence, Florissant, Victor, and Cripple Creek.

First Aid

There is no first aid available on-site. The nearest hospital is in Cañon City.

Additional Information

Two byway routes (Shelf Road and Phantom Canyon Road) are gravel roads that are winding and narrow, and in places are limited to one lane. The route is drivable by passenger vehicle, except for Shelf Road, which may require a four-wheel-drive vehicle under certain conditions, such as heavy rain or snow. Phantom Canyon Road (State Highway 67 north of Florence) is very narrow and cannot accommodate oversize vehicles, tractor-trailers, or large towed trailers. Roads can be slippery when wet.

Contact Information

BLM – Royal Gorge Field Office
3170 East Main Street
Cañon City, CO 81212
Tel: (719) 269-8500
Fax: (719) 269-8599
www.coloradobyways.org/Main.cfm

Activity Codes

other – rock climbing

Travelers on the Gold Belt Tour National Scenic Byway should be prepared for narrow, winding routes and unexpected encounters with local inhabitants, such as these sheep on Shelf Road. *(BLM)*

Gunnison Gorge National Conservation Area

Location
50 miles south of Grand Junction or 10 miles north of Montrose, Colorado.

Description
The Gunnison Gorge National Conservation Area (NCA) encompasses diverse landscapes ranging from abrupt, erosion-sculpted hills of Mancos shale, known as adobe badlands, to rugged pinyon/juniper-covered slopes, to the spectacular double canyon of the Gunnison Gorge Wilderness Area. A variety of recreational activities are available in the NCA—from whitewater boating and rafting to big-game hunting to world-class, Gold Medal trout fishing in the wild river canyon. Off-highway vehicles are allowed, but only in the Peach Valley area, north of Falcon Road (east of U.S. Highway 50 near the town of Olathe, 11 miles north of Montrose). Covering almost 60,000 acres, the NCA abounds with opportunities for back country experiences.

Directions
From Grand Junction, take U.S. Highway 50 south approximately 50 miles, or from Montrose take U.S. Highway 50 north about 10 miles. The best access points are Falcon Road, or County Road 2200, which can be reached by turning east onto U.S. Highway 92 in Delta (21 miles north of Montrose). From Delta, follow U.S. Highway 92 approximately 7 miles to the intersection of County Road 2200, which is near Austin.

Visitor Activities
Back country hiking, picnicking, horseback riding, rafting, kayaking,

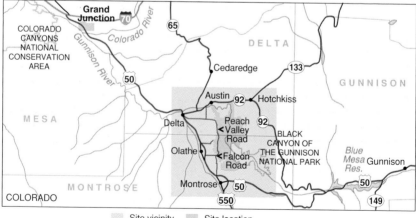

Site vicinity   Site location

fishing, wildlife viewing, big-game hunting, and off-highway driving.

Special Features
The Gunnison Gorge Wilderness Area is an awesome natural beauty, with outstanding wilderness, unique geologic features, sensitive riparian areas, critical wildlife habitat, and diverse recreational opportunities. Wildlife that can be seen in the gorge includes bighorn sheep, mule deer, elk, river otters, ringtail cats, mountain lions, bald and golden eagles, ospreys, chukars, and endangered peregrine falcons.

Permits, Fees, Limitations
There are fees for day use. Annual passes are available.

Accessibility
None.

Camping and Lodging
Camping within the river corridor is permitted, but only in designated sites. There are many such sites along both sides of the river. Camping is also available at Gunnison River Pleasure Park, located on U.S. Highway 92, 14 miles east of Delta (21 miles north of Montrose on U.S. Highway 50), and in Black Canyon of the Gunnison National Park. The park, which borders the southern portion of the NCA, can be reached from the south by way of Montrose (take U.S. Highway 50 for 15 miles east and then turn north on State Highway 347 for 7 miles to the entrance) or from the north by way of Delta (take State Highway 92 east for 31 miles to Crawford. Turn south on North Rim Road and go 11 miles to park entrance). Lodging is available in Delta, Montrose, and Grand Junction.

Food and Supplies
Food and supplies are available in Delta, Montrose, Grand Junction, and Olathe (11 miles north of Montrose on U.S. Highway 50).

First Aid
The nearest first aid is in Delta.

Additional Information
The Gunnison River, which runs through the Gunnison Gorge NCA, offers a technical and remote whitewater experience for rafters, kayakers, and whitewater canoeists. Flows in the gorge are dam-controlled and very dependent on winter snowpack. Visitors should consult the BLM website for current river flows. Hiking down into the gorge is the only way to reach the Gunnison River. Rafters need to carry all equipment for raft trips or hire a horse-packing guide.

The Gunnison River flows through the remote Gunnison Gorge Wilderness, offering whitewater enthusiasts a thrilling ride through a rugged landscape. *(BLM)*

Contact Information

BLM - Uncompahgre Field Office
2505 S. Townsend Avenue
Montrose, CO 81401
Tel: (970) 240-5300
Fax: (970) 240 5367
www.co.blm.gov/ggnca/index.htm

Activity Codes

Kokopelli's Trail

Location

140-mile bike trail between Loma, Colorado, and Moab, Utah.

Description

This is one of Colorado and Utah's premier mountain bike trails. Stretching for 140 miles with elevations that rise to 8,400 feet, Kokopelli's Trail is made up of improved roads, four-wheel-drive roads, and single-track roads. The trail begins in the Colorado Canyons National Conservation Area, west of the Loma boat launch site, and ends in Moab, Utah. It is named for Kokopelli, the hump-backed flute player and fertility symbol in the Native American cultures of the Colorado Plateau.

Directions

From Grand Junction, travel west on Interstate 70 about 15 miles to the Loma exit (Exit 15). Turn left (west) at the top of the exit ramp to cross over the interstate to the south. Turn right at the access road and follow the signs to the trailhead parking area about 0.5 mile down the gravel road.

Visitor Activities

Mountain biking, hiking, horseback riding, and picnicking.

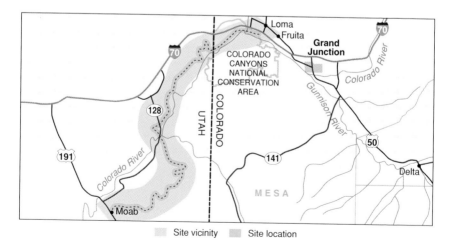

Site vicinity ▪ Site location

Special Features
This 140-mile trail winds through remote desert sandstone and shale canyons, often overlooking or hugging the banks of the Colorado River.

Permits, Fees, Limitations
None.

Accessibility
There is a wheelchair-accessible restroom at the Kokopelli parking area.

Camping and Lodging
No camping is allowed at the Kokopelli trailhead. Primitive camping is available on nearby public lands. The nearest lodging is available in Fruita, 5 miles east on Interstate 70.

Food and Supplies
Food and supplies are available in Fruita.

First Aid
The nearest hospital is in Fruita.

Additional Information
This is a primitive bike trail in an undeveloped area. It is very hot in the summer and subject to intense thunderstorms.

The trail can be very slippery when wet. Drinking water is not available.

Contact Information
BLM - Grand Junction Field Office
2815 H Road
Grand Junction, CO 81506
Tel: (970) 244-3000
Fax: (970) 244-3083
www.co.blm.gov/colocanyons/index.htm

Activity Codes

Kokopelli's Trail is tough in places, but the spectacular scenery makes the effort worthwhile for mountain bikers who are up to the challenge. *(BLM)*

Lowry Pueblo National Historic Landmark

Location
27 miles northwest of Cortez, Colorado.

Description
Located in the Canyons of the Ancients National Monument, this 1,000-year-old Ancestral Puebloan (Anasazi) site was designated a National Historic Landmark in 1967. Lowry has 40 rooms and 8 kivas—round, subterranean rooms that were used for ceremonial and domestic activities. The presence of a great kiva indicates that Lowry may have been a focal point for surrounding communities. Lowry Pueblo was first excavated in 1931 and it remains one of the most significant BLM archaeological sites in the Four Corners region.

The 1,000-year-old walls of Lowry Pueblo, in Colorado's Canyons of the Ancients National Monument, enclose a 40-room village once inhabited by the Ancestral Puebloan people. *(BLM)*

Directions

From Cortez, travel about 18 miles north on U.S. Highway 666 to the "Pleasant View and Lowry" sign at County Road CC. Turn west and follow the signs for about 9 miles.

Visitor Activities

Self-guided interpretive tour, archaeo-logical site, picnicking, and hiking.

Special Features

Lowry Pueblo's stabilized standing walls were constructed of double layers of stone blocks, alternating with bands of smaller stones. The pueblo's 40 rooms were probably home to about 100 people.

Permits, Fees, Limitations

None.

Accessibility

Although the parking lot is gravel, the adjoining picnic area and restroom, as well as the 0.25-mile trail to the pueblo ruins, are all wheelchair-accessible.

Camping and Lodging

Camping is not allowed at Lowry Pueblo. Camping and lodging are avail-able in Cortez and Dolores (about 30 miles southeast on State Highway 145).

Food and Supplies

Food and supplies are available in Cortez and Dolores.

First Aid

No first aid is available on-site. The nearest hospital is in Cortez. First aid and a phone are available in Pleasant View (18 miles north of Cortez on U.S. Highway 666).

Additional Information

A salvaged fragment from a mural at Lowry Pueblo is displayed at BLM's Anasazi Heritage Center, located about

26 miles away on State Highway 184, 3 miles west of Dolores.

Contact Information

BLM - Canyons of the Ancients National Monument/ Anasazi Heritage Center
27501 Highway 184
Dolores, CO 81323
Tel: (970) 882-4811
Fax: (970) 882-7035
www.co.blm.gov/canm/index.html

Activity Codes

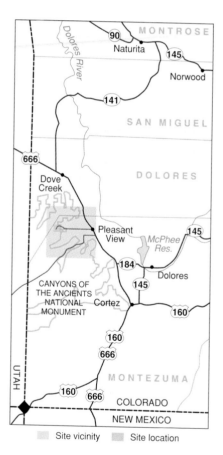

Site vicinity   Site location

Mosquito Pass

Location
10 miles northwest of Fairplay, Colorado.

Description
This beautiful, high-alpine tundra supports significant biodiversity and has been designated a BLM Area of Critical Environmental Concern. There are several small parcels of BLM land here, with unique geologic formations and 18 rare plant species. Remains of historic mining buildings can also be seen along the way.

Directions
From U.S. Highway 285 at Fairplay, turn north on State Highway 9, go about 3 miles to Alma Junction, and then turn west on Mosquito Pass Road. The road continues on to Leadville (on U.S. Highway 24), with the total distance between Fairplay and Leadville being about 22 miles.

Visitor Activities
Four-wheel driving, geologic sightseeing, rare plant viewing, historic site, hiking, mountain biking, and wildlife viewing.

Special Features
The Mosquito Pass road crosses over the Continental Divide (elevation 13,185 feet) and through high-alpine tundra, home to ptarmigans, pikas, marmots, and bighorn sheep. Among the rare plants that can be found in the area are Penland alpine fen mustards and Weber saussureas.

Permits, Fees, Limitations
None.

Accessibility
None.

Camping and Lodging
Primitive camping is allowed on public lands. Lodging is available in Fairplay and Leadville.

The seemingly barren high-alpine tundra of Mosquito Pass is actually home to 18 rare plant species. *(Andy Senti, BLM Colorado State Office)*

Food and Supplies

Food and supplies are available in Fairplay and Leadville.

First Aid

No first aid is available on-site. The nearest hospital is about 20 miles away in Breckenridge on State Highway 9.

Additional Information

This is alpine tundra with elevations between 13,000 and 14,000 feet. It is rugged and subject to harsh and suddenly-changing weather. Summer storms produce lightning and hail. The area is closed from September–June. At other times, there is limited access to the area; a high-clearance or four-wheel-drive vehicle is required.

Contact Information

BLM - Royal Gorge Field Office
3170 East Main Street
Cañon City, CO 81212
Tel: (719) 269-8500
Fax: (719) 269-8599

Activity Codes

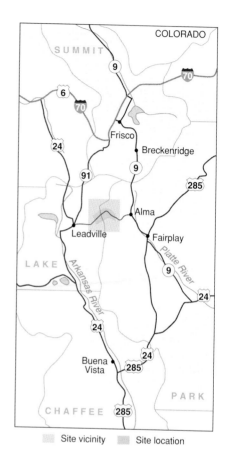

Site vicinity   Site location

Rabbit Valley
Trail Through Time

Location

30 miles west of Grand Junction, Colorado.

Description

Located within the Colorado Canyons National Conservation Area, the Rabbit Valley Trail Through Time is a 1.5-mile interpretive trail that takes hikers past a working fossil quarry and numerous other links to the prehistoric environment of the region. Visitors can view the fossils of 140-million-year-old dinosaurs, which probably gathered at an ancient watering hole here. An interpretive kiosk describes the numerous dinosaurs that have come from Rabbit Valley, which has been designated as an important part of the Dinosaur Diamond National Scenic Byway, a roughly 500-mile route through parts of Colorado and Utah.

Directions
From Grand Junction, drive 30 miles west on Interstate 70 to the Rabbit Valley exit (Exit 2). Turn right into the site parking lot.

Visitor Activities
Fossil viewing, interpretation, and hiking.

Special Features
Numerous dinosaurs, including *Apatosaurus*, *Diplodocus*, and *Brachiosaurus*, roamed this area 140 million years ago.

Permits, Fees, Limitations
None.

Accessibility
None.

Camping and Lodging
Camping is permitted in Rabbit Valley south of Interstate 70. Three developed camping areas are available. Lodging is available in Fruita, 20 miles east on Interstate 70, and in Grand Junction.

Food and Supplies
Food and supplies are available in Fruita.

First Aid
The nearest first aid is available at the hospital in Fruita.

Additional Information
The weather is very hot in summer. Drinking water is not available on-site. During winter, the trail may become impassable because of snow. The trail is slippery when wet.

Contact Information
BLM - Grand Junction Field Office
2815 H Road
Grand Junction, CO 81506
Tel: (970) 244-3000
Fax: (970) 244-3083
www.co.blm.gov/colocanyons/index.htm

Activity Codes

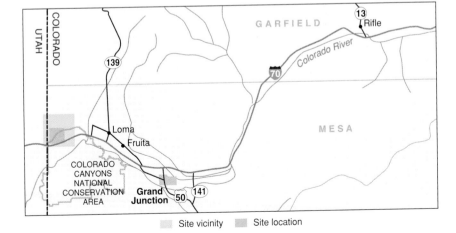

Site vicinity   Site location

Ruby Canyon/Colorado River

Location
15 miles west of Grand Junction, Colorado.

Description
This 25-mile stretch of the Colorado River gets its name from the red-rock canyons that line its shores. Rafters in this scenic section of the Colorado Canyons National Conservation Area can camp overnight and take advantage of side-canyon hikes that are accessible only by river. Prehistoric rock art sites are nestled in some of these side canyons.

Directions
From Grand Junction, travel west on Interstate 70 about 15 miles to the Loma exit, State Highway 139. Use the Loma boat ramp to launch rafts. The site is well marked.

Visitor Activities
Rafting, fishing, wildlife viewing, birdwatching, plant viewing, archaeological site, geologic sightseeing, and hiking.

Special Features
On its journey into Utah, the Colorado River cuts through billion-year-old rocks, which have taken on the rusty red color of the iron oxides they contain. Rafters may see bald eagles, peregrine and prairie falcons, and desert bighorn sheep. Side-canyon hikes, especially the trail near the confluence of McDonald Creek (17.8 river miles from Loma), lead to etched and painted rock art, most likely created by the Ute and Fremont cultures.

Permits, Fees, Limitations
No fees. Floaters are required to sign in at the visitor registration station at the Loma launch site. Commercial rafters must have a permit. Portable toilets and fire pans are required for all trips. Check with the Colorado Division of Wildlife

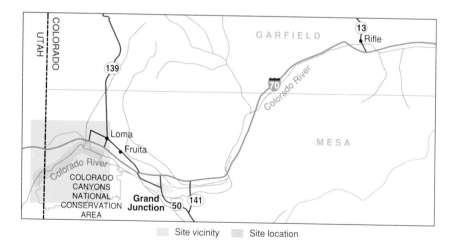

Site vicinity   Site location

The Colorado River travels through 1.5 billion-year-old metamorphic rock, as well as the red rocks of Ruby Canyon, in the Colorado Canyons National Conservation Area.
(Greg Gnesios, BLM Grand Junction Field Office)

for fishing license requirements, (970) 255-6100.

Accessibility
None.

Camping and Lodging
There is no camping at the Loma site. Camping is available in Rabbit Valley, 15 miles west on Interstate 70, or at Highline Lake State Park, 7 miles northwest of Loma on State Highway 139. Lodging is available in Fruita (5 miles east) and in Grand Junction.

Food and Supplies
Food and supplies are available in Grand Junction and Fruita.

First Aid
The nearest first aid is available at the hospital in Fruita.

Additional Information
The Loma boat ramp has an interpretive sign, parking area, and restrooms. Sudden weather changes can occur along the river. This is a desert area, which is very hot in the summer. Drinking water is not available. Visitors should be prepared for difficult conditions and bring all supplies.

Contact Information
BLM - Grand Junction Field Office
2815 H Road
Grand Junction, CO 81506
Tel: (970) 244-3000
Fax: (970) 244-3083
www.co.blm.gov/colocanyons/index.htm

Activity Codes

San Miguel River Corridor

Location
28-mile river corridor northwest of Placerville, Colorado.

Description
The San Miguel River corridor is a fragile riparian ecosystem that contains rare plants and supports numerous species of birds and other wildlife. This special management area is jointly managed by BLM and The Nature Conservancy. Rafting is one way to explore the river, but a scenic drive along the corridor also provides beautiful views and several access points for fishing and picnicking.

Directions
From Placerville, take State Highway 145 (part of the Unaweep-Tabeguache Scenic Byway) for about 33 miles to Naturita. The northern part of this area is accessible via the river, or from the State Highway 90 turn-off, 3 miles east of Naturita.

Visitor Activities
Fishing, rafting, picnicking, and scenic drives.

Special Features
The San Miguel River extends 72 miles from high alpine meadows and waterfalls above Telluride to a deep red sandstone canyon where it joins the Dolores River. The riparian forest lining much of the river includes narrowleaf cottonwoods, thinleaf alders, and Colorado blue spruces. Fish in the river include rainbow trout, brown trout, cutthroat trout, and brook trout.

Permits, Fees, Limitations
No fees or permits. For fishing license requirements, check with the Colorado Division of Wildlife, (970) 252-6000.

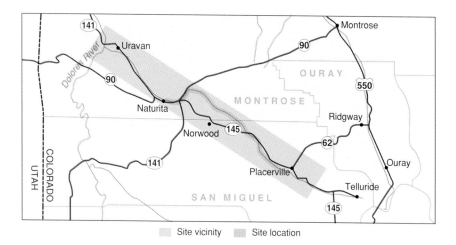

Site vicinity   Site location

Accessibility
None.

Camping and Lodging
Camping and lodging are available in Naturita and in Telluride, located on the San Juan Skyway, 16 miles south of the junction of State Highways 62 and 145 in Placerville. Camping along the river corridor on State Highway 145 is limited to designated areas, with a 7-day limit.

Food and Supplies
Food and supplies are available in Telluride, Placerville, and Naturita.

First Aid
There is no first aid available on-site. The nearest hospital is 50 miles northeast of Placerville on U.S. Highway 550 in Montrose. There are medical clinics in Telluride and Ridgway (22 miles northeast of Placerville on State Highway 62).

Additional Information
The river has been preserved by BLM and The Nature Conservancy as a BLM Area of Critical Environmental Concern. It is jointly managed along a 28-mile corridor.

Contact Information
BLM - Uncompahgre Field Office
2505 South Townsend
Montrose, CO 81401
Tel: (970) 240-5300
Fax: (970) 240-5367
www.co.blm.gov/ubra/sanmigriv.htm

Activity Codes

Morning mist rises from the sparkling waters of the San Miguel River, an important riparian area for wildlife and an enticing destination for travelers. *(Rick Athearn, BLM Colorado State Office (retired))*

BLM-Eastern States recently acquired the Meadowood property, located in the Mason Neck area of Fairfax County, Virginia. *(Don Cabrera, BLM Washington Office (retired))*

More than 30,000 acres of BLM public lands are located in the 31 states bordering upon and east of the Mississippi River. While the collective area of these public lands is relatively small, their diverse locations make them important resources for local communities in the East.

Douglas Point in Maryland and Meadowood in Virginia — both recent BLM acquisitions — offer quick getaways from urban Washington, DC, to quiet, forested solitude. These Potomac River sites offer activities including horseback riding, hiking, and birdwatching, and Meadowood also hosts BLM wild horse and burro adoptions.

Minnesota's Lake Vermilion offers excellent boating and fishing areas. Within the lake, BLM manages 70 small public islands that are popular for picnicking and birdwatching.

The interagency America's Outdoors Center for Conservation, Education, and Recreation in Milwaukee, Wisconsin, furnishes information about many recreation areas. Visitors can purchase Federal Recreation Passports and maps and also learn about citizen-based conservation projects.

The General Land Office (GLO) Records Project in Springfield, Virginia, houses documents about land transfers during U.S. westward expansion. At this office, BLM maintains more than 9 million historic records dating back to 1787.

The Jupiter Inlet Natural Area shelters Florida oak scrub, an imperiled habitat for specialized plants and animals that survive nowhere else. Photographers, birdwatchers, and botanists are sure to enjoy this vestige of old Florida, and history enthusiasts will appreciate tours of the picturesque Jupiter Lighthouse.

If you live in the eastern United States, you may find public lands virtually just beyond your own backyard. These lands boast a wide variety of resources for recreational pursuits, places for city dwellers to get away from it all, and critical habitat for important wildlife.

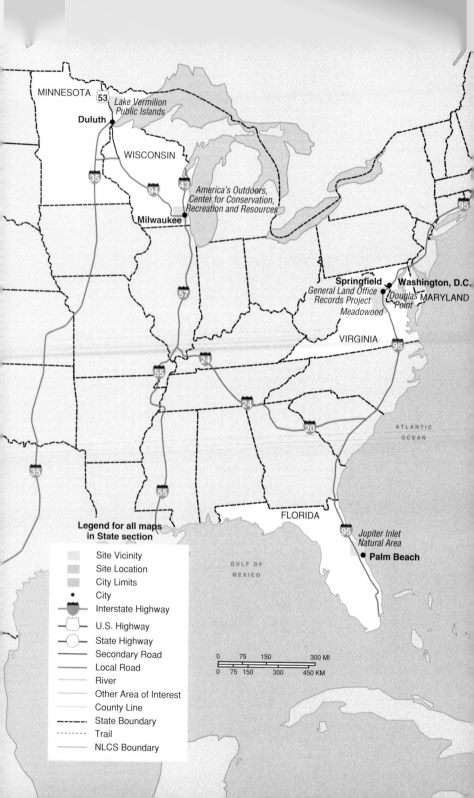

MINNESOTA   (53)   *Lake Vermilion
Public Islands*

Duluth

WISCONSIN

I-35   I-94   I-43   *America's Outdoors,
Center for Conservation,
Recreation and Resources*

Milwaukee

I-57

Springfield   **Washington, D.C.**
*General Land Office
Records Project
Meadowood*   *Douglas
Point*   MARYLAND

VIRGINIA

I-55   I-24

I-24   I-95

I-20

ATLANTIC
OCEAN

I-35

I-55

FLORIDA

I-95   *Jupiter Inlet
Natural Area*

Palm Beach

**Legend for all maps
in State section**

GULF OF
MEXICO

	Site Vicinity
	Site Location
	City Limits
•	City
	Interstate Highway
	U.S. Highway
	State Highway
	Secondary Road
	Local Road
	River
	Other Area of Interest
	County Line
	State Boundary
	Trail
	NLCS Boundary

0	75	150		300 MI

0	75	150	300	450 KM

America's Outdoors Center for Conservation, Education, and Recreation

Location

The Gas Light Building, downtown Milwaukee, Wisconsin.

Description

The America's Outdoors Center offers the public convenient, "one-stop" shopping for a wide range of conservation and educational materials, as well as maps, brochures, and other information on Federal recreation areas and public lands nationwide.

The America's Outdoors Center has a professional staff to assist with citizen-based conservation projects and activities, and offers an array of resource materials, including posters, a lending library of educational trunks, lesson plans, activity guides, CDs, and video-tapes for educators to use to supplement their existing classroom curricula. Federal Recreation Passports and National Forest visitor maps can be purchased to facilitate trips to Federal recreation areas and campgrounds.

America's Outdoors also helps Milwaukee-area communities protect local rivers, trails, and green spaces. By offering resources for successful outreach programs to local schools and organizations, the staff of America's Outdoors helps communities achieve their conservation goals.

Directions

In downtown Milwaukee, follow Inter-state 794 east to the Van Buren Street exit and drive north 2.5 blocks to Wisconsin Avenue. The Gas Light Building is located on the northwest

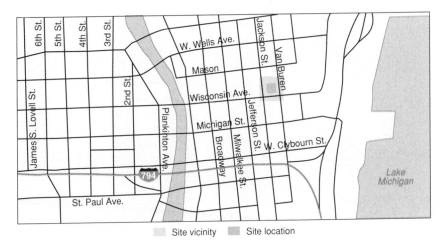

Site vicinity ■ Site location

America's Outdoors, a "one-stop" public information center located in downtown Milwaukee, Wisconsin, provides recreation information on Federal lands, as well as assistance with conservation projects and environmental education programs.
(Sylvia Jordan, BLM Milwaukee Field Office)

corner of Van Buren Street and Wisconsin Avenue.

Visitor Activities
The center offers educational, natural resource, and recreation information to the public.

Special Features
Milwaukee's Urban Tree House Site (located between North 22nd and 23rd Streets and between West McKinley and West Juneau Avenues, 1 mile from the downtown area) is an innovative project that is an excellent example of an America's Outdoors educational program.

Permits, Fees, Limitations
There are fees for some materials.

Accessibility
The center is wheelchair-accessible.

Camping and Lodging
Lodging is available at several nearby hotels. Restaurants and department stores are located within a reasonable walking distance or are accessible by local bus lines. The Grand Avenue Mall is also located in the vicinity.

Food and Supplies
Restaurants are located within several blocks in downtown Milwaukee.

First Aid

First aid kits are maintained at this facility. The nearest hospital is Sinai Samaritan in downtown Milwaukee.

Additional Information

America's Outdoors is a partnership effort among BLM's Eastern States Office; the National Park Service; the U.S. Fish and Wildlife Service; the USDA Forest Service; and the Natural Resources Conservation Service. The facility is open Monday–Friday, 9 a.m.–5 p.m., year-round, except for Federal holidays.

Contact Information

America's Outdoors, Center for Conservation, Education, and Recreation
626 E. Wisconsin Avenue
Milwaukee, WI 53202
Tel: (414) 297-3693
Fax: (414) 297-3660
www.americasoutdoors.gov

Activity Codes

other - public information and environmental education.

Douglas Point

Location

Suburban Maryland, 35 miles south of Washington, DC.

Description

Douglas Point is a 570-acre tract along the Potomac River in Charles County, Maryland. The site, managed cooperatively by BLM and the State of Maryland, offers a variety of public recreation ranging from hiking to seasonal hunting. A relatively old coastal plain, hosting mixed hardwoods and dotted with wetland seeps, provides habitat for a diversity of wildlife, including migratory songbirds and various mammals, reptiles, and amphibians.

Directions

From Washington, DC, take Interstate 295 about 7 miles south to Maryland State Highway 210 south. Follow State Highway 210 south 18 miles to State Highway 225, then take State Highway 225 southeast 2 miles to State Highway 224 at Mason Springs. Travel southwest approximately 6 miles to Douglas Point.

Visitor Activities

Plant viewing, wildlife viewing, hiking, geologic sightseeing, historic site, bird-watching, and deer hunting in season.

Special Features

The shoreline of the Potomac River hosts many cultural and natural resources, including sunken ships from the World War I era, and fossils from the Paleocene epoch about 58 million years ago. Several nesting bald eagles and ospreys have been reported at the site. In addition to the wetland seeps, a wild rice wetland provides for a variety of waterfowl nesting. Mammals include deer, raccoons, muskrats, beavers, and foxes.

Permits, Fees, Limitations

Day use only.

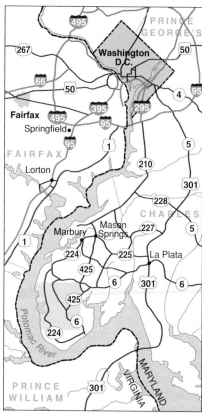

Accessibility
None.

Camping and Lodging
Camping is available in the immediate vicinity at Smallwood State Park, 3 miles north on State Highway 224. Contact the Maryland State Forest and Parks Reservation Center, 1-888-432-2267.

Food and Supplies
Restaurants are located within 8 miles of Douglas Point on State Highway 210.

First Aid
The nearest hospital is in LaPlata, 14 miles east via State Highway 6.

Additional Information
The BLM office is open from 8 a.m.– 5 p.m. daily, including weekends.

Contact Information
BLM - Eastern States
Lower Potomac Field Station
10406 Gunston Road
Lorton, VA 22079
Tel: (703) 339-8009
Fax: (703) 339-3313
www.es.blm.gov/programs/land/ lowerpotomac/index.html

Activity Codes

There are excellent opportunities for wildlife viewing within the wetlands and hardwood forests of Douglas Point, Maryland.
(Bill Davenport, BLM Eastern States Office)

General Land Office Records Project

Location
13 miles south of Washington, DC, at the BLM-Eastern States Office in Springfield, Virginia.

Description
As the successor agency to the original General Land Office (GLO), BLM-Eastern States maintains more than 9 million historic land documents at its Springfield, Virginia, office. Documents include survey plats and field notes, homestead patents, cash entry and serial patents, military warrants, and railroad grants. Some of these historic documents were among the very first land records to develop from the Land Ordinance of 1785, which authorized the disposal of Federal lands for the settlement of our nation.

Directions
From Washington, DC, follow Interstate 395 south 9 miles to its junction with Interstate 95 in Springfield. Follow Interstate 95 south 2 miles to the Backlick Road/Fullerton Road exit. Turn right at the first light onto Fullerton Road. Turn left at the third light onto Boston Boulevard. BLM-Eastern States is approximately 0.25 mile on the right. The visitor entrance and parking lot are located at the rear of the building.

Visitor Activities
Genealogical and historical research.

Special Features
Original documents are stored in acid-free boxes and protected in fire-proof and temperature-controlled vaults. These records are valuable resources, especially for amateur historians and genealogists. For example, a surveyor might have recorded the names of settlers, and included a description of land formations, climate, soil, and plant and animal life in the field notes. The

Site vicinity   Site location

patent (deed) contained the new landowner's name, the legal land description, and date of issue. Often, the information derived from a patent can be the link needed to piece together a family's history.

Permits, Fees, Limitations
None.

Accessibility
The research room, vending room, and restrooms are wheelchair-accessible.

Camping and Lodging
Camping is available at two nearby Northern Virginia Regional Parks. For specific information and directions, contact Bull Run Regional Park (approximately 30 miles west) at (703) 631-0550, or Pohick Bay Regional Park (16 miles south) at (703) 339-6104. Lodging is available at hotels in the Springfield, Virginia, area.

Food and Supplies
Restaurants are located within walking distance. Snack foods and soft drinks are available from vending machines in the building.

First Aid
First aid kits are maintained at this facility. The nearest hospital is located in Fairfax, 10 miles away via Interstate 95 north and Interstate 495 west.

Additional Information
The office is open to the public for research from 8 a.m.–4:30 p.m., Monday–Friday, excluding Federal holidays.

BLM-Eastern States safeguards the first land conveyance records for the public domain states of Alabama, Arkansas, Florida, Illinois, Indiana, Iowa, Louisiana, Michigan, Minnesota, Mississippi, Missouri, Ohio, and Wisconsin. Eastern States also maintains land conveyance records issued by the General Land Office from July 1, 1908, through the mid-1960s for 30 public land states, including some western states. Many of these documents are computerized and can be accessed online at the GLO website at *www.glorecords.blm.gov*.

Because the 13 original colonies and their territories were not part of the Federal lands acquired during national expansion, BLM does not maintain the land records of the District of Columbia or 18 eastern non-public-lands states. Those states are Connecticut, Delaware, Georgia, Kentucky, Maine, Maryland, Massachusetts, New Hampshire, New Jersey, New York, North Carolina, Pennsylvania, Rhode Island, South Carolina, Tennessee, Vermont, Virginia, and West Virginia. Inquiries concerning land records for these states should be directed to the individual states' archives or land record offices.

Contact Information
BLM - Eastern States
7450 Boston Boulevard
Springfield, VA 22153
Tel: (703) 440-1602
Fax: (703) 440-1609
www.glorecords.blm.gov

Activity Codes
other – genealogical and historical research

The BLM Eastern States Office maintains more than 9 million historic land title records dating back to 1787. *(BLM Eastern States Office)*

Jupiter Inlet Natural Area

Location

Approximately 20 miles north of West Palm Beach, Florida.

Description

The Jupiter Inlet Natural Area is a virtual "island" of sand, pine forest, and oak scrub that surrounds the historic Jupiter Lighthouse near the thriving communities of Jupiter and Tequesta, Florida. This vestige of a once-widespread plant community supports a host of rare and endemic plant species, as well as a breeding population of scrub jays, a Federally-listed threatened species.

Directions

From West Palm Beach, follow Interstate 95 north 16 miles to Indiantown Road (State Highway 706) at exit 87A. Follow Indiantown Road east toward Jupiter for approximately

Once choked with invasive, exotic plants, the reconstructed wetlands at the Jupiter Inlet Natural Area in Florida are now an integral part of Indian River Lagoon, one of the most diverse estuaries in the country. *(Jerry Sintz, BLM Utah State Office (retired))*

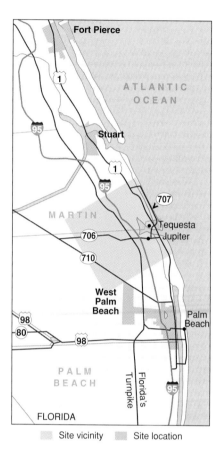

Special Features

An award-winning tidal wetland, constructed along the Intracoastal Waterway, provides habitat for wading birds and a nursery for marine fish. The picturesque Jupiter Lighthouse has been recently restored to mint condition. Tours are offered by the Loxahatchee River Historical Society. Interpretive programs focus on the history of the construction of the lighthouse and the lives of the early lighthouse keepers, providing poignant stories of life in south Florida in the 1800s.

Permits, Fees, Limitations

None.

Accessibility

The lighthouse is not wheelchair-accessible. Deep sand on much of the tract limits access by wheelchairs. The lighthouse visitor center and restrooms are universally accessible.

Camping and Lodging

Lodging is available at numerous nearby hotels and resorts in Jupiter (3 miles south) and West Palm Beach (12 miles southwest). There are several commercial and public campsites within 15 miles of Jupiter.

Food and Supplies

A full range of restaurants and stores is available in the Jupiter area.

First Aid

The Jupiter Urgent Care facility is located at 1335 W. Indiantown Road; the nearest hospital is the Jupiter Medical Center at 1210 S. Old Dixie Highway in Jupiter.

3 miles, and after the drawbridge, turn left and go north on U.S. Highway 1 approximately 1.5 miles to Beach Road (State Highway 707). The natural area and the associated Jupiter Lighthouse Park straddle State Highway 707 immediately east of U.S. Highway 1. The visitor center is located in the white barracks building at the southern end of Lighthouse Park.

Visitor Activities

Wildlife viewing, birdwatching, picnicking, plant viewing, interpretation, historic site, and hiking.

Additional Information

The Jupiter Inlet Natural Area is open to foot traffic only. Vehicles must stay on paved public roads. Lighthouse tours are available through the Loxahatchee River Historical Society. Tickets are available from the lighthouse visitor center located at the southern end of the tract. Tours are available Sunday–Wednesday from 10 a.m.–3:15 p.m., and typically last 40–45 minutes. For safety reasons, shoes must have an enclosed heel or strap, and children must be at least 48 inches tall. The lighthouse's 105 stairs can be challenging, especially during the heat of the summer. For more information and updates, visitors should call the lighthouse visitor center at (561) 747-8380. Portions of the tract continue to be used by the U.S. Coast Guard. These areas are marked by signs and fenced and are not accessible to the public. Nearby attractions include The Nature Conservancy's Blowing Rocks Preserve, Loxahatchee River Historical Museum, Hobe Sound National Wildlife Refuge, and Jonathan Dickerson State Park.

Contact Information

BLM - Jackson Field Office
411 Briarwood, Suite 404
Jackson, MS 39206
Tel: (601) 977-5400
Fax: (601) 977-5440
www.es.blm.gov/programs/land/jupiter/index.html

Activity Codes

Lake Vermilion Public Islands

Location

Approximately 85 miles north of Duluth, Minnesota, stretching 40 miles between the communities of Cook and Tower, Minnesota.

Description

Lake Vermilion, which covers 40,000 acres in northeastern Minnesota, was carved out of bedrock by glaciers. The lake has hundreds of bays and inlets, 1,200 miles of shoreline, and more than 365 islands. Of these, 70 are small, widely-scattered islands of public land. Lake Vermilion is one of the largest lakes in northeastern Minnesota to allow motorized boats. Fishing is the most popular form of recreation associated with the public islands (their shores provide excellent fish habitat), and some of the larger islands provide good sites for lakeside lunches.

Public islands enhance the fishing opportunities for recreationists at Lake Vermilion, Minnesota. *(Sylvia Jordan, BLM Milwaukee Field Office)*

Directions

From Duluth, take U.S. Highway 53 north 61 miles through the town of Virginia. To visit the western end of the lake, continue north on U.S. Highway 53 about 26 miles to Cook and follow State Highway 24 to the lake. To visit the eastern end of the lake, take the State Highway 169 turnoff north of Virginia and travel 25 miles northeast to Tower. The east end of the lake is accessible from a public boat ramp on Hoodoo Point Road, 2 miles north of Tower. The public islands are accessible only by boat.

Site vicinity   Site location

Visitor Activities

Sailing, canoeing, kayaking, motor boating, fishing, picnicking, houseboat mooring, wildlife viewing, birdwatching, and plant viewing.

Special Features

Lake Vermilion is home to more than 18 pairs of bald eagles, hundreds of loons, and dozens of ospreys. Other wildlife in the area includes deer, moose, minks, otters, and occasional wolves. Fish species include walleyes, bass, bluegills, and muskellunges.

Permits, Fees, Limitations

None.

Accessibility

The Wakemup Bay public water-access site (at the western end of Lake Vermilion) provides universal access. Road access to the site is from U.S. Highway 53 and State Highway 24, 10 miles north of Cook. There is a universal-access fishing pier at Hoodoo Point.

Camping and Lodging

McKinley Park Campground is at the eastern end of the lake in Soudan, 2 miles east of Tower and 27 miles northeast of Virginia. Numerous privately-operated lodges and cabins are also located in the area.

Food and Supplies

Food and supplies are available in Cook and Tower.

First Aid

First aid is available in Cook and Tower. A hospital is located in Virginia.

Additional Information

The Minnesota Department of Natural Resources maintains free, public water-access sites. Privately-maintained boat-access sites are also available. The lake receives heaviest use from Memorial Day–Labor Day; less use occurs in late spring and early fall. During winter months, snowmobiles can be run on trails in the vicinity of Lake Vermilion, and on the frozen lake.

Contact Information

BLM - Milwaukee Field Office
626 E. Wisconsin Avenue
Milwaukee, WI 53202

Tel: (414) 297-4400
Fax: (414) 297-4409
www.es.blm.gov/programs/land/ lake_vermilion/index.html

Activity Codes

other - houseboat mooring

Meadowood

Location

Suburban Virginia, 20 miles south of Washington, DC.

Description

Meadowood is an 800-acre special recreation management area recently acquired by BLM for recreation and other public uses. The site contains a 50-stall horse barn and hosts a variety of ecosystems providing habitat for diverse wildlife, including foxes, deer, raccoons, rabbits, and groundhogs, over 100 species of birds, and various amphibians and reptiles.

Directions

From Washington, DC, follow Interstate 395 south 9 miles to Interstate 95 at the Springfield interchange. Continue on Interstate 95 approximately 6 miles to the Lorton exit (Exit 163). At the exit, turn left onto Lorton Road. Follow Lorton Road 0.5 mile to Armistead Road, and turn right. Follow Armistead Road 1 mile to U.S. Highway 1. Turn right onto

U.S. Highway 1 and follow it approximately 2 miles to Gunston Road. Carefully turn left onto Gunston Road, and follow Gunston Road approximately 2 miles to Meadowood on the right.

Visitor Activities

Wild horse and burro viewing, birdwatching, wildlife viewing, hiking, horseback riding, and environmental education.

Special Features

Habitat includes protected areas for blue herons, wood ducks, screech owls, bluebirds, and tree frogs.

Permits, Fees, Limitations

None.

Accessibility

None.

Camping and Lodging

Camping is available at Pohick Bay Regional Park, approximately 2 miles north. Contact the Northern

Virginia Regional Park Authority at (703) 352-5900. Lodging is available at hotels located in the Springfield, Virginia, area, about 16 miles north.

Food and Supplies

Restaurants are located within 2 miles of Meadowood at the intersection of Gunston Road and U.S. Highway 1.

First Aid

First aid kits are maintained at Meadowood. The nearest hospital is in Woodbridge, Virginia, 7 miles south via U.S. Highway 1.

Additional Information

The BLM Office at Meadowood is open from 8 a.m.–5 p.m. daily, including weekends. Under the management plan for Meadowood, wild horses will be brought to the site for periodic adoption events. Eventually, the plan provides for a permanent holding facility for up to 50 wild horses. Contact BLM for current information.

Contact Information

BLM - Eastern States
Lower Potomac Field Station
10406 Gunston Road
Lorton, Virginia   22079
Tel: (703) 339-8009
Fax: (703) 339-3313
www.es.blm.gov/programs/land/meadowood/index.html

Activity Codes

other - environmental education

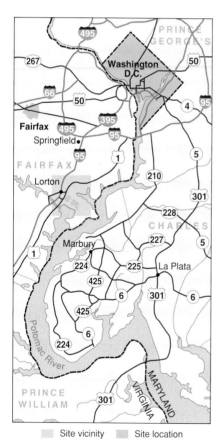

Meadowood provides visitors with a spectacular setting in which to enjoy Virginia's autumn foliage. *(Don Cabrera, BLM Washington Office (retired))*

Idaho's public lands are rugged, beautiful, and largely unchanged since the time of explorers Lewis and Clark. *(Karen Wattenmaker)*

It's not just the natural splendor of Idaho's public lands that enchants visitors—it's also the seclusion of the state's special destinations. With just over a million residents scattered across 53 million acres, Idaho offers ample opportunity to find peace and solitude on the public lands, which comprise 22 percent of the state.

Adventures on Idaho's public lands range from the plush to the primitive. Visitors who want to venture outdoors without leaving the comforts of home will enjoy exploring public lands within the resort atmosphere of Coeur d'Alene Lake, while travelers who want a more rugged and remote experience will find it on the Owyhee Uplands Back Country Byway. Although summer is "high season" on Idaho's public lands, the other seasons offer adventures as well. In the fall, hunters will find abundant birds and big game; in the winter, hearty souls can cross-country ski, tour by snowmobile, and try ice fishing; and in the spring, everyone will find Idaho's wildflowers worth the trip.

Travelers from around the world visit Idaho in the spring to see eagles and other birds of prey soaring in the sky at what may be the world's largest raptor nesting site, the Snake River Birds of Prey National Conservation Area. Anglers relish the opportunity to cast a line in cool, clear river waters in hopes of landing a trophy cutthroat trout. Amateur and professional historians alike can retrace the footsteps of pioneers who trekked west in the 1800s on emigrant trails. One can still see the ruts carved into the earth by settlers' wagon wheels, mute testament to early Americans' courage and adventurous spirit. And truly wild whitewater awaits the intrepid—and well-prepared—boater on Idaho's spectacular rivers.

Idaho

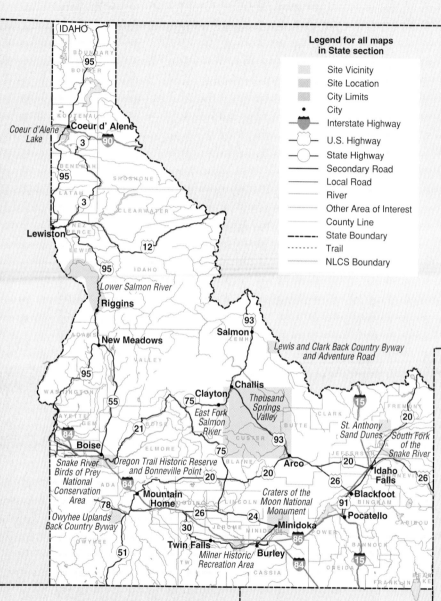

IDAHO

95

Coeur d'Alene
Lake

Coeur d'Alene

3

90

95

3

Lewiston

12

95

Lower Salmon River

Riggins

New Meadows

Salmon

93

Lewis and Clark Back Country Byway
and Adventure Road

95

Clayton

Challis

55

75

Thousand
Springs
Valley

15

21

East Fork
Salmon
River

93

20

84

75

St. Anthony
Sand Dunes

South Fork
of the
Snake River

Boise

Oregon Trail Historic Reserve
and Bonneville Point

Arco

20

20

Snake River
Birds of Prey
National
Conservation
Area

20

26

Idaho
Falls

26

84

Mountain
Home

Craters of the
Moon National
Monument

91

Blackfoot

78

26

24

Pocatello

Owyhee Uplands
Back Country Byway

30

Minidoka

86

51

Twin Falls

Burley

84

15

Milner Historic/
Recreation Area

**Legend for all maps
in State section**

Site Vicinity
Site Location
City Limits
● City
Interstate Highway
U.S. Highway
State Highway
Secondary Road
Local Road
River
Other Area of Interest
County Line
State Boundary
Trail
NLCS Boundary

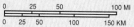

0   25   50   100 MI
0 25 50   100   150 KM

Coeur d'Alene Lake

Location
In and south of the City of Coeur d'Alene in northwestern Idaho.

Description
The sparkling waters of Coeur d'Alene Lake, considered by many to be one of the most beautiful lakes in the world, offer a variety of outdoor recreational activities year-round in a setting of exceptional scenic beauty. The panhandle of Idaho has the greatest concentration of lakes in the northwestern U.S.; Coeur d'Alene Lake is the largest and most popular.

Directions
To drive around the lake: From Coeur d'Alene, travel 11 miles east on Interstate 90 to State Highway 97 (Exit 22), then south on State Highway 97 and State Highway 3 about 46 miles to the town of St. Maries. Continue 19 miles west on State Highway 5 to Plummer, and then north 39 miles back to Coeur d'Alene on U.S. 95. The total distance is about 115 miles. The 36-mile section of State Highway 97 from Interstate 90 to State Highway 3 is designated as an Idaho State Scenic Byway. Eight boat ramps are located along the lakefront in the city of Coeur d'Alene; three are in the town of Wolf Lodge Bay, 5 miles east.

Visitor Activities
Canoeing, kayaking, sailing, motorboating, fishing, swimming, wildlife viewing, hiking, hunting for deer, elk, and wild turkeys.

Special Features
Each winter, a population of bald eagles visits the lake on its southward migration to feed on the abundant supply of kokanee salmon.

Permits, Fees, Limitations
Alcohol and firearms are prohibited at the Mica Bay Boater Park, located 15 miles south of Coeur d'Alene off U.S. 95. Check with the Idaho Department of Fish and Game for hunting and fishing license requirements, (208) 334-3700.

Accessibility
The Blackwell Island Recreation Site, opened in May of 2003, is the newest and largest boat launching site in the

The clear, blue waters of Coeur d'Alene Lake sparkle at Beauty Bay, one of the lake's premier day-use areas.
(Karen Wattenmaker)

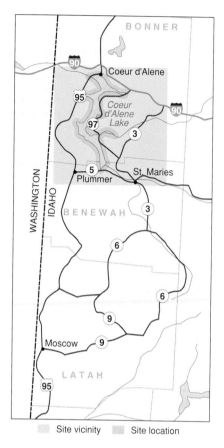

Site vicinity   Site location

Highway 95. Windy Bay and Mica Bay are accessible only by boat. Camping fees and daily parking fees are charged at some sites; check with BLM for details. A 14-day stay limit applies. Lodging is available in Coeur d'Alene.

Food and Supplies
Food and supplies are available in Coeur d'Alene.

First Aid
Kootenai County operates a 911 emergency dispatch for first aid needs. The Kootenai Medical Center is located in Coeur d'Alene.

Additional Information
At an elevation of 2,152 feet, the Coeur d'Alene area has a temperature range from an average of 64°F in the summer to an average of 32°F in the winter. The average annual rainfall is 26 inches.

A prime eagle viewing area in winter is Wolf Lodge Bay, located 5 miles east of Coeur d'Alene. From Coeur d'Alene, travel 4 miles east on Interstate 90 to the Wolf Lodge Bay exit. Travel 1 mile south on State Highway 97 to several shoreline turnouts from which to view these magnificent birds.

Contact Information
BLM - Coeur d'Alene Field Office
1808 N. Third Street
Coeur d'Alene, ID 83814
Tel: (208) 769-5000
Fax: (208) 769-5050
www.id.blm.gov/offices/coeurd'alene

Activity Codes

area and is fully accessible. The site is located near the junction of the lake and Spokane River within the city of Coeur d'Alene, off U.S. Highway 95. The Beauty Bay picnic site and trail, located 20 miles east of Coeur d'Alene off State Highway 97, are also fully accessible.

Camping and Lodging
Camping is available at Mica Bay Boater Park, located about 7 miles south of Coeur d'Alene off U.S. Highway 95, and Windy Bay, located about 18 miles south of Coeur d'Alene off U.S.

Craters of the Moon National Monument

Location
86 miles west of Idaho Falls; 18 miles southwest of Arco, Idaho.

Description
Craters of the Moon National Monument, co-managed by BLM and the National Park Service, is a vast open area that hosts some of the world's finest examples of recent basaltic volcanism, comparable only to the rift volcanic systems of Hawaii and Iceland. The site includes Holocene-age (less than 10,000 years old) lava flows, remnant native plant communities, rift volcanism crack sets, and volcanic caves. The monument also contains "kipukas," islands of native sagebrush-grassland communities surrounded by lava. Black night skies and broad open country characterize this wild landscape.

Directions
From Idaho Falls, follow U.S. Highway 20 west about 68 miles to Arco. Follow U.S. Highway 93 about 18 miles southwest to the Craters of the Moon Visitor Center. Other parts of the monument can be accessed on unpaved roads from the town of Carey, also located on U.S. Highway 93 (25 miles west of the visitor center); from the town of American Falls via Pleasant Valley Road (67 miles west of Idaho Falls); or from two locations on State Highway 24 near the town of Minidoka (132 miles west of Idaho Falls).

Visitor Activities
Hiking, wildlife viewing, geologic sightseeing, and big-game hunting.

Special Features
A main feature of the monument is the Great Rift, a 62 mile-long system of fractures in the Earth's crust and one of the few exposed volcanic rift systems in the world. Despite the harsh environment, many species of wildlife live here, including mule deer, mountain lions, elk, and moose.

Permits, Fees, Limitations
Contact the Idaho Department of Fish and Game at (208) 334-3700 for information on hunting license requirements.

Accessibility
The visitor center and the developed campground nearby have accessible toilets. One campsite in the campground is accessible.

Camping and Lodging
Camping is available at many dispersed primitive sites throughout the monument.

Basaltic fissure volcanic eruptions, such as the ones that produced Idaho's Great Rift pictured here, are characterized by relatively slow extrusion of lavas from fissures or vents. (Jerry Sintz, BLM Utah State Office (retired))

A 14-day stay limit applies. Modern camping and lodging facilities exist in the gateway communities of Arco (18 miles), Minidoka (43 miles on unpaved roads), American Falls (45 miles on unpaved roads), Twin Falls (85 miles), and Shoshone (64 miles), and near the National Park Service visitor center at the monument entrance on State Route 93. Fees are only charged on National Park Service developed campsites.

Food and Supplies
Food, lodging, and fuel are available in Arco, Minidoka, American Falls, Twin Falls and Shoshone.

First Aid
Travelers must possess at least basic first aid skills; assistance is a considerable distance away. The emergency telephone number for this area is 911. Hospitals are located in Twin Falls, Idaho Falls (86 miles), and Ketchum (57 miles).

Additional Information
This is a remote desert setting. Precipitation is less than 12 inches per year, with most falling as winter snow. Proper preparation is critical. Roads are usually impassable from late fall to early spring. In summer, the temperature often reaches more than 100°F, with persistent high winds. Visitors should come prepared for any contingency because assistance can be hours or days away. Plenty of water, a high-clearance, four-wheel-drive vehicle, first aid kit, maps, and a reliable form of communication are strongly advised. In the summer, wildfires are a threat in the monument area. If you see wildfire, dial 911 or #FIRE on your mobile phone.

Contact Information
BLM - Shoshone Field Office
PO Box 2-B
Shoshone, ID 83352
Tel: (208) 732-7200
Fax: (208) 732-7317
www.id.blm.gov/offices/shoshone
www.nps.gov/crmo

Activity Codes

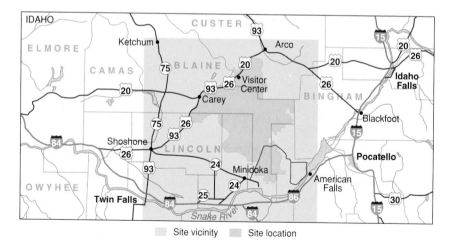

Site vicinity   Site location

East Fork Salmon River

Location
153 miles east of Boise; 20 miles southwest of Challis, Idaho.

Description
The roads that parallel the East Fork of the Salmon River and its feeder streams offer visitors an opportunity to see a wide variety of wildlife, as well as engage in a multitude of outdoor recreational activities. The roads climb from sagebrush plains at 5,400 feet through alpine forests at 10,000 feet.

Directions
From Boise, follow State Route 21 north 120 miles to Stanley, then follow State Route 75 east 33 miles to East Fork Road, which parallels the river upstream.

From Challis, travel south on U.S. Highway 93 for 3 miles. Turn right (southeast) onto State Highway 75 for 17 miles and turn left (southwest) onto East Fork Road. East Fork Road terminates at Bowery Guard Station, approximately 28 miles upstream from State Highway 75.

Visitor Activities
Wildlife viewing, wild horse viewing, hiking, horseback riding, four-wheel driving, mountain biking, fishing, and big-game hunting.

Special Features
Wild horses are likely to be seen on side trips up Spar Canyon and Road Creek Roads, which link East Fork Road to State Highway 75. Chukars, red-tailed hawks, moose, and mule deer frequent the lower elevations, while Rocky Mountain bighorn sheep, elk, and golden eagles can be seen at higher elevations.

Red-tailed hawks are adapted to live and hunt in open country, soaring over vast expanses in search of their principal prey: rabbits and rodents. A large stick nest, sometimes exceeding 30 inches in diameter, is constructed by both sexes in a large tree or on a cliff; breeding pairs often re-occupy the same nest year after year. *(BLM)*

Permits, Fees, Limitations

Along East Fork Road there are four wilderness study areas; travel in these areas is limited to roads which were constructed prior to their designation as wilderness areas in 1980. Winter snowfall restricts vehicle access on most secondary roads.

Accessibility

Accessible vault toilets are located at Herd Lake Overlook, Jimmy Smith Trailhead, and Little Boulder Creek Campground.

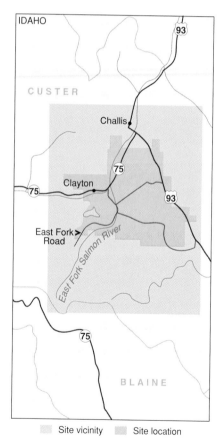

Site vicinity   Site location

Camping and Lodging

Camping is available at East Fork Campground (fee charged), located at the junction of State Highway 75 and East Fork Road; at Little Boulder Creek Campground (fee charged), located on East Fork Road about 22 miles south of its junction with State Highway 75. Dispersed camping is also available. Lodging is available in Challis.

Food and Supplies

Food and supplies are available in Challis, 20 miles northeast of the intersection of East Fork Road and State Highway 75.

First Aid

The closest medical clinic is located in Challis.

Additional Information

During most winters, much of East Fork Road is open and plowed. However, the stretch of East Fork Road that begins about 19 miles south of State Highway 75 is closed from November 30–May 1 to protect wintering big game. All roads leading from East Fork Road, except State Highway 75, are gravel or dirt and are subject to intermittent closure in inclement weather.

Contact Information

BLM - Challis Field Office
801 Blue Mountain Road
Challis, ID 83226
Tel: (208) 879-6200
Fax: (208) 879-6219
www.id.blm.gov/offices/challis

Activity Codes

Lewis and Clark Back Country Byway and Adventure Road

Location
A 39-mile loop road beginning and ending in Tendoy, Idaho, which is 141 miles northwest of Idaho Falls and 20 miles south of Salmon.

Description
The byway winds its way up to the Continental Divide through the scenic Beaverhead Mountains of the Bitterroot Range. From river bottoms through sagebrush hills to forested mountains, the drive offers the opportunity to visit portions of the Lewis and Clark National Historic Trail and the Continental Divide National Scenic Trail.

Directions
From Idaho Falls, follow Interstate 15 north 24 miles to Sage Junction (Exit 143). Then follow State Highway 33 west 12 miles to Mud Lake and State Highway 28. Follow State Highway 28 northwest 105 miles to Tendoy. From Salmon, Idaho, travel south 20 miles on State Highway 28 to Tendoy, and turn

The Lewis and Clark Back Country Byway crosses Lemhi Pass, homeland of the famous Native American guide Sacajawea. The mountains represented a formidable barrier to the explorers' Corps of Discovery in their 1805 quest to find the "Northwest Passage" to the Pacific Ocean. *(Leo Geis, Idaho Airships (used with permission))*

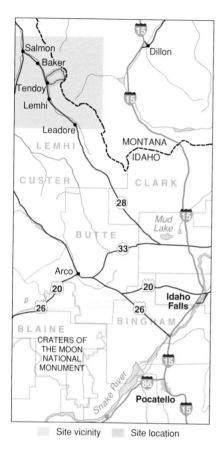

Site vicinity   Site location

toric sites, such as Lemhi Pass (elevation 7,373 feet) where Lewis and Clark crossed the Continental Divide, and access to Sharkey Hot Springs, a developed hot spring complex offering two soaking pools. Wildlife includes deer, elk, moose, bears, pronghorn antelope, and many bird species.

Permits, Fees, Limitations
The road is usually snow-covered from November–early June. During those months, the roadway is groomed for snowmobile use only.

Accessibility
Accessible vault toilets are located adjacent to the Tendoy store, the byway welcome site (3.5 miles north on Warm Springs Wood Road), and the Agency Creek Recreation Site, approximately 5 miles east on Agency Creek Road from Tendoy. Sharkey Hot Springs offers accessible vault toilets and two accessible soaking pools (1.5 miles east on Warm Springs Wood Road). Accessible vault toilets at Lemhi Pass are scheduled for construction in 2003.

Camping and Lodging
There are no campgrounds along the byway itself; primitive camping is available at the Agency Creek Recreation Site. Lodging is available in Salmon.

Food and Supplies
The Tendoy Store offers gas, some food items, byway information and interpretive services, and a post office. Portable toilets are located adjacent to the store.

First Aid
Travelers must possess at least basic first aid skills; assistance is some distance away. Ambulances are available in Salmon and Leadore (25 miles south of

left onto the byway. The byway roads are also known as Warm Spring Wood Road and Agency Creek Road.

Visitor Activities
Historic site, interpretation, wildlife viewing, birdwatching, hiking, mountain biking, big-game hunting, snowmobiling, cross-country skiing, motorboating, scenic drives, and swimming.

Special Features
Sweeping views of mountain ranges and river valleys are typical along the Continental Divide. The byway includes his-

Tendoy via State Highway 28). A hospital is located in Salmon. There is very limited mobile phone service along the byway.

Additional Information

The gravel road is a single lane, with occasional pullouts for passing. From Salmon, the trip takes at least half a day. Vehicle access is best in the summer, as snow blocks the roads during the winter months. Roads are very rough and at least one inflated spare tire is a must. Brochures and information are available at the Tendoy Store and from the BLM/U.S. Forest Service joint office in Salmon. The byway is a cooperative effort of the Salmon Field Office, BLM, and the Salmon-Challis National Forest.

The route has been designated a state Scenic Byway by the State of Idaho.

Contact Information

BLM - Salmon Field Office and
Salmon-Challis National Forest
50 Highway 93 South
Salmon, ID 83467
Tel: (208) 756-5400
Fax: (208) 756-5436
www.id.blm.gov/offices/salmon
www.fs.fed.us/r4/sc/lewis-clark/index.htm

Activity Codes

Lower Salmon River

Location

170 miles northeast of Boise, Idaho

Description

This river features 112 miles of Class III–IV whitewater in the second–deepest canyon in the United States. About 53 miles of the river, from White Bird (29 miles north of Riggins) downstream to the confluence of the Snake and Salmon Rivers, are roadless and accessible only by boat.

Whitewater boaters enjoy exciting rapids and breathtaking beauty on a 112-mile stretch of the Lower Salmon River, the longest free-flowing river in the lower 48 states. *(Karen Wattenmaker)*

Directions

From Boise, follow State Highway 44 west for 7 miles to State Highway 55. Travel on State Highway 55 north 111 miles to U.S. Highway 95 and follow U.S. Highway 95 north 35 miles to Riggins. Access to the river is via U.S. Highway 95 north in Riggins and 29 miles further in White Bird, Idaho.

Visitor Activities

Whitewater rafting, kayaking, fishing, chukar partridge hunting, wildlife viewing, and scenic drives.

Special Features

Extensive white sand beaches, interesting Native American pictographs, and early Chinese mining sites are found along this scenic river corridor. Bighorn sheep, elk, deer, bears, and eagles can be seen along the riverbanks.

Permits, Fees, Limitations

Self-issued boating permits are required for all trips below White Bird. Regulations are printed on self-issue permits, which must be filled out prior to all trips. Portable toilets and fire pans are required. Check with the Idaho Department of Fish and Game for hunting and fishing license requirements, (208) 334-3700.

Accessibility

Hammer Creek Recreation Site, located 1.5 miles northwest of White Bird, and Slate Creek Recreation Site, located 8 miles south of White Bird, are fully accessible.

Camping and Lodging

Camping is available for a fee at Hammer Creek and Slate Creek Recreation Sites. Lodging is available in Riggins

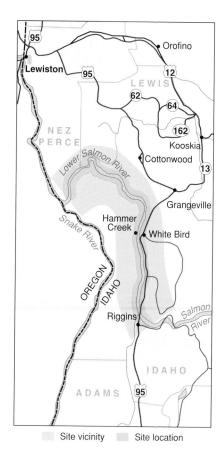

Site vicinity   Site location

(153 miles north of Boise), Grangeville (15 miles north of White Bird), and Cottonwood (30 miles north of White Bird).

Food and Supplies

Food and supplies are available in Riggins and Cottonwood.

First Aid

There is a medical clinic in Riggins, and hospitals are located in Cottonwood and Grangeville. Emergency medical technicians are located in Cottonwood, Riggins, and Whitebird.

Additional Information

July–October are best for boating, with generally hot, dry conditions. The mild winter months are best for fishing; steelhead trout are plentiful. High water from snowmelt in May and June creates dangerous boating conditions. Most popular are 1-day trips in the Riggins area and multi-day trips from White Bird to the Snake River. Commercial outfitter services are available in Riggins and White Bird. The Lower Salmon River Boaters Guide is available from BLM. Whitewater enthusiasts are encouraged to view the video clip "Ride the Lower Salmon River's Bodacious Bounce" at the web address below.

Contact Information

BLM - Cottonwood Field Office
Route 3, Box 181
Cottonwood, ID 83522
Tel: (208) 962-3245
Fax: (208) 962-3275
www.id.blm.gov/offices/cottonwood

Activity Codes

Milner Historic/Recreation Area

Location

31 miles east of Twin Falls and 9 miles west of Burley, Idaho.

Description

This 2,055-acre area, located on the banks of the Snake River, provides visitors with opportunities to hike the Oregon Trail, an important part of Idaho's past, and also to enjoy modern-day outdoor recreational activities. A 1-mile interpretive trail enables visitors to see wagon ruts and learn about the pioneers as well as the ecology of the

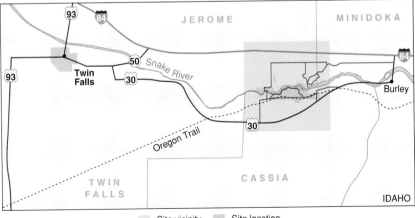

Site vicinity   Site location

Snake River Valley. Boat ramps and docks provide access to the Snake River for anglers and canoeists. Visitors can walk the shoreline, boat on the lake, or travel 3 miles of dirt road in an easterly direction.

Directions

From Twin Falls, follow U.S. Highway 30 east 31 miles. Or, from Burley, follow U.S. Highway 30 west about 9 miles.

At the Milner Historic/Recreation Area sign turn north for 1 mile, then travel west for approximately 3 miles on a gravel road to the parking area. From the parking area, a sign directs visitors to the boat ramp a short distance east, where there is another parking lot and a picnic area.

Visitor Activities

Historic site, wildlife viewing, fishing, motorboating, hiking, picnicking, snowmobiling, and interpretation.

Special Features

An Oregon Trail interpretive shelter and signs are located at Milner, along with several miles of wagon ruts. The Milner Reservoir, which is formed behind a dam on the Snake River at Milner, is a designated Watchable Wildlife Site. Bird species include yellow warblers, American goldfinches, and belted kingfishers.

Permits, Fees, Limitations

There are daily per-vehicle entrance fees. There are also seasonal passes available from BLM. Check with the Idaho Department of Fish and Game for hunting and fishing license requirements, (208) 334-3700.

Accessibility

Vault toilets and a number of picnic tables are fully accessible.

Camping and Lodging

Camping is available along the Snake River at the Milner Boat Ramp, as well as several other dispersed locations within the recreation area. Lodging is available in Burley and Twin Falls.

Food and Supplies

Food and supplies are available in Burley and Twin Falls.

First Aid

The Cassia County Sheriff's Department can provide first aid. The nearest hospital is in Burley.

Additional Information

During late winter, the area can get very muddy and some roads are closed.

Contact Information

BLM - Burley Field Office
15 East 200 South
Burley, ID 83318
Tel: (208) 677-6641
Fax: (208) 677-6699
www.id.blm.gov/burley

Activity Codes

Oregon Trail Historic Reserve and Bonneville Point

Location
The Oregon Trail Historic Reserve is 13 miles east and Bonneville Point is 21 miles east of Boise, Idaho.

Description
The Oregon Trail Historic Reserve and Bonneville Point offer travelers a snap-shot of the past. They will see ruts carved more than 150 years ago by the wagon wheels of westbound emigrants on the Oregon Trail, learn how the city of Boise got its name, and discover how the trail influenced the growth and culture of the city. The Oregon Trail Historic Reserve provides trails for hiking and mountain biking. A mountain biking trail runs west from Bonneville Point to Discovery Park on the Boise River and eventually connects with the Boise Greenbelt System, a regional park system through the city of Boise.

Directions
Oregon Trail Historic Reserve: From Boise, follow Interstate 84 east 10 miles to Gowen Road (Exit 57). Follow Gowen Road (State Highway 21) east for 2.5 miles. Turn left on East Forest Lake Drive and follow it for 0.25 mile to the Oregon Trail Reserve.
Bonneville Point: From Boise, travel east on Interstate 84 for 17 miles to Blacks Creek (Exit 64). Turn left onto Blacks Creek Road, drive about 3.5 miles, turn left at the sign marked "Historical Site," and proceed for 1 mile to the Bonneville Point site.

Visitor Activities
Historic site, hiking, mountain biking, and interpretation.

Special Features
One of the main features at the Oregon Trail Historic Reserve is the Kelton Ramp, part of an old freight and stagecoach road built in the 1860s. This ramp greatly improved access to the Boise Valley, helping the city of Boise

Modern-day history buffs re-enact a portion of the pioneers' westward journey along an Idaho segment of the Oregon Trail. *(BLM)*

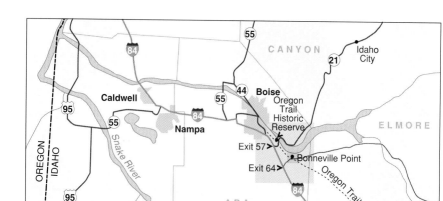

Site vicinity   Site location

grow. Bonneville Point features outstanding panoramic views of the Boise Valley and the Snake River Plain.

Permits, Fees, Limitations
None.

Accessibility
The Oregon Trail Historic Reserve has an accessible flush toilet. The Bonneville Point site can be accessed by wheelchair on a concrete sidewalk.

Camping and Lodging
No on-site camping is available. Lodging and camping are available in Boise.

Food and Supplies
Food and supplies are available in Boise.

First Aid
Two hospitals are located in Boise.

Additional Information
To make the trip more rewarding, visitors may wish to read the book *Emigrant Trails of Southern Idaho*, available from BLM. No restrooms or water are available at the Bonneville Point site.

Contact Information
BLM - Four Rivers Field Office
3948 Development Avenue
Boise, ID 83705
Tel: (208) 384-3300
Fax: (208) 384-3493
www.id.blm.gov/offices/fourrivers

Activity Codes

Owyhee Uplands Back Country Byway

Location
End points are 60 miles southeast of Boise in Grandview, Idaho, and 80 miles southwest of Boise in Jordan Valley, Oregon.

Description
This 101-mile route extends from Grandview, Idaho, to Jordan Valley, Oregon, and offers high-desert scenery at its finest. From expanses of sagebrush and grasslands to sheer, rock-walled river canyons, the drive provides an opportunity to visit a little-known and unchanged corner of the American West. Most of the route is a narrow, winding gravel road. From Boise, it is an all-day trip.

Deep Creek is one of many streams and rivers that drain southward into the Owyhee River. The Owyhee River is known for outstanding floating opportunities in the spring. Poison Creek Recreation Site (near Grandview) is a shady, cottonwood-lined streamside location that is perfect for a picnic.

Directions
The byway extends south and west from State Highway 78 in Grandview, Idaho, or south and east from U.S. Highway 95 in Jordan Valley, Oregon. From Grandview, travel southeast about 2 miles to the turn onto the byway. Part of the route is also called the Mud Flat Road. Or, from Jordan Valley, travel east out of town for 0.5 mile to the beginning of the byway.

Visitor Activities
Wildlife viewing, birdwatching, historic site, geologic sightseeing, cross-country hiking, mountain biking, and scenic drives.

Special Features
A beautiful rhyolite canyon, typical of the spectacular Owyhee Canyonlands country that extends to the south, can be observed at North Fork Campground, located about 30 miles east of Jordan Valley, where the byway crosses the North Fork gorge of the Owyhee

The North Fork of the Owyhee River flows in sheer-walled canyons and narrow gorges carved from a massive expanse of volcanic rock deposited 8–12 million years ago.
(Don Smurthwaite, Natl. Interagency Fire Center)

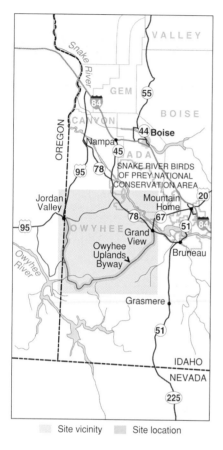

Site vicinity Site location

Camping and Lodging

Primitive camping is available at North Fork Campground. No lodging is available along the byway, but is available in Mountain Home, 23 miles northeast of Grandview, and in Jordan Valley.

Food and Supplies

There are no services along the byway. Limited food and supplies are available in Grandview and Jordan Valley.

First Aid

Travelers must possess at least basic first aid skills, since assistance is some distance away. Ambulances are available in Grandview and Bruneau (18 miles east via U.S. Highway 78). Hospitals are located in Mountain Home (23 miles east), Nampa (57 miles northwest), and Boise.

Additional Information

Hiking is best in spring and fall. Visitors should purchase the appropriate 1:100,000-scale BLM surface management maps and U.S. Geological Survey 7.5′ topographic quadrangles for areas they intend to explore. The byway is usually impassable November–March because of snow; travel is also hazardous when the road surface is moist. The route has been designated a State Scenic Byway by the State of Idaho.

Contact Information

BLM - Owyhee Field Office
3948 Development Avenue
Boise, ID 83705
Tel: (208) 384-3300
Fax: (208) 384-3493
www.id.blm.gov/offices/owyhee

Activity Codes

River. Old stone buildings that are part of the Turmes Homestead from the 1880s can be viewed from the road about 8 miles west of Grandview. Visitors can observe pronghorn, mule deer, and bighorn sheep in the deep canyons.

Permits, Fees, Limitations

None.

Accessibility

Vault toilets at North Fork Campground and Poison Creek Recreation Site (8 miles west of Grandview) are accessible.

Snake River Birds of Prey National Conservation Area

Location
20 miles south of Boise, Idaho.

Description
This 485,000-acre area, located along 81 miles of the Snake River, is home to the densest population of nesting birds of prey (raptors) in North America and perhaps the world. Visitors can see raptors by taking a raft or canoe trip through the area in the spring. Boating and fishing are popular activities, spring through fall, on the Snake River and at C.J. Strike Reservoir, near the southeastern part of the conservation area. Many miles of trails offer outstanding hiking, horseback riding, and mountain biking.

Directions
From Boise, follow Interstate 84 west 10 miles to Meridian (Exit 44). Turn left onto State Highway 69 and follow it 8 miles south to the town of Kuna. Turn south onto Swan Falls Road and follow signs 15 miles to Dedication Point.

Crags and crevices, the deep canyon of the Snake River, and a broad plateau rich in small wildlife provide habitat for the greatest concentration of nesting birds of prey in North America. *(Larry Ridenhour, BLM Lower Snake River District)*

Visitor Activities

Birdwatching, rafting, canoeing, kayaking, archaeological site, duck hunting, hiking, horseback riding, mountain biking, scenic drives, and interpretation.

Special Features

Approximately 700 pairs of hawks, eagles, falcons, and owls nest in the lava cliffs and surrounding desert plateau. Dedication Point, an outstanding scenic overlook, is about 15.5 miles south of the town of Kuna on Swan Falls Road. Visitors can walk about 0.25 mile from the road down a gravel path to the canyon rim to get the best view of the Snake River Canyon. Continue on Swan Falls Road for another 4.5 miles to Swan Falls Dam, the oldest hydroelectric dam on the Snake River. Prehistoric Native American rock art can be seen at nearby Celebration Park, where petroglyphs line both sides of the canyon. There is an interpretive kiosk at Dedication Point.

Permits, Fees, Limitations

Hunting restrictions are in effect in some areas. Check with the Idaho Department of Fish and Game, (208) 334-3700, for hunting and fishing license requirements. All vehicles must stay on designated routes.

Accessibility

Wheelchair-accessible restrooms are available at Dedication Point, 15.5 miles south of Kuna on Swan Falls Road; Swan Falls Dam, 21 miles south of Kuna on Swan Falls Road; and Celebration Park, 20 miles south and west of Kuna.

Camping and Lodging

Cove Recreation Site on C.J. Strike Reservoir, approximately 85 miles south and east of Kuna, is the only improved public camping facility in the area. On the south side of the reservoir and immediately west of Cove Recreation Site is the Black Sands RV Resort, offering campsites with full hookups, a restaurant/bar, and boat launch. Primitive camping is allowed throughout the National Conservation Area, but campers should avoid areas where birds are nesting. Use of fire pans is recommended. Lodging is available in

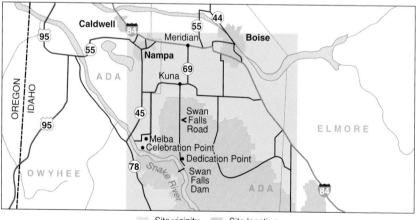

Site vicinity   Site location

Meridian (10 miles north), Nampa (18 miles northwest), Caldwell (27 miles northwest), and Boise.

Food and Supplies
At the western end of the National Conservation Area, food and supplies are available in the towns of Kuna, Melba (2 miles west), Meridian, and Boise. At the upstream end of the area, food and supplies are available in Bruneau (2 miles east) and Mountain Home (22 miles northeast).

First Aid
An Emergency Medical Technician Quick Response Unit is located in the town of Melba. Hospitals are located in Nampa, Meridian, and Boise.

Additional Information
The best viewing of birds of prey is at the Dedication Point Overlook from

March 1–June 15. A visitor contact station in Kuna, staffed on weekends, can provide more information about the area and local conditions. A visitor's guide with map is available from BLM along with other brochures and publications.

Contact Information
BLM - Snake River Birds of Prey NCA
3948 Development Avenue
Boise, ID 83705
Tel: (208) 384-3300
Fax: (208) 384-3205
www.birdsofprey.blm.gov

Activity Codes

St. Anthony Sand Dunes

Location
51 miles north of Idaho Falls, Idaho.

Description
The St. Anthony Sand Dunes are comprised of multiple dune complexes forming the largest tract of sand dunes in Idaho and covering an area of approximately 175 square miles. The active dune field trends northeast for 35 miles and is 5 miles wide, with dunes ranging from 50–600 feet high. The largest of the active dune complexes (11,000 acres) is within the Sand Mountain Wilderness Study Area. These high and expansive dunes attract off-highway-vehicle riders from

throughout the United States. Other visitors prefer to explore the dunes on horseback or on foot.

Directions
From Idaho Falls, follow U.S. Highway 20 east 40 miles to Rexburg and the North Rexburg exit. Proceed west onto Route 1900 East (Parker-Salem Highway and the Red Road). Travel 6.3 miles north to the second flashing light. To access the eastern end of the largest dune complex, continue north 3.5 miles. To go to the Egin Lakes Recreation Site access, turn left at the flashing light and travel 0.85 mile to the split in the road. Travel right over the railroad

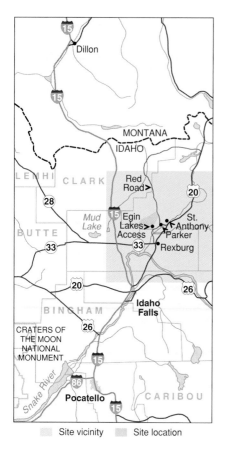

Site vicinity ■ Site location

tracks and continue on Route 500 North for 2.9 miles. At the Egin Lakes Access sign, turn right onto a gravel road that leads to the Egin Lakes Recreation Site.

Visitor Activities
Hiking, horseback riding, off-highway driving riding on open sand dunes, all-terrain driving, motorcycle riding, mountain biking on designated roads and trails, picnicking, sledding/snow tubing, snowmobiling, and wildlife viewing.

Special Features
The dunes are composed mostly of white quartz sand lightly peppered with grains of black basalt. Surrounding the dunes are thousands of acres of native grasses, junipers, and sagebrush. Dead-horse Bowl, an area 1 mile in circumference and 400 feet deep, is located within the western section of the largest dune complex. The sand dune complexes are also host to two species of special concern: the Idaho dunes tiger beetle and the Saint Anthony evening primrose. The area also provides critical winter range habitat for more than 1,000 mule deer and 2,000 elk.

Permits, Fees, Limitations
Portions of the area are affected by seasonal closures to all forms of human entry from January 1–March 31 or April 30 each year, depending on snow conditions. No highway-licensed vehicle is allowed on the sand dunes. All off-highway vehicles must be equipped with 6-foot whip masts and brightly colored flags.

Accessibility
The restrooms at Egin Lake Recreation Site are accessible.

Camping and Lodging
Dispersed camping is available at the Egin Lakes Access and along Red Road adjacent to the largest active dune complex. When completed (estimated for spring 2005), the Egin Lakes Recreation Site will feature expanded day-use parking for a variety of recreational users, a developed camping area with RV and group sites, and a visitor contact station. There are also two private campgrounds adjacent to this dune complex: Desert

With their stark natural beauty, the St. Anthony Sand Dunes complexes provide outstanding riding opportunities for all-terrain vehicles, dune buggies, and sand rails. *(Karen Wattenmaker)*

Oasis RV Park located 1 mile east of Egin Lakes, and Sand Hills Resort located on Red Road. Lodging is also available in St. Anthony (8 miles east) and Rexburg (11 miles south). A 14-day stay limit applies.

Food and Supplies
Food and supplies are available in Rexburg and St. Anthony. Limited supplies are available at Egin Lakes Access next to the largest active dune complex, Desert Oasis RV Park (1 mile east), and Sand Hills Resort in St. Anthony.

First Aid
The nearest hospital is located in Rexburg.

Additional Information
Spring through fall are the best times to visit the sand dunes. During the summer, temperatures on the sand can reach over 100°F. The sand dunes are constantly changing; visitors should be very careful even if they have been to the area before. BLM began to improve and expand the

Egin Lakes Access Recreation Site in 2002. During construction, estimated to take more than 2 years, there will be periods when BLM will restrict overnight camping and day-use access to this site. OHV users are strongly encouraged to avoid damage to vegetation and impacts to wildlife so use of this unique area may continue. Open campfires are prohibited on the sand dunes and in the Sand Mountain Wilderness Study Area, with the exception of the Red Road Open Sand Campfire Area.

Contact Information
BLM – Idaho Falls Field Office
1405 Hollipark Drive
Idaho Falls, ID 83401
Tel: (208) 524-7500
Fax: (208) 524-7505
www.id.blm.gov/offices/idahofalls

Activity Codes

South Fork of the Snake River

Location
Beginning 22 miles northeast of Idaho Falls, Idaho.

Description
This highly diverse river corridor, which stretches upstream for 62 miles, contains one of the largest cottonwood gallery forests in the West, and is home to 13 nesting pairs of bald eagles. The South Fork of the Snake River is known throughout the country as a premier "Blue Ribbon" trout fishery and was selected as the host site for the 1997 World Fly Fishing Championship.

Directions
From Idaho Falls, take U.S. Highway 26 north and east 22 miles to the Byington boat access point 1 mile south of Heise. The other major boat access points are at Conant (off U.S. Highway 26, 16 miles southeast of Byington) and the

Boaters get ready for a day of fishing and sun on the beautiful South Fork of the Snake River. *(Karen Wattenmaker)*

Palisades Dam (off U.S. Highway 26, 37 miles southeast of Byington).

Visitor Activities
Fishing, canoeing, kayaking, rafting, jet boating, hiking, environmental education, interpretation, scenic drives, mountain biking, off-highway vehicle riding, birdwatching, wildlife viewing, and picnicking.

Special Features
Wildlife abounds, including bald eagles, moose, elk, white-tail deer, black bears, and mountain lions. This area is amongst the most unique and biodiverse ecosystems in Idaho — more than 125 bird species can be found in the South Fork drainage.

Permits, Fees, Limitations
A daily facility-use and parking fee is required at 10 river access sites along the South Fork of the Snake River. Anyone using facilities or parking a vehicle at any of the sites must pay a daily fee or purchase a season pass. To protect bald eagle nesting sites, a number of areas are closed to riverbank occupancy from February 1–July 31 each year. Check with the Idaho Department of Fish and Game for fishing license requirements, (208) 334-3700.

Accessibility
Accessible restrooms, picnic areas, and a boat ramp are available at the Byington River Access, located off U.S. Highway 26 about 22 miles northeast of Idaho Falls. Accessible facilities are available at the Conant River Access, located off

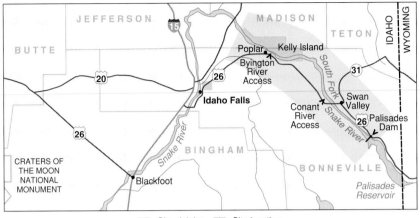

Site vicinity   Site location

U.S Highway 26 about 40 miles east of Idaho Falls. Accessible restrooms are available at Kelly Island Campground, located off U.S. Highway 26, about 25 miles northeast of Idaho Falls. A wheelchair-accessible fishing dock is available at the Palisades Creek River Access, located off U.S. Highway 26 about 50 miles east of Idaho Falls.

Camping and Lodging
Self-issued permits are required to camp in 11 designated, signed areas along 12 miles of the river between Conant River Access and Lufkin Bottom (14 miles southeast of Byington). These designated camp areas are only accessible by boat. Campers must obtain a permit from the boat access areas and keep it with them during all overnight river visits. Portable toilets are required in this section. Drive-in camping is available at the following locations: Kelly Island Campground (at Byington), Wolf Flat Dispersed Campsites (4 miles southeast of Byington), Tablerock Campground (7 miles southeast of Byington) and

Falls Creek Campground (29 miles southeast of Byington). Lodging is available in Idaho Falls.

Food and Supplies
Food and supplies are available in Idaho Falls.

First Aid
The nearest hospital is located in Idaho Falls.

Additional Information
The South Fork is a flat-water river, but hazards do exist. Inexperienced boaters should call BLM for specific information before visiting. Developed and undeveloped launch areas offer river access for fishing and boating. To protect bald eagle nesting sites, a number of areas are closed to riverbank occupancy from February 1–July 31 each year. Additional information about outdoor recreational opportunities in the area is available from the Eastern Idaho Visitor Information Center, 630 W. Broadway, Idaho Falls, ID 83402, (866) 365-6943.

Contact Information

BLM - Idaho Falls Field Office
1405 Hollipark
Idaho Falls, ID 83442
Tel: (208) 524-7500
Fax: (208) 524-7505
www.id.blm.gov/offices/idahofalls

Activity Codes

other - environmental education

Thousand Springs Valley

Location

98 miles west of Idaho Falls; 5 miles
north of Mackay, Idaho.

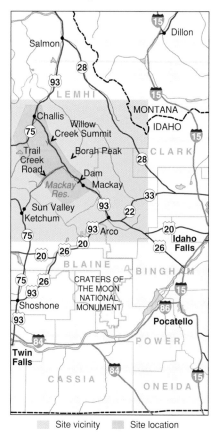

Site vicinity   Site location

Description

Thousand Springs Valley stretches nearly
30 miles from Mackay northwest to
Willow Creek Summit along U.S.
Highway 93. This broad valley features
innumerable seeps and springs that coa-
lesce into the Chilly Springs wetland
and Mackay Reservoir. Recreational
climbing is popular in the mountains
surrounding the valley.

Directions

From Idaho Falls, follow U.S. Highway
26 to Arco (58 miles) and U.S. Highway
93 about 27 miles to Mackay. From
Mackay, drive north on U.S. Highway
93. The southern end of the valley
begins just outside the town of Mackay.
Willow Creek Summit marks the
northern end of the valley.

Visitor Activities

Birdwatching, wildlife viewing, fishing,
geologic sightseeing, bird and big-
game hunting, hang gliding, and
interpretation.

Special Features

The most stunning aspect of the
Thousand Springs Valley is the surround-
ing mountain ranges. The Lost River
Range, which includes Mount Borah,

Idaho's tallest peak at 12,662 feet, rises to the east and the White Knobs rise to the southwest. The earthquake fault line along the base of Mount Borah provides an excellent opportunity to see evidence of geologic forces at work. Bird life includes bald eagles, herons, and ducks. Sagebrush dominates mid-elevation slopes, giving way briefly to evergreens before vegetation finally disappears on the glaciated peaks of the Lost River Range. Mule deer, antelope, and coyotes are frequent inhabitants of the valley.

Permits, Fees, Limitations
The Borah Peak Wilderness Study Area, 30 miles northwest of Mackay on the east slope of the Valley, has vehicle travel restrictions.

Accessibility
The BLM Mackay Reservoir's Joe T. Falinni Campground is scheduled for reconstruction and will meet accessibility standards by late 2004.

Camping and Lodging
Camping is available at the Joe T. Falinni Campground on Mackay Reservoir (fee charged), Garden Creek Campground 18 miles west on Trail Creek Road, and the Mount Borah Trailhead, 22 miles northwest of Mackay. Dispersed camping is also available. A 14-day stay limit applies. Lodging is available in Mackay and in Challis, approximately 35 miles north via U.S. Highway 93.

Food and Supplies
Food and supplies are available in Challis, Mackay, and the Sun Valley/ Ketchum area (38 miles west).

First Aid
Full medical services are located in Sun Valley/Ketchum. A medical clinic is located in Challis. A part-time medical clinic is located in Mackay.

Additional Information
Trail Creek Road from Thousand Springs Valley to the Sun Valley/ Ketchum area is closed during the winter months. An earthquake fault interpretive center is located 1 mile north of the Mount Borah trailhead, 23 miles north of Mackay.

Contact Information
BLM - Challis Field Office
801 Blue Mountain Road
Challis, ID 83226
Tel: (208) 879-6200
Fax: (208) 879-6219
www.id.blm.gov/offices/challis

Activity Codes

other – hang gliding

The crystal-clear waters and tall-grass marshes of Thousand Springs' Chilly Slough are home to a wide variety of wildlife, in-cluding willets, sandhill cranes, and tundra swans, as well as wintering pronghorn and mule deer. *(Karen Wattenmaker)*

Northeast of Ft. Benton, near Loma, Montana, the confluence of the Missouri and Marias Rivers presented explorers Lewis and Clark with a dilemma: which river was the all-important Missouri? The Expedition members camped at this spot, now known as Decision Point, in June 1805, while they explored the area and cached supplies for their return trip. *(Wayne Mumford (used with permission))*

The journals of the 1803–1805 Lewis and Clark Expedition extolled the natural beauty and diversity of this region. Later in the 19th century, the promise of precious metals and homesteading lands lured miners, farmers, and ranchers to settle the area. Today, the spectacular scenery, uninterrupted vistas, clean air, and an abundance of elbow room attract recreationists and other visitors to Montana as well as North and South Dakota.

Public lands in Montana and the Dakotas present tremendous diversity in topography, climate, and spectacular natural resources. The designations of two national monuments in Montana—Pompeys Pillar and Upper Missouri River Breaks—attest to the exceptional cultural and natural values featured on these lands. Encompassing 8 million acres in Montana and 330,000 acres in the Dakotas, public lands range from the vast high plains of the western Dakotas and eastern Montana to the majestic peaks of the Rocky Mountains in western Montana. Included are semi-arid regions as well as high-elevation areas where snow can fall in any given month. Temperatures range as widely as the geography, accommodating activities tailored to all seasons.

Visitors will enjoy exploring historic sites and viewing wildlife, as well as a host of other recreational activities, including cross-country skiing, camping, fishing famous "Blue Ribbon" trout streams, and driving scenic highways and back country byways. Whether one seeks primitive solitude or activities in a more developed environment, public lands in Montana and the Dakotas offer choices that will fit the bill.

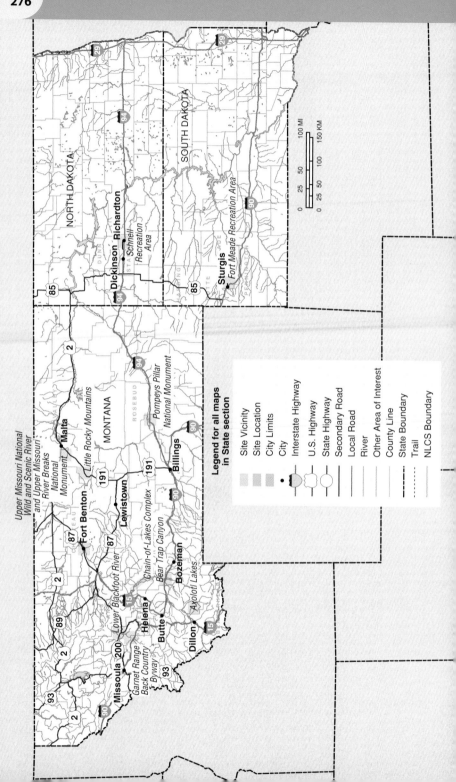

Axolotl Lakes

Location
70 miles northeast of Dillon, Montana.

Description
The Axolotl ("Ak-suh-*lot*-ul") Lakes Wilderness Study Area and 40 adjacent acres make up this unique and relatively remote recreation area. Axolotl Lakes lies on the northern edge of the Greenhorn Mountains at an elevation of roughly 6,900 feet. The entire Madison Range and valley are visible from the heights of the property. The land is characterized by lush meadows interspersed with rolling foothills, rocky ledges, and outcrops. The area is known for its scenic beauty, fishing opportunities, and diversity of wildlife. Several small, unnamed lakes and potholes throughout the area are inhabited by rainbow and cutthroat trout.

Directions
From Dillon, travel north 40 miles on State Highway 41 to Twin Bridges. Then travel 50 miles east on State Highway 287. Turn south on Gravelly Range Road and drive about 7 miles. Turn west on Axolotl Lakes Road and go about 5 miles to the recreation area entrance.

Visitor Activities
Hiking, fishing, picnicking, wildlife viewing, and hunting.

Special Features
Riparian and wetland areas are interspersed throughout the area. In addition, fluvial Arctic graylings are reared in Upper Twin Lake, accessible via the recreation area, providing brood stock for the reintroduction and recovery of the grayling in Montana. A great diversity of wildlife inhabits the area, including elk, antelope, mule deer, moose, bald and golden eagles, nesting ospreys, and many other species.

Permits, Fees, Limitations
None.

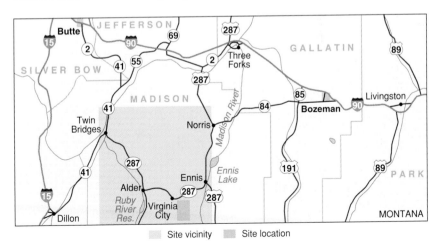

Site vicinity   Site location

Accessibility
None.

Camping and Lodging
Only dispersed, primitive camping is permitted. The nearest lodging is in Virginia City, 10 miles east on State Highway 287, and Ennis, 30 miles east on State Highway 287.

Food and Supplies
Food, supplies, and commercial services are available in Virginia City and Ennis.

First Aid
The nearest hospital is in Ennis.

Additional Information
Vehicle travel in this area is limited to designated routes. Roads in this area are not maintained; a high-clearance vehicle is required. Foot travel may be necessary.

Contact Information
BLM - Dillon Field Office
1005 Selway Drive
Dillon, MT 59725
Tel: (406) 683-2337
Fax: (406) 683-2970
www.mt.blm.gov/dfo

Activity Codes

Numerous small lakes and potholes in the remote Axolotl Lakes area provide high-elevation habitat for rainbow and cutthroat trout. *(BLM)*

Bear Trap Canyon

Location
30 miles west of Bozeman, Montana.

Description
The 6,000-acre Bear Trap Canyon Wilderness was the first unit of the National Wilderness Preservation System to be managed by the BLM. The canyon cuts its way through 1,500 feet of granite in the Madison Range, and the fast-flowing Madison River features a 9-mile day run of mostly Class IV rapids, culminating in the famous Class V "Kitchen Sink" rapids. The area also features outstanding scenery, opportunities for wildlife viewing, and a "Blue Ribbon" trout fishery. The Bear Trap Canyon National Recreation Trail and Trail Creek/Pot Trail are both located within the wilderness.

In addition to the recreational opportunities found in the wilderness, BLM manages several established recreation sites along the lower Madison River and Ennis Lake. These include the Red Mountain Campground, Warm Springs Boat Launch, Clute's Landing Boat Launch, Kobayashi Beach, and Trail Creek Day Use Area.

Directions
From Bozeman, travel 30 miles west on State Highway 84 and turn left at the Madison River onto Bear Trap Road. Travel 7 miles to the northern boundary of the wilderness area.

From Ennis, travel 6 miles north on U.S. Highway 287, turn east at the town of McAllister onto Ennis Lake Road, and continue 7 miles to the end of the road and the southern boundary of the wilderness area.

Visitor Activities
Hiking, floating, fishing, boating, swimming, water skiing, jet skiing, picnicking, whitewater rafting, and wildlife viewing.

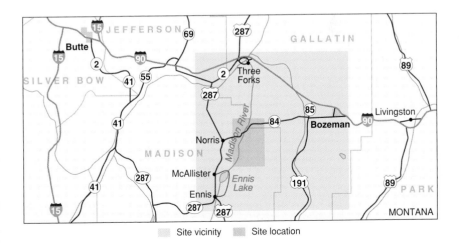

Site vicinity   Site location

Rafters negotiate expert-class rapids on the Madison River as it flows through Bear Trap Canyon. (BLM)

Special Features

The canyon has healthy populations of rainbow and brown trout. A variety of wildlife inhabits the area, including elk, deer, ospreys, hawks, geese, and eagles. Grizzly bears occasionally visit the area.

Permits, Fees, Limitations

Permits are not required for private float groups, but registration is necessary at the launch. Commercial floats are available.

Accessibility

All restrooms, developed campsites, and most picnic areas are accessible.

Camping and Lodging

Camping is allowed only in developed and dispersed/designated campsites, with a maximum of three vehicles per site. Per-night fees are charged. Developed camping is available at Red Mountain Campground and Clute's Landing. To get to Red Mountain Campground from Ennis, travel 10 miles north on U.S. Highway 287 to the town of Norris, then travel 8 miles east on State Highway 84 to the river. Clute's Landing, on Ennis Lake, is accessible from Bear Trap Road, just north of the town of Ennis. Lodging is available in Bozeman (30 miles east on State Highway 84), McAllister (7 miles west on Ennis Lake Road), and Ennis (7 miles west on Ennis Lake Road, then 6 miles south on U.S. Highway 287).

Food and Supplies

Food, supplies, and commercial services are available in Bozeman, McAllister, Ennis, and Norris (10 miles north of Ennis on U.S. Highway 287).

First Aid

The nearest hospitals are in Bozeman and Ennis.

Additional Information

Vehicle travel is limited in this area to designated routes. The use of firearms is prohibited within the Bear Trap Canyon Wilderness except during open hunting season. Open fires must be completely contained within one of the permanently installed metal fire grates provided. Visitors should be aware of the presence of rattlesnakes, ticks, and *Giardia* (an intestinal parasite found in some fresh water). A hiking trail follows the river for the length of the canyon, but cannot be accessed from the southern end. *The Bear Trap Canyon Wilderness Visitor's Guide* is available free of charge from BLM. Canyon floaters must be skilled in negotiating whitewater.

Contact Information

BLM - Dillon Field Office
1005 Selway Drive
Dillon, MT 59725
Tel: (406) 683-2337
Fax: (406) 683-2970
www.mt.blm.gov/dfo

Activity Codes

Chain-of-Lakes Complex

Location

This 115-mile-long series of lakes stretches from Three Forks to Wolf Creek, Montana, with its midpoint about 15 miles east of Helena.

Description

The Chain-of-Lakes Complex is a series of four north-south-trending, manmade lakes along the Missouri River, interspersed with segments of free-flowing water. From south to north, the four lakes in the "chain" are Toston, Canyon Ferry, Hauser, and Holter; Toston is the smallest at 5 miles long, and Canyon Ferry is the largest at 24 miles long. Each lake hosts BLM, Bureau of Reclamation, and/or private recreation areas, campgrounds, and other facilities, such as marinas.

The lake complex is a popular fishing, sightseeing and boating area, with spectacular mountain settings along portions of the corridor. The Chain-of-Lakes Complex provides boat access to excellent hiking, fishing, camping, and hunt-

ing opportunities. The area also includes the Sleeping Giant Wilderness Study Area, about 11,000 acres of steep, irregular topography with elevations ranging from 3,600–6,800 feet.

Directions

Toston Lake: From Three Forks, drive 3 miles west on Interstate 90. Take exit 274 to U.S. Highway 287, and drive north about 21 miles. Turn east onto Toston Road (improved gravel) and go 6 miles to Toston Dam. The road dead-ends at BLM's Upper Toston Recreation Site, just above the dam. *Canyon Ferry Lake:* From Helena, travel east on U.S. Highway 287 about 10 miles. Turn north onto Route 284 and go 8 miles to Canyon Ferry Dam. *Hauser Lake:* From Helena, take Exit 193 (Cedar Street) off Interstate 15. Turn right onto Washington Street and go past the airport entrance to Custer Avenue. Turn right, and travel for 1.5 miles to York Road. Turn north onto York, and travel 10 miles to Lakeside, a

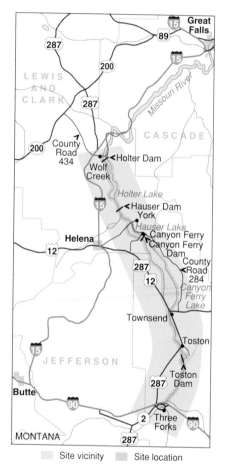

Site vicinity   Site location

Visitor Activities

Picnicking, fishing, boating, hiking, wildlife viewing, hunting, and ice fishing (during winter).

Special Features

The "Gates of the Rocky Mountains" create an optical illusion that occurs while one travels upriver on Holter Lake: these cliffs, on opposite sides of a narrow section of the lake, appear to swing open, revealing mountain peaks behind them. In 1805, Lewis and Clark named this phenomenon during their historic expedition; the entire Chain-of-Lakes Corridor is now part of the Lewis and Clark National Historic Trail. Today the Gates' base is flooded by the waters of Holter Lake, and visitors glide in aboard tour boats along the explorers' route.

Mountain goats, elk, antelope, ospreys, bald eagles, mule deer, bighorn sheep, and other native wildlife can often be seen in this area. Popular fishing species include kokanee salmon, brown and rainbow trout, walleyes, perch, and smallmouth bass. The Sleeping Giant, a feature along the Beartooth Mountain ridgeline that resembles the profile of a reclining giant, is a well-known area landmark, readily visible from Helena and Interstate 15.

Permits, Fees, Limitations

Day-use fees are in effect at all sites. Fishing and hunting licenses can be obtained at numerous stores throughout the lake corridor.

Accessibility

Restrooms and developed campgrounds are accessible.

private resort. Travel 2 more miles to Devil's Elbow, where BLM manages two recreation areas.

Holter Lake: From Helena, drive north on Interstate 15 about 35 miles and take Exit 226 at Wolf Creek. Travel east from Wolf Creek to the east side of the Missouri River bridge, and then turn right onto a paved county road. Travel south about 3 miles to the BLM recreation areas: Holter Dam, Holter Lake, Log Gulch, Departure Point, and Beartooth Landing.

The Chain-of-Lakes Complex along the Missouri River in central Montana offers numerous opportunities for camping, picnicking, and water-based recreation in a peaceful, wooded setting. *(Wayne Mumford (used with permission))*

Camping and Lodging

Primitive camping is available at all BLM sites, with a 14-day camping limit and per-night fees. Group camping is offered at some locations; please contact BLM for more details. The Bureau of Reclamation manages six recreation campgrounds at Canyon Ferry Lake. Developed overnight camping for RVs and tents is available at several campgrounds within the complex. There are also about 50 undeveloped, boat-in camping sites at Holter Lake and other points in the corridor. Camping is on a first-come, first-served basis. Checkout time is 3 p.m. RV dump stations are available in Helena (8 miles south on Route 84, then 10 miles west on U.S. Highway 287), Cascade (25 miles north of Wolf Creek along Interstate 15), and Townsend (at the southern tip of Canyon Ferry Lake, about 30 miles south on U.S. Highway 287).

Food and Supplies

Food, supplies, and commercial services are available in the towns of Wolf Creek, Townsend, Three Forks (6 miles west on Toston Road, then 21 miles north on U.S. Highway 287, then 3 miles east on Interstate 90), and Craig (5 miles north of Wolf Creek), along the eastern shore of Holter Lake, and in Helena.

First Aid

The nearest hospital is in Helena. Wolf Creek and other communities within the corridor have volunteer fire departments, search and rescue teams, and paramedics.

Additional Information

A towing service is located in Wolf Creek. The Gates of the Mountains boat tour, which operates on Upper Holter Lake, is a favorite local attraction. There are also swimming beaches, fish cleaning stations, boat ramps, and docks at Holter Lake (at Holter Lake and Log Gulch recreation sites) and Hauser Lake (Devil's Elbow site).

Contact Information

BLM - Butte Field Office
106 N. Parkmont
Butte, MT 59701
Tel: (406) 533-7600
Fax: (406) 533-7660
www.mt.blm.gov/bfo

Activity Codes

other - ice fishing

Fort Meade Recreation Area

Location
Immediately east of Sturgis, South Dakota.

Description
The Fort Meade Recreation Area consists of about 6,700 acres of forest and grasslands. The area is managed to protect, preserve, and enhance its cultural, historic, recreational, and wildlife values. Fort Meade was established on August 28, 1878, on the east side of Bear Butte Creek as the first military outpost in the Black Hills, becoming home to the U.S. Army's famed 7th Cavalry until 1889. The Fort is the northern end point of the 5-mile-long Fort Meade Back Country Byway.

Directions
From Sturgis, travel 3 miles southeast on Interstate 90 to the Black Hills National Cemetery interchange, Exit 34. Turn left under the overpass, and then follow signs to the site.

Alternatively, from Sturgis, travel 1 mile east on State Highway 34. The site entrance is just west of the first entrance to the Fort Meade Veterans Affairs Hospital.

Visitor Activities
Self-guided auto and walking tours, scenic drives, wildlife viewing, bird-watching, bow-hunting, hiking, fishing, and historic site.

Special Features
During the late 19th century, most of the U.S. Army's cavalry units, including the "Buffalo Soldiers" of the 10th Cavalry, served at Fort Meade. Prior to World War I, the 4th Cavalry began its long association with Fort Meade. In early World War II, the 4th Cavalry was dismounted and trained as a mechanized

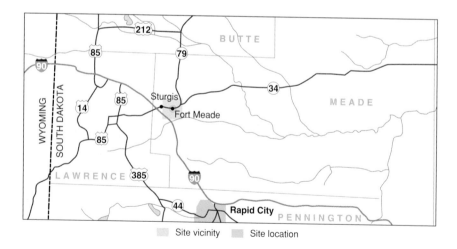

Site vicinity   Site location

Headstones in the Post Cemetery memorialize the lives of the U.S. Cavalry soldiers who were once stationed at Fort Meade. *(BLM)*

reconnaissance unit that later fought in Normandy, northern France, the Battle of the Bulge, and Germany.

Attractions in the area include the historic Fort Meade Cavalry Post, the Old Fort Meade Cavalry Museum, the Fort Meade Post Cemetery, and the Centennial Trail. About a third of the 6,700-acre area is on the National Register of Historic Places. The Fort Meade Back Country Byway and a portion of the 110-mile Centennial Trail cross the recreation area. The southern portion of this unit has a large population of Merriam's wild turkeys, which can be observed there at all times of the year.

Permits, Fees, Limitations
Motor vehicle use is restricted to maintained roads. The Centennial Trail is for non-motorized use only. Fires are allowed only in fire pits or grates.

Accessibility
Most picnic areas and one campsite are wheelchair-accessible.

Camping and Lodging
There is a daily camping fee from May–September. Six tent campsites and a six-unit campground for horseback riders are available. Picnic facilities include 22 family picnic units and three group picnic units. The campgrounds are closed around the time of the Sturgis Motorcycle Rally in August.

Please call BLM for more information. RVs are welcome at the BLM campgrounds and at Bear Butte State Park, 12 miles from the site along State Highway 34 east and State Highway 79 north, but no hookups are provided.

Food and Supplies
Food and supplies are available in Sturgis.

First Aid
The nearest hospital is in Sturgis.

Additional Information
In most of the recreation area, only hunting with bows is permitted. Fort Meade has a mild climate with seasonal variations. Little snow accumulates during the winter months, but snowfall varies from year to year. Nearly 70 percent of the precipitation occurs during April, May, and June. Water is available on-site from May–September.

Contact Information
BLM - South Dakota Field Office
310 Roundup Street
Belle Fourche, SD 57717
Tel: (605) 892-7000
Fax: (605) 892-7015
www.mt.blm.gov/sdfo

Activity Codes

Garnet Range
Back Country Byway

Location
40 miles east of Missoula, Montana.

Description
The 12-mile-long Garnet Range Back Country Byway climbs 2,000 feet through the scenic Garnet Range to historic Garnet Ghost Town. Thanks to extensive preservation efforts, the 30 buildings in this former gold mining town look much the same as they did in 1895.

Directions
From Missoula, drive about 9 miles east on Interstate 90 and exit at State Highway 200. Continue traveling east on Highway 200 about 23 miles to the clearly marked turnoff to Garnet. This road is the start of the Garnet Range Back Country Byway, which leads directly to the ghost town.

Visitor Activities
Scenic drives, hiking, historic site, interpretation, geologic sightseeing, wildlife viewing, plant viewing, birdwatching, snowmobiling, and cross-country skiing.

Special Features
The rounded slopes of the Garnet Range hide evidence of the geologic upheavals that created an interior laced with enough gold to create a stampede in the 1860s. The key to Garnet's gold and minerals lies in the area's granite, which cooled in fractures within sedimentary rocks, causing quartz and gold to crystallize into distinct veins. Rock weathering then sent gold flakes into local streams—and ultimately into the pans of eager prospectors.

Montana's most intact ghost town, Garnet—named for the garnet crystals

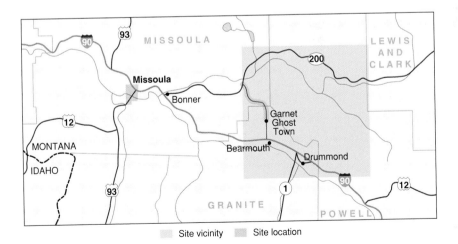

Site vicinity   Site location

During the winter months, Garnet Ghost Town is an appealing destination for cross-country skiers and snowmobilers. *(Travel Montana)*

frequently found with gold—endures, along with the spirits of the rugged gold miners who once carved a community into the heart of the Garnet Mountain Range. In 1898, some 1,000 people called Garnet home; by 1905, only 150 remained. Today, Garnet's fame lies not in its gold, but in the rich history of the town.

Permits, Fees, Limitations
There is a day-use fee at the Ghost Town.

Accessibility
Restrooms are wheelchair-accessible.

Camping and Lodging
During the winter, two rustic cabins at the ghost town can be rented for overnight stays. Contact BLM for more information. Other nearby lodging can be found at the Bearmouth Chalet, located at the Bearmouth exit off Interstate 90 (about 1 mile east of the intersection of the byway with Interstate 90), and in Missoula and Drummond (about 10 miles east of the intersection of the byway with Interstate 90). The Bearmouth Chalet also has RV facilities.

Food and Supplies
There are no commercial facilities at Garnet Ghost Town; however, tour maps and limited sales items are available at the visitor center. The nearest food and supplies are in Drummond or Potomac, about 12 miles east of Missoula on Interstate 90.

First Aid

The nearest hospital is in Missoula.

Additional Information

Travel on the Garnet Range Back Country Byway is limited to over-the-snow travel methods (i.e., no wheeled vehicles) from January 1–April 30. A 32-mile network of trails called the Garnet National Winter Recreation Trail is accessible from Garnet Ghost Town. The trails are open from January 1–April 30 for snowmobiling and cross-country skiing, with warming shelters provided along some of the trails. The visitor center at Garnet Ghost Town is open daily from June–September, and on a limited basis during the rest of the year. Maps and additional information are available from BLM.

Contact Information

BLM – Missoula Field Office
3255 Fort Missoula Road
Missoula, MT 59804
Tel: (406) 329-3914
Fax: (406) 329-3721
www.mt.blm.gov/mifo/index.html
www.garnetghosttown.org

Activity Codes

Little Rocky Mountains

Location

40 miles southwest of Malta, Montana.

Description

This isolated, heavily-timbered volcanic mountain range near the Canadian border rises abruptly from the surrounding plains, providing habitat for a unique mix of mountain and prairie wildlife. Many species found infrequently in eastern Montana are found here. The highest points in Phillips County, the Little

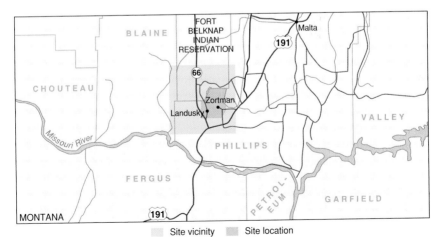

Site vicinity   Site location

The tree-covered Little Rockies are typical of the isolated "island ranges" that dot the plains of eastern Montana. *(BLM)*

Rocky Mountains are an "island range" surrounded by rolling prairies; a 15-minute drive can take a visitor from the vast expanse of prairie to the shelter of pine trees. The Little Rocky Mountains are rich in gold-mining history and offer diverse mountain recreational experiences.

Directions
From Malta, drive about 40 miles south on U.S. Highway 191. Watch for a sign pointing west toward Zortman, and follow that road about 7 miles, turning at the Camp Creek Campground turnoff.

Alternatively, from Malta, drive about 55 miles south on U.S. Highway 191 to its intersection with State Highway 66. Turn north onto State Highway 66, drive about 8 miles, and turn right at the sign pointing east to Landusky. BLM's Montana Gulch Campground is a short distance up this road.

Visitor Activities
Picnicking, hiking, scenic drives, wildlife viewing, birdwatching, and cross-country skiing.

Special Features
Local rivers and ponds are havens for walleye, historic paddlefish, trout, and many more fish varieties. Bighorn sheep can often be seen on the south side of Saddle Butte and Silver Peak, especially in the winter. The remains of hadrosaurs and other types of dinosaurs have been unearthed in this area.

Permits, Fees, Limitations
None.

Accessibility
None.

Camping and Lodging

Camp Creek Campground is about 2 miles northeast of Zortman; Montana Gulch Campground is 2 miles southwest of Landusky. Both charge nightly fees and can accommodate RVs and tents, but there are no plug-ins. Limited lodging may be found in Zortman; more extensive lodging choices are available in Malta.

Food and Supplies

Some food and supplies are available in Zortman; more supplies and services are available in Malta. Potable water is available at Camp Creek from May through September.

First Aid

The closest hospital is in Malta.

Additional Information

Additional information and maps are available from BLM.

Contact Information

BLM - Malta Field Office
501 South Second Street East
HC 65 Box 5000
Malta, MT 59538-0047
Tel: (406) 654-5100
Fax: (406) 654-5150
www.mt.blm.gov/mafo

Activity Codes

Lower Blackfoot River

Location

Approximately 40 miles east of Missoula, Montana.

Description

The spectacular Blackfoot River was the subject of the best-selling book and popular movie entitled, "A River Runs Through It." The river's deep pools, charming riffles, mossy overhangs, and challenging whitewater runs provide exhilarating floating, as well as great habitat for trout and world-class fly fishing for visitors. Firs, willows, and larches line the river, whose clear, emerald water flows between banks that are an average of 75 feet across.

Directions

From Missoula, drive about 9 miles east on Interstate 90, exit at State Highway 200, and continue east. The highway crosses the river four times within 30 miles, and offers several marked river access points.

The Lower Blackfoot River sets a scene typical of Montana's big sky, spectacular mountains, and clear water. *(Wayne Mumford (used with permission))*

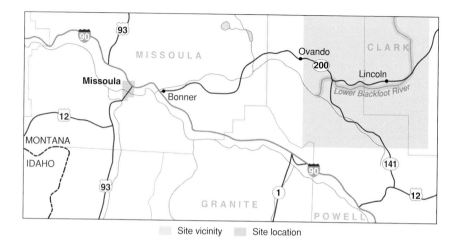

Site vicinity ▨ Site location

Visitor Activities
Wildlife viewing, rafting, boating, birdwatching, scenic drives, and fishing.

Special Features
Millions of tons of ice and a glacial lake formed the modern Blackfoot Valley; glaciers once extended from the high peaks to the valley floor, grinding and sculpting the landscape as they moved. In their wake, they left extravagant handiwork, including the boulders and cobbles now jutting from the river's surface.

The Blackfoot Valley provides habitat for a wide variety of plants and animals, including grizzly bears, bighorn sheep, moose, elk, ospreys, bald eagles, pileated woodpeckers, and neo-tropical migrant songbirds. Both native bull and westslope cutthroat trout are abundant in the river —a "Blue Ribbon" trout stream— which provides crucial habitat for these and other fish species. Explorer Meriwether Lewis and his party followed a Native American trail that paralleled the Blackfoot River on the 1806 return trip from their famous expedition.

Today, this mountain river remains largely pristine.

Permits, Fees, Limitations
None.

Accessibility
Restrooms are accessible.

Camping and Lodging
Several small campgrounds and day-use areas are located along this stretch of river, which is accessible via McNamara Road, off State Highway 200. Parking areas are provided, but there are no RV hookups. The nearest lodging is in Missoula.

Food and Supplies
Food and supplies are available in Missoula.

First Aid
The nearest hospital is in Missoula.

Additional Information
Maps and additional information are available from BLM.

Contact Information
BLM - Missoula Field Office
3255 Fort Missoula Road
Missoula, MT 59804
Tel: (406) 329-3914
Fax: (406) 329-3721
www.mt.blm.gov/mifo

Activity Codes

Pompeys Pillar National Monument

Location
30 miles northeast of Billings, Montana.

Description
Pompeys Pillar National Monument contains exceptional cultural, recreational, and wildlife values, and bears the only known physical evidence of the Lewis and Clark Expedition. Captain William Clark, his Shoshone expedition guide, Sacagawea, her 18-month old son (nicknamed "Pompey," or "little chief"), and a crew of 11 men stopped near this 121-foot-high rock outcropping on the return trip of the Lewis and Clark Expedition. On July 25, 1806, Clark carved his signature and the date into the rock and recorded doing so in his journal. The historic signature remains today, and is accessible to visitors via a boardwalk.

Directions
From Billings, drive 30 miles east on Interstate 94 to the Pompeys Pillar Exit (#23). Signs clearly point the way to the site, which is 0.5 mile off the Interstate.

Visitor Activities
Interpretive tours, historic site, wildlife viewing, birdwatching, picnicking, and hiking.

Special Features
Pompeys Pillar is located at a natural ford in the Yellowstone River. As a result, the area has been a crossroads throughout history for hunters and their prey, such as once-prominent buffalo herds. Native Americans, early explorers, fur trappers, U.S. Cavalrymen, railroad developers, and early homesteaders all used the pillar as a registry of their passing. In addition to Clark's signature, the sandstone is marked with literally hundreds of other etchings and drawings, including Native American animal figures. A large and diverse wildlife popu-

Pompeys Pillar is a massive sandstone outcrop that rises from a 2-acre base on the banks of the Yellowstone River. Its geologic distinction as the only major landform in the area has helped to make Pompeys Pillar a celebrated landmark and outstanding observation point for more than 11,000 years of human occupation. *(BLM)*

lation is drawn to the site's thriving riparian zone, a healthy plant community of grasses, willows, and cottonwood trees that stabilizes the river bank and provides important habitat. Today's existing ecosystem at the pillar is typical of the Yellowstone Valley as Clark would have seen it in 1806.

Permits, Fees, Limitations

A per-vehicle, day-use fee is charged during the summer season. No fees are charged during the rest of the year, but in the off-season, the site is open to walk-in traffic only.

Accessibility

The visitor center, gift shop, and restrooms are fully accessible.

Camping and Lodging

Daytime RV parking is available during the summer, but no overnight camping is permitted. The nearest lodging is in Billings.

Food and Supplies

There are several small towns west of Pompeys Pillar along Interstate 94

where food and supplies may be purchased. These include Ballantine, Worden, and Huntley, all within 17 miles of the site.

First Aid

The nearest hospital is in Billings.

Additional Information

The visitor center is open from 8 a.m.–8 p.m. daily Memorial Day–Labor Day, and 9 a.m.–5 p.m. through the end of September. The boardwalk and restrooms are open year-round. Winter walk-in access requires a walk of less than 1 mile to the site.

Contact Information

BLM - Billings Field Office
5001 Southgate Drive
Billings, MT 59101
Tel: (406) 896-5013
Fax: (406) 896-5281
www.mt.blm.gov/bifo/index.html
www.mt.blm.gov/pillarmon

Activity Codes

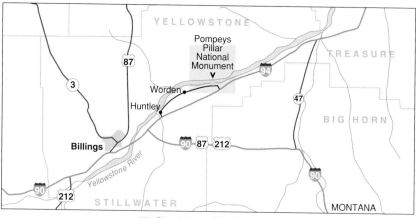

Site vicinity   Site location

Schnell Recreation Area

Location
25 miles east of Dickinson, North Dakota.

Description
Schnell Recreation Area features 2,000 acres of native mixed-grass prairie and woody draws that have been set aside for wildlife habitat, environmental education, and outdoor recreation.

Directions
From Dickinson, drive about 25 miles east on Interstate 94. Take Exit 84 and go 1 mile north on State Highway 8 to Richardton. Turn right at the stop sign onto State Highway 10, and go east from Richardton about 1 mile. Then turn left onto the gravel County Road and follow it 1 mile north and 1 mile east to the campground. Signs direct visitors to the recreation area.

Visitor Activities
Picnicking, wildlife viewing, birdwatching, cross-country skiing, hunting, hiking, fishing, mountain biking, and horseback riding.

Special Features
Schnell Recreation Area features diverse native prairie, riparian areas, ponds, and hardwood draws, where centuries-old

The woody draws of North Dakota's Schnell Recreation Area provide protected habitat for a variety of wildlife. (BLM)

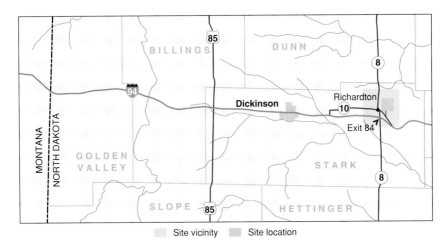

Site vicinity   Site location

bur oaks thrive. Abundant wildlife on the property include ducks, ring-necked pheasants, sharp-tailed grouse, Hungarian partridges, whitetail and mule deer, turkeys, rabbits, squirrels, porcupines, and neotropical migratory birds, such as bluebirds, warblers, and flickers.

Permits, Fees, Limitations
The site is closed to motorized vehicles.

Accessibility
Restrooms are wheelchair-accessible.

Camping and Lodging
Primitive camping is allowed. Visitors can also enjoy solitude while camping in one of six sheltered, spacious campsites. Each campsite has a table, fire ring, grill, lantern post, and drinking water. There is a per-night fee for campsites, and a 14-day maximum stay.

Food and Supplies
Food and supplies are available in Richardton (1 mile west and 1 mile

south on the gravel County Road, then 1 mile west on State Highway 10).

First Aid
First aid is available in Richardton. The nearest hospital is in Dickinson.

Additional Information
None.

Contact Information
BLM - North Dakota Field Office
2933 Third Avenue West
Dickinson, ND 58601
Tel: (701) 227-7700
Fax: (701) 227-8510
www.mt.blm.gov/ndfo

Activity Code

Upper Missouri National Wild and Scenic River and Upper Missouri River Breaks National Monument

Location
Fort Benton, Montana, marks the western extent of both the river and the monument. From Fort Benton, the river and monument wind their way 149 miles east, to the Fred Robinson Bridge, where U.S. Highway 191 crosses the Upper Missouri River. The James Kipp Recreation Area is also located at the eastern terminus.

Description
The 149-mile section of the Missouri River that flows through the Upper Missouri River Breaks National Monument is the only major portion of the river that has been preserved in a natural and free-flowing state. The remote nature of this segment of the Upper Missouri River has buffered the area from most human influence and maintained

the same vistas that awed the Lewis and Clark Expedition in 1805 and 1806.

The river offers remarkable opportunities for both floaters and those who use motorized watercraft. Canoers and kayakers at all levels of experience will find a river trip to be a comfortable, enjoyable experience. Along the way, habitats change from rolling pastures and grasslands to soaring white cliffs and rugged badlands.

Directions

The most frequently used put-in/take-out points are:

- Fort Benton;
- Coal Banks Landing, about 12 miles southwest of Big Sandy. (From Big Sandy, drive about 7 miles west on U.S. Highway 87, and turn left onto a clearly marked graveled road. Continue for about 4 miles, following the signs to Coal Banks Landing.);
- Judith Landing, approximately 44 miles south of Big Sandy on County Road 236; and
- Kipp Recreation Area, where U.S. Highway 191 crosses the Upper Missouri River.

Visitor Activities

Canoeing, boating, scenic drives, hunting, historic site, fishing, hiking, picnicking, wildlife viewing, and birdwatching.

Special Features

The monument boasts diverse wildlife and bird populations; the river corridor is a designated Watchable Wildlife site. The monument also contains the Missouri Breaks Back Country Byway and six wilderness study areas. Glaciers, volcanic activity, and erosion have folded, faulted, uplifted, and sculpted the landscape into the majestic form it takes today. The river, which is along the Lewis and Clark National Historic Trail, looks much the same as it did 200 years ago.

The banks of the Upper Missouri National Wild and Scenic River provide habitat for wild turkeys and bighorn sheep. *(BLM)*

The monument is home to one of the premier bighorn sheep herds in the continental United States. It also provides essential winter range for sage grouse as well as habitat for prairie dogs, antelope, and whitetail and mule deer. Cliff faces provide perching and nesting habitat for many raptors, including sparrow hawks, ferruginous hawks, peregrine falcons, prairie falcons, and golden eagles. Two pairs of bald eagles nest along the river, and many others visit during the late fall and early winter. Shoreline areas provide habitat for great blue herons, pelicans, and a wide variety of other waterfowl. The river and its tributaries host 48 fish species, including goldeyes, drums, saugers, walleyes, northern pikes, channel catfish, and smallmouth buffalos. The river also supports blue suckers, shovel nose sturgeons, sicklefins, sturgeon chubs, and endangered pallid sturgeons. The heads of the coulees and breaks contain archaeological and historical sites, from teepee rings and remnants of historic trails to abandoned homesteads and lookout sites used by explorers Lewis and Clark.

Permits, Fees, Limitations

For safety reasons, all floaters are asked to register at their put-in site.

Accessibility

None.

Camping and Lodging

Camping is permitted on BLM land along the river, with a 14-day limit. There is a per-night campsite fee at Kipp Recreation Area. Vault toilets are available at some sites; see Upper Missouri Wild and Scenic River maps 1, 2, 3, and 4, available from BLM, for exact locations.

Food and Supplies

Supplies can be purchased in Fort Benton; Big Sandy; Winifred (60 miles south of Big Sandy on County Road 236); Havre (35 miles north of Big Sandy on U.S. Highway 87); and Lewistown (65 miles south of the Robinson Bridge on U.S. Highway 191). Visitors should check a road map to determine which of these towns is along their approach route. There is a

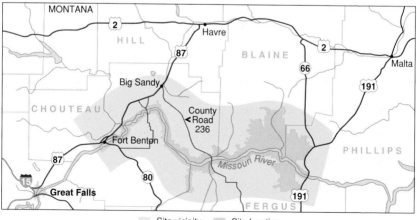

Site vicinity ■ Site location

potable water supply at Coal Banks Landing, but availability is never guaranteed. Visitors should obtain drinking water before reaching their launch point.

First Aid

The nearest hospitals are in Fort Benton, Havre, and Malta, about 70 miles north of the Robinson Bridge on U.S. Highway 191.

Additional Information

The Fort Benton Visitor Center is located along the town's Main Street, directly across from the river put-in site. The center offers books, maps, slide shows, and other displays about the river and its historical significance. Weather forecasts, safety information, and detailed brochures about the river are also available here. It is open from Memorial Day–Labor Day each year. Visitors

should contact staff there or at the BLM office for more information on planning a float trip.

Contact Information

BLM – Lewistown Field Office
P.O. Box 1160
Airport Road
Lewistown, MT 59457-1160
Tel: (406) 538-7461
Fax: (406) 538-1904
www.mt.blm.gov/ldo

BLM – Fort Benton Visitor Center
1718 Front Street
P.O. Box 1389
Fort Benton, MT 59442
Tel: (406) 622-5185

Activity Codes

White cliffs line the course of the Upper Missouri National Wild and Scenic River, supporting hawks, eagles, and other birds of prey. *(BLM)*

Created in 1936–1937 to address dwindling local water supplies, Wildhorse Reservoir is one of Nevada's premier fishing destinations. *(Bob Goodman (used with permission))*

Nevada's rugged beauty may be the nation's best-kept secret. Its public lands extend from the Sierra foothills across vast, open spaces to pinyon/juniper woodlands. Nevada boasts more than 150 mountain ranges, making it the nation's most mountainous state and providing miles of possibilities for mountain bikers, hikers, and equestrians.

Natural wonders are found throughout the state, from colorful sandstone cliffs and desert bighorn sheep at Red Rock Canyon, to aspen trees and golden eagles at Blue Lakes and Pine Forest. Cultural artifacts include Native American petroglyphs at Grimes Point/Hidden Cave and the quirky Gold Rush-era ghost town of Rhyolite, featuring a house with walls constructed of glass bottles and mud.

Adventure is a lifestyle in Nevada, especially for creative visitors seeking alternatives to the usual recreational fare. Public lands offer superb opportunities for rock and ice climbing, hang gliding, and the unique sport of land sailing. Distinctive desert playas provide land sailors with the raw materials for reaching truly invigorating speeds. Nevada even features Sand Mountain, which can be "surfed" on a board or crested by sand rail, a special type of open-cage, off-road vehicle.

With 48 million acres of public lands in Nevada, visitors are apt to travel through public lands on both major highways and rural roads. Those who tour in the spring and summer may choose to visit northern Nevada, characterized by warm, dry days and cool nights. In the fall and winter, visitors often head for southern Nevada, where the northern Mojave Desert offers plentiful sunshine and pleasant temperatures.

Recreationists of all types will discover opportunities of a lifetime on Nevada's public lands. Photographers will relish the clear air, breathtaking mountain landscapes, and spectacular rangeland tableaus. And Nevada is a rockhound's paradise: in many areas, semi-precious gemstones, mineral specimens, and certain plant and invertebrate fossils may be collected. Primitive, isolated, and infused with the adventurous spirit of the West—that's the unique charm of Nevada's public lands.

Nevada

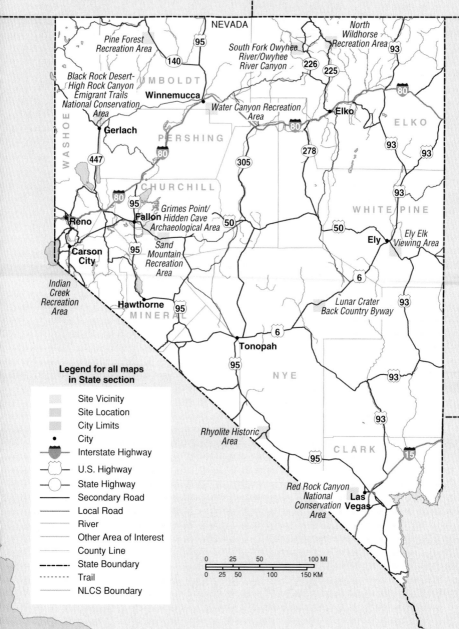

NEVADA

Pine Forest
Recreation Area

140

95

South Fork Owyhee
River/Owyhee
River Canyon

226

225

North
Wildhorse
Recreation Area

93

Black Rock Desert-
High Rock Canyon
Emigrant Trails
National Conservation
Area

Winnemucca

Water Canyon Recreation
Area

80

Elko

80

ELKO

Gerlach

PERSHING

278

93

447

80

305

93

93

95

CHURCHILL

WHITE PINE

Reno

Fallon

Grimes Point/
Hidden Cave
Archaeological Area

50

50

Ely

Ely Elk
Viewing Area

Carson
City

95

Sand
Mountain
Recreation
Area

6

Indian
Creek
Recreation
Area

Hawthorne

95

MINERAL

6

Lunar Crater
Back Country Byway

93

Tonopah

95

NYE

93

Legend for all maps
in State section

93

Site Vicinity

Site Location

City Limits

• City

Interstate Highway

U.S. Highway

State Highway

Secondary Road

Local Road

River

Other Area of Interest

County Line

------ State Boundary

.... Trail

NLCS Boundary

Rhyolite Historic
Area

CLARK

95

15

Red Rock Canyon
National
Conservation
Area

Las
Vegas

0   25   50   100 MI

0   25 50   100   150 KM

Black Rock Desert-High Rock Canyon Emigrant Trails National Conservation Area

Location
90 miles north of Reno, Nevada.

Description
The terrain of this 795,000-acre area consists of canyons, playas, and mountains. The famous Applegate-Lassen Emigrant Trail, a section of the California National Historic Trail that runs through the heart of the area, played a pivotal role in American western migration and the California Gold Rush. The Black Rock Desert Playa, a vast dry lakebed, is one of the largest and most spectacular playas in the world and is well known as the proving grounds for the current land speed record.

Directions
From Reno, take Interstate 80 east to Wadsworth. Travel north for 75 miles on State Highway 447 to Gerlach. Drive 4 miles north to Playa West Access Point #1, or 6 miles north to Playa West Access Point #2.

Visitor Activities
Hiking, scenic drives, mountain biking, hunting, horseback riding, off-highway driving, geologic sightseeing, historic site, land sailing, model rocketry, and wild horse viewing.

Special Features
This area features 120 miles of nationally significant segments of historic California emigrant trails and the trails

used by John C. Fremont, with settings that remain nearly unchanged since pioneer days. Wagon ruts and historical inscriptions are in evidence. With an area of more than 160,000 acres, the Black Rock Desert Playa once formed the bed of ancient Lake Lahontan,

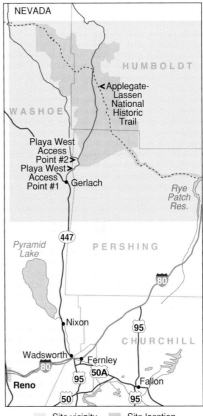

Site vicinity   Site location

Under ideal conditions and with expert handling, "land yachts" such as the ones pictured here can achieve speeds many times faster than ambient wind speeds. Specially built racers are capable of sailing at more than 100 miles per hour in winds of only 30 miles per hour. *(Mike Bilbo, BLM Roswell Field Office)*

which covered this region with 500 feet of water as recently as 60,000 years ago. Many prehistoric animal remains have been found here, including those of saber tooth cats and woolly mammoths. Within the national conservation area, wild horses may be found in the Black Rock Range East and West, and the Calico, Jackson, and Kamma Mountain ranges. Horses and burros coexist in Lava Beds and Warm Spring Canyon.

Permits, Fees, Limitations
None.

Accessibility
None.

Camping and Lodging
Camping is primitive. Lodging is available in Gerlach, 4–6 miles south on State Highway 447.

Food and Supplies
Food and camping supplies are available in Reno. A more limited selection of food and supplies is available in Empire, 4 miles south of Gerlach on State Highway 447.

First Aid
First aid is not available in this isolated area. Visitors should be prepared for any emergency. Gerlach has a small clinic. The nearest hospital is located in Reno.

Additional Information
This high-desert location can experience temperature extremes in summer, from 100°F at midday to nighttime chill. Visitors should bring plenty of extra food and water and some cool-weather clothing, even in summer. Lip balm and sunscreen are also

recommended. The best time to visit is from June–September. Visitors unfamiliar with the area are cautioned not to wander into this vast region alone! Roads are only passable in dry weather; when wet, the playa becomes an impassable sea of mud. Visitors should call BLM for current playa conditions. Permitted events, such as the annual Burning Man Festival, take place on portions of the playa at various times of the year; call BLM for information.

Contact Information

BLM - Winnemucca District Office
5100 East Winnemucca Boulevard
Winnemucca, NV 89445
Tel: (775) 623-1500
Fax: (775) 623-1503
www.nv.blm.gov/winnemucca

Activity Codes

 other - rockhounding, land sailing, model rocketry

Ely Elk Viewing Area

Location

11 miles south of Ely, Nevada.

Description

This area offers motorists a chance to stop and see Nevada's largest native animal, the Rocky Mountain elk. The biggest herd of elk in Nevada can be observed feeding during the fall and spring seasons, both along the paved highway south of Ely and at the viewing area pull-out. Peak viewing times are October through November and March through April, with elk sometimes also seen in mid-winter. Fall is the rutting season, when mature elk bulls join does, calves, and young bulls.

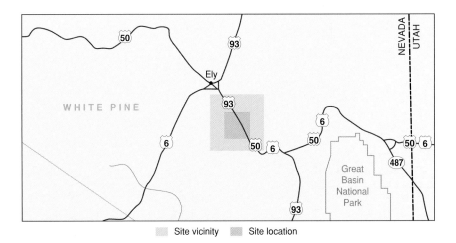

Site vicinity   Site location

Directions

From Ely, drive south on U.S. Highway 6/50/93. Elk can be seen on either side of the highway, starting about 6 miles from the town. Elk viewing signs along the highway designate the best viewing areas.

Visitor Activities

Wildlife viewing, interpretation, picnicking, and birdwatching.

Special Features

A mile-long corridor has been dedicated to allow visitors a chance to stop and view elk right from their vehicles. Hawks, ravens, and eagles perch on poles along the highway, and golden eagles are common year-round. Bald eagles arrive in late fall and spend the winter here. Other animals commonly seen in the area include golden eagles, black-tailed jackrabbits, badgers, and chipmunks.

Permits, Fees, Limitations

Day-use only.

Accessibility

The facilities at the main parking area are wheelchair-accessible.

Camping and Lodging

No camping is available on-site. Parking is available for RVs, but no hookups are provided. The nearest developed camping facilities are at the KOA Campground located 3 miles south of Ely on U.S. Highway 6/50/93. Numerous motels are also available in Ely.

Food and Supplies

No supplies are available on-site. Food and supplies may be purchased in Ely.

First Aid

There are a hospital with an emergency room and two clinics in Ely.

Additional Information

Elks usually feed at dawn and dusk. Elks are large animals—adults weigh from 450–1,000 pounds and stand 5–6 feet high. Bulls have large, swept-back antlers that can be up to 5 feet long. Visitors are cautioned not to approach them. Motorists should be particularly cautious at night, because elk sometimes bed down on warm highway pavement. Wildlife viewers share the area with hunters in the fall.

Contact Information

BLM - Ely District Office
HC33 Box 33500
Ely, NV 89301-9408
Tel: (775) 289-1800
Fax: (775) 289-1910
www.nv.blm.gov/ely

Activity Codes

Grimes Point/Hidden Cave Archaeological Area

Location
11 miles east of Fallon, Nevada.

Description
Grimes Point was first visited by Native Americans at least 8,000 years ago. One of the largest and most accessible petroglyph (rock art) sites in northern Nevada, the area contains about 150 basalt boulders covered with prehistoric art. The site also features Hidden Cave, a prehistoric storage cave.

Directions
From Fallon, go east on U.S. Highway 50 approximately 11 miles until you see the archaeological site sign.

Visitor Activities
Hiking, archaeological site, picnicking, and interpretation.

Special Features
This area is listed on the National Register of Historic Places. Hidden Cave is nationally recognized as one of the most significant archaeological sites in the Great Basin. The petroglyphs probably date from between 5,000 BC and AD 1500. Grimes Point petroglyphs are of magico-religious significance; they were likely created to ensure the success of large game hunts, and were located near former Native American seasonal migration routes. Running east and west

Near the waters of ancient Lake Lahontan, indigenous peoples left carvings in the rocks and boulders of Grimes Point, which was once part of the lake's shoreline. *(Bob Goodman (used with permission))*

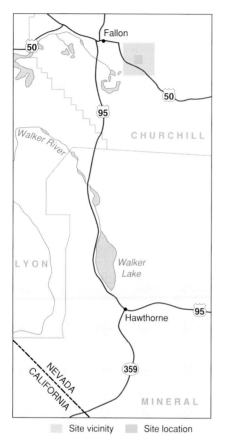

Site vicinity ■ Site location

Camping and Lodging

There is no camping on-site. Lodging is available in Fallon.

Food and Supplies

No supplies are available on-site. Food and supplies may be purchased in Fallon.

First Aid

First aid is not available on-site. A regional hospital is located in Fallon.

Additional Information

Summer temperatures can be very hot, exceeding 100°F on some days. Visitors should not enter this area during the summer without carrying sufficient water. In addition to the self-guided interpretive trails at Grimes Point, there is a guided educational tour to Hidden Cave for those interested in learning more about Great Basin prehistory. Public tours of Hidden Cave are conducted by the Churchill County Museum (1050 S. Maine, Fallon) on the second and fourth Saturdays of each month. Call the museum at (775) 423-3677 for additional information.

Contact Information

BLM - Carson City Field Office
5665 Morgan Mill Road
Carson City, NV 89701
Tel: (775) 885-6000
Fax: (775) 885-6147
www.nv.blm.gov/carson

Activity Codes

along the ridge above the petroglyphs, there is evidence of an aboriginal drift fence that was used for driving deer or antelope.

Permits, Fees, Limitations

No fees. Only day use is permitted.

Accessibility

Facilities near the highway at the Grimes Point Petroglyph Trail are wheelchair-accessible. Hidden Cave is located in steep topography and is not accessible.

Indian Creek Recreation Area

Location
9 miles north of Markleeville, California, 20 miles southeast of Lake Tahoe, Nevada.

Description
Indian Creek Recreation Area is located on Indian Creek Reservoir, within a pine forest at an elevation of 6,000 feet. The area lies at the edge of the scenic Sierra Nevada Mountains, approximately 20 miles southeast of Lake Tahoe. The surrounding area transitions from high mountains, rivers, and streams in the west, to Great Basin desert with pinyon pine and sagebrush in the east. Recreational facilities include a 160-acre reservoir, a developed recreation site, and hiking trails. The nearby Carson River is managed as a trophy trout fishery.

Directions
From Carson City, Nevada, take U.S. Highway 395 south for 12 miles to State Highway 88. Go south 15 miles on State Highway 88 to Woodfords, California. At Woodfords, turn south onto State Highway 89 toward Markleeville, and go approximately 5 miles to the directional sign for Indian Creek Reservoir.

Visitor Activities
Mountain biking, hiking, wildlife viewing, fishing, picnicking, boating, birdwatching, and rafting.

Special Features
Hiking trails lead down to the East Fork of the Carson River, a designated component of the California Wild & Scenic Rivers system. The reservoir is used by shorebirds, gulls, ducks, double-crested cormorants, white pelicans, bald eagles, and ospreys. Lewis's woodpeckers, western bluebirds, and kestrels are often found in the trees along the east side of the reservoir. The waters north of the dam often host hundreds of ducks, mergansers, and geese.

Permits, Fees, Limitations
None.

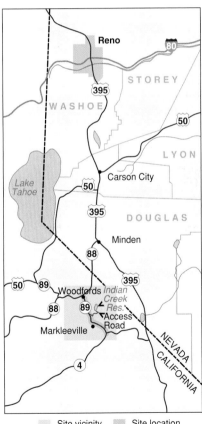

Site vicinity   Site location

Accessibility
Recreational facilities are accessible to wheelchairs, but only with difficulty and if assistance is available. The main restrooms and shower facility are accessible.

Camping and Lodging
Camping is permitted in designated areas on-site. Per-night fees are charged. The campground is open from early May–early October, weather permitting. Reservations are required for the group site. The length limit for RVs is 30 feet. The nearest lodging is in Markleeville.

Food and Supplies
No supplies are available on-site. The nearest supplies are available in Markleeville.

First Aid
First aid is not available on-site. Emergency aid is available through the Alpine County Sheriff in Markleeville,

California. The nearest hospital is located in Carson City, Nevada.

Additional Information
This developed recreation area is popular during the summer and campsites can fill up quickly, especially on holiday weekends. It is closed during the winter months.

Contact Information
BLM - Carson City District Office
5665 Morgan Mill Road
Carson City, NV 89701
Tel: (775) 885-6000
Fax: (775) 885-6147
www.nv.blm.gov/carson

Activity Codes

Lunar Crater Back Country Byway

Location
75 miles east of Tonopah, Nevada.

Description
Meandering among the bold volcanic features of the Lunar Crater Volcanic Field, the 24-mile byway follows an unpaved road through terrain characteristic of the Great Basin desert. Maars, cinder cones, mesas, cuestas, ash flows, lava flows, fault ridges, and alkali playas can be viewed along the route.

Directions
From Tonopah, travel 75 miles east along U.S. Highway 6. The byway forms a loop bisected by U.S. Highway 6, and is marked by signs at its eastern and western entrances along the highway.

Visitor Activities
Geologic sightseeing, hiking, picnicking, scenic drives, and off-highway driving. Although there is no wild horse and burro population within the Lunar Crater

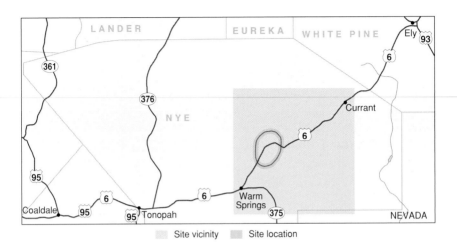

Site vicinity Site location

Volcanic Field, one might glimpse these animals along the way, as the Sand Springs West Herd Management Area is located on the north side of U.S. Highway 6.

Special Features
Lunar Crater, Easy Chair Crater, The Wall, Black Rock Lava Flow, Lunar Lake, and Palisade Mesa are some of the dominant landscape features that are visible from the byway. Lunar Crater, a bowl-shaped depression almost devoid of vegetation, looks more like a meteor-impact crater than what it is: a volcanic cinder cone that has collapsed in upon itself. In 1973, Lunar Crater was recognized as an outstanding example of the nation's natural heritage and designated as a National Natural Landmark.

Permits, Fees, Limitations
No fees.

Accessibility
Limited to existing roads.

Camping and Lodging
No developed camping facilities are available. Primitive camping is subject to

a 14-day stay limit. The site is accessible to RVs; however, no RV facilities are available. The nearest lodging is in Tonopah and in Ely, 90 miles east of the site on U.S. Highway 6.

Food and Supplies
No potable water, food, supplies, toilets, or services are available on-site. Food and supplies are available in Tonopah and Ely.

Once used by the National Aeronautics and Space Administration as a training ground for Apollo astronauts, the eerie moonscape of Lunar Crater Volcanic Field covers more than 100 square miles. *(Chris Ross, BLM Nevada State Office)*

First Aid

There is no first aid available on-site. Medical clinics are located in Tonopah and Ely.

Additional Information

Late spring, summer, and early fall are the best times to travel the byway. The area is open all year, but the byway receives minimal maintenance and can become impassable during wet or snowy weather. High-clearance vehicles are recommended.

Contact Information

BLM - Tonopah Field Station
P.O. Box 911
Tonopah, NV 89049-0911
Tel: (775) 482-7800
Fax: (775) 482-7810
www.nv.blm.gov/bmountain

Activity Codes

North Wildhorse Recreation Area

Location

70 miles north of Elko, Nevada.

Description

Fed by the East Fork Owyhee River, 2-mile-long Wildhorse Reservoir, adjoining the recreation area, is an important northeastern Nevada year-round fishery. The reservoir even offers excellent ice fishing in the winter, when lake ice can grow to a foot thick. Elevations rise to more than 6,000 feet in this beautiful, high-desert environment.

Directions

From Elko, travel north 70 miles on State Highway 225. The BLM North Wildhorse Campground is along the northbound side of the highway. (State Park and Bureau of Indian Affairs campgrounds are on the southbound side of the highway, fronting on the reservoir.)

Visitor Activities

Hiking, mountain biking, horseback riding, fishing, boating, scenic drives, wildlife viewing, birdwatching, snowmobiling, water skiing, windsurfing, and cross-country skiing.

Special Features

The reservoir contains channel catfish, rainbow trout, German brown trout, and other trout species. Golden eagles frequent the area, and waterfowl and shorebirds are common. Other resident bird species include downy woodpeckers, mountain bluebirds, and many types of warblers. Long-tailed weasels, coyotes, and yellow-bellied marmots may also be spotted.

Permits, Fees, Limitations

None.

Accessibility

None.

Camping and Lodging

There are 18 developed campsites. Three of these are shaded group sites that can each accommodate 20–30 people. Fees are charged for overnight

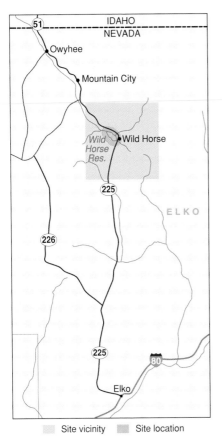

Site vicinity   Site location

camping from May 15–November 15. In addition to BLM's North Wildhorse Campground, both Nevada State Parks and the Bureau of Indian Affairs offer complete campgrounds and boat launch facilities. State Park and Bureau of Indian Affairs fees are slightly higher than BLM fees.

The nearest lodging is available at Wild Horse Ranch and Resort, 3 miles south of the campgrounds on U.S. Highway 225. Lodging is also available in Mountain City, 15 miles north on State Highway 225, and in Elko.

Food and Supplies

There are no supplies or services available on-site. Food and supplies are available in Elko and Mountain City. Limited supplies and a restaurant are available at Wild Horse Ranch and Resort.

First Aid

First aid is not available on-site. The nearest hospital is located in Elko. A medical clinic for emergencies is located

The glistening waters of Wildhorse Reservoir provide visitors with year-round recreational opportunities in a stunning mountain setting. *(BLM Nevada State Office)*

in Owyhee, 12 miles north of Mountain City.

Additional Information
The BLM campground provides beautiful vistas of the reservoir and surrounding mountains. The campground is only open from May–November, as the area's winter weather is very harsh. The recreation area is open year-round, but access may be hampered by extreme cold and snow in winter months.

Contact Information
BLM - Elko District Office
3900 East Idaho Street
Elko, NV 89801
Tel: (775) 753-0200
Fax: (775) 753-0255
www.nv.blm.gov/elko

Activity Codes

other - windsurfing, water skiing

Pine Forest Recreation Area

Location
95 miles northwest of Winnemucca, Nevada.

Description
Three popular recreation sites are located within the alpine environment of the Pine Forest Recreation Area, high in the Pine Forest Range, one of the scenic glories of Nevada's Black Rock Desert country. The glacial Blue Lakes and the Onion and Knott Creek Reservoirs all boast superb scenery, and the Knott Creek Reservoir is famous for its trophy-size rainbow trout. The cold, interconnected Blue Lakes, nestled in a cirque, are fed by snowmelt and abundant springs. The topography of the area is generally steep.

Directions
From Winnemucca, drive 30 miles north on U.S. Highway 95 to State Highway 140, and then travel 50 miles west. Turn left at Alta Creek Road. The Blue Lakes trailhead and the reservoirs are about 15 miles from State Highway 140.

Visitor Activities
Fishing, hiking, birdwatching, bird and big-game hunting, picnicking, off-highway driving, horseback riding, wildlife viewing, mountain biking, and winter sports.

The interconnected Blue Lakes, nestled in a basin carved by a retreating glacier, provide excellent opportunities for fishing and wildlife viewing. *(BLM Nevada State Office)*

Special Features
Evidence of glaciation includes polished rock, moraines, glacial canyons, and rock striations. The area supports subalpine and sagebrush steppe ecosystems and extensive riparian zones. Limber and whitebark pine live in portions of the higher elevations. Abundant wildlife includes mule deer, antelope, mountain lions, sage grouse, chukars, and bighorn sheep.

Permits, Fees, Limitations
None.

Accessibility
None.

Camping and Lodging
Camping is primitive, and there are no fees. The nearest lodging is located in Denio Junction, 35 miles northwest of the site on State Highway 140. There are no RV facilities.

Food and Supplies
Food and supplies are available in Denio Junction and Winnemucca.

First Aid
First aid is not available in this isolated area. Visitors should be prepared for any emergency. The nearest hospital is located in Winnemucca.

Additional Information
Summer temperatures at this high-desert location can range from daytime highs in the 90s to nighttime chill. Visitors should carry extra food and water. Lip balm and sunscreen are also recommended. The best time to visit is from May–September. All roads into this remote area are made of dirt, and the road to Knott Creek Reservoir is particularly rough. Four-wheel-drive vehicles are highly recommended. Roads are only passable in dry weather, and are often snow-covered in winter. Call BLM to check on conditions.

Contact Information
BLM - Winnemucca District Office
5100 East Winnemucca Boulevard
Winnemucca, NV 89445
Tel: (775) 623-1500
Fax: (775) 623-1503
www.nv.blm.gov/winnemucca

Activity Codes

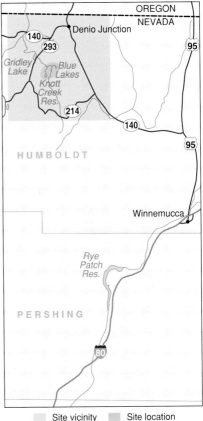

Site vicinity   Site location

Red Rock Canyon National Conservation Area

Location
20 miles west of Las Vegas, Nevada.

Description
This is a beautiful, 197,000-acre area in which to experience the natural wonders of the Mojave Desert, the driest and smallest of the American deserts. Red Rock Canyon's 3,000-foot-high, cross-bedded, red- and cream-colored Aztec Sandstone cliffs have been used as a scenic backdrop for countless motion pictures and television programs. Rock climbers dot the crags and rock faces in this world-class climbing area, which features fossilized sand dunes and sheer rock walls. Thirty miles of easy to difficult hiking trails and a 13-mile paved, scenic loop drive offer additional opportunities to experience the grandeur of the site.

Directions
From central Las Vegas, travel west on Charleston Boulevard, which becomes State Highway 159 after 5 miles. Travel west 15 miles to the Red Rock Canyon entrance.

Visitor Activities
Mountain biking, rock climbing, hiking, picnicking, archaeological site, bird-watching, burro viewing, interpretation, wildlife viewing, horseback riding, geologic sightseeing, and scenic drives.

Special Features
The most significant geologic feature of Red Rock Canyon is the Keystone Thrust Fault. Movement along this and other faults has forced older layers of sedimentary and metamorphic rock on top of younger ones. Many plants within the Mojave Desert are endemic species, including Joshua trees. Desert wildflowers, such as Mojave asters and desert marigolds, are plentiful in spring. Red Rock's fauna includes desert

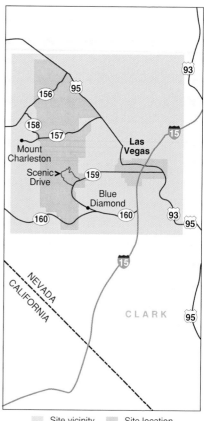

Site vicinity   Site location

tortoises and wild burros. Some rock faces feature prehistoric petroglyphs. A spring that flows year-round and a seasonally cascading waterfall are located at Lost Creek, a short, 0.3-mile hike from the visitor center.

Permits, Fees, Limitations

There is a per-vehicle site entrance fee, and a nightly fee is charged at the campground. Permits are required for back country use, sample collecting, commercial use, filming, rock climbing, special events, and weddings. Camping and climbing are prohibited at archaeological sites, including rock faces on which rock art is present. Climbing on or within 50 feet of any rock art is prohibited by law. Visitors should obtain a map at the visitor center.

Accessibility

The visitor center offers accessible restrooms and picnic tables. The Willow Spring picnic area (check the area map at the visitor center for directions) has accessible tables and one accessible restroom. The following pull-offs have accessible restrooms along the scenic loop: Sandstone Quarry, Willow Spring, and Pine Creek Canyon. (See visitor center map for exact locations.) Accessible campsites and restrooms are also located at Mile 13 of the loop, at the Red Rock Canyon Campground.

Camping and Lodging

Primitive camping is available on a first-come, first-served basis, with 22 car sites and 5 walk-in sites. The Red Rock Canyon Campground is accessible from the loop drive and also from West

Charleston Boulevard. Backpack camping above 5,000 feet along the Rocky Gap Road (see visitor center map) is also popular. The Red Rock Canyon Campground can accommodate RVs, but there are no hookups.

Food and Supplies

Other than drink vending machines at the visitor center, no food or supplies are available on-site. Supplies may be purchased in Las Vegas.

First Aid

There is no first-aid station on-site. The nearest hospital is the University Medical Center, 15 miles east on Charleston Boulevard in Las Vegas.

Additional Information

Horses are available for rental via the visitor center. The visitor center also offers naturalist-guided walks, programs, talks, and a museum and gift shop.

Contact Information

BLM - Las Vegas District Office
HCR 33, Box 5400
Las Vegas, NV 89124
Tel: (702) 515-5000
Fax: (702) 363-6779
Tel: (702) 363-1921 (Red Rock Canyon Visitor Center)
www.nv.blm.gov/vegas
www.redrockcanyon.blm.gov

Activity Codes

other - rock climbing

A majestic sandstone escarpment dominates the Red Rock Canyon National Conservation Area. Narrow canyons along the escarpment are popular day-hike destinations.
(Peggy Hamlen (used with permission))

Rhyolite Historic Area

Location
4 miles west of Beatty, Nevada.

Description
This former boomtown was born when gold was discovered in the area in 1904; by 1908, Rhyolite was the third-largest city in Nevada. The town grew steadily until the decline of the nearby Montgomery-Shoshone Gold Mine and the Bullfrog Mining District, and by 1911, Rhyolite had faded to ghost town status. Visitors to California's Death Valley National Park frequently tour Rhyolite because the townsite is located along one of the major park access roads.

Directions
From Beatty, travel southwest on State Highway 374 approximately 2 miles. Then turn right and proceed 2 miles to Rhyolite.

Visitor Activities
Historic site, hiking, wild burro viewing in general vicinity. (Rhyolite is near the Bullfrog Herd Management Area.)

In its heyday, Rhyolite was served by three train lines. The Spanish Mission-style Las Vegas Tonopah Railroad Station pictured here was expensively constructed entirely of concrete blocks and full-gauge train rails. *(Suzy McCoy, BLM volunteer, Tonopah Field Station)*

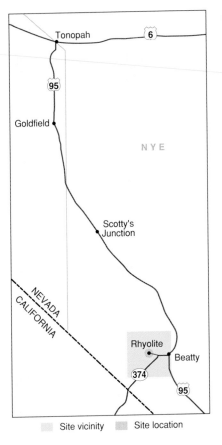

Site vicinity ▮ Site location

Special Features

This popular turn-of-the-20th-century, Gold Rush–era ghost town includes the most photographed building ruin in the West: the Cook Bank Building, once the largest and most expensive building in Rhyolite. Among several other buildings, the townsite also boasts the Tom Kelly House, Nevada's best preserved glass-bottle house and one of three originally built in the town.

Permits, Fees, Limitations

No fees. The area is for day use only.

Accessibility

Limited to the paved road.

Camping and Lodging

No camping or RV facilities are available on-site. Lodging is available in Beatty.

Food and Supplies

No food, supplies, or restroom facilities are available on-site. Food and supplies are available in Beatty.

First Aid

There is no first aid available on-site. A medical clinic is available in Beatty.

Additional Information

There are BLM volunteer site caretakers who provide site tours and interpretive presentations about the history of Rhyolite and its buildings. Free information and a guide booklet are available at the Bottle House. The area is open all year, but summer temperatures are very hot, exceeding 100°F on most days from May–September. The best time to visit Rhyolite is during the winter months. Since the area is managed by multiple landowners, visitors are urged to respect private property rights and not climb on or near structures.

Contact Information

BLM - Tonopah Field Station
P.O. Box 911
Tonopah, NV 89049-0911
Tel: (775) 482-7800
Fax: (775) 482-7810
www.nv.blm.gov/bmountain

Activity Code

Sand Mountain Recreation Area

Location
26 miles east of Fallon, Nevada.

Description
Sand Mountain is a 600-foot-high sand dune that is over a mile wide and more than 3 miles long. It is a popular destination for off-highway-vehicle enthusiasts, who bring their sand rails, all-terrain vehicles, motorcycles, and dune buggies to climb the mountain and traverse the sand. The huge dune also provides a perfect environment for sand surfing.

Directions
From Fallon, take U.S. Highway 50 east 26 miles to the signed turnoff for Sand Mountain.

Visitor Activities
Off-highway vehicle riding, hiking, wildlife viewing, geologic sightseeing, interpretation, and nature study.

Special Features
Sand Mountain is the largest single sand dune within the Great Basin physiographic province. Prevailing winds constantly move and reshape the dune, and sounds created by this movement cause Sand Mountain to "sing"; it is one of only a few such "singing dunes" in the world. The recreation area also is home to the Sand Mountain blue butterfly, first discovered in 1981 and thus far found only at Sand Mountain. Sand Springs Station is one of the best-preserved Pony Express stations still in existence. In addition, the recreation area contains a desert study area that provides interpretation of the area's plants and wildlife.

Permits, Fees, Limitations
Day-use fees are charged. Visitors may purchase either a weekly or yearly pass.

Accessibility
Toilets are wheelchair-accessible; however, the undeveloped portions of the area (including the Pony Express

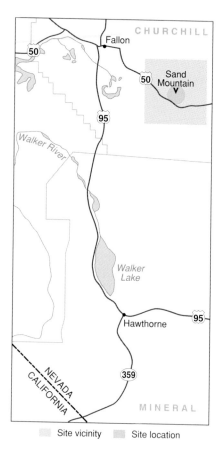

Site vicinity ▢ Site location

The product of thousands of years of blowing sands, the 4,795-acre Sand Mountain Recreation Area provides challenge and excitement for off-highway vehicle users and sandboarders. *(Bob Goodman)*

station and the desert study area) are extremely sandy and therefore inaccessible to most visitors with disabilities.

Camping and Lodging
Camping is primitive and is allowed on a first-come, first-served basis within a designated camping area. Vault toilets and trash dumpsters are located onsite. The nearest lodging is available in Fallon. The area can accommodate RVs, but no hookups are provided.

Food and Supplies
There are no food, water, or services on-site. Food and supplies are available in Fallon.

First Aid
There is no first aid available on-site. The nearest hospital is located in Fallon

Additional Information
The area is open all year, but summer daytime temperatures are very high, often exceeding 100°F. Spring and fall are the best times to visit the recreation area. It is imperative that visitors bring sufficient water to last them for their entire visit. Several thousand people may visit the area on major holiday weekends.

Contact Information
BLM – Carson City Field Office
5665 Morgan Mill Road
Carson City, NV 89701
Tel: (775) 885-6000
Fax: (775) 885-6147
www.nv.blm.gov/carson

Activity Codes

other – sand surfing, OHV open-play area

South Fork Owyhee River/ Owyhee River Canyon

Location
The headwaters are 120 miles north of Elko, Nevada.

Description
From its headwaters in north-central Nevada, the South Fork Owyhee River flows north in a deep, steep-walled canyon, meandering through the remote Owyhee Desert and eventually joining the river's East Fork in southwestern Idaho. The South Fork of the Owyhee offers floats lasting 2 to 3 days, along 23 miles in Nevada and 28 miles in Idaho.

Directions
From Elko, travel 27 miles north on State Highway 225. Turn west onto State Highway 226, and travel for 40 miles until the pavement ends. Follow the signs for Wilson Reservoir, traveling 3.5 miles on a dirt road. Then travel north on County Road 728 for 7.5

miles to the Petan Ranch. To launch a watercraft, you must first obtain permission at the Ranch. Visitors may also launch watercraft at the Pipeline Crossing, 4 miles south of the Nevada-Idaho border on County Road 728.

Visitor Activities
Hiking, fishing, hunting, kayaking, boating, swimming, wildlife viewing, geologic sightseeing, and rafting.

Special Features
River rapids range from Class I–IV. Desert bighorn sheep, mule deer, pronghorn antelope, mountain lions, golden eagles, and chukars frequent the canyon area's 6 million acres of volcanic rock and sagebrush. Fish species include squawfish and rainbow and redband trout. The canyon has cut through a number of layers of volcanic rock, and in places reveals buried ash and welded

Bighorn sheep thrive on the steep, rocky slopes of Owyhee River Canyon. Excellent rock climbers, bighorns have hooves that are hard at their outer edges and spongy in the center, providing good traction even on sheer rock. *(Jerry Sintz, BLM Utah State Office (retired))*

tuff layers that are characteristic of the region. The canyon has also opened up springs along the watercourse; while much of the water in the Owyhee system enters the drainage via precipitation, there is significant contribution to the system from these springs. Gravel bench and terrace deposits along the river contain placer gold.

Permits, Fees, Limitations
No fees or permits are required, but registration at the Petan Ranch is mandatory.

Accessibility
None.

Camping and Lodging
BLM campgrounds are located at Wilson Reservoir, 10 miles south of the Ranch on County Road 728, then 12 miles following signs to Wilson Reservoir. The Bureau of Indian Affairs offers camping at Sheep Creek Reservoir, 18 miles west of the town of Owyhee on County Road 728. RVs are welcome here, and there is a dumping station. The nearest lodging is in Owyhee and in Mountain City, 13 miles southeast of Owyhee on State Highway 225.

Food and Supplies
The nearest food and supplies are available in Owyhee and Mountain City. Full services and camping supplies are available in Elko.

First Aid
First aid is available at the clinic in Owyhee.

Additional Information
This area is not accessible from winter through early spring, because of harsh

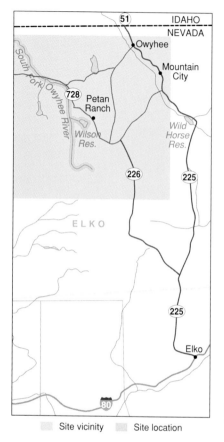

Site vicinity   Site location

weather. The best floating opportunities are available from early May–late June, when the river is at peak flow. The canyon is remote, and vehicle access is limited at all times. *The Owyhee and Bruneau River System Boating Guide* is available for purchase from the BLM offices, as is information regarding guided river trips with licensed outfitters.

Contact Information

BLM - Elko District Office
3900 East Idaho Street
Elko, NV 89801
Tel: (775) 753-0200
Fax: (775) 753-0255
www.nv.blm.gov/elko
BLM - Lower Snake River
District Office
3948 Development Ave.
Boise, ID 83705
Tel: (208) 384-3300
Fax: (208) 384-3493
www.id.blm.gov/offices/lsrd

Activity Codes

Water Canyon Recreation Area

Location

Approximately 4 miles east of Winnemucca, Nevada

Description

Secluded Water Canyon offers a rugged, picturesque setting along the canyon's upper reaches and a lush riparian area of cottonwood and aspen trees along the stream at the canyon bottom. A few primitive roads travel up into the

Sonoma Mountains from the recreation area, offering a variety of back country adventures. A 4-mile trail in Water Canyon links mountain bikers to the 40-mile-long Bloody Shins Trail System within the Santa Rosa-Paradise Peak Wilderness.

Directions

From Winnemucca Boulevard in Winnemucca, turn south onto Hanson

Street, which turns into Water Canyon Road after 2 miles. Continue 2 miles on Water Canyon Road into the recreation area.

Visitor Activities
Hiking, mountain biking, and horseback riding.

Special Features
The recreation area features one of the few riparian (streamside) habitats within this otherwise desert environment.

Permits, Fees, Limitations
No permits or fees. Motor vehicles must stay on existing roads.

Accessibility
None

Camping and Lodging
Primitive camping is available, with a 3-night camping limit. Winnemucca has several motels and RV campgrounds.

Food and Supplies
Food and supplies are available in Winnemucca. Most stores are open 7 days a week, including evenings.

First Aid
The nearest first aid is available at Humboldt General Hospital in Winnemucca.

Additional Information
The best time to visit is April-October. All roads within the recreation area are made of dirt. Visitors must use four-wheel-drive vehicles to travel past the main recreation area. Roads are only passable in dry weather and are snow-covered in winter months. The stream can dry up during exceptionally arid summers.

Contact Information
BLM - Winnemucca Field Office
5100 E. Winnemucca Blvd.
Winnemucca, NV 89445
Tel: (775) 623-1500
Fax: (775) 623-1503
www.nv.blm.gov/winnemucca

Activity Codes

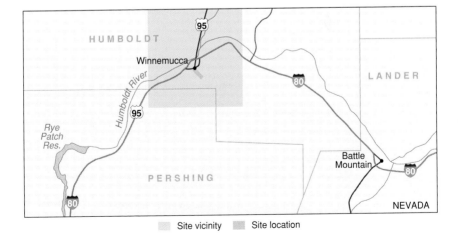

Site vicinity   Site location

The breathtaking canyon wall of the Taos Overlook provides a scenic backdrop for two mountain bikers as they enjoy a day's ride. *(Jane Bernard, Trust for Public Land (used with permission))*

Whether you crave a Rio Grande whitewater trip or a leisurely drive along the Guadalupe Back Country Byway, you'll find New Mexico to be true to its nickname: the "Land of Enchantment." Public lands encompass 12.8 million acres, or about 17 percent of the state, and feature a variety of landscapes, from the rugged lava flows of the Valley of Fires to the spectacular scenery of the Rio Grande gorge.

Public lands in New Mexico are rich in major cultural and natural resources. For example, near La Union, paleontologists unearthed the shell of a 2-million-year-old ancestor of the armadillo. Discoveries of dinosaur bones and skin impressions have ensured New Mexico's place on the map of world-class fossil sites.

Artifacts from Ancestral Puebloans (or Anasazi) and other prehistoric peoples can be found throughout BLM lands in New Mexico. And the "King's Highway," El Camino Real, still bears witness to the European colonists who built early settlements in what is now the United States. Abandoned ranch houses, old mining towns, and military forts are evidence of more recent arrivals.

New Mexico offers both wildlife enthusiasts and birdwatchers their choice of destinations and almost boundless target species. And though Oklahoma hosts only limited public lands, it nevertheless offers an exceptional destination for animal lovers: Pauls Valley, an equine paradise that invites visitors to observe— or even "adopt"—wild horses and burros gathered from public lands.

New Mexico's mild, varied climate allows travel to scenic public land sites at just about any time of year. Although all are accessible by vehicle, some areas can be reached only via rugged dirt roads, providing journeys that are part of the adventure. Visitors will be delighted by the diverse recreation opportunities on public lands in this enchanting state.

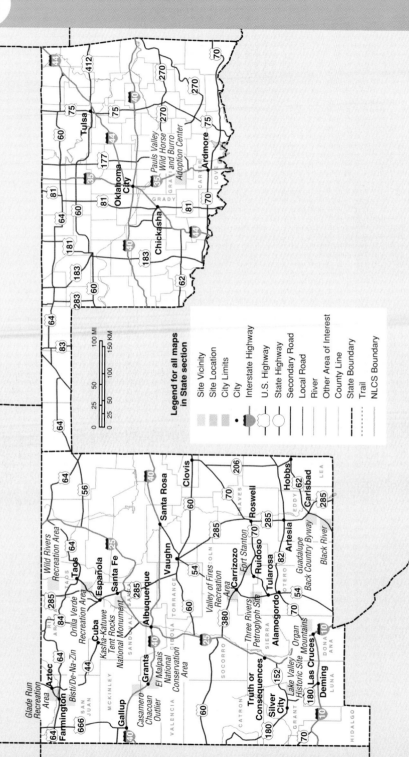

Legend for all maps in State section

Site Vicinity
Site Location
City Limits
City
Interstate Highway
U.S. Highway
State Highway
Secondary Road
Local Road
River
Other Area of Interest
County Line
State Boundary
Trail
NLCS Boundary

0   25   50   100 MI
0 25 50 100 150 KM

Bisti/De-Na-Zin

Location
About 30 miles south of Farmington, New Mexico.

Description
The Bisti/De-Na-Zin Wilderness is a remote, desolate area of steeply eroded badlands that offers some of the most unusual scenery found in the Four Corners region. Time and the natural elements have etched a fantasy world of strange-looking rock formations amid one of the most fossil-rich areas in the West. This ever-changing environment offers the visitor unique, remote wilderness experiences.

During the Late Cretaceous period, approximately 65–80 million years ago, the area was home to many reptiles, large dinosaurs, and some very small, primitive mammals. Fossils here are of great importance because they provide a record of changes in plant and animal life at the end of the Age of Dinosaurs.

The red hills within this wilderness are the result of clay soils having been baked by underground coal fires while buried millions of years ago. The billowy mounds, made up of a crumbling layer of caked soils, are the result of rapidly-eroded silts and clays.

Directions
From Farmington, take State Highway 371 south for 36.5 miles. Turn left on San Juan County Road 7290. Drive 2 miles to the visitor parking lot. From Crownpoint, take State Highway 371 north for about 40 miles to County Road 7500, which accesses the parking area.

Visitor Activities
Hiking, horseback riding, fossil viewing, and geologic sightseeing.

Special Features
The two major geological formations found in the wilderness are the Fruitland Formation and the Kirtland Shale. The Fruitland Formation contains layers of sandstone, shale, mudstone, coal, and silt. The weathering of the sandstone forms the many spires and hoodoos (sculpted landforms) found throughout

The fantastic formations of the Bisti/De-Na-Zin Wilderness appear even more surreal under a full moon. (M'Lee Beazley, BLM Albuquerque Field Office)

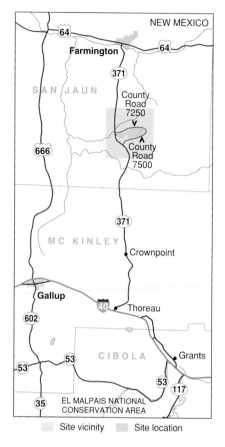

Site vicinity   Site location

Food and Supplies
There are no services on-site. Food and supplies are available in Farmington and Crownpoint, 40 miles south on State Highway 371.

First Aid
The nearest hospital is in Farmington.

Additional Information
The area is open all year. Potential dangers include rattlesnakes. Visitors are cautioned not to light campfires or any type of fire. Collecting fossils or petrified wood is prohibited, as is climbing on delicate geologic formations. Traveling in groups is encouraged. There are no water sources or designated trails in the wilderness. Because of the extremely hot summer climate and unpredictable winter snowfall, visiting the area in late spring, early summer, and fall is recommended. San Juan County Road 7500 may become impassable in the winter.

Contact Information
BLM - Farmington Field Office
1235 La Plata Highway, Suite A
Farmington, NM 87401
Tel: (505) 599-8900
Fax: (505) 599-8998
www.nm.blm.gov/ffo/ffo_home.html

Activity Codes

the area. The Kirtland Shale contains rock of various colors and dominates the eastern part of the wilderness. This shale caps the mushroom-shaped landforms of the area.

Permits, Fees, Limitations
None.

Accessibility
Motorized or mechanized vehicles, including wheelchairs, are not allowed in the wilderness.

Black River

Location
25 miles southwest of Carlsbad, New Mexico.

Description
The Black River is an oasis in the Chihuahuan Desert. Rare species of plants, fish, and reptiles make their home in and around the river. During migration seasons, the area teems with a variety of birds, including waterfowl, shorebirds, and songbirds. Lush desert vegetation and clear pools of water provide opportunities for viewing wildlife. This thriving riparian community includes 15 plants and animals that rarely occur in New Mexico.

Directions
From Carlsbad, take U.S. Highway 62/180 south about 25 miles and turn west onto County Road 418. Travel another 2 miles and turn left at the fork to the BLM Cottonwood Day Use Area, which is in the Black River Special Management Area.

Visitor Activities
Hiking, wildlife viewing, fishing, bird-watching, and plant viewing.

Special Features
Bird populations in this small area fluctuate from day to day. Visitors may observe green-backed herons, orchard orioles, yellow-billed cuckoos, and roadrunners. Some less common plants include gypsum ringstems, gypsum milkvetches, and Scheer's pincushion cacti. River cooter turtles basking on downed trees in the watercourse will also delight wildlife enthusiasts.

Permits, Fees, Limitations
None.

Accessibility
Trails that lead to the water are wheelchair-accessible; however, they are hard-packed, not paved.

Camping and Lodging
Developed camping and lodging are available 5 miles north on U.S. Highway 62/80 in Whites City.

Food and Supplies
Food and supplies are available in Carlsbad and Whites City.

Fed by springs, the tranquil Black River provides habitat for many rare species of plants and animals. (Howard Parman, BLM Roswell Field Office)

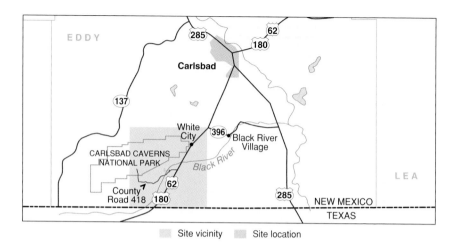

Site vicinity Site location

First Aid
There is no first aid on-site. Emergency services are available at Carlsbad Medical Center.

Additional Information
The site is open all year, but summer daytime temperatures can be over 100°F. The best time to visit is the fall months. BLM manages 1,200 acres along the river, including the springs that feed it.

Contact Information
BLM - Carlsbad Field Office
620 East Greene
Carlsbad, NM 88220
Tel: (505) 234-5972
Fax: (505) 885-9264
www.nm.blm.gov/cfo/cfo_home.html

Activity Codes

Casamero Chacoan Outlier

Location
20 miles west of Grants, New Mexico.

Description
Casamero Pueblo was occupied by the Ancestral Puebloans from AD 1000–1125. It is an excellent example of a Chacoan outlier (an outlying community connected to Chaco Canyon by prehistoric roads), displaying many of the same cultural and architectural traits found at Chaco Canyon. Casamero Pueblo was a community building that served a number of nearby farmsteads. It was used for social and religious activities that were aimed at uniting individual families into a cohesive community. This historic building (along with Chaco Cultural National Historical Park and six other outliers) is included on the World Heritage List.

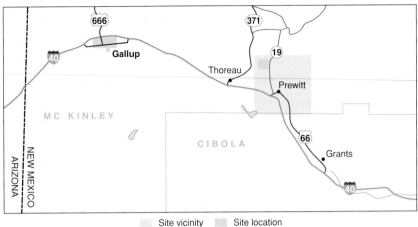

Site vicinity   Site location

Directions

From Grants, drive 15 miles west on Interstate 40. Take the Prewitt Exit, turn right, and drive 0.25 mile north to Old U.S. Highway 66 (Route 66). Turn right on Route 66 and drive 0.25 mile east to the intersection with County Road 19. Turn left and drive 4.5 miles north on the paved County Road to a small parking lot on the left (west) side of the road. The ruin is visible 200 yards further west.

Visitor Activities

Archaeological site, hiking, interpretive trails, and scenic drives.

Special Features

Many of the characteristics that distinguish public architecture of the Chacoan Anasazi are visible at Casamero Pueblo, such as a surface kiva and intricate masonry. The towering red sandstone cliffs of Tecolote Mesa form a dramatic backdrop for this ruin.

Permits, Fees, Limitations

None.

Accessibility

None.

Camping and Lodging

The nearest lodging is available in Grants. For information on lodging and camping, contact the Grants Chamber of Commerce, 100 North Iron Ave., Grants, NM 87020, (505) 287-4802.

At Casamero Pueblo, visitors view remnants of a community building used by the Ancestral Puebloans from AD 1000–1125.
(John Roney, BLM Albuquerque Field Office)

Food and Supplies

The nearest food and supplies are near Bluewater, about 10 miles east on Route 66.

First Aid

The nearest medical facilities are in Grants.

Additional Information

The surrounding lands are private. Visitors should stay within the fenced parcel of public land.

Contact Information

BLM - Albuquerque Field Office
435 Montano NE
Albuquerque, NM 87107
Tel: (505) 761-8700
Fax: (505) 761-8911
www.nm.blm.gov/aufo/aufo_home.html

Activity Codes

El Malpais National Conservation Area

Location

5 miles southeast of Grants and 80 miles west of Albuquerque, New Mexico.

Description

El Malpais, (pronounced "Mall-pie-*ees*"), "the badlands" in Spanish, aptly describes the tens of thousands of acres of

craggy lava flows, some up to 800,000 years old, that cover much of the 263,000-acre El Malpais National Conservation Area. The black basalt, far from lifeless, has been reinvaded by ponderosa pine and pinyon and juniper trees, as well as by various grasses and shrubs. This sparsely-vegetated, rocky terrain provides

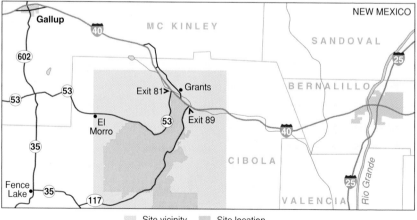

Site vicinity   Site location

habitat for reptiles, small mammals, birds (including hawks and eagles), and coyotes. Two wilderness areas, West Malpais and Cebolla, encompass almost 100,000 acres. West Malpais Wilderness includes Hole-in-the-Wall, a large expanse of grasslands underlain by 700,000-year-old lava and surrounded by younger lava flows. Cebolla Wilderness is dotted with historic homesteads and archaeological sites that provide connections to the past.

Directions

From Albuquerque, take Interstate 40 west to Exit 89. Continue along State Highway 117 to traverse the east side of the conservation area. West of Grants, take Exit 81 along State Highway 53 to travel along the northwestern edge of the area.

Visitor Activities

Hiking, picnicking, wildlife viewing, birdwatching, plant viewing, wildflower viewing, historic site, archaeological site, scenic drives, geologic sightseeing, interpretation, caving, and rock climbing.

Special Features

La Ventana Natural Arch, one of the most visible and accessible features of El Malpais National Conservation Area, is a huge, sandstone arch carved by wind and water.

Permits, Fees, Limitations

None.

Accessibility

The visitor center, restrooms, and picnic tables are accessible. Trails are gravel-packed, not paved.

Camping and Lodging

Primitive camping is encouraged for users of El Malpais. Developed, private campgrounds and other lodging are available in and near Grants, 5 miles northeast of El Malpais. Most of the developed campgrounds provide access for RVs.

Food and Supplies

There are no services on-site. Food and supplies are available in Grants and along Interstate 40.

First Aid

There is no first aid station on-site. Many park rangers are trained in limited first aid. The nearest hospital is located in Grants.

Additional Information

The area is open all year, but summer daytime temperatures can be high. July, August, and the first part of September receive the most rainfall and roads may be impassable at times. The best time to visit is during the autumn months. Lava is sharp and unforgiving; visitors should wear appropriate footwear and gear. Visitors should also respect private lands that are intermixed with public lands. Some back country roads are impassable when wet.

Contact Information

BLM - Grants Field Station
2001 E. Santa Fe Ave.
P.O. Box 846
Grants, NM 87020
Tel: (505) 287-7911
Fax: (505) 285-5041
www.nm.blm.gov/aufo/el_malpais/el_malpais.html

Activity Codes

other - caving, rock climbing

Pinyon- and juniper-studded sandstone soars into La Ventana, a high natural arch within the El Malpais National Conservation Area. *(BLM New Mexico State Office)*

Fort Stanton

Location
65 miles west of Roswell, New Mexico.

Description
The 24,000-acre Fort Stanton area has been designated as a BLM Area of Critical Environmental Concern to protect its biological, archaeological, and scenic qualities while also providing quality recreation opportunities. The area features approximately 20 miles of equestrian trails, 18 miles of mountain bike trails, the Rio Bonito Petroglyph National Recreation Trail, and Fort Stanton Cave, the third-largest cave in New Mexico. The area is rich in military history and includes historic Fort Stanton, an 1860s-vintage cavalry fort and museum located in the middle of the area. Eight miles east of the site is the historic village of Lincoln, scene of the 1870s Lincoln County War, in which the legendary outlaw Billy the Kid participated.

The Lincoln National Forest borders Fort Stanton on the north and south. Fort Stanton provides habitat for elk, deer, and turkeys.

Directions
From Roswell, travel 65 miles west on U.S. Highway 70 to its junction with State Highway 220, and turn south for approximately 4 miles to Fort Stanton. Or, from Ruidoso, travel north 7 miles on State Highway 48. Turn east on State Highway 220 toward the Sierra Blanca Regional Airport and travel south 10 miles to Fort Stanton.

Visitor Activities
Hiking, mountain biking, horseback riding, caving, wildlife viewing, historic site, interpretation, big-game hunting, plant viewing, archaeological site, geologic sightseeing, and scenic drives.

Special Features
The area is rich in remnants of prehistoric Native American culture. The Rio Bonito Petroglyph site is a "must-see." It features Jornada Mogollon rock carvings of animals,

An endurance rider enjoys one of the many equestrian trails in historic Fort Stanton.
(Paul Happel, BLM Roswell Field Office)

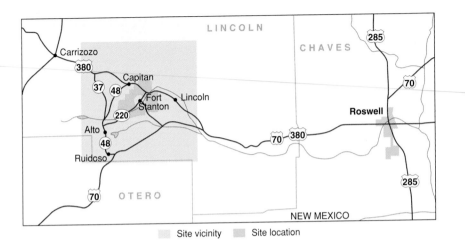

Site vicinity   Site location

footprints, geometric patterns, and mask-like images. The site can be accessed via a dirt road off State Highway 214, just east of the airport. Fort Stanton Cave contains 11 miles of cave passages.

Permits, Fees, Limitations

A permit is required for entry into Fort Stanton Cave. Permits are available from BLM from April 15–October 31.

Accessibility

Toilet facilities at the Horse Trails parking lot on State Highway 220 and at the Fort Stanton Cave are accessible.

Camping and Lodging

The Fort Stanton area contains undeveloped campsites. RV campgrounds are located in Capitan (7 miles west on U.S. Highway 380) and Ruidoso (26 miles southwest on U.S. Highway 70). A variety of lodging is also available in Lincoln (10 miles west on U.S. Highway 380), Capitan, and Ruidoso.

Food and Supplies

Food and supplies are available in Ruidoso and Capitan.

First Aid

The nearest hospital is located in Ruidoso, or visitors can dial 911.

Additional Information

The Fort Stanton area is open year-round. The fort structure itself is managed by the State of New Mexico. The Fort Stanton Museum is open Friday–Sunday, 9 a.m.–4 p.m.

Contact Information

BLM - Roswell Field Office
2909 West Second Street
Roswell, NM 88201
Tel: (505) 627-0272
Fax: (505) 627-0276
www.nm.blm.gov/rfo/index.htm

Activity Codes

other - caving

Glade Run Recreation Area

Location
Immediately north of Farmington, New Mexico.

Description
The approximately 19,000 acres of public land within the Glade Run Recreation Area encompass diverse topography, from rolling hills to sandy arroyo bottoms to sandstone slickrock. Vegetation is sparse, primarily consisting of common grasses, rabbitbrush, sagebrush, junipers, and pinyons. There are 42 miles of marked trails for motorized trailbike riders and mountain bikers. A portion of the area is open to off-highway vehicle use and is used for a number of competitive rock crawling (off-road vehicles across rocks) events each year. Glade Run is the site of the Road Apple Rally, which is the oldest continuously-held mountain bike race in the world.

Rock crawlers at an American Rock Crawling Association event watch a jeep maneuver its way up one of the trails within the Glade Run system. *(Richard Simmons, BLM Farmington Field Office)*

Directions
From Farmington, turn north off Pinon Hills Boulevard onto the main Glade Road and travel north approximately 1.5 miles to the off-road vehicle open area.

Visitor Activities
Motorcycling, trailbiking, all-terrain driving, off-road touring, mountain biking, hiking, and horseback riding.

Special Features
The trail system affords spectacular, panoramic views of the Colorado mountains to the north and of Shiprock, a sacred Navajo "rock with wings" that rises 1,800 feet from the desert floor.

Permits, Fees, Limitations
A free BLM permit is required for overnight camping. Any competitive or commercial use also requires a permit. Check with BLM for applicable fees and other requirements.

Accessibility
Much of the area is wheelchair-accessible, although it tends to be rough and sandy. The single-track trails are too narrow for wheelchairs.

Camping and Lodging
A wide variety of lodging is available in Farmington.

Food and Supplies
Food and supplies are available in Farmington.

First Aid
There is no on-site first aid. The closest medical facilities are in Farmington.

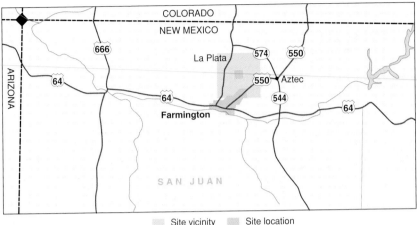

COLORADO

NEW MEXICO

666

La Plata

574

550

64

550 Aztec

64

544

ARIZONA

64

Farmington

64

SAN JUAN

☐ Site vicinity ☐ Site location

Additional Information

The trail system is used year-round; however, occasional heavy rain or winter snows may make routes temporarily impassable. There are no water or restroom facilities within the Glade System. It is a multiple-use area, including recreational activities, oil and gas development, grazing, and private inholdings. Because there are multiple access points in the Glade Run Recreation Area, it is recommended that visitors secure a map of the marked trail system from BLM prior to visiting. Color maps of the trail may be purchased at local bike shops. Visitors should respect other users and private property.

Contact Information

BLM - Farmington Field Office
1235 La Plata Highway, Suite A
Farmington, NM 87401
Tel: (505) 599-8900
Fax: (505) 599-8998
www.nm.blm.gov/ffo/ffo_home.html

Activity Codes

Guadalupe Back Country Byway

Location

The beginning of the byway is located 12 miles north of Carlsbad, New Mexico.

Description

Over the course of 30 miles, the Guadalupe Back Country Byway leads visitors from the cholla cacti and creosote bushes of the Chihuahuan Desert to the pines of the Guadalupe Mountains Escarpment. Travelers can see mule deer, pronghorn antelope, gray foxes, scaled quail, mourning doves, a variety of songbirds, and small mammals. The plains give way to steep limestone out-

Along the Guadalupe Back Country Byway, a visitor stops at a roadside kiosk that highlights both the geology and local petroleum industry of the area.
(Bill Stoughton, Reno, Nevada (used with permission))

crops cut by dry arroyos and containing hundreds of wild caves. With significant petroleum reserves, this area has an interesting history of oil and gas development.

Directions

From Carlsbad, take U.S. Highway 285 north about 12 miles and turn west on State Highway 137. There are signs on U.S. Highway 285 directing visitors to the byway, and the byway itself has signs marking the route.

Visitor Activities

Hiking, wildlife viewing, big-game and bird hunting, birdwatching, geologic sightseeing, historic site, plant viewing, scenic drives, interpretation, and caving.

Special Features

Geologically, the byway is situated along the Capitan Reef complex, which marks one edge of the Permian Basin. The byway highlights the local petroleum industry, the geology of the ancient reef, and the area's caves through a series of roadside kiosks.

Permits, Fees, Limitations

A BLM permit is required for caving.

Accessibility

The byway is a paved state highway with several accessible gravel pullouts.

Camping and Lodging

Developed camping and lodging are available 12 miles south in Carlsbad, and

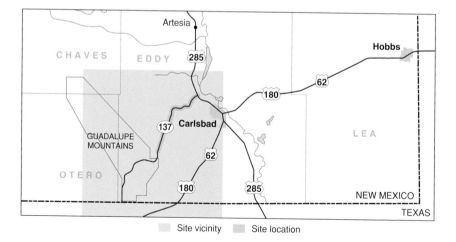

Site vicinity   Site location

20 miles north on U.S. Highway 285 in Artesia. Approximately 27 miles past the byway is the Dog Canyon Campground in Guadalupe National Park. Primitive camping is permitted on both BLM and national forest lands along the byway.

Food and Supplies
Food and supplies are available in Carlsbad and Artesia.

First Aid
Emergency services are available at Carlsbad Medical Center in Carlsbad.

Additional Information
The byway is open all year, but spring and fall wildflower seasons may be the best time to visit. Gasoline and vehicle services are very limited; visitors should be prepared. Carlsbad Caverns and Lechuguilla Cave are located in nearby Carlsbad Caverns National Park.

Contact Information
BLM - Carlsbad Field Office
620 East Greene
Carlsbad, NM 88220
Tel: (505) 234-5972
Fax: (505) 885-9264
www.nm.blm.gov/cfo/cfo_home.html

Activity Codes

other - caving

Kasha-Katuwe Tent Rocks National Monument

Location
55 miles northeast of Albuquerque, New Mexico.

Description
Located on the Pajarito Plateau in north-central New Mexico, Kasha-Katuwe Tent Rocks National Monument is a remarkable outdoor laboratory. The cone-shaped "tent rock" landforms are composed of the products of volcanic eruptions that occurred 6–7 million years ago and left pumice, ash, and tuff deposits over 1,000 feet thick. Over time, wind and water eroded these deposits, creating canyons and arroyos, scooping holes in the rock, and contouring the ends of small, inward-leading ravines into smooth semi-circular features. While fairly uniform in shape, the tent rocks vary in height from a few feet to 90 feet. Bands of gray are interspersed with beige and pink rock along the cliff faces.

"Kasha-Katuwe" means "white cliffs" in the traditional Keresan language of the Native American people of the adjacent Pueblo de Cochiti. The people of the Pueblo have always considered Kasha-Katuwe Tent Rocks a significant place of spirituality and renewal, as well as a place in which to collect plants for medicinal and ceremonial purposes.

A 2-mile national recreation trail within the monument contains two segments that provide opportunities for birdwatching, geologic observation, plant identification, and scenic viewing.

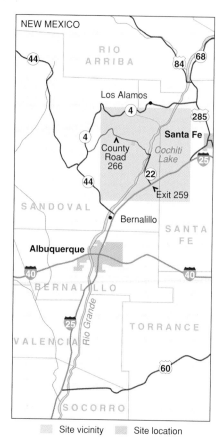

NEW MEXICO

Site vicinity　　Site location

259) onto State Route (SR) 22. Follow the signs on SR 22 to Cochiti Pueblo and Kasha-Katuwe Tent Rocks National Monument. Turn right off SR 22 at the Pueblo water tower (painted to resemble a drum) onto Tribal Route 92. Turn right onto Forest Service Road 266 and travel 5 miles on a gravel road to the monument's designated parking/picnic area, fee station, and trailhead.

Visitor Activities

Hiking, picnicking, birdwatching, wildlife and plant viewing, and geologic sightseeing.

Special Features

Spilling from cracks and crevices on cliff faces, the vibrant green leaves and red bark of the manzanita shrub stand in sharp contrast to the muted colors of the rocks. This hardy evergreen produces a lustrous, pinkish-white flower in the spring. Other desert plants found in the area include Indian paintbrush, Apache plumes, rabbitbrush, and desert marigolds.

Depending on the season, visitors are likely to see a variety of birds. Red-tailed hawks, American kestrels, violet-green swallows, western bluebirds, and an occasional golden eagle soar above the area or use pinyon-covered terrain near the cliffs. The hollows and crags of the cliff faces provide nesting sites. The area also provides habitat for big-game and non-game animals. Elk, mule deer, and wild turkeys frequent the higher elevations with adequate ground cover and food. Coyotes, chipmunks, and ground squirrels can be found almost everywhere.

The Cave Loop Trail, 1.2 miles long, is rated as easy. The more difficult Canyon Trail is a 1.5-mile, one-way trek into a narrow canyon, past the tent rocks, and up a steep, 630-foot hill to a lookout point on the mesa top for outstanding views of the Sangre de Cristo, Jemez, and Sandia Mountains and the Rio Grande Valley.

Directions

From Albuquerque, take Interstate 25 north to the exit for Santo Domingo/Cochiti Lake Recreation Area (Exit

Within New Mexico's Kasha-Katuwe Tent Rocks National Monument, volcanic tuffs have been shaped by wind and rain into unique, conical landforms. *(M'Lee Beazley, BLM Albuquerque Field Office)*

Permits, Fees, Limitations

A per-vehicle day-use fee is charged. An annual day-use pass is available. Motorized vehicles and mountain bikes are permitted only on the access road and in designated parking areas. Pets must be kept on a leash; a fine may be assessed for non-compliance. Camping, fires, shooting, and climbing on the tent rocks are prohibited.

Accessibility

The parking area and facilities are accessible. The trail is not accessible to wheelchairs because of the soft volcanic tuff.

Camping and Lodging

The monument is a day-use area only. Camping, boating facilities, and RV hookups are available at the Cochiti Lake Recreation Area, located 7 miles east of the monument on SR 22.

Food and Supplies

Snacks, water, soda, sandwiches, and gas can be obtained at the convenience store located near the town of Cochiti Lake, approximately 8 miles east of the monument on SR 22.

First Aid

First aid is available from the Pueblo de Cochiti staff who patrol the monument. Emergency services are available through local law enforcement and search and rescue teams. Visitors may call 911 for the Sandoval County Sheriff's Office. The nearest hospitals are in Santa Fe (40 miles northeast on Interstate 25) and Albuquerque.

Additional Information

Kasha-Katuwe Tent Rocks is open 8 a.m.–5 p.m., November 1–March 31, and 7 a.m.–7 p.m., April 1–October 31. Please respect the traditions and privacy of Pueblo de Cochiti residents. Photography, drawings, and recordings are not permitted within the Pueblo. Observe the posted speed limit to reduce dust and noise at the Pueblo.

During rainy weather and thunderstorms, flash-floods may occur in the canyon and lightning may strike the ridges. During periods of inclement weather, the access road may wash out or become impassable. Contact BLM or the Pueblo de Cochiti, (505) 465-2244, for current road conditions.

Contact Information

BLM - Albuquerque Field Office
435 Montano NE
Albuquerque, NM 87107
Tel: (505) 761-8700
Fax: (505) 761-8911
*www.nm.blm.gov/aufo/tent_rocks/
tent_rocks.html*

Activity Codes

Lake Valley Historic Site

Location

15 miles south of Hillsboro, New Mexico.

Description

At this site, visitors can drive the scenic Lake Valley Back Country Byway, visit a historic schoolhouse, or take a self-guided walking tour through Lake Valley ghost town, an old mining town established in 1878. This is the site of the purest silver discovery ever made in the U.S., and was at one time the transportation and commercial center of the local mining district. After the mining bust of 1893, the town's population declined. The community continued as a supply center for

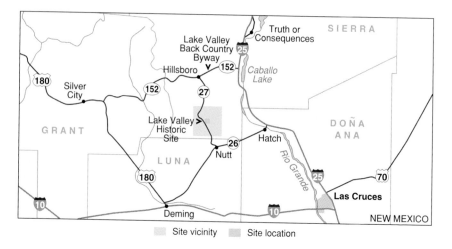

surrounding sheep and cattle ranchers, until an 1895 fire destroyed half of the town, causing the population to further dwindle.

Lake Valley is listed on the State Register of Cultural Properties and is one of the better-preserved ghost towns in New Mexico. Several homes, a one-room schoolhouse, a chapel, and the coal depot remain. The schoolhouse and chapel have been restored to include interior furnishings such as desks and the original clock in the school, and pews, the altar, and the organ in the chapel. Other buildings in the townsite have been stabilized to slow further deterioration.

Directions

From Truth or Consequences, drive south 12 miles on Interstate 25 to the Hillsboro exit and State Highway 152. Go west on State Highway 152 to Hillsboro. From Hillsboro, go 15 miles south on State Highway 27 to the townsite.

Or, from Las Cruces, travel 41 miles north on Interstate 25 and exit at Hatch. Take State Highway 26 west, toward Deming, and go 19 miles to the town of Nutt. Turn north onto State Highway 27 and travel 12 miles to the Lake Valley townsite.

Visitor Activities

Scenic drives, interpretation, and historic site.

Special Features

The restored schoolhouse provides a glimpse of what schooling in a rural area was like in the early 20th century. It also serves as a small museum of the area, exhibiting books, maps, desks, and other materials used by the students of the era. Artifacts from the town of Lake Valley, such as coins, tools, utensils, and photographs, are also housed in the museum.

The restored, historic 1904 schoolhouse in Lake Valley's ghost town is listed on New Mexico's Register of Cultural Properties and now also serves as a museum and local event center. *(Dwayne Sykes, BLM New Mexico State Office)*

Permits, Fees, Limitations

There are no entrance fees, but donations are accepted.

Accessibility

All sites are accessible to the hearing- and sight-impaired, but are not wheelchair-accessible.

Camping and Lodging

There are no picnic facilities, camping, or lodging available at Lake Valley. The nearest lodging is available in Hillsboro, 15 miles north on State Highway 27, and Hatch, 31 miles southeast on State Highways 27 and 26.

Food and Supplies

There are no supplies available at Lake Valley. Food and supplies are available in Hatch and Hillsboro.

First Aid

Emergency medical assistance is available through the Sheriff's Department in Hillsboro. The nearest hospital is in Truth or Consequences.

Additional Information

The site is open year-round. School-house hours are Friday–Tuesday, 9 a.m.–5 p.m.; Wednesday and Thursday, 9 a.m.–3 p.m.; and Sunday, 11 a.m.–5 p.m. Volunteers staff this site; hours sometimes vary with volunteer availability. Portable toilets are located near the schoolhouse.

Contact Information

BLM - Las Cruces Field Office
1800 Marquess Street
Las Cruces, NM 88005
Tel: (505) 525-4300
Fax: (505) 525-4412
www.nm.blm.gov/lcfo/lcfo_home.html

Activity Codes

Organ Mountains

Location

10 miles east of Las Cruces, New Mexico.

Description

The Organ Mountains, ranging in elevation from 5,000–9,000 feet, host a diversity of vegetation and habitat types, from desert grasslands to ponderosa pine and oak. Designated a BLM Area of Critical Environmental Concern, these mountains host approximately 80 species of mammals, 185 species of birds, and 60 species of reptiles and amphibians.

The Dripping Springs Natural Area is located on the west side of the Organ Mountains. Nestled at the base of towering gray granite spires and massive purple rhyolite cliffs, this area is home to several rare plants and animals. Hiking trails, picnic areas, historic sites, and interpretive displays at the A.B. Cox Visitor Center provide a variety of recreational opportunities.

The Aguirre Spring Campground is on the eastern slope of the Organ Mountains. Set among oak and juniper wood-lands and framed by jagged granite spires, the campground overlooks the Tularosa Basin and White Sands Missile Range.

Directions

From Interstate 25 in Las Cruces, take U.S. Highway 70 east approximately 10 miles to Baylor Canyon Road, which runs along the western base of the mountains for 6 miles.

Or, continue east on Highway 70 through San Augustine Pass, turn south on the first paved road, and go 6 miles to the Aguirre Spring Campground. If traveling west on U.S. Highway 70, go 5 miles past the main-gate access road of the White Sands Missile Range, and turn south on the first paved road to Aguirre Spring Campground.

To access Dripping Springs Natural Area, take Exit 1 off Interstate 25, turn east on University Avenue/Dripping Springs Road, and continue for 8 miles to the A.B. Cox Visitor Center.

Visitor Activities

Hiking, picnicking, bird and big-game hunting, horseback riding, birdwatching, wildlife viewing, geologic sightseeing, historic site, archaeological site, and rock climbing.

Special Features

The ruins of a 19th-century resort hotel and an early 20th-century tuberculosis sanitarium are located at Dripping Springs. La Cueva is a small cave or rock shelter from which numerous prehistoric artifacts have been excavated. Local history also chronicles the life of a hermit who lived in the cave and was killed by wandering Apaches in the 1870s.

Permits, Fees, Limitations

A day-use fee is charged at the Aguirre Spring Campground and the Dripping Springs Natural Area. There is no fee for use of other portions of the mountains.

Accessibility

Both Aguirre Spring Campground and Dripping Springs Natural Area have wheelchair-accessible facilities.

Camping and Lodging

Developed camping and picnic sites are available at Aguirre Spring

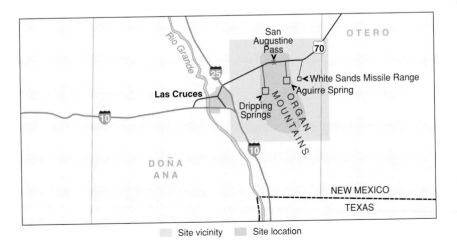

Site vicinity   Site location

Campground. Water is available at the campground host residence on the access road. Back country areas in the mountains are open to primitive camping. Lodging is available in Las Cruces.

Food and Supplies

Food and supplies are available in Las Cruces.

First Aid

First aid is available from the Aguirre Spring Campground hosts, who reside on the campground access road, 3 miles south of Highway 70, and at the Dripping Springs Visitor Center. Emergency services are available through local law enforcement and search and rescue teams. The nearest hospital is in Las Cruces.

Additional Information

Much of the southeastern portion of the Organ Mountains is within the Ft.

Bliss Military Reservation. This area is not open to the public; however, in many areas, the boundary is not marked. Potential dangers in the mountains include rattlesnakes, mountain lions, and precipitous cliffs.

Contact Information

BLM - Las Cruces Field Office
1800 Marquess
Las Cruces, NM 88005
Tel: (505) 525-4300
Fax: (505) 525-4412
www.nm.blm.gov/lcfo/lcfo_home.html

Activity Codes

other − rock climbing

Orilla Verde Recreation Area

Location

1.5 miles west of Pilar, New Mexico.

Description

Orilla Verde Recreation Area, nestled along the banks of the Rio Grande, offers visitors a wide variety of recreational opportunities. All facilities are located within the steep-walled Rio Grande Gorge. Because of the dramatic changes in elevation (over 600 feet) and the diversity of plant life, Orilla Verde draws many species of animals, including raptors (such as eagles and hawks), songbirds, waterfowl, beavers, cougars, ringtails, and mule deer. Gentle waters with occasional small rapids flow through Orilla Verde,

providing an ideal setting for many water-based recreational activities. Five campgrounds along the river provide a tranquil setting for relaxation. La Vista Verde Trail, Las Minas Trail, and the West Rim Trail are developed hiking/biking trails within the recreation area and provide opportunities for nature study and scenic vistas of the gorge and surrounding area.

Directions

From Española, take State Highway 68 north approximately 23 miles (toward Taos) to the village of Pilar. Turn left on State Highway 570, just north of the Rio Grande Gorge Visitor Center. Follow signs to Orilla Verde.

Visitor Activities

Canoeing, kayaking, floating, wildlife viewing, fishing, hiking, mountain biking, picnicking, birdwatching, and interpretation.

Special Features

The cottonwoods and willows along this section of the Rio Grande provide habitat for a variety of resident, nesting, and migrant bird species. The more illustrious include great blue herons, bald eagles, and golden eagles. This is the most accessible, yet almost entirely undeveloped, part of the 70-mile long Rio Grande Gorge. Petroglyphs offer evidence of human occupation over thousands of years. Visitors should check with BLM rangers for the locations of petroglyphs.

Permits, Fees, Limitations

There is a per-vehicle, day-use fee. A day-use pass, good for 1 calendar year, is available from the BLM Taos Field Office or the Rio Grande Gorge Visitor Center, (505) 751-4899.

Accessibility

All facilities at the Rio Grande Gorge Visitor Center are wheelchair-accessible. There are also several wheelchair-accessible campsites at Orilla Verde Recreation Area. Information on accessible campsites is available at the visitor center.

Camping and Lodging

There are nightly camping fees at the Orilla Verde Recreation Area's campgrounds, two with RV hookups (first come, first served), and privately-owned campgrounds in Taos. Lodging is available in Taos. For further information on camping and lodging, contact or visit

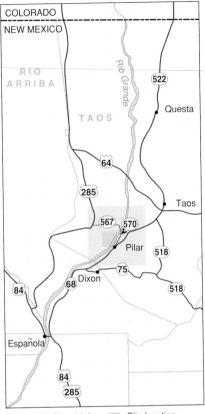

Site vicinity   Site location

Just south of Orilla Verde Recreation Area, whitewater rafters maneuver through the challenging "rock garden" rapids of the Rio Grande's "BLM Racecourse" segment.
(M'Lee Beazley, BLM Albuquerque Field Office)

the Taos County Chamber of Commerce Visitor Center located approximately 20 miles north at the intersection of State Highways 68 and 64, Taos, NM 87571, (505) 758-3873.

Food and Supplies

Food and supplies are available in Taos, and, during the summer, in Pilar.

First Aid

First aid is available at the Rio Grande Gorge Visitor Center. The nearest hospitals are located in Taos and Española; a clinic is available during the day in Embudo (11 miles southwest of Pilar on State Highway 68).

Additional Information

The climate is semi-arid, with thunderstorms common in July and August, and snow possible from October–March. The weather is unpredictable; summer temperatures range from

60–95°F, and in winter from 20–60°F. The visitor center, open from May 1–early September, is located on the east side of State Highway 68, directly across from the Village of Pilar. The center offers interpretive displays about the Rio Grande Gorge, a bookstore, and information about recreation opportunities in the area.

Contact Information

BLM - Taos Field Office
226 Cruz Alta Road
Taos, NM 87571
Tel: (505) 758-8851
Fax: (505) 758-1620
www.nm.blm.gov/tafo/tafo_home.html

Activity Codes

Pauls Valley Wild Horse and Burro Adoption Center

Location

Approximately 45 miles south of Oklahoma City, Oklahoma.

Description

Stretching across 200 acres of land covered with lush green grass, the Pauls Valley Wild Horse and Burro Adoption Center provides wild horses and burros with a natural and safe environment before their placement in new homes.

The lands on which the wild horses and burros graze are divided into eight

pastures, which can hold a maximum of 500 animals. The number of animals residing on-site varies throughout the year, depending on the number of BLM adoption events held in other states. Equipped to care for the animals on a daily basis, the facility is also set up to provide emergency care when needed.

Directions

From Oklahoma City, travel south on Interstate 35 to exit 74, Kimberlin Road. Head west 0.25 mile and then

Wild horses and burros on public lands are recognized as a "living legacy" of the West. Over the course of BLM's 30-year adoption program, more than 185,000 animals have found their way into the hearts of recreational riders, as well as western and English show arenas. Burros have been successfully used as guard and companion animals, as well as for mountain packing. *(Feran Revard-Anderson, BLM Oklahoma Field Office)*

north 0.25 mile to the Pauls Valley Facility. The center can be seen from the Interstate.

Visitor Activities

Wild horse and burro viewing and interpretation.

Special Features

Monthly adoptions are held at the center on the second Tuesday of each month.

Permits, Fees, Limitations

Admission is free. The public is welcome to attend adoptions and learn more about the competitive bid process. Adopters must be 18 years of age, have no animal abuse records, and have suitable facilities that will accommodate a wild horse or burro. There are minimum adoption fees.

Accessibility

The facility and viewing location are accessible by vehicle. The packed-earth entrance and walk-up areas may not be suitable for wheelchairs during wet seasons.

Camping and Lodging

There are no camping facilities on-site. The closest lodging is in Pauls Valley, 2 miles away on exit 72 off Interstate 35.

Food and Supplies

There are no vendors on-site, except during monthly adoption events. Food and supplies are available in Pauls Valley.

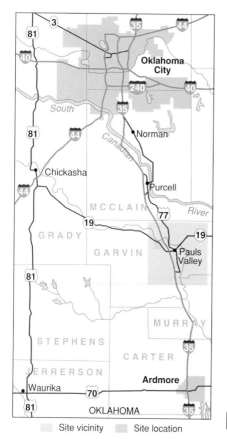

Site vicinity   Site location

First Aid

The nearest hospital is in Pauls Valley.

Additional Information

Visitors are welcome to walk near corrals and fences for better viewing opportunities, but may not enter pastures. Interpretive panels and drive-up viewing sites are accessible year-round, and open during daylight hours only. The BLM's Wild Horse & Burro Program conducts adoptions across the United States throughout the year. For more information on national adoption events, call toll free 1-866-4MUSTANGS, or visit the BLM national website at *www.wildhorseandburro.blm.gov.*

Contact Information

BLM - Oklahoma Field Office
221 North Service Road
Moore, OK 73160
Tel: (800) 237-3642
Fax: (405) 790-1050
www.nm.blm.gov/okfo/okfo_home.html

Activity Codes

Three Rivers Petroglyph Site

Location

17 miles north of Tularosa, New Mexico.

Description

The Three Rivers Petroglyphs are outstanding examples of prehistoric Jornada Mogollon rock art. The basaltic ridge rising above the Three Rivers Valley contains over 21,000 petroglyphs, including masks, sunbursts, wildlife images, handprints, and geometric designs. The number and concentration of petroglyphs make this one of the largest and most interesting rock art sites in the Southwest. A rugged, 0.5-mile trail begins at the visitor shelter and links many of the most interesting petroglyphs. Another short trail begins on the east side of the picnic area and leads to a partially-excavated prehistoric village.

Directions

From Tularosa, take U.S. Highway 54 north for 17 miles. Turn right (east) onto County Road 579, and travel 5 miles on the paved road, following the signs.

Visitor Activities

Hiking, petroglyph viewing, archaeological site, interpretation, and picnicking.

Special Features

The partially excavated pithouse village offers a glimpse of how early inhabitants of the area lived. The petroglyphs, other archeological features, and the river valley location itself indicate that this area was probably occupied for many hundreds, if not thousands, of years. It is estimated that the petroglyphs were created during the period from AD 900–1400.

Permits, Fees, Limitations

There is a day-use vehicle fee. Pets and smoking are not allowed on trails. Charcoal grills are available, but campfires are not permitted.

Accessibility

There are two wheelchair-accessible toilets and an accessible picnic shelter, with accessible trails leading to them. There are also wheelchair-accessible

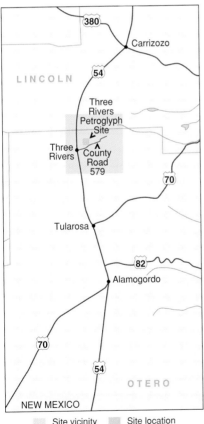

Scattered over 50 acres in the Chihuahuan Desert, more than 21,000 petroglyphs were etched into oxidized rock surfaces by Jornada Mogollon people using stone tools. (M'Lee Beazley, BLM Albuquerque Field Office)

trails to the visitor shelter and up to the base of the main petroglyph hill, where a spotting scope enhances viewing.

Camping and Lodging

The site offers seven shelters with tables, barbecue grills, trashcans, restrooms, and water. Camping is permitted on-site. The nearest lodging is in Alamogordo, 30 miles south on State Highway 54.

Food and Supplies

The Three Rivers Trading Post at the entrance to County Road B30 offers limited food and supplies. A variety of food and supplies can be found in the towns of Tularosa and Carrizozo (28 miles north on State Highway 54).

First Aid

Medical emergency assistance is available through the Sheriff's Department in Tularosa. The closest hospital is in Alamogordo.

Additional Information

The site is open to the public year-round. Rugged trails, extreme temperatures, and poisonous snakes may be encountered. A guide to the petroglyphs is available from the site host.

Contact Information

BLM - Las Cruces Field Office
1800 Marquess Street
Las Cruces, NM 88005
Tel: (505) 525-4300
Fax: (505) 525-4412
www.nm.blm.gov/lcfo/lcfo_home.html

Activity Codes

Valley of Fires Recreation Area

Location

4 miles west of Carrizozo, New Mexico.

Description

The Valley of Fires Recreation Area is a multi-faceted area adjacent to one of the most recent lava flows in the continental United States. The 40-mile flow intrigues visitors with its many varieties of flowers and cacti typical of the Chihuahuan Desert. The flow, 4–6 miles wide and 2,500–5,000 years old, also supports a notable number of melanistic (black) individuals of several animal species.

Directions

From Alamogordo, take U.S. Highway 54 north for 58 miles to Carrizozo. Travel 4 miles west on State Highway 380 to Valley of Fires. Or, from Interstate 25, exit at San Antonio and travel 62 miles east on State Highway 380 to Valley of Fires.

Visitor Activities

Hiking, wildlife viewing, birdwatching, plant viewing, self-guided accessible nature trail, and geologic sightseeing.

Special Features

Juniper trees up to 400 years old and a surprisingly wide variety of wildlife, including bats, cottontails, lizards, roadrunners, great horned owls, burrowing owls, turkey vultures, cactus wrens, and golden eagles, inhabits the seemingly inhospitable lava flows.

Permits, Fees, Limitations

There is a day-use fee.

Accessibility

Four campsites, restrooms, and the Malpais Nature Trail area are wheelchair-accessible. The trail to the lava flow is fully accessible and interpreted along its entire length.

Camping and Lodging

Valley of Fires has 30 developed campsites with drinking water, sun shelters, picnic tables, and grills. Some sites have 30-amp electrical service. Five tent-only camping sites are available. RV campgrounds are located in Carrizozo, Capitan (20 miles east on U.S. Highway 380) and Ruidoso (32 miles southeast on State Highway 48). A variety of lodging is also available in Carrizozo, Lincoln (32 miles east on State Highway

A snag forms a picturesque frame for Little Black Peak, a lava bed extruded by extinct volcanoes at Valley of Fires. *(Michael Grant, BLM Roswell Field Office)*

380), Capitan, and Ruidoso. Two group shelters are available by reservation.

Food and Supplies

Food and supplies are available in Carrizozo, Ruidoso, and Capitan.

First Aid

The nearest hospital is located in Ruidoso, or visitors can call 911.

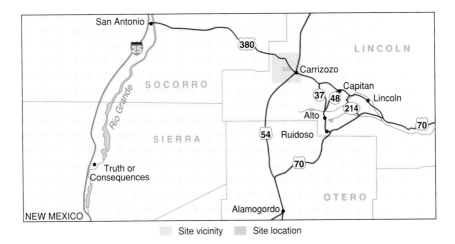

Site vicinity   Site location

Additional Information

Valley of Fires is open year-round. BLM's Fort Stanton area and Three Rivers Petroglyph Site are 25 miles and 35 miles from the site, respectively. White Sands National Monument, the National Space Exploration Hall of Fame in Alamogordo, and the historic village of Lincoln are all nearby. The Smokey Bear Museum is located in Capitan.

Contact Information

BLM - Roswell Field Office
2909 West Second Street
Roswell, NM 88201
Tel: (505) 627-0272
Fax: (505) 627-0276
www.nm.blm.gov/rfo/index.htm

Activity Codes

Wild Rivers Recreation Area

Location

Approximately 42 miles northwest of Taos, New Mexico.

Description

The Rio Grande Gorge is a rugged, steep-walled canyon that cuts into the volcanic plateaus of north-central New Mexico. The Wild Rivers Recreation Area provides splendid views into this 800-foot-deep gorge. The recreation area takes its name from two wild and scenic rivers, the Rio Grande and the Red River, which join in the gorge below La Junta Point. The Wild Rivers Back Country Byway, winding its way along the rim of the Rio Grande Gorge, offers access to spectacular overlooks, including one above the confluence of the two rivers. Most visitor facilities are located along the rim, but several trails provide access to the river and to facilities located within the gorge. The Wild Rivers Visitor Center features interpretive displays about the geologic and natural history of the gorge and the surrounding area.

Directions

From Taos, follow State Highway 68 north 7 miles to its end. Continue north on State Highway 522 approximately 20 miles to Questa. Travel 3 miles past the stoplight in Questa to State Highway 378. Turn left onto State Highway 378, and follow signs approximately 12 miles west to Wild Rivers Recreation Area. To reach the Wild Rivers Visitor Center, follow the signs as you enter the gate.

Visitor Activities

Hiking, fishing, wildlife viewing, bird-watching, geologic sightseeing, plant viewing, interpretation, scenic drives, and mountain biking.

Special Features

The 800-foot deep canyon hosts a unique ecosystem that supports a variety of plant and animal life. Sightings of mule deer, prairie dogs, red-tailed hawks, ravens, pinyon jays, and mountain bluebirds are common. Black bears may occasionally visit the area.

Permits, Fees, Limitations

There is a day-use fee. Day-use passes, good for 1 calendar year, are available.

Accessibility

The BLM Wild Rivers Visitor Center, restrooms, a few trails, and some campsites are wheelchair-accessible.

Camping and Lodging

There are BLM campgrounds in or adjacent to the gorge at Wild Rivers Recreation Area. Sites are available for tent camping and RVs. There are camping fees and a maximum of two vehicles permitted per campsite. Walk-in river campsites are available for a reduced rate. There are also privately-owned campgrounds in Taos, Questa (13 miles east on State Highway 522), and Red River (30 miles east on State Highway 38), and U.S. Forest Service campgrounds are nearby. Lodging is available in Questa, Taos, and Red River. For further information on camping and lodging, contact or visit the Taos County Chamber of Commerce Visitor Center, at the intersection of State Highways 68 and 64, Taos, NM, 87571, (505) 758-3873.

Food and Supplies

Food and supplies are available in Taos and in limited quantity in Questa and Red River.

First Aid

First aid is available at the BLM Wild Rivers Visitor Center. First aid is also available in Questa and Taos. There is a hospital in Taos.

Additional Information

Facilities are located at elevations ranging from 7,200–7,800 feet. The

The Rio Grande cuts through the high plains of northern New Mexico at Wild Rivers, where an 800-foot-deep volcanic canyon attracts rugged recreationists as well as raptors, elk, and beaver.

(M'Lee Beazley, Albuquerque District Office)

climate is semi-arid, with thunderstorms common in July and August. Snow is likely to occur from November–March. The area is open year-round, but winter access may be difficult. The weather is unpredictable. Call for New Mexico Road Conditions, 1-800-432-4269. Visitors should anticipate changeable weather conditions and bring warm clothing. The BLM Wild Rivers Visitor Center is open daily from 9 a.m.– 5 p.m., Memorial Day–Labor Day.

Contact Information

BLM - Taos Field Office
226 Cruz Alta Road
Taos, NM 87571
Tel: (505) 758-8851
Fax: (505) 758-1620
www.nm.blm.gov/tafo/tafo_home.html

Activity Codes

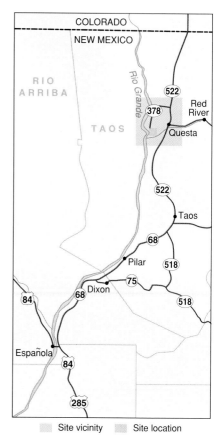

Site vicinity   Site location

"A view from the top": Manby Springs offers a spectacular vista of rafters floating south on the **Rio Grande Wild and Scenic River.** *(Guadalupe Martinez, BLM Taos Field Office)*

Each spring, abundant rhododendron blossoms add sparkling color to the forest under-story within Oregon's Molalla River Recreation Site. *(Trish Hogervorst, BLM Salem District Office)*

From the sculpted Owyhee Canyonlands of eastern Oregon to the Pacific Coast tidepools of Yaquina Head, the public lands of Oregon and Washington provide a variety of climates, beautiful natural landscapes, important wildlife habitats, and outstanding recreation opportunities.

The Cascade Mountains and the eastern portion of Oregon are high desert, where sagebrush, prairie grasses, and junipers provide cover and forage for a variety of wildlife, birds, and livestock. Recreation opportunities include rafting the whitewater of the Deschutes River and hiking within the Steens Mountain Cooperative Management and Protection Area.

West of the Cascades, there are deciduous and evergreen forests. These lands provide habitat for a variety of fish and wildlife. During the spring and summer, wildflowers are abundant in the Cascade-Siskiyou National Monument area, and throughout most of the year, Roosevelt elk can be seen at the Dean Creek Elk Viewing Area near Reedsport.

Visitors to the National Historic Oregon Trail Interpretive Center near Baker City will hear the story of the hopes, dreams, and heartaches of Oregon Trail-era pioneers. Near Mt. Hood, the Cascade Streamwatch facility at the Wildwood Recreation Site provides visitors with a unique opportunity to explore natural stream and wetland ecosystems along barrier-free interpretive trails and boardwalks.

Whether inspired by the vastness of the desert, the mystery of the forest, or the wonder of ocean tidepools, visitors to the public lands in Oregon and Washington will experience an unforgettable glimpse of our spectacular natural world.

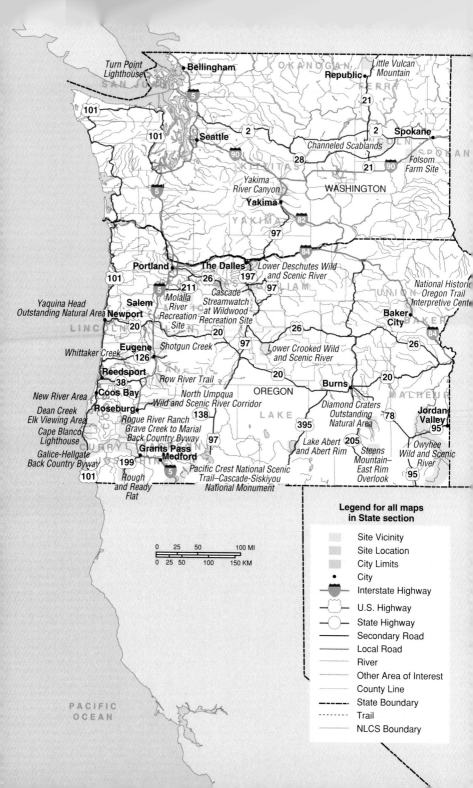

Turn Point Lighthouse

Little Vulcan Mountain

Bellingham

Republic

OKANOGAN

FERRY

21

SAN JUAN

101

101

Seattle

2

Spokane

Channeled Scablands

SPOKAN

28

Folsom Farm Site

LINCOLN

21

90

KITTITAS

WASHINGTON

YAKIMA

Yakima River Canyon

Yakima

82

97

84

Portland

The Dalles

197

Lower Deschutes Wild and Scenic River

26

97

National Historic Oregon Trail Interpretive Center

UNION

211

Molalla River Recreation Site

Cascade Streamwatch at Wildwood Recreation Site

Salem

Yaquina Head Outstanding Natural Area

Newport

20

20

Baker City

BAKER

26

84

Eugene

126

Shotgun Creek

97

26

Lower Crooked Wild and Scenic River

Whittaker Creek

Reedsport

38

Row River Trail

20

Burns

20

New River Area

Coos Bay

North Umpqua Wild and Scenic River Corridor

OREGON

LAKE

78

Jordan Valley

MALHEUR

Dean Creek Elk Viewing Area

Roseburg

138

Diamond Craters Outstanding Natural Area

95

Cape Blanco Lighthouse

Rogue River Ranch Grave Creek to Marial Back Country Byway

395

205

Lake Abert and Abert Rim

97

Owyhee Wild and Scenic River

Galice-Hellgate Back Country Byway

199

Grants Pass

Medford

Steens Mountain–East Rim Overlook

95

101

Rough and Ready Flat

5

Pacific Crest National Scenic Trail–Cascade-Siskiyou National Monument

PACIFIC OCEAN

Legend for all maps in State section

Site Vicinity
Site Location
City Limits
• City
Interstate Highway
U.S. Highway
State Highway
Secondary Road
Local Road
River
Other Area of Interest
County Line
State Boundary
Trail
NLCS Boundary

0 25 50 100 MI

0 25 50 100 150 KM

Cape Blanco Lighthouse

Location
10 miles northwest of Port Orford, Oregon.

Description
Cape Blanco Lighthouse is the oldest standing lighthouse on the western point of the Oregon coast, and holds at least four Oregon records: oldest continuously operating light; most westerly; highest above the sea (245 feet); and the first to have a woman keeper. The lighthouse was commissioned in 1870 to aid in the shipping of products for the gold-mining and lumber industries. Binoculars and a camera are a must to view and photograph some of the roughest and most scenic portions of the Oregon coastline.

Directions
From Port Orford, go 5 miles north on U.S. Highway 101 to Cape Blanco Highway, then 5 miles west to the site.

Visitor Activities
Historic site, interpretation.

Special Features
A 64-step climb up a freestanding, circular staircase leads visitors to the lantern room, which houses the spectacular lens invented by Augustin Jean Fresnel. The lantern is 4 feet, 8 inches in diameter, and 6 feet, 8 inches high. The lighthouse is identifiable at night by its "signature," a bright light that flashes for 1.8 seconds at intervals of 18.2 seconds. The lighthouse is listed on the National Register of Historic Places.

Permits, Fees, Limitations
There are no required fees, but donations are accepted.

Accessibility
The visitor center and associated restrooms are wheelchair-accessible; the lighthouse is not.

Windswept Cape Blanco Lighthouse once warned ships away from offshore reefs and islands with a light that could be seen by vessels more than 22 nautical miles offshore. *(Jim Brende, BLM Coos Bay District Office)*

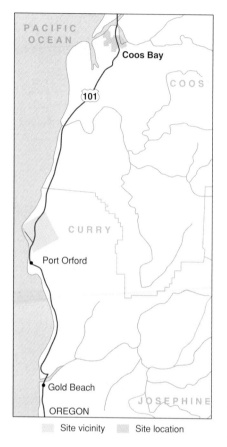

Site vicinity   Site location

Camping and Lodging

Camping is available at the Cape Blanco State Park, within walking distance of the site. Lodging is available in Port Orford.

Food and Supplies

Food, supplies, and restaurants are available in Port Orford.

First Aid

Volunteer site hosts are trained in basic first aid. The nearest hospital is in Gold Beach, 25 miles south of Port Orford on U.S. Highway 101.

Additional Information

There is a visitor center with interpretive information and photographs of coastal tribes, geologic history, and maritime use. Lighthouse tours (five persons per group) are offered from April 1–October 30. Visitor hours are 10 a.m.–4 p.m., Thursday-Monday; the center is closed Tuesday and Wednesday. The weather at the lighthouse is very unpredictable, but is usually windy and cool. Lighthouse tours are managed by Oregon State Parks; for tour information, visitors should call (541) 332-6774.

Contact Information

BLM - Coos Bay District Office
1300 Airport Lane
North Bend, OR 97459
Tel: (541) 756-0100
Fax: (541) 751-4303
www.or.blm.gov/coosbay/recreation/blanco.htm

Activity Codes

Cascade Streamwatch at Wildwood Recreation Site

Location
39 miles east of Portland, Oregon.

Description
Located along the Salmon Wild and Scenic River, Wildwood Recreation Site is a day-use area that is home to the Cascade Streamwatch and Wildwood Wetland Trails. These trails provide visitors with a unique opportunity to explore natural stream and wetland ecosystems along barrier-free interpretive trails and boardwalks. From the Cascade Streamwatch Trail, visitors can view young salmon and steelhead in a natural stream through an in-channel glass viewing structure. Wildwood offers family picnic units, group day-use shelters, playing fields, Salmon River access trails, and walking trails. The historic Barlow Road, which crosses Wildwood, is an Oregon Trail site, easily accessible from U.S. Highway 26.

Directions
From Portland, take Interstate 84 east to Exit 16, towards Wood Village. Turn right onto 238th Drive and follow it for approximately 4 miles. Turn left onto Burnside Street, which becomes U.S. Highway 26. Proceed east on U.S. Highway 26; the Wildwood Recreation Site is located on the south side of the highway, 1 mile west of the community of Welches.

Visitor Activities
Self-guided interpretive walks, picnicking, wildlife viewing, birdwatching,

The developed facilities at Cascade Streamwatch include a unique underwater stream-viewing chamber along a restored side channel of the Salmon Wild and Scenic River. *(BLM)*

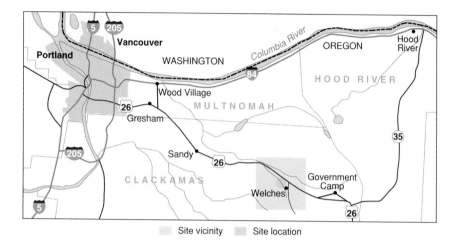

Site vicinity   Site location

swimming, historic site, fishing, and hiking.

Special Features

The Cascade Streamwatch project, a collaborative effort among BLM, the U.S. Forest Service, and the non-profit Wolftree, Inc., has restored over 2 miles of fisheries habitat and developed facilities that offer visitors a chance to view and learn firsthand about anadromous fish in their natural habitat. The network of barrier-free trails is highlighted by creative sculptures, models, interpretive signing, and kiosks.

Permits, Fees, Limitations

Fees vary. Please contact BLM for more information.

Accessibility

Both the Cascade Streamwatch and Wildwood Wetland Trails are wheelchair-accessible, as are restrooms, paved trails, and picnic sites.

Camping and Lodging

There is no overnight camping on-site. There are several private overnight accommodations in nearby towns, including Welches (1 mile east), Government Camp (13 miles west), and Sandy (16 miles east).

Food and Supplies

Food and supplies are available in Welches.

First Aid

Emergency services are available in Gresham (28 miles northwest) or Portland.

Additional Information

Contact BLM with any additional questions.

Contact Information

BLM - Salem District Office
1717 Fabry Road, SE
Salem, OR 97306
Tel: (503) 375-5646
Fax: (503) 375-5622
www.or.blm.gov/salem/html/rec/cascade.htm

Activity Codes

Channeled Scablands

Location
Numerous locations in Lincoln County (in and around Davenport), Washington.

Description
The Channeled Scablands of eastern Washington are home to geologic features not found anywhere else in the world. Catastrophic floods raced through the area during the last Ice Age, carving channels through the mostly flat land. Today, rolling hills of cropland and sagebrush steppe habitat are interspersed with canyons of carved basalt columns. A completely unique world exists within those canyon walls. Creeks and lakes support grasslands and trees. Wildlife and wildflowers thrive. Remnants of early Native American settlements and pioneer homesteads speak of the first inhabitants. Visitors have easy access to scenic canyons along 6 miles of roads open for motorized vehicle travel in the Lakeview area.

Directions
From Spokane, take U.S. Highway 2 west 30 miles to Davenport. Or, from Seattle, take Interstate 90 east for 203 miles, then State Highway 21 north for 19 miles.

Visitor Activities
Picnicking, hiking, mountain biking, horseback riding, fishing, wildlife viewing, birdwatching, wildflower viewing, and geologic sightseeing.

Special Features
The area consists of scarred black rock cut by canyons, channels, pools, rock basins, ragged buttes, and cliffs. Sagebrush is often interspersed with bluebunch wheatgrass, basin wild rye, and wildflowers. Mule deer often browse along uplands, and many migratory birds flock to the area's lakes and wetlands. Thrushes, warblers, mountain finches, and other small birds

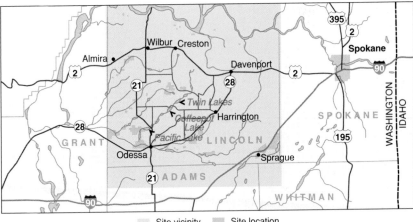

Site vicinity   Site location

not ordinarily found in arid, open country congregate here in fall and spring.

Permits, Fees, Limitations
None.

Accessibility
There are wheelchair-accessible outhouses and boat docks at the following sites:

Twin Lakes: From State Highway 28, turn west on Coffeepot Road for 12 miles, then turn right into Highline Road. Drive 1.5 miles to the entrance on the right and follow this access road for about 2 miles to reach the recreation site.

Coffeepot Lake: From State Highway 28, turn west onto Coffeepot Road and travel about 12 miles to the gravel entrance on the left.

Pacific Lake: Take State Highway 21 north from Odessa, go 2 miles to Lakeview Ranch Road, turn left, and travel 5 miles on a gravel road to Lakeview Ranch sites. The Cache Crater Trail, 6 miles north of Odessa on State Highway 21, is wheelchair-accessible.

Camping and Lodging
All public lands in Lincoln County are open to camping, but there are no developed campsites. RV parking and lodging are available in the communities of Davenport, Odessa, Harrington (13 and 38 miles, respectively, west of Davenport on State Highway 28), and Wilbur (29 miles west of Davenport on U.S. Highway 2).

Food and Supplies
No supplies are available on-site. Supplies may be purchased in Davenport, Odessa, Wilbur, or Harrington.

First Aid
First aid is not available on-site. The nearest hospitals are located in Davenport and Odessa. Enhanced 911 service is available countywide.

Additional Information
Lincoln County, Washington, is sparsely populated and contains rough terrain. No drinking water is provided on public lands; visitors should bring their own, especially during the summer months, when temperatures can climb above 90°F. Visitors may encounter rattlesnakes and poison ivy. Vehicles are limited to designated roads and trails, and campfires must be self-contained. Visitors can obtain a free recreation map of the Channeled Scablands from BLM. At the Lakeview Ranch, visitors will find picnic areas with grills for cooking. Just a short distance east of the ranch, on the Pacific Lake shoreline, are recreational facilities, including a boat launch, fishing dock, and several camping and picnic sites.

Contact Information
BLM - Spokane District Office
1103 N. Fancher Road
Spokane, WA 99212
Tel: (509) 536-1200
Fax: (509) 536-1275
www.or.blm.gov/Spokane

Activity Codes

Dean Creek Elk Viewing Area

Location
3 miles east of Reedsport, Oregon.

Description
Dean Creek is a premier Watchable Wildlife site providing visitors an up-close look at wildlife in its natural habitat. The 1,040-acre area is a mosaic of pastures, woodlands, and wetlands, providing a variety of wildlife-viewing experiences. There are two viewing areas with nearby parking, an interpretive center, viewing scopes, and restrooms. The area is contiguous with the scenic Umpqua River.

Directions
From Reedsport, go 3 miles east on State Highway 38. The viewing area begins at that point and extends for an additional 3 miles along the highway.

Visitor Activities
Wildlife viewing and birdwatching.

Special Features
Roosevelt elk are visible almost every day of the year, sharing the pastures, wetlands, ponds, and adjacent forest with snowy egrets, ospreys, and red-winged blackbirds.

Permits, Fees, Limitations
There are no fees. Hunting, overnight camping/parking, and hiking are not permitted.

Accessibility
The viewing areas are fully wheelchair-accessible.

Camping and Lodging
There is no camping permitted on-site. Camping is available at nearby Umpqua Lighthouse State Park, 5 miles south of Reedsport on U.S. Highway 101, and at BLM's Loon Lake Recreation Area, 7 miles east on State Highway 38, and then 6 miles south on Loon Lake Road. Reedport offers several motels and RV parks.

Food and Supplies
There are no food or supplies available on-site. Groceries and restaurants are available in Reedsport.

Resident Roosevelt elk roam freely in the pastures, woodlands, and wetlands of the Dean Creek Elk Viewing Area. Oregon's largest land mammals, adult bulls may weigh as much as 1,100 pounds and stand 5 feet at the shoulder. (Will B. Golden, BLM Coos Bay District Office)

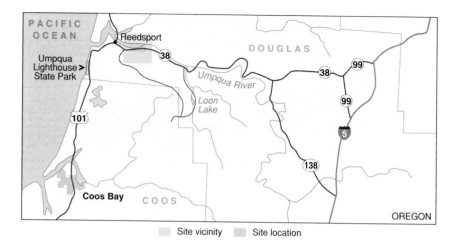

First Aid
There is no first aid on-site. The nearest hospital is in Reedsport.

Additional Information
Elk roam the area freely, and their numbers fluctuate with the seasons. During the summer months, the best times to view elk are the early morning and before dusk. During the other three seasons, viewing is best during the day. Daytime temperatures tend to be cool or cold, even during the summer, and the area is generally windy.

Contact Information
BLM - Coos Bay District Office
1300 Airport Lane
North Bend, OR 97459
Tel: (541) 756-0100
Fax: (541) 751-4303
www.or.blm.gov/coosbay/recreation/dean.htm

Activity Codes

Diamond Craters Outstanding Natural Area

Location
55 miles south of Burns, Oregon.

Description
Diamond Craters contains hundreds of pristine volcanic features. Geologists maintain that the 17,000-acre area has some of the best and most diverse examples of basaltic volcanism in the United States. The 64-mile Diamond Loop Back Country Byway meanders through a sagebrush-covered landscape, which is punctuated by buttes and rimrock above broad, water-filled valleys. Wild horses,

Little Red Cone is one of the many well-preserved volcanic features that highlight the landscape at Diamond Craters. *(Mark Armstrong, BLM Burns District Office)*

including the famous Kiger mustangs (thought to be one of the purest herds of Spanish mustangs existing in the wild today), mule deer, pronghorn antelope, hawks, and eagles are among the many species of wildlife that can be seen.

Directions
From Burns, take State Highway 205 south approximately 41 miles to the Diamond turn-off. Travel east 7 miles to Diamond Craters junction, turn left on Lava Beds Road, and follow signs 2 miles north to Diamond Craters.

Visitor Activities
Picnicking, geologic sightseeing, scenic drives, wildflower viewing, wild horse viewing, and wildlife viewing.

Special Features
Features include blast craters, small calderas, unusual lava flow formations, a water-filled crater (known as a maar), and unusual plant communities. A self-guided tour identifies the craters, cinder cones, lave tubes, and other features. Wildflowers are in bloom from May–August.

Permits, Fees, Limitations
No permits or fees are required. Vehicle access is permitted on designated roads only. No removal of rock materials, plants, or animals is permitted.

Accessibility
None.

Camping and Lodging
There are no facilities on-site. Year-round camping (36 sites) is available at BLM's Page Springs Campground near Frenchglen, 23 miles south on State Highway 205. No services are available from October–April. In season, a fee is charged, which includes some amenities (toilets, water, picnic tables, fire rings, parking pads, but no waste water disposal). Lodging is available in Diamond (5 miles east of Diamond Crater junction on Diamond Grain Camp Road), Frenchglen, and Burns.

Food and Supplies
Supplies are available in Diamond, Frenchglen, and Burns.

First Aid
There is no first aid available on-site.
The nearest hospital is in Burns.

Additional Information
The area is open all year; however, winter
weather can restrict travel. This is an isolated area of rocky terrain, inhabited by
rattlesnakes and ticks. The best times
to visit are May–June and September–
October. The weather is very hot and dry
in July and August. There are no facilities
of any kind on-site. The Kiger Mustang
Viewing Area, located approximately
14 miles east of Diamond and accessible
from Happy Valley Road, requires a high-
clearance vehicle and is reachable only in
dry weather.

Contact Information
BLM - Burns District Office
28910 Highway 20 West
Hines, OR 97738
Tel: (541) 573-4400
Fax: (541) 573-4411
www.or.blm.gov/Burns

Activity Codes

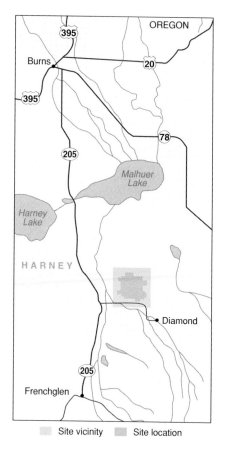

Site vicinity ▨ Site location

Folsom Farm Site

Location
8 miles northeast of Sprague,
Washington.

Description
The Folsom Farm site consists of an early
1900s homestead overlooking Smick
Meadows, a restored wetland. In the late
1800s and early 1900s, explorers, traders,
and settlers converted this

landscape to farms, ranches, and small
communities. From a scenic overlook,
visitors can observe wildlife, including
nesting waterfowl, deer, and raptors. A
foot trail leads down to the wildlife
viewing station for closer observation.

Directions
From Sprague, take Interstate 90 north
to Exit 254. Proceed south 2.25 miles to

Scroggie Road. Turn east, and proceed 0.75 mile to the entrance.

Visitor Activities

Hiking, picnicking, wildlife viewing, historic site, birdwatching, fishing, and horseback riding.

Special Features

This wetland is especially vibrant with songbirds in the springtime. From the viewing station, visitors can catch a glimpse of northern shovelers and spotted sandpipers.

Permits, Fees, Limitations

No fees or permits. Motor vehicle use is limited to the parking lot and access road.

Accessibility

The trail to Folsom Farm overlook is wheelchair-accessible.

Camping and Lodging

Adjacent BLM lands are open to primitive camping. Fishtrap Resort, 0.25 mile east of the Folsom Farm entrance on Scroggie Road, has facilities for RVs.

Food and Supplies

Food and supplies can be purchased in Sprague or at the Fishtrap Resort.

First Aid

There is no first aid available on-site. The closest medical facility is located in Cheney, 25 miles north via Interstate 90 and State Highway 904.

Additional Information

There are no restroom facilities on-site. Support facilities are limited to a parking lot, picnic area, hiking trail, and scenic overlook.

Contact Information

BLM – Spokane District Office
1103 North Fancher
Spokane, WA 99212
Tel: (509) 536-1200
Fax: (509) 536-1275
www.or.blm.gov/Spokane

Activity Codes

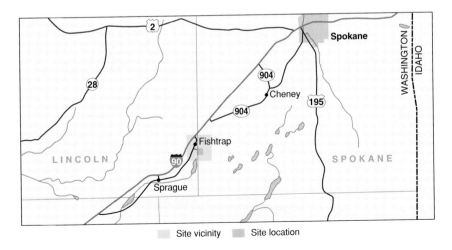

Site vicinity   Site location

Galice-Hellgate
Back Country Byway

Location

The eastern end of the byway is located 4 miles east of Merlin, Oregon. The western end is located 58 miles east of Gold Beach, Oregon.

Description

The Galice-Hellgate Back Country Byway is a 39-mile scenic motor route starting from Interstate 5 near Merlin ("Gateway to the Rogue") and progressing along the Rogue National Wild and Scenic River. The byway winds past majestic vistas of a deep and rocky river canyon, densely wooded hillsides, and whitewater rapids. Along one portion of the route, motorists drive into the Siskiyou Mountains, climbing up and away from the river and topping out into a high-altitude forest environment offering spectacular views of nearby mountains and stands of Douglas fir.

This portion of the route eventually takes travelers to Gold Beach and the Oregon coast. The byway offers numerous Rogue River access points and developed recreation sites.

Directions

From Grants Pass, take Interstate 5 north 2 miles to the Merlin exit (#61). Travel west on Merlin Galice Road 9 miles through the town of Merlin to the river canyon. Continue on the Merlin Galice Road to the Rand Visitor Center, where written information about the area is available. To reach the coast, travel another 58 miles to the end of the byway, on narrow, winding mountain roads. The Galice Access Road (#34-8-36), an 8-mile-long side route off the byway, leads you to the Bear Camp Road (#FS 23). When you reach the Rogue River again near

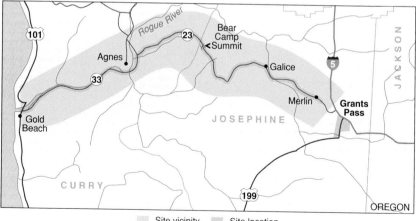

Site vicinity   Site location

Agnes, proceed on road #FS 33 to the coast.

Visitor Activities
Boating, swimming, rafting, powerboat rides, wildlife viewing, historic site, scenic drives, fishing, and hiking.

Special Features
Much of the drive provides a view of the deep river canyon with impressive rock walls and forested slopes. The remains of old mining operations, some visible from the byway, offer glimpses into the area's past. The Rogue River is a national wild and scenic river.

Permits, Fees, Limitations
No fees. Travelers wishing to boat down the adjacent Rogue River wild section must obtain a permit from the Rand Visitor Center from May 15– October 31.

Accessibility
There are numerous wheelchair-accessible overlooks and one major accessible campground (Indian Mary Park) with full, barrier-free facilities.

Camping and Lodging
Grants Pass, just 6 miles southeast of the byway's eastern terminus, offers a variety of lodging and camping opportunities. Indian Mary Park is located along the byway route, on the Rogue River, 11 miles northwest of Interstate 5.

Food and Supplies
Food and supplies are available in Grants Pass, Merlin, and Galice. The historic community of Galice is located 11 miles northwest of Merlin along the byway, just past the junction to the coastal route.

First Aid
Ambulance service is available throughout the route. The nearest hospitals are in Grants Pass, in the northwestern part of town.

The byway offers stunning views of the Rogue River's rocky canyon and whitewater rapids, against the backdrop of the fir-studded Siskiyou Mountains. *(BLM)*

Additional Information

For the most part, the byway is a well-maintained, two-lane country road that narrows as it progresses into the Siskiyou Mountains, requiring very careful driving. In winter months, this mountainous portion of the byway is generally closed by snow accumulations. As travelers progress into the more remote portions of the byway, telephone availability diminishes. The best time of year to visit the area is from May–October.

Contact Information

BLM – Medford District Office
3040 Biddle Road
Medford, OR 97504
Tel: (541) 618-2200
Fax: (541) 618-2400
www.or.blm.gov/Medford

Activity Codes

Grave Creek to Marial Back Country Byway

Location

8 miles north of Galice, Oregon.

Description

Upon entering this gateway into the back country, visitors can feel the cool mist surrounding Rainie Falls, a cascade along the wild and scenic portion of the Rogue River. The byway climbs out of the Rogue River Canyon and winds through the beautiful Klamath Mountains before descending back to the river and leading to the historic Rogue River Ranch.

A boat cruises serenely after successfully navigating the Grave Creek rapids on the Rogue River. *(BLM)*

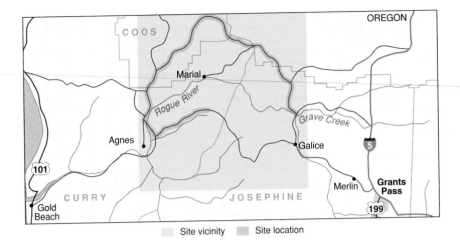

Site vicinity ▮ Site location

Directions

From Galice, head north on Galice Road 8 miles to the Grave Creek Bridge. The byway route starts here; follow the back country byway signs, or the following directions:

Cross the Grave Creek Bridge and bear left uphill on paved BLM Road #34-8-1 for 5 miles. At the junction with Whisky Creek Road (#33-8-26), bear right and continue on #34-8-1 (sign reads "Marial 28 Miles") for 3 miles. At the junction with BLM Road #33-8-13 (on the right), bear left and continue on #34-8-1 for 8 miles. At the junction with BLM Road #32-8-31, bear left and continue on a paved road for 5 miles to the junction with BLM Road #32-8-9.2. Bear left and continue on #32-8-31 for 1 mile to Anaktuvuk Saddle Junction. Turn left on BLM road #32-9-14.2 for 3 miles to Marble Gap Junction. Continue ahead (pavement will end) for another 3 miles to Fourmile Saddle junction. Bear left and stay on #32-9-14.2 for another 9 miles to the Rogue River Ranch.

Visitor Activities

Picnicking, scenic drives, swimming, boating, rafting, plant viewing, wildlife viewing, birdwatching, and hiking.

Special Features

A strenuous hike along the historic Rogue River or the Mule Creek Canyon Trail offers visitors an invigorating challenge. Wildlife observers will want to look for elk, deer, and wild turkeys. Black bears also inhabit the area.

Permits, Fees, Limitations

There are no fees. Boating on the Rogue River requires a permit, which can be obtained at the Rand Visitor Center near Galice, at the eastern terminus of the route.

Accessibility

The Rogue River Ranch is wheelchair-accessible.

Camping and Lodging

There is a primitive BLM campground approximately 0.5 mile from the Rogue River Ranch. There are no fees.

Food and Supplies

All food and supplies should be obtained prior to beginning the trip. There are no gas stations in the area. Travelers should fill their tanks when they purchase supplies in Grants Pass or Merlin. (From Galice, travel east approximately 20 miles on the Merlin-Galice Road to Interstate 5. Grants Pass is 2 miles south on Interstate 5.) Drinking water is not available.

First Aid

There is no phone service or medical care. During the peak-use season of May-September, caretakers are on duty at the site and can provide first aid supplies and radio communication. The nearest hospital is in Grants Pass.

Additional Information

This site is extremely remote, with no visitor services. Travelers should be well prepared for a long trip on mostly one-lane dirt roads, which are well maintained and passable by passenger vehicles. Access to the area is often impossible during the winter months because of snow accumulations. The best time of year to visit the site is from May–September.

Contact Information

BLM - Medford District Office
3040 Biddle Road
Medford, OR 97504
Tel: (541) 618-2200
Fax: (541) 618-2400
www.or.blm.gov/Medford

Activity Codes

Lake Abert and Abert Rim

Location

25 miles north of Lakeview, Oregon.

Description

Lake Abert is the third-largest body of saline water in North America. It is a remnant of a much larger lake that existed thousands of years ago, when the climate provided far more moisture. The lake is in a flat basin with no outlet; as a result, mineral salts that originally dissolved into the larger prehistoric lake have been concentrated in Lake Abert. The lake is home to an abundance of brine shrimp, which provide food for many birds during their migrations.

Abert Rim is a block of rock that was tilted along a fault line, creating a sheer cliff, or fault scarp.

Directions

From Lakeview, drive 25 miles north on U.S. Highway 395 through Valley Falls. Continue north 3 miles. The highway parallels the lake for the next 18 miles.

Visitor Activities

Wildlife viewing, geologic sightseeing, birdwatching, hiking, and hang gliding.

Special Features

Visitors will find excellent birdwatching opportunities at the north end of Lake

Abert, where up to 10,000 waterfowl and shore birds may feed at any given time. Abert Rim, one of the highest fault scarps in the world, rises 2,500 feet above Lake Abert and runs for 30 miles. Visitors can travel to the foot of Abert Rim's rugged cliffs to the Abert Lake Watchable Wildlife site to learn more about brine shrimp, the only creatures that can survive in this alkaline lake. The Watchable Wildlife site is located 26 miles north of Lakeview on U.S. Highway 395.

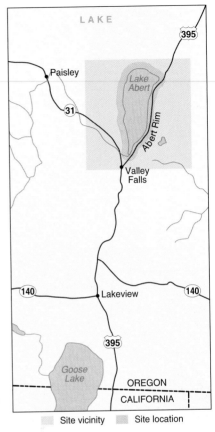

Permits, Fees, Limitations
None.

Accessibility
The Watchable Wildlife site is wheelchair-accessible. The rim itself and surrounding terrain are extremely steep, and consequently are not wheelchair-accessible.

Camping and Lodging
Developed campgrounds are available near Lakeview. Motel lodging is available in Lakeview and Paisley, 20 miles north of Lakeview on State Highway 31.

Eastern Oregon's Lake Abert offers visitors majestic views and excellent birdwatching opportunities. In this photo, the sharp profile of Abert Rim is visible in the distance.
(Chuck Telford, BLM Roseburg District Office)

Food and Supplies
There are a small store and gas station at Valley Falls (3 miles south on U.S. Highway 395).

First Aid
The nearest hospital is located in Lakeview.

Additional Information
There are no restroom facilities available at Lake Abert. Hang-glider pilots launch south from the rim and can often be seen flying in the area during the summer months.

Contact Information
BLM – Lakeview District Office
1300 South G Street
Lakeview, OR 97630
Tel: (541) 947-2177
Fax: (541) 947-6399
www.or.blm.gov/Lakeview

Activity Codes
 other – hang gliding

Little Vulcan Mountain

Location
6 miles west of Curlew, Washington.

Description
The combination of elevation (4,940 feet), aspect, and rock outcroppings within this vegetative community provides the unique qualities that create excellent bighorn sheep habitat and outstanding viewing opportunities. Other wildlife that can be observed include deer and bears.

Directions
Take State Highway 21 to Curlew. Turn west on East Kettle River Road,

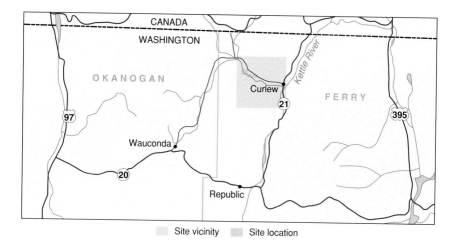

Site vicinity   Site location

Located just a few miles from the Canadian border, Little Vulcan Mountain provides the three most important components of bighorn sheep habitat: forage, water, and escape terrain. *(BLM)*

and travel 6 miles to Little Vulcan Mountain.

Visitor Activities
Hiking and wildlife viewing.

Special Features
This 600-acre area provides critical winter range, escape cover, and lambing areas for the local herd of bighorn sheep.

Permits, Fees, Limitations
None.

Accessibility
None.

Camping and Lodging
Primitive camping is permitted. Lodging is available in Curlew and Republic, 21 miles south of Curlew on State Highway 21.

Food and Supplies
Food and services are not available on-site. Supplies can be purchased in Curlew.

First Aid
The closest first aid is available in Curlew. The nearest hospital is located in Republic.

Additional Information
Because of the critical nature of the habitat, visitors should refrain from entering the area during the spring lambing period (April 1–July 15). Temperatures range from 90°F in the summer to below 0°F in the winter.

Contact Information
BLM - Spokane District Office
1103 North Fancher Road
Spokane, WA 99212
Tel: (509) 536-1200
Fax: (509) 536-1275
www.or.blm.gov/Spokane

Activity Codes

Lower Crooked
Wild and Scenic River

Location
12 miles south of Prineville, Oregon.

Description
Located along a national back country byway, the 8-mile Chimney Rock segment of the Lower Crooked River boasts diverse scenery and wildlife, and provides opportunities for year-round recreation activities. The segment of river along the byway is a national wild and scenic river. The river provides excellent fishing for native rainbow trout. Wildlife seen along this stretch of the byway includes deer, coyotes, and numerous birds of prey. Black bears inhabit the area, as do bald eagles during winter.

Directions
From Prineville, Lower Crooked River can be accessed via State Route 27. The designated river canyon begins approximately 12 miles south of Prineville and continues upstream to the Prineville Reservoir. From Bend, follow U.S. Highway 20 east and turn north on State Route 27 and continue to the Prineville Reservoir on the gravel road.

Visitor Activities
Picnicking, fishing, rafting, hiking, wildlife viewing, and scenic drives.

Special Features
The Lower Crooked River is nationally known for its rainbow trout fly-fishing opportunities. The Rim Rock trailhead, across from the Chimney Rock campground (on State Route 27, 17 miles south of Prineville), leads to a 2-mile hike to the top of Chimney Rock. The trail and summit provide outstanding views of the river corridor and surrounding areas.

Permits, Fees, Limitations
The discharge of firearms within any campground or day-use area is prohibited.

Accessibility
Stillwater, Lower Palisades, Chimney Rock, Cobble Rock, Poison Butte, and Big Bend campgrounds (located from 13.5–19.2 miles south of Prineville on State Highway 27) all include accessible facilities. Palisades and Chimney Rock campgrounds include both accessible trails and accessible fishing platforms.

Camping and Lodging
A nightly fee is charged for camping. Campfires are generally allowed year-round; check for fire closures before

The Crooked River Back Country Byway provides motorists with outstanding views of the river corridor. *(BLM)*

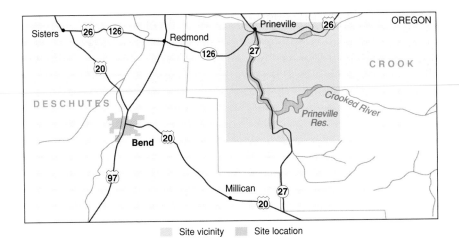

Site vicinity   Site location

you visit. Two day-use sites and nine developed campgrounds are available year-round on a first-come, first-served basis. Facilities include picnic tables, vault toilets, and garbage dumpsters. Each campground includes 6–30 camp-sites, but potable water is only available at the Chimney Rock Campground.

Food and Supplies

No food or supplies are available on-site. Supplies are available in Prineville.

First Aid

No first aid facilities are available on-site; however, some BLM personnel have first aid skills. The nearest hospital is in Prineville.

Additional Information

Oregon Highway 27 is a two-lane paved road for 21 miles from Prineville; the rest is gravel.

Contact Information

BLM - Prineville District Office
3050 NE 3rd Street
Prineville, OR 97754
Tel: (541) 416-6700
Fax: (541) 416-6798
www.or.blm.gov/Prineville

Activity Codes

Lower Deschutes River

Location

The Lower Deschutes Wild and Scenic River stretches 100 miles from the Pelton Reregulating Dam downstream to the river's confluence with the Columbia River. Towns along its course include Maupin, Warm Springs, Madras, and The Dalles.

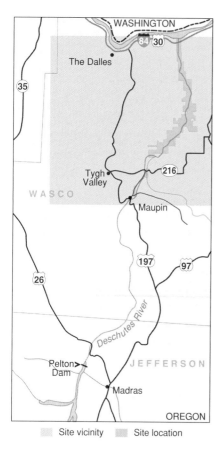

Site vicinity ▓ Site location

Description

The Lower Deschutes is central Oregon's whitewater playground. The river is characterized by a rimrock-lined canyon that ranges from 900–2,600 feet in depth. The river corridor hosts a diverse community of fish, wildlife, and vegetation, and offers an abundance of recreation opportunities, from whitewater rafting and swimming to hiking and biking.

Directions

Starting from Madras, follow U.S. Highway 197 north 47 miles to Maupin.

River access is available in Maupin. (U.S. Highway 197 crosses the river at this point, and intersects the Deschutes River Access Road and the Deschutes State Park.) Traveling east from Portland, follow Interstate 84 for 84 miles to The Dalles. Take U.S. Highway 197 south, 41 miles to exit 84 to Maupin, the southern end of the corridor.

Visitor Activities

Hiking, fishing, rafting, wildlife viewing, interpretation, birdwatching, and scenic drives.

Special Features

This popular whitewater river offers day-long and overnight float trips, as well as "Blue Ribbon" trout and steelhead fishing in the summer and Chinook salmon fishing in the spring. Along the river, one may see ospreys, deer, and bighorn sheep.

Permits, Fees, Limitations

Boater passes are required on the Lower Deschutes River for any individual using a boat or other device as a means of water transport. Day-use picnic areas do not require a fee.

Accessibility

Most sites along the Deschutes River Access Road are wheelchair-accessible and have accessible vault toilets. The campgrounds have some sites that are wheelchair-accessible.

Camping and Lodging

There are about 20 drive-in campgrounds and 5 picnic areas along the river. Camping is available year-round at all campgrounds. At developed sites, facilities include picnic tables, vault toilets, garbage dumpsters, sink-water

At River Mile 75, Whitehorse Rapids on the Lower Deschutes River offers rafters the opportunity to "pinball" from one haphazardly-placed boulder to the next as the river drops 35–40 feet over a distance of 1 mile. *(BLM)*

sumps, boat ramps, and interpretive displays. Drinking water is available only at the Beavertail and Macks Canyon campgrounds, which are 21 and 29 miles north of Maupin on the Deschutes River Access Road, respectively. Wood and charcoal fires are not permitted from June 1–October 15.

Food and Supplies

There are no food or supplies on-site. Supplies are available in Maupin.

First Aid

No first aid facilities are available on-site; however, many BLM personnel have first aid skills. Maupin has an ambulance service. The nearest hospitals are located in Madras and The Dalles.

Additional Information

BLM, the State of Oregon, and the Confederated Tribes of the Warm Springs Reservation jointly manage the Deschutes River. Visitors to the Lower Deschutes should expect high levels of visitation during summer weekends. Information on recreation opportunities along the river and instructions for reserving, purchasing, or canceling a boater pass can be obtained online at *www.boaterpass.com*. For current fishing regulations in effect on the Deschutes River, visitors should contact the Oregon Department of Fish and Wildlife, (541) 440-3353.

Contact Information

BLM - Prineville District Office
3050 NE 3rd Street
Prineville, OR 97754
Tel: (541) 416-6700
Fax: (541) 416-6798
www.or.blm.gov/Prineville/Deschutes_River

Activity Codes

Molalla River Recreation Site

Location

40 miles southeast of Portland, Oregon.

Description

The scenic Molalla River Corridor is a wonderful place to recreate, relax, and enjoy the great outdoors. A drive along Molalla Road offers miles of easy river access and year-round recreation opportunities. Visitors can hike, ride horses, or mountain bike within the Molalla River Shared-Use Trail System, specifically developed for non-motorized travel. It is an extensive network of forested trails that offer scenic glimpses of the Molalla River and the Cascade Range. The Molalla River Recreation Corridor includes over 5,000 acres of land along 12 miles of the scenic upper Molalla River. It extends 1.5 miles south of the Glen Avon area to the Table Rock Wilderness.

Directions

The Molalla River Recreation Site is located 9 miles southeast of Molalla. From Portland, take Interstate Highway 5 to the Woodburn Exit 271. Proceed east on State Highway 211 to Molalla. Follow signs to Dickey Prairie. Continue south on Dickey Prairie Road about 4 miles. Turn right onto the Molalla Forest Road and cross the Glen Avon Bridge. The Hardy Creek trailhead is located 3.5 miles south of the Glen Avon Bridge.

Visitor Activities
Swimming, fishing, horseback riding, hiking, kayaking, mountain biking, picnicking, and birdwatching.

Special Features
The river provides spawning grounds for steelhead and salmon, and is stocked with rainbow trout throughout the season. A wide variety of songbirds, as well as wood ducks, grouse, and great blue herons, are known to nest in the area.

Permits, Fees, Limitations
None.

Accessibility
Limited. Contact BLM for more information.

Camping and Lodging
There are no developed campgrounds. Camping is allowed at designated undeveloped campsites along and near the Molalla River. Feyrer Memorial Park, located approximately 10 miles from the corridor, provides developed campsites.

Food and Supplies
Food and supplies are available in Molalla.

First Aid
Emergency services are available in Molalla, and the closest hospital is in Silverton (24 miles south on U.S. Highway 5).

Flowing through the forested foothills of the Western Cascades to the Willamette River, the Molalla and its tributaries host a wide variety of streamside ecosystems. *(BLM)*

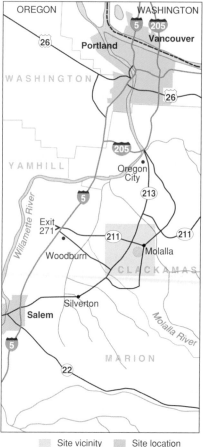

Site vicinity ▨ Site location

Additional Information

The first 1.5 mile-stretch of the river south from the bridge is bordered by private property. Visitors should not trespass on these lands. The river can be dangerous, especially in the winter and spring when the water is high and cold. Visitors should check with the Oregon Department of Fish and Wildlife, (503) 872-5268, for current fishing regulations. Development and management of the 50-mile trail system is part of a cooperative effort with Molalla RiverWatch, Inc. (a non-profit group) and several hiking, mountain biking, and equestrian groups. Contact BLM with any additional questions.

Contact Information

BLM - Salem District Office
1717 Fabry Road
Salem, Oregon 97306
Tel: (503) 375-5646
Fax: (503) 375-5622
www.or.blm.gov/salem

Activity Codes

National Historic Oregon Trail Interpretive Center

Location

5 miles east of Baker City, Oregon.

Description

Using life-size displays and multi-media and living-history presentations, this center dramatically tells the story of the lives and journeys of Oregon Trail-era pioneers. A visit to the center offers a unique opportunity to walk through a wagon train, join a group of emigrants as they cross the frontier, and experience history come to life. An outdoor trail system provides 4 miles of hiking to see

Pioneer figures, replica wagons, and native wildlife and vegetation give life to the story of the emigrant experience at the National Historic Oregon Trail Center. *(BLM)*

scenic vistas of the Blue Mountains, the Wallowa Mountains, the Baker Valley, and Virtue Flat. The original route of the Oregon Trail can be clearly seen from atop Flagstaff Hill. Visitors may hike down to the trail itself, and walk in the actual ruts made by pioneer wagons.

Directions
From Baker City, go east on State Highway 86 for 5 miles. Turn at the National Historic Oregon Trail Interpretive Center sign.

Visitor Activities
Interpretive exhibits and hiking.

Special Features
In addition to an outdoor pioneer wagon encampment and the remnants of a mining site, the center features the 150-seat Leo Adler Theater. Gleaning stories from pioneer diaries and other documents, living-history presenters in period dress offer factual and emotional perspectives on the trail era through music, songs, props, and soliloquies.

Permits, Fees, Limitations
Entrance fees, which vary during the year, are charged at the center. Call the center at (541) 523-1845 for information.

Accessibility
The center is fully wheelchair-accessible.

Camping and Lodging
Motels are available in Baker City. There are also two RV parks in Baker

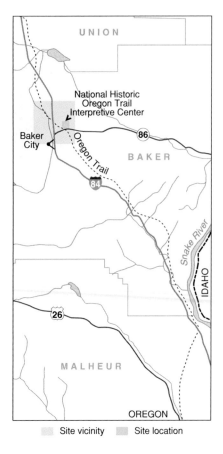

Site vicinity   Site location

City. There are no full-service camp-grounds within 15 miles of the site.

Food and Supplies
Vending machines are located on-site. A wide range of supplies and services are available in Baker City.

First Aid
First aid is available at the center. The nearest hospital is in Baker City.

Additional Information
The Center is open daily from 9 a.m.–6 p.m., April–October; and 9 a.m–4 p.m., November–March, except Thanksgiving, Christmas Day, and New Year's Day.

Contact Information
BLM - Baker Resource Area
22267 Oregon Highway 86
Baker City, OR 97814
Tel: (541) 523-1843
Fax: (541) 523-1834
oregontrail.blm.gov

Activity Codes

New River Area

Location
8 miles south of Bandon, Oregon.

Description
The New River runs through an area of rich biological diversity. The area en-compasses 1,168 acres, and provides quality habitat for native communities of plants, birds, animals, and fish. Its varied ecosystems include meadows, wind-eroded plains, forests, estuaries, open sand dunes, brackish and fresh waters, and wetlands. The wide range of ecosystems is used by a variety of avian species, including bald eagles, peregrine falcons, brown pelicans, neo-tropical birds, and wintering waterfowl. Because of its outstanding biological values, the New River was designated a BLM Area of Critical Environmental Concern in

North Umpqua Wild and Scenic River Corridor

Location
The corridor begins 23 miles east of Roseburg, Oregon, and extends 34 miles east to Soda Springs, Oregon.

Description
The beautiful North Umpqua Wild and Scenic River Corridor features world-class fly-fishing opportunities, exhilarating whitewater for rafters and kayakers, picture-postcard scenery, and a hiking and biking trail that follows the river for the entire length of the corridor and beyond. Barrier-free trails wind through the forest and provide views of migrating fish and soaring ospreys searching for food. At Deadline Falls Watchable Wildlife site, anadromous (sea run) fish may be viewed jumping falls as they return to spawn during the summer months. Almost all of the wild and scenic section of the North Umpqua River (31 miles) is limited to fly-fishing only.

Directions
From Roseburg, travel 23 miles east on State Highway 138, through Glide, to the Swiftwater Recreation Site. Here, Rock Creek joins the North Umpqua River and the wild and scenic river corridor begins. From the North Umpqua Trailhead, an easy 0.25-mile trail leads to the Deadline Falls Watchable Wildlife viewing area.

Visitor Activities
Scenic drives, fishing, whitewater rafting, kayaking, hiking, mountain biking, wildlife viewing, birdwatching, geologic sightseeing, and picnicking.

The North Umpqua River flows through a distinctive canyon landscape of vertical rock cliffs and spires, within a mosaic of mountain meadows and Douglas fir and western hemlock forests. *(Chuck Telford, BLM Roseburg District Office)*

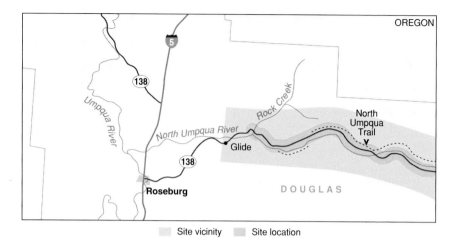

OREGON

North
Umpqua
Trail

Rock Creek

Umpqua River

North Umpqua River

Glide

Roseburg

DOUGLAS

Site vicinity   Site location

Special Features

Anglers from all parts of the nation are lured to the emerald-green waters of the North Umpqua River for its seasonal runs of steelhead and salmon. These anadromous fish migrate upriver from the ocean to spawn in the tributary waters. The river rapids are rated from Class I–V, ranging from mild water to moderately short, but raging, rapids. Numerous geologic features are visible along the river, including columnar basalt, basalt cliffs, boulders, and spires.

Permits, Fees, Limitations

Dogs must be leashed and all pets must be controlled. Commercial river outfitters are required to have a special recreation use permit.

Accessibility

Many facilities and trails are wheelchair-accessible. The first 0.25 mile of the North Umpqua Trail is accessible all the way to Deadline Falls Watchable Wildlife Site. Several day-use areas, trails, and campgrounds are also accessible. Contact BLM for a full list.

Camping and Lodging

The 31-unit Susan Creek Day-Use Area and Campground (7 miles upriver on Highway 138) is open from May–October. A nightly fee is charged for camping at Susan Creek Campground (29.5 miles east of Roseburg on State Highway 138). Voluntary donations are accepted for showers. There is a 14-day limit. Additional campgrounds upriver are managed by the Umpqua National Forest and include Bogus Creek, Canton Creek, Island, Apple Creek, Horseshoe Bend, Eagle Rock, and Boulder Flat Campgrounds. Cabins are also available for rent on private lands within the corridor.

Food and Supplies

Convenience stores are located along State Highway 138, near or within the corridor. A broader selection of groceries and other items is available in Glide, approximately 6 miles west of the beginning of the corridor on State Highway 138. Full services and complete supplies are available in Roseburg.

First Aid
The Glide Rural Fire Department/ Ambulance Service responds to 911 calls. Two hospitals are located in Roseburg. There are no first aid stations within the corridor.

Additional Information
The Swiftwater Recreation Site is a day-use area popular for steelhead and salmon fishing. An easy, 0.8-mile hike from the day-use area ends at moss-lined Susan Creek Falls. The difficulty of rapids of the North Umpqua River for rafts and kayaks is dependent primarily on water flow levels. Several rapids on the North Umpqua become more difficult as the water level decreases because of exposed rocks and the currents around them.

Mountain biking should not be attempted during wet conditions because rutting can result in severe trail damage.

For information on current fishing regulations, visitors should contact the Oregon Department of Fish and Wildlife at (541) 440-3353.

Contact Information
BLM - Roseburg District Office
777 Northwest Garden Valley Blvd.
Roseburg, OR 97470
Tel: (541) 440-4930
Fax: (541) 440-4948
www.or.blm.gov/roseburg/rec/nuws.html

Activity Codes

Owyhee National Wild and Scenic River/Owyhee Canyonlands

Location
The main river access is in Rome, 32 miles southwest of Jordan Valley, Oregon.

Description
This national wild and scenic river invites visitors to float more than 120 miles through rugged, high-desert canyonlands and view spectacular spires and cliffs towering 1,000 feet overhead. The Owyhee Wild and Scenic River Corridor flows through southeastern Oregon from the Idaho/Oregon state line to the Owyhee Reservoir. It is not unusual for visitors to come across a band of California bighorn sheep, many wildflowers, or a waterfall.

Directions
From Jordan Valley, take U.S. Highway 95 southwest 32 miles to Rome. The Rome Launch Site is located just before Highway 95 crosses the river, on the south side of the road.

Visitor Activities
Whitewater rafting, wildlife viewing, fishing, geologic sightseeing, and birdwatching.

Special Features
Visitors should keep a sharp eye out for bighorn sheep, river otters, and golden eagles. Columns, spires, needles, and arches are some of the

magnificent landforms found in the canyon.

Permits, Fees, Limitations
All river floaters must register. Also required are a firepan and a portable toilet system. Float group size is limited to 15 people upriver from Rome, and 20 people downriver from Rome.

Accessibility
None.

Camping and Lodging
Camping is available at BLM's Three Forks (15 miles southwest on U.S. Highway 95, then south on Three Forks Road for 35 miles) and Birch Creek (8 miles north on U.S. Highway 95, then west on Cow Creek road at Jordan Craters sign, then follow BLM Owyhee River access signs for 28 miles) Campgrounds, Rome Launch site, and at BLM's Antelope Reservoir Campground (22 miles northeast of Rome on Highway 95). Lodging, including

The Owyhee River's spectacular canyon cuts through ancient volcanic ash flows in southeastern Oregon. *(BLM)*

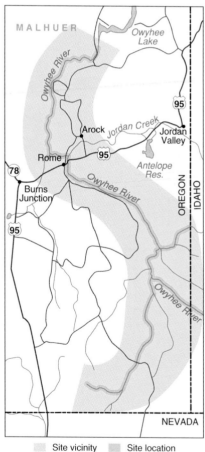

RV facilities, is available in Rome and Jordan Valley.

Food and Supplies

Gas and limited supplies are available in Rome and Burns Junction (12 miles west of Rome). Jordan Valley has gas, food, groceries, and a small medical clinic.

First Aid

The nearest hospitals are in Ontario, Oregon (approximately 120 miles north via U.S. Highway 95 to U.S. Highways 20/26) and Caldwell, Idaho (100 miles north via U.S. Highway 95 and Idaho State Highway 55).

Additional Information

The Owyhee Canyon is rugged country with limited access. Floating the river requires a high degree of technical skill.

River flows are seasonal, with peak flow times usually occurring in early spring–early summer. The river has several sections to float: the lower section is from Rome downstream; the middle section is from Three Forks to Rome; and the upper section is the entire river upstream of Three Forks, including segments in Idaho and Nevada. Visitors should call BLM for details.

Contact Information

BLM - Vale District Office
100 Oregon Street
Vale, OR 97918.
Tel: (541) 473-3144
Fax: (541) 473-6213
www.or.blm.gov/Vale

Activity Codes

Pacific Crest National Scenic Trail–Cascade-Siskiyou National Monument

Location

14 miles south of Ashland, Oregon.

Description

Hikers and horseback riders can traverse significant portions of the monument on the Pacific Crest National Scenic Trail. The trail meanders through wildflower-strewn meadows, old-growth forests, and juniper-covered hillsides. A portion of the trail stretches between Pilot Rock and Soda Mountain, offering scenic views to the south of Agate Flat, the Soda Mountain Wilderness Study Area, and Mount Shasta.

Directions

From Interstate 5, take Exit 14 near Ashland and turn east on State Highway 66 toward Klamath Falls. Take State Highway 66 for 17 miles to the Greensprings Summit. A trailhead and parking area are located at the summit. From there, follow the Pacific Crest Trail 6 miles north to Hyatt Reservoir or 12 miles south toward Pilot Rock.

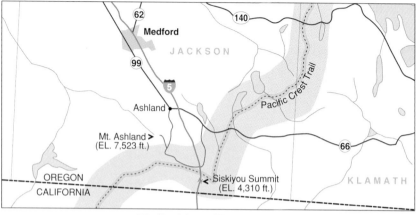

Site vicinity ▦ Site location

Within the monument, a short hike leads visitors from the quiet of a cool forest to wildflower meadows brimming with butterflies. *(Terry Tuttle, BLM Medford District Office)*

Trailhead locations are at Mt. Ashland Road, 5 miles west of Siskiyou summit, at Interstate 5, Exit 6; Callahan's Restaurant, at Interstate 5, Exit 6; and Greensprings summit, Mile 17 on State Highway 66.

Visitor Activities

Hiking, horseback riding, rock climbing, wildflower viewing, wildlife viewing, scenic drives, geologic sightseeing, snowshoeing, and cross-country skiing.

Special Features

The 200-foot columnar basalt cliffs of Pilot Rock provide viewers with a look inside a remnant of an ancient volcano, and offer a prime practice spot for rock climbers. Fossil sites in the vicinity of Pilot Rock contain leaf impressions and conifer cones that became embedded in volcanic ash beds 25–35 million years ago. The monument is also home to one of the highest diversities of butterfly species in the United States.

Permits, Fees, Limitations

None.

Accessibility
None.

Camping and Lodging
Developed campsites, including hot showers, are available at the BLM Hyatt Lake campground from May–September. Hyatt Lake campground is 18 miles east of Ashland on State Highway 66.

Food and Supplies
Food and supplies are available at the Greensprings Inn, located on State Highway 66, 16 miles east of Ashland.

First Aid
The nearest hospital is located in Ashland, an average of 20 miles from the Pacific Crest Trail. No first aid is available on-site.

Additional Information
Sections of the trail pass through private property; please respect private property owners' rights.

Contact Information
BLM - Medford District Office
3040 Biddle Road
Medford, OR 97504
Tel: (541) 618-2200
Fax: (541) 618-2400
www.or.blm.gov/csnm

Activity Codes

other - rock climbing

Rogue River Ranch

Location
45 miles northwest of Galice, Oregon.

Description
Whether visitors seek the excitement of a whitewater rafting trip or the quiet pleasure of watching a hawk circle above, the Rogue River offers outdoor escapes for every mood. Nestled in the heart of the Rogue River's wild section is the Rogue River Ranch, which is listed on the National Register of Historic Places. It can be reached by automobile or by hiking in on the Rogue River National Recreation Trail.

Directions
From Galice, head north on Galice Road 8 miles to the Grave Creek Bridge. Cross the Grave Creek Bridge and bear left uphill on paved BLM Road #34-8-1 for 5 miles. At the junction with Whisky Creek Road (#33-8-26), bear right and continue on #34-8-1 (sign reads "Marial 28 Miles") for 3 miles. At the junction with BLM Road #33-8-13 (on the right), bear left and continue on #34-8-1 for 8 miles. At the junction with BLM Road #32-8-31, bear left and continue on a paved road for 5 miles to the junction with BLM Road #32-8-9.2. Bear left and continue on #32-8-31 for 1 mile to Anaktuvuk Saddle Junction. Turn left on BLM road #32-9-14.2 for 3 miles to Marble Gap Junction. Continue ahead (pavement will end) for another 3 miles to Fourmile Saddle Junction. Bear left and stay on #32-9-14.2 for another 9 miles to the Rogue River Ranch.

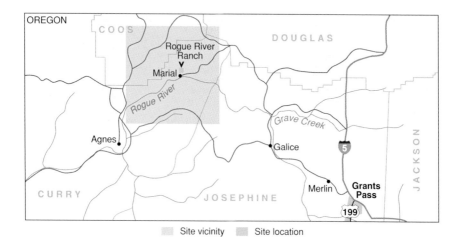

OREGON

COOS

DOUGLAS

Rogue River
Ranch
∨
Marial

Rogue River

Grave Creek

Agnes

Galice

JACKSON

CURRY

JOSEPHINE

Merlin

Grants
Pass

199

▨ Site vicinity ▨ Site location

The Rand Visitor Center is 3 miles northwest of Galice, on the route to the Ranch. Information and brochures about the ranch can be obtained from the visitor center.

Visitor Activities

Boating, rafting, swimming, wildlife viewing, birdwatching, plant viewing, historic site, interpretation, scenic drives, and hiking.

Nestled in the heart of the Rogue River's wild section, the Ranch is a welcome stopping place for day visitors. (B. Brown, BLM Medford District Office)

Special Features

Once a major Native American habitation site, the area has enjoyed a rich human history of over 9,000 years. After Europeans arrived, the site evolved into a small gold-mining community, with up to 100 residents trying to scratch a living from the gold-bearing gravel bars of the mighty Rogue River. The ranch structures remaining today represent the center of the early 1900s community, which had a trading post with upstairs lodging, a blacksmith's shop, and numerous outbuildings that filled the early residents' social and commercial needs. There is a museum on-site.

Permits, Fees, Limitations

Permits are not required for vehicle access or foot travel at the site; however, boating on the Rogue River does require a permit, obtainable at the Rand Visitor Center.

Accessibility

The main museum building is wheelchair-accessible. Other areas necessitate assisted access.

Camping and Lodging

There is a primitive BLM campground approximately 0.5 mile from the historic site. It is a no-charge site with a primitive toilet and no water. There is a lodge 1 mile west of the ranch. Two other lodges along the river can be reached by driving 2 miles west from the Ranch and then hiking 4 miles west on the Rogue River Trail. Primitive camping is allowed on surrounding public lands. Other lodging and camping can be found 45–75 miles east on Interstate 5 in Galice, Glendale, Merlin, and Grants Pass.

Food and Supplies

Supplies and gas are available in Galice, Glendale, Merlin, and Grants Pass.

First Aid

This is a remote site with no phone service or medical facilities. During the peak-use season of May–September, caretakers are on duty and can provide radio communication. The nearest hospitals are in Grants Pass, in the northwestern part of town.

Additional Information

This site is extremely remote, with no visitor services. All food and supplies should be obtained prior to beginning the trip. There are no gas stations in the area. Travelers should expect to come well-prepared for a long trip on mostly one-lane, winding, mountain dirt roads. Roads are maintained and are passable by passenger vehicles. Access to the area is often impossible during the winter months because of snow accumulations. The best time of the year to visit the site is from May–September.

Contact Information

BLM - Medford District Office
3040 Biddle Road
Medford, OR 97504
Tel: (541) 618-2200
Fax: (541) 618-2400
www.or.blm.gov/Rogueriver/Rec_areas_and_maps/roguerriverranch.htm

Activity Codes

Rough and Ready Flat

Location

6 miles south of Cave Junction, Oregon.

Description

Rough and Ready Flat is located within an area that is recognized as one of 200 biologically outstanding eco-regions in the world. A unique botanical habitat along Rough and Ready Creek, it harbors a multitude of rare or special-status plants endemic to the serpentine soils of the Siskiyou Mountains. The area has been a popular wildflower-watching spot for decades, and hybrid plant species are actively evolving here. A total of 1,164 acres surrounding Rough and Ready Creek have been designated a BLM Area of Critical Environmental Concern to protect botanical, wildlife, fisheries, hydrological and other natural systems and processes. The impetus to protect the area was provided by the Illinois Valley Garden Club in 1937.

With only a fraction of its area having been surveyed by botanists, more than 300 plant species have already been identified within the Rough and Ready Creek watershed so far. (John Craig, BLM Oregon State Office)

Directions
From Cave Junction, travel 4.5 miles south on U.S. Highway 199. Parking is available at the turnout on the right, just before the highway crosses Rough and Ready Creek. A botanical wayside sign designates the area.

Visitor Activities
Plant viewing, hiking, and biking.

Special Features
Ancient, gnarled cedars and pines, tenaciously rooted along the creek, are hardy survivors of flood and drought. Native bunch grasses, wild azaleas, and rare willows grace the banks, punctuated by springs that form unique wetlands hosting rare and carnivorous plants, lilies, and orchids.

Permits, Fees, Limitations
No fees. Off-highway vehicle use is prohibited.

Accessibility
None.

Camping and Lodging
Lodging is available in Cave Junction. Several RV campgrounds are located near Cave Junction, and 2 U.S. Forest Service campgrounds are located on State Highway 46 (Caves Highway) between Cave Junction and the Oregon Caves National Monument. Campgrounds are only open in the summer months.

Food and Supplies
Food and supplies are available in Cave Junction.

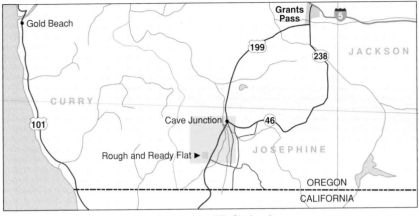

 Site vicinity █ Site location

First Aid

There is no first aid available on-site.
A clinic is located in Cave Junction.
The closest hospital is in Grants Pass,
approximately 30 miles north on U.S.
Highway 199.

Additional Information

No facilities are available on-site. An
interagency visitor center is located in
Cave Junction; this is the best source for
information on the area.

Contact Information

BLM – Medford District Office
3040 Biddle Road
Medford, OR 97504
Tel: (541) 618-2200
Fax: (541) 618-2400
www.or.blm.gov/Medford/recreationsites/
Medroughreadybot.html

Activity Codes

🚲 🚶 🏕

Row River Trail

Location

20 miles southeast of Eugene, Oregon.

Description

This 14-mile, paved, multi-use trail
follows the route of the now-abandoned
Oregon Pacific & Eastern Railroad line,
along the scenic shores of the Row
(rhymes with "cow") River and Dorena
Reservoir. There are many trailheads and
places to stop and enjoy views of Dorena
Lake and the surrounding farm country.

Several quaint, covered bridges are located
nearby, as is the historic Bohemia Mining
Area, which features remnants of late
1800s gold mines. The trestle bridge at
Harms Park is one of several locations
immortalized on the silver screen. Movies
filmed along the railway include "Stand
By Me" with River Phoenix, "Emperor
of the North" with Ernest Borginine,
and, in 1926, "The General" with Buster
Keaton.

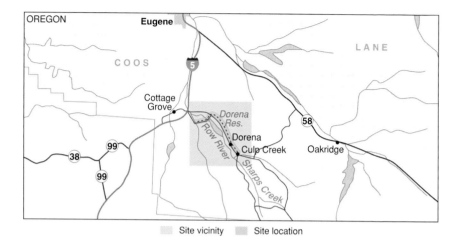

Site vicinity   Site location

Directions

From Eugene, take Interstate 5 south to the Cottage Grove exit (#174), and turn east onto Row River Road. Travel for 3.5 miles. Turn right onto Layng Road and proceed 1.2 miles to the corner of Layng and Mosby Creek Roads.

Visitor Activities

Picnicking, hiking, biking, horseback riding, and wildflower viewing, wildlife viewing, interpretation, and historic site.

Sharpes Creek is one of many refreshing stops along the Row River Trail. *(Doug Huntington, BLM Eugene District Office)*

Special Features

The Mosby Creek Covered Bridge, located just off the trail, is a white bridge built in 1920. Extensive restoration work was completed in 1990. Row Point survives as a remnant of a native prairie community, featuring showy displays of wildflowers during spring.

Permits, Fees, Limitations

None.

Accessibility

The trail is an 8-foot-wide paved path that allows for wheelchair access.

Camping and Lodging

No camping is allowed along the trail.

Food and Supplies

No food or water is available on the trail. Several general stores are located in Cottage Grove, Dorena (across Row River Road from the trail), and Culp Creek (0.25 mile east on Row River Road).

First Aid

No first aid is available along the trail. BLM Rangers or Lane County Sheriff's

Deputies may be on patrol in the area to provide assistance. The nearest hospital is located in Cottage Grove.

Additional Information

The trail is located in a forested environment. Visitors can expect warm, dry conditions in the summer, and cool, damp conditions in the spring, fall, and winter. Travel to the site is on two-lane, rural roads, which often have heavy truck traffic. Parking and restroom facilities are located at 2- to 3-mile intervals along the trail. This day-use area is open daily from dawn to dusk. Trailhead and interpretive facilities are provided.

Visitors should not enter old mine tunnels, which are both hazardous and located on private property.

Contact Information

BLM - Eugene District Office
2890 Chad Drive
Eugene, OR 97408
Tel: (541) 683-6600
Fax: (541) 638-6981
www.edo.or.blm.gov

Activity Codes

Shotgun Creek

Location

17 miles northeast of Springfield, Oregon.

Description

This day-use site is situated in the foothills of the Cascade Mountains.

Ten acres have been developed for recreation and 268 acres retain the natural characteristics typical of the region's temperate coniferous rainforest. In addition to the Douglas firs that are dominant, the area boasts many other species of plant life. Visitors on mountain bikes

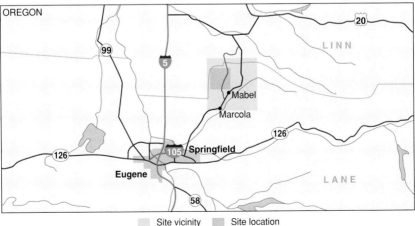

Site vicinity   Site location

can explore the additional miles of roads and trails outside the recreation site boundaries.

Directions
From Interstate 105 in Springfield, take the 42nd Street exit, and turn onto Marcola Road heading north. Travel 3 miles past the town of Marcola, and turn left onto Shotgun Creek Road. Proceed about 1.5 miles to the site.

Shotgun Creek entices young visitors to explore their surroundings.
(Doug Huntington, BLM Eugene District Office)

Visitor Activities
Picnicking, hiking, biking, swimming, playground activities, and historic site.

Special Features
Historical highlights of the surrounding area include evidence of the early native Kalapuya people, traces of pioneer homesteaders, and reminders of the colorful days of logging and timber booms.

Permits, Fees, Limitations
There is a vehicle entrance fee and the option of a calendar-year pass is available. Daily group shelter rental fees vary depending upon the size of the group.

Accessibility
All the high-use areas of the site are wheelchair-accessible. Trails within developed areas are paved, and some playground equipment is designed for people with special needs.

Camping and Lodging
No camping is allowed on-site. Dispersed camping is permitted on adjacent BLM lands up to 14 days per calendar year. Lodging is available in Springfield, 15 miles south on Marcola Road.

Food and Supplies
No food is available on-site. The nearest store is located in Marcola.

First Aid
Basic first aid is available on-site from BLM employees. First aid supplies and radio/telephone units are available for emergencies. The nearest hospital is located in Springfield.

Additional Information

Shotgun Creek is located in a forested environment. Visitors can expect warm, dry conditions in summer and cool, damp conditions in spring, fall, and winter. Travel to the site is on two-lane, rural roads, which often have heavy truck traffic. There are picnic areas, group shelters, beach and swimming areas, a volleyball court, a softball diamond, horseshoe pits, and several miles of nature trails. The two large group shelters, with amenities, are ideal for reunions, office parties, school outings, and weddings.

Contact Information

BLM - Eugene District Office
2890 Chad Drive
Eugene, OR 97440-2226
Tel: (541) 683-6600
Fax: (541) 683-6981
www.edo.or.blm.gov

Activity Codes

other - playground activities

Steens Mountain–East Rim Overlook

Location

85 miles southeast of Burns, Oregon.

Description

Whether your passion is summer wild-flower displays or big-game hunting, outdoor adventures in the Steens Mountain Cooperative Management and Protection Area (CMPA) are as big as the desert sky. Rising 9,700 feet above sea level, Steens Mountain is the highest peak in the northern Great Basin desert. The East Rim Overlook provides a stunning view of this rugged country, including the Alvord Desert, a dizzying vertical mile below your feet. Bighorn sheep can be spotted in the rugged cliffs of the east face. The 66-mile Steens Mountain Back Country Byway offers visitors a chance to see prairie falcons, American kestrels, and other birds of prey.

Directions

From Burns, drive south 60 miles on State Highway 205 to Frenchglen. From

Hikers are treated to majestic views into glacially-carved Kiger Gorge at Steens Mountain. *(Mark Armstrong, BLM Burns District Office)*

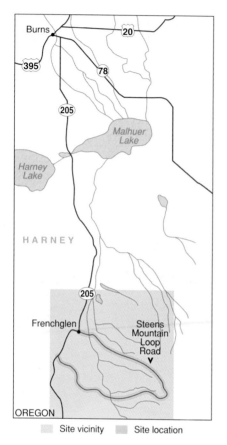

Site vicinity   Site location

stunning, colorful alpine wildflower meadows; high-desert vegetation; and wildlife such as pronghorn antelope, elk, and mule deer.

Permits, Fees, Limitations
None.

Accessibility
None.

Camping and Lodging
BLM campsites are available at Jackman Park, Fish Lake, and Page Springs, which are located along the Steens Mountain Loop Road (north segment), 5 miles, 7 miles, and 22 miles west of the East Rim Viewpoint, respectively. Another BLM campground (South Steens) is located 9 miles southwest of the East Rim viewpoint along the Steens Mountain Loop Road (south segment).

Food and Supplies
Frenchglen (25 miles west on Steen Mountain Loop Road) and Burns have the closest food and supplies.

First Aid
The nearest hospital is in Burns. No closer first aid is available.

Additional Information
Steens Mountain Loop Road is closed during the winter and usually does not reopen until June or July.

Contact Information
BLM – Burns District Office
28910 Highway 20 West
Burns, OR 97738
Tel: (541) 573-4400
Fax: (541) 573-4411
www.or.blm.gov/steens

there, follow signs to Steens Mountain Loop Road and turn left. The East Rim Overlook is at the 25-mile mark.

Visitor Activities
Scenic drives, nature study, hiking, wildlife viewing, geologic sightseeing, and wildflower viewing.

Special Features
Steens Mountain CMPA offers exceptional ecologic and geologic diversity. The mountain provides spectacular views of deep, glacial gorges; seasonal playa lakes; hot springs; sand dunes;

Activity Codes

Turn Point Lighthouse

Location
The western tip of Stuart Island, San Juan Islands, Washington.

Description
The light at Turn Point Lighthouse has been in continuous operation on the northwestern end of Stuart Island since 1893. While the point marks the spot where migrating orca (killer) whales turn south in the early summer, the name actually is derived from the fact that the light warns vessels of a sharp turn in Haro Strait. This location features grassy bluffs, coastal forest, and the historical buildings of the Turn Point Lighthouse Station. While the buildings are closed to the public at this time, Turn Point remains a beautiful spot in which to picnic, whale-watch, and explore the past.

Directions
Stuart Island is in the northwestern portion of the San Juan Islands, and is without commercial ferry service. Access is by private boat or airplane. Upon arrival at Prevost Harbor on the southwestern end of Stuart Island, follow the gravel road west 0.75 mile to its end at Turn Point Lighthouse.

Visitor Activities
Hiking, picnicking, historic site, and wildlife viewing, and plant viewing.

Special Features
From mid-March–May, migrating whales make their way into bays and inlets; a popular time to watch the orcas is April–September. The best time to view wildflowers is in May. White chickweed and yellow buttercups can be found throughout the grasslands.

Permits, Fees, Limitations
None. Site use is limited by the lack of public transportation to Stuart Island.

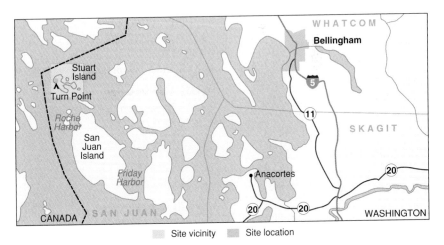

Site vicinity ▪ Site location

Historic Turn Point is a beautiful spot in which to picnic, whale-watch, and enjoy spectacular sunsets. *(John Craig, BLM Oregon State Office)*

Accessibility
A wheelchair-accessible outhouse is located on-site.

Camping and Lodging
Turn Point is a day-use site only. Public camping facilities are available at Reid Harbor State Park on the western end of Stuart Island.

Food and Supplies
No supplies are available on-site. Supplies may be purchased at Roche Harbor and Friday Harbor on San Juan Island.

First Aid
First aid is not available on-site. There is a hospital located at Friday Harbor on San Juan Island.

Additional Information
The best time to visit Turn Point is in the summer. Visitors should bring water, food, hiking shoes, binoculars, and a jacket to guard against changing weather. Weather ranges from warm, dry summers to cold, wet, stormy winters. At times, storms might prevent entry onto, or exit from, the island. The lighthouse facility is set high on a bluff; visitors should avoid getting too close to hazardous cliffs. Washington State Ferries make multiple daily departures to San Juan, Lopez, Shaw, and Orcas Islands from Anacortes, Washington, on the mainland. Private water taxi services and boat rentals and charters are available to Stuart Island from larger islands. Commercial flights to San Juan Island are available from Seattle, Washington.

Contact Information
BLM - Wenatchee Resource Area
915 N. Walla Walla
Wenatchee, WA 98801
Tel: (509) 665-2100
Fax: (509) 665-2121
www.or.blm.gov/Spokane

Activity Codes

Whittaker Creek

Location
30 miles west of Eugene, Oregon.

Description
Whittaker Creek serves as a cool oasis for travelers along State Highway 126. This 16-acre campground offers several unique features. In addition to its 31 rustic campsites, it hosts a Watchable Wildlife site for fish migration and a national recreation trail (Old Growth Ridge Trail). This trail, ascending 1,000 feet above the Siuslaw River, is a hiker's sanctuary nestled in the Coast Range Mountains. The moderately difficult trail takes hikers through a stand of old-growth Douglas fir, and offers wildlife, geologic, and botanic wonders. Whittaker Creek provides a setting for summertime water-play activities, featuring a swimming beach, picnic gazebo, children's playground, and a nearby boat ramp for access to the Siuslaw River.

Directions
From Eugene, travel State Highway 126 west for approximately 30 miles, and turn left onto Siuslaw River Road. Travel 2 miles south, turn right to cross the Siuslaw River, and travel 0.25 mile to the campground entrance on the right.

Visitor Activities
Hiking, swimming, fishing, wildlife viewing, and picnicking.

Visitors can get unparalleled views of spawning salmon in Whittaker Creek by crossing the footbridge from the campground and then walking upstream. *(John Craig, BLM Oregon State Office)*

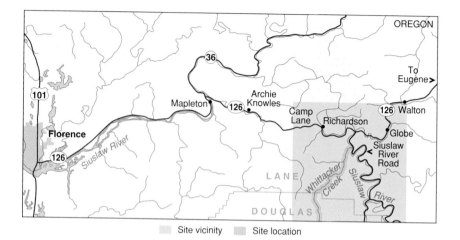

Site vicinity   Site location

Special Features

Whittaker Creek is noted for its annual runs of native Chinook, Coho salmon, and steelhead. In the fall, visitors can see fish spawning in the gravel beds; migrating fish can be seen during the fall and spring.

Permits, Fees, Limitations

None.

Accessibility

There are wheelchair-accessible out-houses, a gazebo, and some camping sites.

Camping and Lodging

An overnight camping fee is required. There are 31 campsites, including eight trailer sites. Only water and vault toilets are available.

Food and Supplies

No food or supplies are available on-site. Supplies may be purchased in Florence and Mapleton (30 and 15 miles west on State Highway 126, respectively), and Eugene.

First Aid

The nearest hospitals and clinics are located in Florence and Eugene.

Additional Information

The campground is usually closed during the winter months. Visitors should call to check on dates of operation. A small, day-use gazebo can accommodate 10 visitors. There is a boat ramp accessing the Siuslaw River near the campground, and a covered bridge a few miles away.

Contact Information

BLM - Eugene District Office
2890 Chad Drive
Eugene, OR 97440-2226
Tel: (541) 683-6600
Fax: (541) 683-6981
www.edo.or.blm.gov

Activity Codes

Yakima River Canyon

Location
5 miles south of Ellensburg, Washington.

Description
The Yakima River Canyon meanders through 25 miles of rolling desert hills and basalt cliffs between Ellensburg and Yakima. The river is part of a thriving sagebrush-steppe ecosystem, with birds of prey and bighorn sheep sharing the high cliffs. Yakima River is popular for family rafting, and as a high-quality, "catch and release" trout stream.

Directions
From Ellensburg, travel south 5 miles on State Highway 821 to the entrance of the Yakima River Canyon. The Um-tanum Recreation Site is located 8 miles beyond this point. Drive 4 more miles to the Lmuma Recreation Site, and Roza Recreation Site is located 5 miles further still.

Visitor Activities
Catch and release fishing, hunting (bird and big-game), floating, picnicking, hiking, wildlife viewing, boating, plant viewing, and swimming.

Special Features
The Yakima River is considered a "Blue Ribbon" trout fishery, home to wild rainbow and cutthroat trout.

Permits, Fees, Limitations
Day-use fees are charged.

Originating near the crest of the Cascade Range, the Yakima River is celebrated as one of Washington's premier trout streams. *(Bill Schurger, BLM Spokane District Office)*

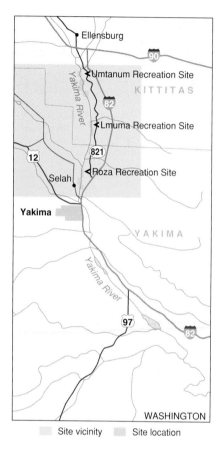

Site vicinity   Site location

Accessibility

There are wheelchair-accessible out-houses at Roza and Lmuma Recreation Sites. All three recreation sites (Lmuma, Roza, and Umtanum) are flat, and Lmuma has asphalt-hardened, wheelchair-accessible camping spots.

Camping and Lodging

Umtanum and Roza permit camping in designated sites. The camping stay limit is 7 days total at BLM areas within the canyon. Other nearby camping facilities and motels are in Ellensburg and in Yakima and Selah (14 and 10 miles south of Roza on State Highway 821, respectively).

Food and Supplies

No food or supplies are available on-site. Visitors may purchase supplies in Ellensburg or Selah, at either end of the canyon.

First Aid

First aid is not available on-site. Hospital and first aid facilities are located in Ellensburg and Yakima. Emergency medical services serve the Yakima River Canyon.

Additional Information

Spring, fall, and winter are good times to view wildlife and enjoy the solitude of the canyon, while summer brings large crowds to enjoy water activities. Some motorized boat activities are permitted in the Roza Dam pool, which extends for 1.5 miles north to the Roza Recreation Site. Visitors should bring water, food, binoculars, and appropriate clothing. Temperatures range from more than 100°F in the summer to below 0°F in the winter. Visitors should respect the rights of private property owners and other recreationists.

Contact Information

BLM - Wenatchee Resource Area
915 N. Walla Walla
Wenatchee, WA 98801
Tel: (509) 665-2100
Fax: (509) 665-2121
www.or.blm.gov/Spokane

Activity Codes

Yaquina Head
Outstanding Natural Area

Location
3 miles north of Newport, Oregon.

Description
Jutting into the Pacific Ocean, Yaquina Head was formed by a series of lava flows that spread across Oregon and Washington millions of years ago. This headland provides visitors with one of the most accessible wildlife and ocean viewing locations on the Pacific Coast. Harbor seals and whales are visible offshore year-round. In spring and summer, thousands of seabirds flock to the near-shore islands to breed and raise their young; birdwatchers can experience incredibly close views of these nesting seabirds. At low tide, visitors can observe pools filled with many different species of intertidal life. Oregon's tallest (93 feet) and second-oldest lighthouse has illuminated this promontory since 1873. Archaeologists have also discovered evidence of Native American visits to the site.

Site vicinity   Site location

Directions
From Newport, drive north on U.S. Highway 101 for 3 miles. Look for the Yaquina Head sign. Turn left on Lighthouse Drive.

Visitor Activities
Tidepool study, wildlife viewing, birdwatching, historic site, interpretation, and summer lighthouse tours.

Special Features
Quarry Cove, a former rock quarry, is the world's only manmade, accessible tidepool, offering close views of intertidal ecosystems. The Cobble Beach tidepools provide visitors with views of purple sea urchins and sea lemons. From December–February, whales can be seen traveling south to calving and breeding grounds in Baja, and from March–May,

they can be seen heading north to feeding grounds in the Bering Sea. In the summer, medium-sized whales and cows with calves spend their time feeding along the Oregon coast. Tufted puffins and common murres are among the 25,000 birds that form a nesting area, or rookery, during the spring and summer.

Permits, Fees, Limitations
Entrance fees vary. Please call BLM for information.

Accessibility
There are wheelchair-accessible trails through tidepools, around the outside of the lighthouse, and at wildlife-viewing decks.

Camping and Lodging
Newport has several hotels and motels, and the central Oregon coast includes state parks with camping facilities.

Food and Supplies
Newport has several large grocery stores and a department store.

First Aid
The nearest hospital is located in Newport.

Additional Information
This day-use area is open daily from dawn to dusk. The lighthouse is open 10 a.m.–4 p.m. for viewing (weather permitting). Winter hours are variable. A telephoto lens will help visitors take close-up pictures of whales, seals, and birds from one of the nation's closest mainland viewpoints of seabird nesting colonies, and a visit to the lighthouse interpretive center and store will round out the experience. Visitors should consult local tide tables to plan a tide-pool visit coinciding with low tide.

Contact Information
BLM – Yaquina Head
Outstanding Natural Area
P.O. Box 936
Newport, OR 97365
Tel: (541) 574-3100
Fax: (541) 574-3141
www.or.blm.gov/salem/html/yaquina/index.htm

Activity Codes
 other – tidepool study

A classic example of 1870s lighthouse design, the Yaquina Head Lighthouse's 93-foot tower was built with supplies brought in by boat. *(BLM)*

One of the outstanding landscape features of the Grand Staircase-Escalante National Monument, 40-foot-high Phipps Arch is a colorful formation named for a 19th-century Escalante rancher who pastured livestock nearby. *(Jerry Sintz, BLM Utah State Office (retired))*

Utah's public lands feature some of the most spectacular scenery in the world, from the snow-capped peaks of remote mountain ranges to the colorful red-rock canyons of the Colorado Plateau. There are over 22 million acres of public lands in Utah, representing about 42 percent of the state. These lands are located mostly in western and southeastern Utah. The terrain is varied, ranging from rolling uplands in the Uintah Basin to sprawling lowlands in the Mojave Desert.

Utah's public lands offer unparalleled opportunities for activities including mountain biking, desert backpacking, and whitewater rafting on the Green, San Juan, and Colorado Rivers. Visitors can also explore a number of significant archaeological and historical sites, including those along a 165-mile segment of the Pony Express National Historic Trail. The John Jarvie Historic Site, having hidden such famous outlaws as Butch Cassidy and the Sundance Kid, provides visitors with a flavor of the Wild West. Aspiring paleontologists may find their special experience at the Cleveland-Lloyd Dinosaur Quarry, an active operation from which 12,000 bones have been excavated so far.

BLM's first national monument is located on public lands in Utah. Situated in the stunningly beautiful red-rock country of south-central Utah, the Grand Staircase-Escalante National Monument is a dramatic, multi-hued landscape that encompasses 1.9 million acres. Rich in natural and human history, the area boasts a unique combination of archaeological, historical, paleontological, geological, and biological resources. One of the last places in the United States to be mapped, this national monument is definitely worth the trip for those with a sense of adventure and a little time to explore.

Utah

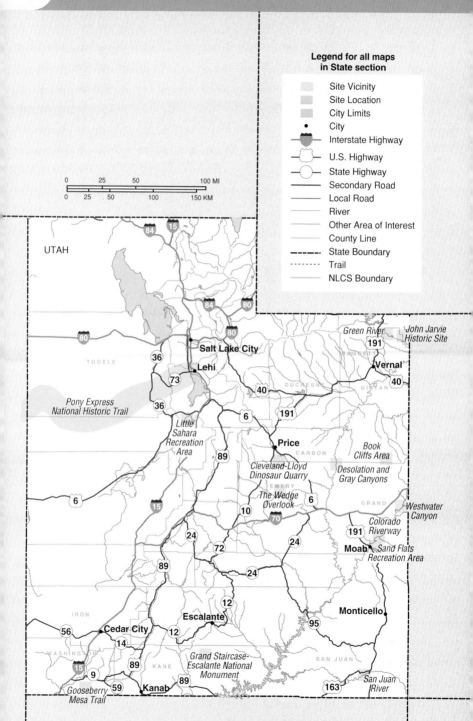

Legend for all maps
in State section

Site Vicinity
Site Location
City Limits
• City
Interstate Highway
U.S. Highway
State Highway
Secondary Road
Local Road
River
Other Area of Interest
County Line
State Boundary
Trail
NLCS Boundary

UTAH

Salt Lake City
Lehi
TOOELE
Pony Express
National Historic Trail
Little
Sahara
Recreation
Area

Green River
John Jarvie
Historic Site
Vernal
DUCHESNE
UINTAH
Price
CARBON
Cleveland-Lloyd
Dinosaur Quarry
Book
Cliffs Area
Desolation and
Gray Canyons
EMERY
The Wedge
Overlook
GRAND
Westwater
Canyon
Colorado
Riverway
Moab
Sand Flats
Recreation Area

Escalante
Monticello

Cedar City
IRON
WASHINGTON
KANE
Grand Staircase-
Escalante National
Monument
SAN JUAN
Kanab
Gooseberry
Mesa Trail
San Juan
River

Book Cliffs Area

Location
60 miles south of Vernal, Utah.

Description
This area contains 455,000 acres of diverse vegetation and wildlife. Sagebrush, greasewoods, and junipers are found at the lower elevations around 5,500 feet, while Gamble oaks, mountain mahoganies, aspens, and Douglas firs are at the highest elevations around 8,200 feet. Although only 60 air miles south of Vernal, Utah, the area remains remote, with rough and dusty dirt roads. Several old ranch sites, mining remains, and an abundance of wildlife give the area a "frontier" mystique. The vista is broken by deeply incised canyons rising up from the sagebrush, through tall aspens and pines, to the panoramic Book Cliffs Divide. Willow, Bitter Creek, and Sweetwater are the perennial streams that gently wind their way out of the high country to feed the slowly moving Green River.

Directions
Stop at the BLM office to obtain a map, directions, and information on road conditions. Many gravel roads are unmarked.

Visitor Activities
Wildlife viewing, hiking, birdwatching, fishing, big-game and small-game hunting, plant viewing, scenic drives, and horse packing.

Special Features
Visitors may see deer, elk, and black bears. Blue and sage grouses, numerous

Vistas at the remote Book Cliffs Area present a spectrum of landscapes, from desert to lush hills, deep valleys to cliff-top overlooks. *(Jerry Sintz, BLM Utah State Office (retired))*

hawks, antelope, mountain lions, small mammals, birds, reptiles, and amphibians also inhabit this diverse and unique landscape.

Permits, Fees, Limitations

There are no fees or permits required. Check with the Utah Division of Wildlife Resources for information on hunting and fishing license requirements (152 East 100 North, Vernal, UT 84078, (435) 789-9453).

Accessibility

None.

Camping and Lodging

There are no developed facilities in the area. Primitive camping is available throughout the area in the spring, summer, and fall. Commercial camping and motel accommodations are available in Roosevelt and Vernal, both about 60 miles away.

Food and Supplies

Gas, food, and supplies are available in Vernal (60 miles) and Price (80 miles), Utah, and in Rangely (25 miles) and Grand Junction (50 miles), Colorado.

First Aid

There is no first aid on-site. The nearest hospitals are in Vernal, Utah, and Grand Junction, Colorado.

Additional Information

This is a very remote, rugged area accessible only by gravel and dirt roads. The roads often have a sharp, shale surface that causes numerous flat tires. Carrying two spare tires is recommended. Some roads are impassable when wet. Uintah County maintains a majority of the roads year-round, except for some at the highest elevations in

winter. A high-clearance or four-wheel-drive vehicle is recommended. Visitors should carry extra water and food, and have a full tank of gas.

Contact Information

BLM - Vernal Field Office
170 South 500 East
Vernal, UT 84078
Tel: (435) 781-4400
Fax: (435) 781-4410
www.blm.gov/utah/vernal

Activity Codes

other - horse packing

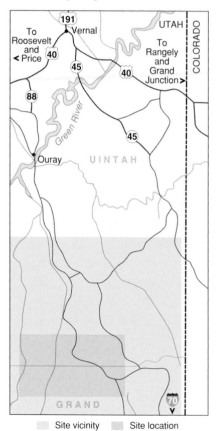

Site vicinity   Site location

Cleveland-Lloyd Dinosaur Quarry

Location
30 miles south of Price, Utah.

Description
The Cleveland-Lloyd Dinosaur Quarry contains the greatest accumulation of Jurassic dinosaur bones in the world. Since the 1920s, paleontologists have collected more than 12,000 fossil bones at the quarry. At least 70 individual dinosaurs died here about 145 million years ago during the Jurassic Period, and their jumbled skeletons were covered by sediments of the Morrison Formation. The remains of the carnivorous dinosaur *Allosaurus* are unusually common, and visitor center displays include an *Allosaurus* skeleton. Visitors can also view part of the quarry that has been enclosed for specimen protection. There are restrooms, picnic tables, and self-guided trails. The Cleveland-Lloyd Dinosaur Quarry was designated BLM's first National Natural Landmark in 1966.

Directions
From Price, drive south about 12 miles on State Highway 10. Turn left onto State Highway 155, and follow the signs to Elmo for 5–6 miles. Just east of Elmo, turn right onto a graded dirt road and follow the signs 12 miles through the Desert Lake Waterfowl Reserve and on to the Cleveland-Lloyd Dinosaur Quarry. Visitors should pick up a map at the BLM office in Price. The road to the quarry is well marked, but there are a number of turns on the dirt road leading to the visitor center.

Visitor Activities
Picnicking, fossil viewing, interpretive exhibits, wildlife viewing, and hiking.

The Cleveland-Lloyd Dinosaur Quarry has produced thousands of prehistoric animal bones, from which more than 60 casts and original skeletons have been assembled for display in museums around the world.
(Jerry Sintz, BLM Utah State Office (retired))

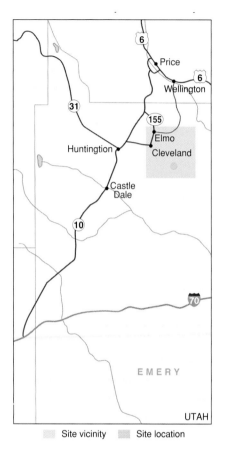

Site vicinity   Site location

Special Features

In addition to seeing dinosaur bones, in-cluding a mounted *Allosaurus* skeleton, visitors will experience towering rock outcrops, and miles of empty space. The area surrounding the quarry is semi-arid and sparsely vegetated with pinyon pines, Utah junipers, sagebrush, salt-brush, and cacti. The San Rafael Swell, a large, 900-square-mile bulge in the earth, is the dominant feature to the south. From atop Raptor Point, a high spot a few hundred yards west of the quarry, one can look out across 30 miles of land and see high cliffs arranged in a

great horseshoe to the east, north, and west. These cliffs are the abrupt edges of the Tavaputs Plateau to the east and north, and the Wasatch Plateau to the west.

Closer to the quarry, room-size boulders are strewn across the land. Ridges and steep-sided hills contain evidence that dinosaurs once walked here, and ranger guides lead the hardiest visitors on "track tours" to dinosaur footprints recorded in the rock. Large and small hoodoos dot the landscape along the way to the bones and tracks. Reddish barite roses—barium-rich mineral crystals in the shape of flow-ers—litter the ground in places, giving scientists clues to what the climate was like when allosaurs prowled ancient flood plains.

Permits, Fees, Limitations

There is a fee for admission to the visitor center and covered quarry.

Accessibility

The restrooms and buildings are wheelchair-accessible. The path to the quarry is a 4-foot-wide concrete surface that can accommodate wheelchairs.

Camping and Lodging

Most of the public lands outside the quarry area are open to dispersed camp-ing. The closest State campground is in Huntington, near State Highway 10, about 21 miles south of Price and about 20 miles from the quarry. Motel accommodations are available in Price, Huntington, and Castle Dale, on State Highway 10, 32 miles south of Price.

Food and Supplies

Food, gas, and supplies are available in Price, Huntington, and Castle Dale.

in Price and Green River. Price is about 83 miles from Sand Wash; Green River is about 149 miles from Sand Wash.

Food and Supplies

Shuttles, outfitters, gasoline, equipment rentals, and food are available in Price and Green River.

First Aid

Boaters are required to carry a complete first aid kit on all trips. No first aid is available on-site. The nearest hospital is in Price.

Additional Information

The area is remote and not serviced by roads or communication facilities; therefore, visitors are dependent upon self-rescue in emergencies. Class III boating skills are recommended. Open canoes are not advised. The character of individual rapids fluctuates greatly with changing river flows; flash floods from side canyons can create new rapids or change existing ones. Scouting those rapids that are not clearly visible from upstream is recommended.

There are several boat take-out points. The best is the Swasey Beach Boat Ramp just below Swasey Rapid at Mile 12. (This is 84 miles downstream from Sand Wash and 12 miles upstream from the town of Green River. To drive to this point, from Green River, travel north on the Hastings Road for 12 miles. This road parallels the river.) Those who choose to extend the river trip past this point should be aware that there is a low-head dam that blocks the river 3 miles below Swasey Rapid. This dam forms a Class IV drop, which must be scouted. The river traverses private

A visitor contemplates a deceptively placid stretch of the Green River, whose 84 miles in Desolation and Gray Canyons boast 60 Class II and III rapids. *(Kelly Rigby, BLM Utah State Office)*

lands below this point for the next 30 miles to Ruby Ranch.

The water in the river should be treated before drinking. Visitors are encouraged to carry in drinking water. There are 17 outfitting companies offering professionally-guided, full-service trips through Desolation Canyon. Contact information on these companies, as well as other additional information, is provided on the BLM website.

Contact Information:
BLM - Price Field Office
125 South 600 West
Price, UT 84501
Tel: (435) 636-3622
Fax: (435) 636-3657
www.blm.gov/utah/price

Activity Codes

Gooseberry Mesa Trail

Location
35 miles northeast of St. George, Utah.

Description
The Gooseberry Mesa trail, featured in numerous trade publications and sports videos, is a unique technical mountain biking trail that combines slickrock obstacles with a single-track trail to create a series of interconnecting loops bi-sected by a rugged jeep road. The trail is rated as one of Utah's supreme riding opportunities, and may be one of the best trails in the nation. The layout allows the mountain biker to customize the length and technical difficulty of the ride. Each component of the trail can be ridden in any direction, allowing the rider to combine loops to suit interest or ability.

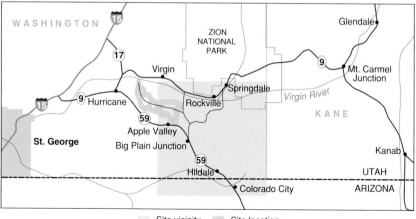

Site vicinity   Site location

Directions

From St. George, travel north on Interstate 15, then go east on State Highway 59 through Hurricane City to Big Plains Junction (the first left past Apple Valley). Travel 2.75 miles to Gooseberry Mesa Road and turn left. Or, from Springdale, travel west on State Highway 9 to Rockville. Turn left on Bridge Road and follow it 7.5 miles to Gooseberry Mesa Road and turn right.

Then travel 3.5 miles on Gooseberry Mesa Road to the left fork road. You will see a restroom. Turn left and travel 1 mile to the main trailhead or continue straight 1 mile to the oversized-vehicle parking area on the Windmill Loop. All commercial vehicles are required to use this parking area. Other low-clearance vehicles should park here as well.

Visitor Activities

Technical mountain biking and hiking

Special Features

The "Point" and other viewing stops along the trail offer a 360° view featuring such attractive points of interest as Zion National Park, Smithsonian Butte, The Virgin Terraces, Pine Valley Mountains, Little Creek Mountain, and the St. George Basin. These views are greatly enhanced during sunsets in the fall.

Permits, Fees, Limitations

None.

Accessibility

The restrooms along Gooseberry Mesa Road are wheelchair-accessible. The White Trail and Gooseberry Mesa Road are accessible by four-wheel-drive vehicle or all-terrain vehicle to the Rim View points. The South and North Rim Trails are not wheelchair-accessible

A mountain biker approaches Rattlesnake Rim on the South Rim Trail at Gooseberry Mesa. *(Chuck Haney (used with permission))*

as they were designed for technical mountain biking and contain narrow passages and rock obstacles.

Camping and Lodging

There are no BLM-operated camping facilities near Gooseberry Mesa, although there are 10 primitive camp sites along the Gooseberry Mesa and Left Fork Roads. The town of Springdale offers everything from private RV parks to three-star accommodations. Springdale is 15.5 miles from the trailhead. Zion National Park, just east of Springdale on State Highway 9, offers tent and RV camping for a fee.

Food and Supplies
Food, gas, and supplies are available in Springdale and at a gas station in Apple Valley along State Highway 59. Apple Valley is about 10 miles from the trailhead.

First Aid
A hospital and after-hours clinic are located in St. George. Emergency services are available in St. George or Colorado City. (This is a 911 search and rescue service.)

Additional Information
Gooseberry Mesa is located in a desert climate on the edge of the Colorado Plateau. The riding seasons are September 1–November 15 and February 1–May 15. The total mileage of this trail system is 18.3 miles. Each loop section is between 1 and 3 miles long, with the Yellow Trail being the shortest at 0.4 mile and the White Trail the longest at 3.5 miles. A round-trip ride to the "Point" is 8 miles long.

There is a map of the trails in the area on the trailhead sign. The trail route is officially marked with reflective, white color dots. However, old trail markings may still be encountered along the trail, and may vary from dark green to light blue or long white stripes. To avoid getting lost, visitors should only follow the white dot markings, as changes in the trail's route have been made since its creation.

Contact Information
BLM - St. George Field Office
345 East Riverside Dr.
St. George, UT 84790
Tel: (435) 688-3200
Fax: (435) 688-3252
www.ut.blm.gov/st_george/index.html

Activity Codes

Grand Staircase-Escalante National Monument

Location
85 miles east of St. George, Utah.

Description
Grand Staircase-Escalante National Monument is located on the Colorado Plateau in the pristine and spectacular canyonlands of Utah. It contains some of the most remote country in the lower 48 states. The monument's 1.9 million acres of vast and austere landscape embrace a spectacular array of scientific and historic resources in an unspoiled natural setting. This rugged and remote region of high plateaus and multi-hued cliffs was the last place in the continental United States to be mapped. The monument contains extensive and remote back country hiking opportunities.

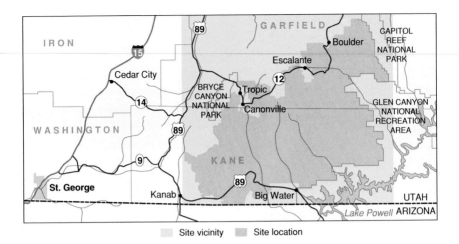

Site vicinity   Site location

The lands of the monument are divided into three distinct regions: The Grand Staircase, Escalante Canyon, and Kaiparowits Plateau. The Grand Staircase is a series of great geological "steps" that ascend northward across the southwestern corner of the Monument, spanning five different life zones, from Sonoran Desert to coniferous forest. The Escalante River cascades off the southern flank of the Aquarius Plateau, winding through a 1,000-mile maze of interconnected canyons. This magical labyrinth is one of the scenic wonders of the West. The Kaiparowits Plateau is a vast, wedge-shaped block of mesas and deeply incised canyons that tower above the surrounding canyonlands. The isolated, rugged plateau is refuge for wildlife and rare plants, and a depository for countless fossils.

Directions

The monument is surrounded by the towns of Kanab, Cannonville, Boulder, Bigwater, and Escalante. Each of these towns has a visitor center offering maps and information. Scenic All American Highway 12 (State Highway 12) runs along the northern portion of the monument, and State Highway 89 is located on the southern boundary. Bryce Canyon National Park abuts the monument near Cannonville. Glen Canyon National Recreation Area and Capitol Reef National Park lie adjacent to the monument on the east, and Dixie National Forest borders the monument to the north. To get to Devil's Garden, one of the striking landscape features in the monument, go about 4.5 miles south on State Highway 12 from Escalante. Turn right on Hole-in-the-Rock Road. Proceed another 7.5 miles to the site. Proceed another 7.5 miles to the parking area for Devil's Garden.

Visitor Activities

Hiking, scenic drives, mountain biking, wildlife viewing, birdwatching, four-wheel driving, horseback riding, geologic sightseeing, and interpretive exhibits.

Special Features

Calf Creek Falls is one of the most well-known features in the Grand

Hikers find solitude and beauty in the Escalante Canyon area of the Grand Staircase-Escalante National Monument. *(Kelly Rigby, BLM Utah State Office)*

where visitors can hike a short trail system to meander among striking hoodoos, arches, and other sandstone formations. The Paria Movie Set and the Pahreah Cemetery and Town Site are well worth a visit, just 5 miles off of State Highway 89 in the southern portion of the monument. Visitors will be treated to a newly reconstructed movie set complete with interpretive panels and a walking tour brochure that explores life on the Paria River.

Permits, Fees, Limitations
Fees may be required in the future. Special-use permits are required for commercial users such as guides, outfitters, and large groups.

Accessibility
The visitor centers at Anasazi State Park and in Big Water, Cannonville, Escalante, and Kanab all have building entry ramps, wheelchair-accessible toilets, and wheelchair-accessible exhibit facilities. Within the monument, Grosvenor Arch, about 18 miles south of Cannonville on Cottonwood Canyon Road, has a wheelchair-accessible toilet and picnic site, and a hardened surface trail to view the arch. (Cottonwood Canyon Road is paved to Kodachrome State Park.) The Blues Overlook on State Highway 12 has wheelchair-accessible toilets and paved access to viewing spots. Calf Creek Recreation Area has wheelchair-accessible toilets and a few wheelchair-accessible picnic and camping sites. Deer Creek campsite, 9 miles east of Boulder on the paved portion of Burr Trail, has a wheelchair-accessible toilet. Devil's Garden, about 10 miles east of Boulder on Burr Trail Road, has wheelchair-accessible toilets.

Staircase-Escalante National Monument. A trail leads visitors along Calf Creek to a 126-foot-high, spectacular waterfall. The hike is 6 miles round-trip and takes 3–4 hours. A trail brochure highlights features along the way. Another easily accessible feature is Devil's Garden,

Camping and Lodging

Lodging is available in Kanab, Cannonville, Escalante, Boulder, and Tropic, about 5 miles northwest of Cannonville on State Highway 12. Within the monument, campgrounds are located at Calf Creek and Deer Creek, 5 miles east. Primitive camping is also permitted within the monument. Back country permits are required for all overnight stays (backpacking, car camping, horse packing, and boating). State park campgrounds are located adjacent to the monument at Kodachrome Basin, 10 miles west of Cannonville, and in Escalante Petrified Forest, 5 miles west. Other public and private campgrounds are nearby. Check with a visitor center for details.

Food and Supplies

No services are available within the monument. Services are available in nearby Kanab, Cannonville, Tropic, Escalante, and Boulder, and in Page, Arizona, 9 miles southeast of Bigwater on U.S. Highway 89.

First Aid

No first aid is available within the monument. The nearest hospitals are located in Page, Arizona, and Panguitch (about 60 miles northwest of Escalante) and Kanab, Utah. Limited medical services are available in Escalante.

Additional Information

Visitors should check with BLM staff before visiting the monument. Visitors must be cautious, whether riding in a vehicle or hiking. State Highways 89 and 12 and the Burr Trail (a partially paved route from Boulder to Capital Reef National Park), are the only roads within the monument that are paved. Unpaved portions of Burr Trail require a four-wheel-drive, high-clearance vehicle. Dirt roads can become impassable when wet.

Contact Information:

BLM – Grand Staircase-
  Escalante National Monument
190 E. Center
Kanab, UT 84741
Tel: (435) 644-4300
Fax: (435) 644-4350
www.ut.blm.gov/monument

Activity Codes

Green River

Location

The launch site at Little Hole is located 50 miles north of Vernal, near Dutch John, Utah.

Description

The Green River flows east from Flaming Gorge Dam in northeastern Utah toward the Utah/Colorado state line. Along its shores, cottonwood trees provide habitat for wildlife. The cold, clear water is a "Blue Ribbon" trout fishery and provides for various types of water recreation. Visitors can float into the sprawling Brown's Park section and stop at the historic John Jarvie Ranch

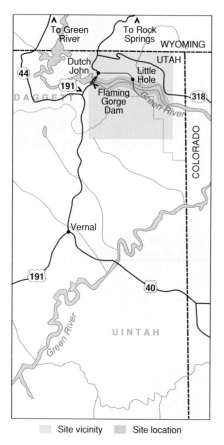

Site vicinity   Site location

Visitor Activities

Fishing, rafting, hiking, wildlife viewing, swimming, canoeing, kayaking, historic site, and big-game, small-game and waterfowl hunting (along the lower third, near Brown's Park).

Special Features

Starting at the base of the 500-foot Flaming Gorge Dam, boaters quickly find themselves floating on crystal-clear water flanked by the 2,000-foot-high walls of Red Canyon. Seven miles below the dam is the historic river crossing known as Little Hole, which was once used by Native Americans and fur trappers. The miles below Little Hole continue to offer unique scenery, excitement, solitude, and excellent wildlife viewing. When the opening between the canyon walls begins to widen, boaters enter yet another unique ecosystem named Brown's Park, with such attractions as the historic John Jarvie Ranch, Outlaw Trail, Swallow Canyon, and State and Federal wildlife refuge complexes.

Permits, Fees, Limitations

Permits are required for commercial floating only. Motors are not allowed. Fishing is limited to artificial bait only. Check with the Utah State Division of Wildlife Resources for fishing and hunting license requirements, (801) 789-9453.

Accessibility

Indian Crossing Campground has wheelchair-accessible toilets and two accessible picnic sites. John Jarvie Historic Ranch has a wheelchair-accessible picnic site and accessible toilets. Bridge Hollow campground has wheelchair-accessible toilets.

to glimpse what frontier life was like and picnic or camp. (See also the separate entry on John Jarvie Ranch.) The float trip from Little Hole to the last take-out on BLM lands is about 20 miles.

Directions

To get to the launch point at Little Hole, from Vernal, travel north for 45 miles on U.S. Highway 191. Turn right onto a paved road 0.3 mile east of Dutch John. Follow this road for 5 miles to the launch point.

Campers try their luck in the crystal-clear waters of the Green River, a world-class trout fishing destination. *(BLM)*

Camping and Lodging

From the put-in point at Little Hole, any of 28 float camps can be accessed. The first 15 camps are clearly marked; the last 13 are below the Indian Crossing take-out at Jarvie Ranch, and are not as clearly marked but visible from the river.

Two campgrounds are accessible by car: Bridge Hollow and Indian Crossing; there are fees at both. Located 0.25 mile from the John Jarvie Historic Site, both have potable water. Swallow Canyon raft ramp is the last take-out from BLM-managed waters (a distance of 20 miles downriver from Little Hole).

Lodging is available in the following towns (distances are approximate and are from the Little Hole launch site): Green River (74 miles) and Rock Springs, Wyoming (75 miles); Maybell, Colorado (101 miles); and Vernal (50 miles), Manila (43 miles), and Dutch John (5 miles), Utah. To reach Rock Springs from Brown's Park, follow signs to U.S. Highway 191 and proceed north to Rock Springs, approximately 75 miles. To reach Vernal from Brown's Park, follow signs to U.S. Highway 191 and proceed south through Dutch John for 65 miles.

Food and Supplies

Gas, food, and supplies are available in Green River, Rock Springs, Maybell, Vernal, Manila, and Dutch John. Gas, food, and phone services are available at the Brown's Park Store in Colorado, approximately 20 miles east of the John Jarvie Historic Site, just off State Highway 318. Visitors should follow the signs. Fishing gear, boat rentals, and other services and supplies are available in Dutch John, Manila, and Green River.

First Aid

The nearest hospitals are in Rock Springs and Vernal. Emergency medical technicians and an ambulance are available in Dutch John.

Additional Information

There are 10 Class II rapids between the Flaming Gorge Dam and Little Hole. There is one Class III rapid (Red Creek Rapid) between Little Hole and the Jarvie Historic Ranch. Fishing is usually best during the evening, when the level of the river is dropping. Lifejackets must be worn. Extra gas for land vehicles should be carried for travel in the area.

Contact Information

BLM - Vernal Field Office
170 South 500 East
Vernal, UT 84078
Tel: (435) 781-4400
Fax: (435) 781-4410
www.blm.gov/utah/vernal

Activity Codes

John Jarvie Historic Site

Location
75 miles northeast of Vernal, Utah.

Description
Visitors can experience a bit of the Wild West at the John Jarvie Historic Site in Brown's Park, a small mountain valley in the remote northeastern corner of Utah. Originally used by mountain men and trappers for shelter in the early 19th century, Brown's Park was settled in 1880 by Jarvie, who operated a Green River ferry as well as a store and a post office. In addition to being a common stopping place for travelers, the area became known as an outlaw hideout frequented by Butch Cassidy and the Sundance Kid, Matt Warner, Isom Dart, and Ann Bassett, "Queen of the Rustlers." Today, several historic structures are maintained by BLM, and the facility is open to the public.

Directions
From Vernal (via Crouse Canyon), go north on Vernal Avenue to Fifth North, then east for 25 miles on Fifth North to Diamond Mountain and the signed turnoff to Brown's Park. Travel 16 miles north on an infrequently maintained dirt road to Brown's Park. There is a fork in the road at the bottom of Crouse Canyon, providing two travel options:

West (left) side of fork (jeep trail): After approximately 10 miles, cross Taylor Flats, which is a sparse arrangement of cabins. After passing the cabin area, the trail drops down to the Green River and crosses the steel bridge. Turn left (west) and travel 0.5 mile to the historic site.

East (right) side of fork: Travel about 4 miles to the Utah/Colorado line, and another 1 mile to the Swinging Bridge. Cross the bridge (and it does swing!), and then proceed north about 4 miles to the paved State Highway. Turn west (left) and proceed 8 miles to the historic sign turnoff. Proceed west 1 mile (upriver) to the historic site.

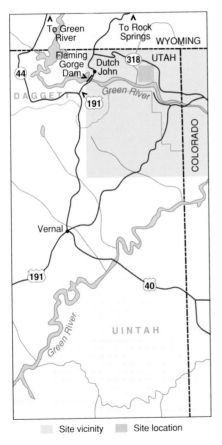

Site vicinity   Site location

The total distance along either route is approximately 75 miles.

Visitor Activities
Rafting, fishing, hiking, historic site, and four-wheel driving.

Special Features
Along with the restored Jarvie General Store and irrigation waterwheel, four original structures, each over 100 years old, still exist. These include a two-room dugout, a one-room stone house (built by outlaw Jack Bennett), a blacksmith shop, and corrals. The historic Jarvie property truly provides an atmosphere of turn-of-the-century frontier life in what still remains a remote part of famous Brown's Park.

Permits, Fees, Limitations
A permit is required for commercial outfitters and guides.

Accessibility
The parking area, restrooms, and some paths and structures at the John Jarvie Historic Site are wheelchair-accessible; however, the store and some other

Visitors can view 19th-century artifacts at this faithful replica of the original 1881 John Jarvie General Store. *(Garth Portillo, BLM Utah State Office)*

structures are not. The restrooms at both Bridge Hollow and Indian Crossing Campgrounds are wheelchair-accessible.

Camping and Lodging
Bridge Hollow and Indian Crossing Campgrounds are operated by BLM adjacent to the John Jarvie site. They are open all year, charge a fee, and provide water and toilets. Indian Crossing has picnic tables and grills. Lodging is available in Green River (79 miles) and Rock Springs, Wyoming (80 miles); Maybell, Colorado (66 miles); and in the towns of Vernal (75 miles), Manila (66 miles), and Dutch John (28 miles), Utah.

Food and Supplies
Food and supplies are available in the towns of Green River, Rock Springs, Maybell, Dutch John, Manila, and Vernal. In addition, gas, food, and supplies, as well as telephone service, are available at the Brown's Park Store in Colorado. (Brown's Park extends into Colorado.)

First Aid
The nearest hospitals are in Vernal and Rock Springs. Emergency medical technicians and an ambulance are available at Dutch John.

Additional Information
Visitors should be aware that John Jarvie Historic Site is in a remote location with an infrequently maintained dirt access road; trips should be planned accordingly. The site is open for tours from May–October each year. There is a resident BLM Park Ranger. Ramps for launch-

ing river rafts are located along the Green River in Brown's Park. Visitors should purchase gas, food, and supplies for the entire trip prior to leaving the last town en route to the area. Carrying extra gas, tire chains, a shovel, and adequate food and water is recommended.

Contact Information
BLM – Vernal Field Office
170 South 500 East
Vernal, UT 84078

Tel: (435) 781-4400
Fax: (435) 781-4410
John Jarvie Park Ranger
Tel: (435) 885-3307
www.blm.gov/utah/vernal

Activity Codes

Little Sahara Recreation Area

Location
Approximately 115 miles south of Salt Lake City.

Description
Little Sahara Recreation Area is a designated and managed off-road-vehicle (OHV) open area. It features 60,000 acres of sand dunes, trails, and sagebrush flats. The main attraction is a system of giant, free-moving sand dunes that creates a constantly changing playground for motorcycles, all-terrain vehicles (ATVs), and sand rails (steel-tubed enclosed sand vehicles). Sand Mountain, a wall of sand climbing nearly 700 feet, is the primary focal point for hill climbing. White Sands Dunes, on the northern side of the recreation area, has plentiful riding "bowls." The low-lying dunes southwest of Black Mountain provide good terrain for beginners or for those who just want to get away from the crowds. Black Mountain provides a network of dirt trails up, over, and around a peak, offering excellent trail riding for just about any kind of OHV.

A plentiful sand source and strong prevailing winds have combined to create Little Sahara, a 124-square-mile system of free-moving sand, one of the largest sand dune fields in Utah. *(Kelly Rigby, BLM Utah State Office)*

Directions

From Salt Lake City, travel south on Interstate 15 to Exit 225. Turn right and take State Highway 132 toward Nephi. Continue west from Nephi on State Highway 132 for about 13 miles, then northwest for 9 miles on Juab County Route 1812 to Jericho Junction. The entrance road to Little Sahara is 4 miles west of Jericho Junction. There is a visitor center near the pay station at the entrance.

Visitor Activities

All-terrain driving, dirt-bike riding, dune-buggy riding, picnicking, hiking, sand surfing, and sand playing.

Special Features

Rockwell Outstanding Natural Area, which is also a wilderness study area, is set aside as a vehicle-free zone. This 9,000-acre unit is a miniature version of the larger surrounding desert ecosystem and provides a place to experience the quiet side of Little Sahara.

Permits, Fees, Limitations

There is a daily use fee. Annual permits are also available.

Accessibility

Wheelchair-accessible toilets are located at the visitor center, and at White Sands, Oasis, Jericho, and Sand Mountain campgrounds.

Camping and Lodging

Camping is available within the recreation area along the 9-mile main road at these sites: White Sands Campground has 100 campsites nestled among the junipers with immediate access to the dunes. It has flush toilets (vault in winter), drinking water, and a fenced play

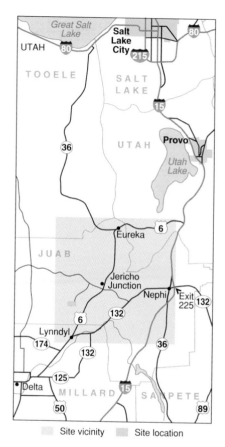

Site vicinity   Site location

area. Oasis, the most developed campsite, has paved trailer access close to the dunes, making this a popular family destination. It has 114 campsites, flush toilets (vault in winter), drinking water, and an RV dump station. Jericho serves as an overflow or large-group camping area. It has 40 picnic tables with shade armadas, flush toilets (vault in winter), drinking water, an amphitheater, and a fenced play area. Sand Mountain, at the end of the road, is a popular primitive camping/staging area. It has three paved parking loops, a flush toilet, vault toilets, drinking water and tent spaces. The closest motels are located in Nephi.

Food and Supplies
Food and supplies are available in the neighboring communities of Nephi (about 28 miles from the visitor center), Delta (37 miles), Eureka (22 miles), and Lynndyl (20 miles).

First Aid
The staff at Little Sahara provides first-response medical assistance and there is a medical room at the visitor center. The nearest hospital is in Nephi.

Additional Information
The visitor center is open primarily during spring and fall, which are heavy use periods. Hours of operation vary; visitors should call BLM for information.

Contact Information
BLM – Fillmore Field Office
35 East 500 North
Fillmore, UT 84631
Tel: (435) 743-3100
Fax: (435) 743-3135
Visitor Center Office
Tel: (435) 433-5960
Weather Information
Tel: (435) 433-5961
Fax: (435) 433-596
www.ut.blm.gov/recsite/little.html

Activity Codes

Pony Express National Historic Trail

Location
The eastern terminus of the trail is located at Stagecoach Inn State Park in Fairfield, Utah, 55 miles southwest of downtown Salt Lake City. The western terminus of the trail is located at Ibapah, Utah, 60 miles south of Wendover, Nevada.

Description
A trip down the Pony Express Trail is a celebration of the beautiful desert through which the route winds. It is an opportunity to enjoy and explore the romance, vastness, history, and solitude of America's outback. From Fairfield to Ibapah, the legendary road snakes south and west across the Bonneville Basin of west-

The restored structure of Simpson Springs Station, named for 1858 mail-route explorer Captain J.H. Simpson, is still considered a dependable desert watering hole on the historic Pony Express Trail.
(Jerry Sintz, BLM Utah State Office (retired))

central Utah. Fourteen station sites, markers, or ruins are spaced every 6–13 miles along the trail, which crosses broad valleys and mountain passes, and links small, isolated settlements. The first 5 miles are asphalt, as are the last 2, but in between lie 126 miles of what the pioneers called "Piute Hell." The trail crosses 2 million acres of topographical extremes including alpine forests and desert hot springs. The exact routes taken by the Pony Express riders are unknown; the trail shifted frequently with changes in weather, schedule, or the rider's whim.

Directions

To reach Fairfield from Salt Lake City, travel south on Interstate 15 approximately 30 miles to Lehi. Get off at exit 282 (Lehi), and proceed west on State Highway 73 (Lehi's main thoroughfare). Continue 5 miles west through Lehi to the junction of State Highways 68 and 73, then approximately 20 more miles west on State Highway 73 to Fairfield and the Stagecoach Inn State Park. The Pony Express Trail kiosk is located in the southwestern corner of the park

grounds. To get to the trail's eastern terminus, continue west from Fairfield another 5 miles to the Five Mile Pass turnoff and the start of the Pony Express Trail dirt road. A large sign points the way west toward Nevada.

Visitor Activities

Scenic drives, biking, hiking, and historic site.

Special Features

Historic markers dot the Pony Express Trail. Wild horses (during certain seasons) may be viewed in the Government Creek area, just east of Simpson Springs campground. There are many sites of interest along the trail. At Stagecoach Inn State Park in Fairfield, open from Easter–October, the original adobe inn structure is still standing. Camp Floyd, established in 1858, is adjacent to Stagecoach Inn. This historic military installation once housed 3,000 troops. Simpson Springs Station is a restored structure closely resembling the original (circa 1860) station that was located on that site.

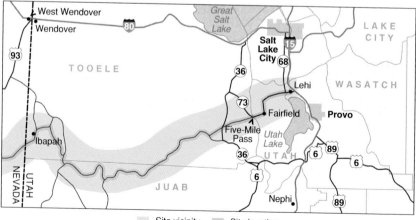

Site vicinity   Site location

Permits, Fees, Limitations
None.

Accessibility
Three wheelchair-accessible vault toilets are located at the Simpson Springs Campground.

Camping and Lodging
The Simpson Springs Campground, 44.5 miles west of Fairfield, is the only developed campground along the trail. There is a per-vehicle, per-night fee. Dispersed, primitive camping is permitted on BLM lands along the trail. Contact BLM for details. There is no charge for picnicking or for day use at the campground. There are motels along Interstate 15, within 20 miles of Fairfield. There are no motels at the western terminus (Ibapah). The closest motels to that terminus are in Wendover, Nevada, 60 miles north.

Food and Supplies
Food and supplies are available at either end of the Pony Express Trail, in Lehi and in Wendover. Along the trail, gas and snacks are available at Vernon, 5 miles south of the intersection of the Pony Express Trail with State Highway 36, and occasionally in Ibapah. Travelers are encouraged to be prepared for a long drive with no services between Vernon and Wendover.

First Aid
There is no first aid facility between Lehi and Wendover. Hospitals are located in Tooele, 35 miles north of Vernon, and approximately 110 miles east of Wendover; in Salt Lake City; and in American Fork, 1 mile north of Lehi. There is also a medical clinic in Wendover.

Additional Information
There is no staff, but the Simpson Springs Campground is open year-round—it is the only campground on the Pony Express Trail. A portion of the Pony Express Historic Trail is paved; however, the greater length of the route is graded or graveled dirt road until pavement is reached again at Ibapah. The desert environment can be harsh. Extreme summer and winter weather is possible, with summer temperatures in excess of 100°F. Dry lightning storms are common during the summer in the western desert. Winter weather is often extremely cold, with snow and ice common. Spring and fall are typically more moderate. Visitors should plan ahead and be prepared. Road conditions vary with the weather, and the road surface may be muddy and unstable in wet weather. Travelers are advised to carry adequate fuel, water, food, two spare tires (if possible), and other supplies for the entire trip. There is no place along the trail where a visitor can have a tire repaired. Visitors are also encouraged to carry at least a Utah State Highway Map. Those planning to camp on BLM-managed lands at undeveloped locations along the trail should have BLM 1:100,000-scale maps showing land ownership.

Contact Information
BLM - Salt Lake Field Office
2370 South 2300 West
Salt Lake City, UT 84119
Tel: (801) 977-4300
Fax: (801) 977-4397

Activity Codes

San Juan River

Location
Between Bluff and Mexican Hat, Utah.

Description
Ancient cultures, rugged landscapes, and relatively mild rapids combine to enchant boaters of all ages and abilities on this remote river in Utah's high-desert country. Boaters may run the 26-mile section from Sand Island to Mexican Hat (2–3 days), the 58-mile section from Mexican Hat to Clay Hills Crossing (about 5 days), or the total length of 84 miles (about 6 days). Trips can also be started from Montezuma Creek upstream from Sand Island. Montezuma Creek is 14 miles east from Bluff via U.S. highway 191.

Directions
From Bluff, travel 3 miles west along the Trail of the Ancients, U.S. Highway 191, to the launch area at Sand Island Recreation Site, or 23 miles further west to the launch area in the town of Mexican Hat.

Visitor Activities
Rafting, canoeing, kayaking, geologic sightseeing, hiking, archaeological site, and wildlife viewing.

Special Features
The San Juan River cuts deep canyons through southern Utah's red rock and reveals dramatic artifacts from the Ancestral Puebloans who made their homes along the river. Located near Sand Island is a large panel of rock art (petroglyphs) along the cliffs of the San Juan River. The petroglyphs are most noted for their numerous figures of Kokopelli, the hump-backed flute player in Native American stories. There are several other ancient sites accessible from the river, including the outstanding Butler Wash Petroglyph Panel and the River House Ruin. Prehistoric

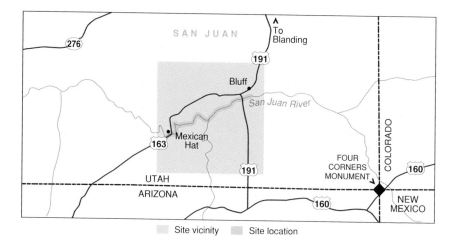

Site vicinity   Site location

Pueblo farmers lived in this cliff dwelling from AD 900 to 1300.

Bighorn sheep can be viewed along the river's south side, so visitors should remember to bring binoculars.

Permits, Fees, Limitations

A BLM permit is required to float any section of the San Juan River downstream of Montezuma Creek. Permits are issued through a lottery system, or by post-lottery telephone reservations. Applications must be received by January 31 to be included in the drawing. A fee is charged for permits to float from Sand Island to Clay Hills Crossing from March 1–October 31. The 17-mile portion of the river from Montezuma Creek to Sand Island also requires a permit, but there is no fee charged for this section. Check with BLM for details.

For approximately 3 miles downstream from the river bridge at Montezuma Creek, both sides of the river are bordered by the Navajo Nation reservation. Beyond that point, the center of the deepest channel marks the border of the reservation. Everything south of that, from Montezuma Creek to Oljato Wash, is Navajo land. A Navajo permit is needed to camp and hike on this land. For permit information, call or write the Navajo Parks and Recreation Department, P.O. Box 9000, Window Rock, AZ 86515, (928) 871-6647, fax: (928) 871-6637. Allow at least 30 days for the Navajo permit to be issued.

Accessibility

Wheelchair-accessible toilets are located at the Sand Island campground and at Mexican Hat. Sand Island also has wheelchair-accessible campsites. There are no other developed sites along the river.

The San Juan River's sinuous course through Utah's high-desert country offers visitors satisfying whitewater in a remote wilderness environment. *(Jerry Sintz, BLM Utah State Office (retired))*

Camping and Lodging

Sand Island Recreation Area has a campground with drinking water, picnic areas, pit toilets, 20 campsites with tables and fire grills, and a boat launch. There is also a large group site that may be reserved. Contact BLM for reservations.

Although there are plenty of campsites on the upper portion of the river (Sand Island to Mexican Hat), visitors are encouraged to share their campsite intentions with other river parties. Larger campsites are intended for bigger groups. Campsites on the lower 58 miles of the river are limited, and it is necessary to reserve any of the nine sites from Slickhorn Gulch (Mile 66) downstream. Campsites may be reserved at the time the river permit is obtained. Camping is not allowed at the Butler Wash Petroglyph Panel.

Food and Supplies

Food and supplies may be purchased in nearby Bluff or Mexican Hat. Information about outfitter services, accommodations, and shuttles is available from the Utah's Canyon Country Visitor Services, 117 South Main Street, Monticello, UT 84535, 1-800-574-4386 or (435) 587-3235.

First Aid

The nearest hospital is in Monticello, Utah, 50 miles north on US Highway 191.

Additional Information

The river corridor is quite remote, especially the lower 58 miles. Novice river-runners should always be accompanied by those who are more experienced. Lifejackets are required. Although the river has been controlled by the Navajo Dam in New Mexico since 1963, its level can change rapidly as a result of thunderstorms and flash floods. Boaters should always tie boats securely when stopping. The river moves surprisingly fast, and has some Class II and III rapids. Water temperatures vary between 41°F in April and 67°F in July. Boaters

should bring drinking water; there are no reliable, potable sources of drinking water on the San Juan. During the summer, 1 gallon per person per day is recommended. Pets are not allowed on the river. All boaters must carry a firepan and toilet system. A non-formaldehyde toilet chemical is recommended. Artifacts at historic and cultural sites along the way are protected by law; visitors are reminded to please not remove or disturb them.

Contact Information

BLM - Monticello Field Office
435 N. Main St.
P.O. Box 7
Monticello, UT 84532
Tel:(435) 587-1544 or (435) 587-1504
Fax: (435) 587-1518
*www.blm.gov/utah/monticello/
rec_fr.htm#river*

Activity Codes

Sand Flats Recreation Area

Location

2 miles east of Moab, Utah.

Description

One of the most famous mountain biking trails in the world, the Slickrock Bike Trail, is located at the Sand Flats Recreation Area. This trail was pioneered by motorcyclists in the 1960s, but adopted by mountain bikers in the 1980s. The hilly and steep 12-mile trail can be strenuous, and is suitable only for experienced mountain bikers. But the

beauty of the area can be enjoyed by all. The trail is set on sandstone "slickrock," with spectacular views of Arches National Park, the Colorado River, and the snow-capped La Sal Mountains. Sand Flats is also famous for the Porcupine Rim Bike Trail, and two four-wheel-drive challenges, the Fins & Things Jeep Trail and the Hell's Revenge Jeep Trail. Visitors should be prepared to share these trails. This popular area, just outside of Moab, enjoys heavy visitor use, especially in the spring and fall.

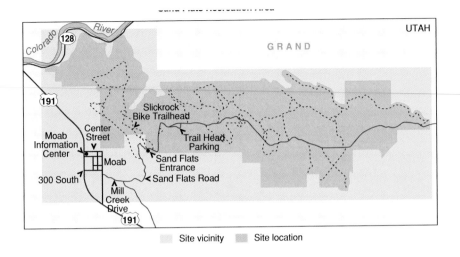

UTAH

GRAND

Colorado River

128

191

Slickrock
Bike Trailhead

Center
Street

Moab
Information
Center

Moab

Trail Head
Parking

Sand Flats
Entrance

300 South

Sand Flats Road

Mill
Creek
Drive

191

Site vicinity   Site location

Directions

From the center of Moab, drive south on U.S. Highway 191 to 300 South. Turn left (east) on this street, and follow the signs to the Slickrock Bike Trail. The Sand Flats Entrance Booth is 2 miles from Moab.

Visitor Activities

Biking, hiking, four-wheel driving, and dirt-bike riding.

Special Features

This 7,240-acre wonderland of rock fins and sandstone slabs is minutes from the

A mountain biker climbs the Porcupine Rim Trail, one of many slickrock trails in the Sand Flats Recreation Area. *(Bill Stevens, BLM Moab Field Office)*

community of Moab. The ever-present backdrop of the LaSal Mountains frames the scenery, providing spectacular views in every direction.

Permits, Fees, Limitations
There is an entrance fee for the Sand Flats Recreation Area. All vehicles are limited to designated roads.

Accessibility
The restrooms at the Slickrock Bike Trailhead are wheelchair-accessible.

Camping and Lodging
A fee is charged for camping. A full range of lodging is available in Moab, including many commercial campgrounds. The Sand Flats Recreation Area also has campgrounds with toilets and fire rings. Additionally, there are 10 BLM campgrounds within 20 miles of the recreation area. (See the Colorado Riverway site description for locations.)

Food and Supplies
Food, supplies, and gas are available in Moab.

First Aid
Allen Memorial Hospital is located in Moab.

Additional Information
Information on four-wheel-drive trails is available at the Sand Flats Entrance Booth.

Contact Information
BLM - Moab Field Office
82 East Dogwood
Moab, UT 84532
Tel: (435) 259-2100
Fax: (435) 259-2158
www.ut.blm.gov/moab

Activity Codes

The Wedge Overlook

Location
15 miles east of Castle Dale, Utah.

Description
The Wedge Overlook is located in the San Rafael Swell of southeastern Utah, in the Canyonlands area of the Colorado Plateau. The overlook provides a striking view of the "Little Grand Canyon," the San Rafael River, and a spectacular expanse of the Sids Mountain Wilderness Study Area. This is the heart of the San Rafael Swell, a 2,000-square-mile expanse of public land featuring stunning scenery, important scientific resources, and a fascinating historical record of the forces that helped shape the American West. The rim at the Wedge Overlook offers an easy and spectacular mountain bike trail.

Directions
From Price, take State Highway 10 south for about 30 miles. About a mile north of Castle Dale, turn left onto a well-maintained gravel county road. Go about 13 miles to a 4-way intersection. There is a BLM sign there indicating The Wedge. Turn right and stay on the well-maintained dirt road for about 6

The Wedge Overlook offers spectacular views of the San Rafael Swell. *(Jerry Sintz, BLM Utah State Office (retired))*

miles until you get to The Wedge Overlook.

Visitor Activities

Picnicking, mountain biking on designated roads, birdwatching, wildlife viewing, and horseback riding.

Special Features

The road along the rim leads the motorist or hiker to several viewpoints. From the easternmost point, a visitor can see where the Buckhorn Draw empties into the San Rafael River at the historic Swinging Bridge. To the west are views of the Wasatch Plateau, an extension of the Wasatch Mountains. Given the normally clear conditions, one usually can see the La Sal Mountains to the southeast. The Swell provides excellent habitat for wildlife. From the overlook, visitors may see desert bighorn sheep and birds of prey such as golden eagles, peregrine falcons, and red-tailed hawks.

Permits, Fees, Limitations

All vehicles are restricted to designated roads due to sensitive plant communities. Visitors should camp only in designated camping areas and bring in firewood and drinking water.

Accessibility

The restroom and viewing area are wheelchair-accessible.

Camping and Lodging

Camping is permitted in designated camping areas only. Motel accommodations are available in Price (30 miles away), Huntington (20 miles), Castle Dale (15 miles), and Green River (45 miles).

Food and Supplies

Food, gas, and supplies are available in Price, Huntington, Castle Dale, and Green River.

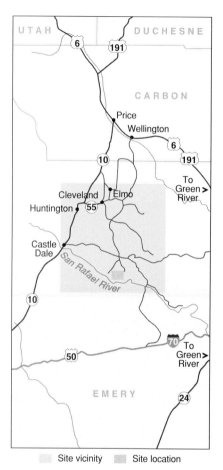

Site vicinity   Site location

First Aid
Medical services are available in Price, Green River, and Castle Dale. The nearest hospital is in Price.

Additional Information
This is a day-use area; for those wishing to stay overnight, limited camping is available. A vault toilet is provided at the overlook. Contact the Price Field Office for information about this and other places of interest in the area.

Contact Information
BLM - Price Field Office
125 South 600 West
Price, UT 84501
Tel: (435) 636-3600
Fax: (435) 636-3657
www.blm.gov/utah/price/ SanRafaelDesert.htm

Activity Codes

Westwater Canyon

Location
70 miles northeast of Moab, Utah.

Description
The Westwater Canyon area provides a wild stretch of renowned whitewater opportunities for both rafters and kayakers. The black, uplifted rocks in the canyon represent the oldest exposed formations in eastern Utah. Heading west from Colorado, this is the first canyon along the Colorado River within Utah. The 17-mile river trip is not for beginners.

Directions
From Moab, drive 30 miles north on U.S. Highway 191 to Interstate 70.

From this junction, proceed 45 miles east on Interstate 70 to exit 225 (Westwater Exit). Turn east and travel on the paved road approximately 6 miles. At the main intersection, turn left and proceed another 2 miles to the Westwater ranger station. The launch site is located at the ranger station. The most popular take-out is 17 river miles downstream at Cisco Landing.

Visitor Activities
Rafting, kayaking, geologic sightseeing, and historic site.

Special Features
Many species of wildlife inhabit the canyon, including deer, beavers, turkeys, golden eagles, and peregrines. There are also several historic sites along the river corridor, including "Miner's Cabin," built in the early 1900s, and "Outlaw Cave," a legendary hiding spot for old-time bank robbers.

Permits, Fees, Limitations
Because of the heavy demand for launches, BLM permits and advance reservations are required for both commercial outfitters and private boaters to run this section of the river. A per-person fee applies. Call the BLM River Permit Office for more information.

Accessibility
Toilet facilities at the launch and take-out are wide enough to accommodate wheelchairs; however there are no paved walkways. Many commercial outfitters are equipped to provide trips for those requiring special accommodations.

Camping and Lodging
There are 10 campsites in Westwater Canyon. These are assigned at the ranger station at launch time. Camping is limited to 1 night, with a limit on party size of 25. Minimum-impact camping techniques are required; all solid waste must be packed out, and river-runners' toilets are mandatory. Commercial lodging is available in

Colorado River rafters negotiate Westwater Canyon's Skull Rapid at low water, 9 miles into their trip. *(Kyler Carpenter, BLM Moab Field Office)*

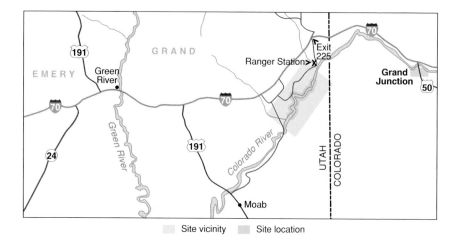

Site vicinity   Site location

Moab and Grand Junction, Colorado, about 40 miles east on Interstate 70.

Food and Supplies
Food and supplies are available in Moab and Grand Junction.

First Aid
There is no first aid on-site. The nearest hospital is in Grand Junction.

Additional Information
Only experienced boaters should pilot rafts through the canyon. Lifejackets must be worn, as required under Utah State Law. The river is not suitable for open canoes. As a general rule, the river peaks at about 20,000 cubic feet per second (cfs) in late May or early June, and recedes throughout the summer and autumn months to reach a low flow of less than 3,000 cfs. The character of the river varies with each change in river flow. Some rapids are most challenging at high water, while others require greater skill at low water. Within Westwater Canyon, there are 11 rapids that range in difficulty from 1–9,

on a scale in which the most dangerous rapids have a rating of 10. The rapids of note are Funnel Falls, Skull, and Sock-It-To-Me. From the ranger station, it is approximately 17 river miles to the first available take-out point at Cisco Landing. In this distance, the river drops 125 feet. First aid and repair kits are required, as well as an extra oar, air pump, fire pan, and life jackets. Artifacts at historic and cultural sites along the way are protected by law; visitors are reminded to please not remove or disturb them.

Contact Information
BLM - Moab Field Office
82 East Dogwood
Moab, UT 84532
Tel: (435) 259-2100
Fax: (435) 259-2158
River Permit Office
Tel: (435) 259-7012
www.blm.gov/utah/moab/ww-info.html

Activity Codes

Adult golden eagles, so named for their flaxen neck feathers, are some of the top predators within Westwater Canyon. Utah's largest resident raptors, the birds are protected by law under the Federal Bald and Golden Eagle Protection Act. *(BLM)*

A rainbow of colors paints the sky, mountains, and vegetation at Red Gulch. *(BLM)*

High-desert plains, sand dunes, badlands, and rugged mountains characterize the 18.4 million acres of public lands in Wyoming. Representing about 20 percent of the state, these public lands are concentrated in the western two-thirds of Wyoming, with additional small parcels scattered throughout the state.

The public lands managed by BLM in Wyoming offer exceptional opportunities for recreational activities away from the crowd. Remote and primitive open spaces provide "Blue Ribbon" trout fishing, world-class hunting, primitive camping, hiking, and snow-mobiling. Although public lands offer mostly primitive recreational experiences, there are also a number of developed sites with easy access.

Visitors to Wyoming's vast high plains and deserts stand a good chance of seeing pronghorn antelope, wild horses, and golden eagles. The Whiskey Mountain Bighorn Sheep Area hosts the largest wintering herd of Rocky Mountain bighorn sheep in North America.

Wyoming's public lands also help tell the story of the West through several interpretive sites. Some of the nation's most significant paleontological discoveries have been made on Wyoming's public lands, including the first fully-jointed *Allosaurus*. Visitors will also enjoy historic sites, including Native American petroglyphs, emigrant etchings, as well as portions of trails used by settlers moving westward. Original wagon ruts along National Historic Trails, such as the Oregon Trail, can still be seen. Gold Rush buffs will appreciate a visit to the South Pass Historic Mining District, which includes the ghost town of Miner's Delight.

With Wyoming's diverse geography and rich history, a visit to the "Cowboy State" will only confirm that the public lands offer a world of unlimited outdoor adventures.

Wyoming

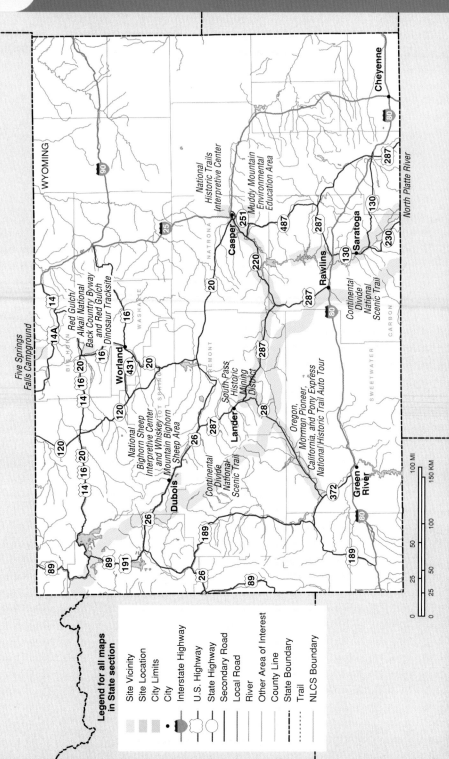

WYOMING

Cheyenne

80

287

North Platte River

National
Historic Trails
Interpretive Center

Muddy Mountain
Environmental
Education Area

90

130

Saratoga

130

251

487

287

230

Casper

25

NATRONA

220

Rawlins

130

Five Springs
Falls Campground

14

14

Red Gulch/
Alkali National
Back Country Byway
and Red Gulch
Dinosaur Tracksite

20

287

80

Continental
Divide
National
Scenic Trail

CARBON

14A

BIG HORN

16

16

16–20

14

WASHAKIE

Worland

431

20

120

FREMONT

HOT SPRINGS

South Pass
Historic
Mining
District

287

287

SWEETWATER

14–16–20

National
Bighorn Sheep
Interpretive Center
and Whiskey
Mountain Bighorn
Sheep Area

26

287

Lander

28

Oregon,
Mormon Pioneer,
California, and Pony Express
National Historic Trail Auto Tour

120

Continental
Divide
National
Scenic Trail

Dubois

26

372

Green
River

189

80

89

89

191

26

26

189

89

100 MI

150 KM

50

100

25

50

0   25   50
0

Continental Divide National Scenic Trail

Location
The northern trailhead is 35 miles south of Lander, Wyoming.

Description
The Continental Divide National Scenic Trail (CDNST) is a Congressionally-designated trail through the Rocky Mountain states of Montana, Idaho, Wyoming, Colorado, and New Mexico. The 3,100-mile trail extends from the Canadian border on the north to the Mexican border on the south, and provides access to some of the most beautiful and rugged terrain in the West.

The 165-mile portion of the trail in Wyoming follows a combination of trails and primitive two-track roads, but also requires cross-country travel in some portions.

Directions
From Lander: Take U.S. Highway 287 south for 9 miles. Take U.S. Highway 28 south for another 24 miles. Turn left toward South Pass City (Fremont County Road 515) and proceed 2 miles to the town of South Pass City where the northern CDNST trailhead is located.

A llama carries the load as hikers traverse rugged Wyoming terrain on The Continental Divide National Scenic Trail. *(BLM)*

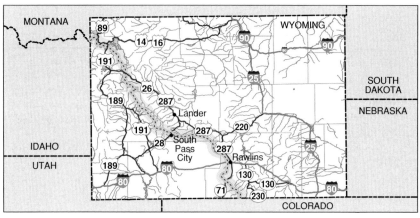

Site vicinity ░ Site location

From Rawlins: Take State Highway 71 south for 10 miles, where it becomes Carbon County Road 401. Continue south for 25 miles to the southern trailhead location.

On the northern end, the trail is in the southern Wind River Range (30 miles southwest of Lander); it then heads southeast through public lands into the Great Divide Basin before entering the Sierra Madre Range on the southern end (35 miles south of Rawlins).

Visitor Activities

Hiking, horseback riding, mountain biking, wildlife viewing, birdwatching, and plant viewing.

Special Features

The CDNST crosses the Great Divide Basin in Wyoming. This geologic and hydrologic feature is unique in the United States. No streams flow out of the basin, meaning that the precipitation falling within it never reaches the Pacific or Atlantic Ocean. This austere and beautiful landscape is characterized by sagebrush and dry lakebeds, and supports a variety of wildlife such as elk, mule deer, pronghorn antelope, mountain lions, bobcats, raptors, and wild horses.

Permits, Fees, Limitations

None.

Accessibility

None.

Camping and Lodging

BLM campgrounds off the trail on the northern end are located near Atlantic City. On the southern end, a BLM campground is located 15 miles south of Rawlins. U.S. Forest Service campgrounds are located off the route at both the northern and southern ends of the trail.

Food and Supplies

Grocery and sporting goods stores are located in Lander and Rawlins (125 miles southeast of Lander). Restaurants are available in Lander, Rawlins and Atlantic City (30 miles south of Lander).

First Aid
Emergency first aid is available from local law enforcement. Hospitals are located in Lander and Rawlins.

Additional Information
Warm days and cool nights are to be expected in summer. Thunderstorms are common. In the spring and fall, snowstorms may occur. Winter storms can be severe. Winds are common throughout the year. The elevation ranges from 6,800–8,000 feet.

Contact Information
BLM - Lander Field Office
P.O. Box 589
1335 Main Street
Lander, WY 82520
Tel: (307) 332-8400
Fax: (307) 332-8447
www.wy.blm.gov/recreation/cdnst/info.htm

Activity Codes

Five Springs Falls Campground

Location
22 miles east of Lovell, Wyoming.

Description
This BLM-administered campground is nestled at the base of the Bighorn Mountains along Five Springs Creek. It is centrally located between the U.S. Forest Service's Medicine Wheel National Historic Landmark and the National Park Service's Bighorn Canyon National Recreation Area. A short hike on the trail from the parking area leads visitors to a viewing area for Five Springs Falls. The upper loop of the campground road provides a breathtaking scenic overlook of the Bighorn Basin, and the Bighorn, Pryor, and Absaroka Mountains beyond, and access to trails leading to the Bighorn National Forest. The campground is located within the Five Springs Falls Area of Critical Environmental Concern, which was designated to protect existing

Five Springs Falls is a short hike from the campground parking area. *(Jerry Jech, BLM Cody Field Office)*

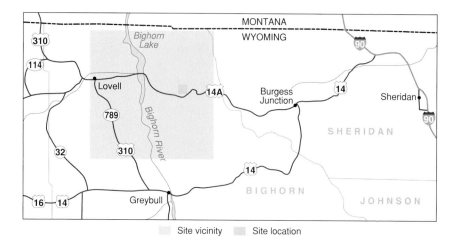

Site vicinity ▨ Site location

populations of four rare and sensitive plant species.

Directions
From Lovell, travel 22 miles east on U.S. Highway 14A, and turn left at the Five Springs Falls Campground sign. Travel this steep, narrow access road 2 miles to the campground loop road.

Visitor Activities
Hiking, horseback riding, geologic sightseeing, picnicking, birdwatching, plant viewing, and wildlife viewing.

Special Features
The elevation ranges from 6,250 feet at the campground to 7,240 feet at the national forest boundary. Rare plants include bristly fleabane, Cary beard-tongue, princes plume, and Sullivantia. Wildlife in the area includes mule deer, elk, black bears, and mountain lions.

Permits, Fees, Limitations
None.

Accessibility
The campground has eight wheelchair-accessible campsites. The campground's central water faucet and toilet facilities are also accessible.

Camping and Lodging
There is a fee for overnight camping. The campground features 19 developed campsites. Campsites are occupied on a first-come, first-served basis; there is no reservation system. There is a 14-day camping limit. The campground loop road features nine campsites with tent pads, fire rings, picnic tables, and a central toilet facility and water faucet. The sites in the lower loop are suitable for tent camping or picnicking only. The upper loop of the campground contains 10 campsites, and a central toilet facility. Many of the campsites in the upper loop are designed as pull-through sites suitable for camp trailers. Lodging is available in Lovell, 22 miles west on U.S. Highway 14A.

Food and Supplies
There are no first aid services on-site. Food and supplies are available in Lovell.

First Aid

There are no services on-site. There is a hospital located in Lovell.

Additional Information

The best time to visit is from May–October. The site is open year-round, but is often not accessible during the winter months because of snowpack. The access road is steep and narrow with many switchbacks, and is not suitable for RVs over 25 feet in length.

Contact Information:

BLM - Cody Field Office
1002 Blackburn Avenue
Cody, WY 82414
Tel: (307) 578-5900
Fax: (307) 578-5939
www.wy.blm.gov/cyfo/info.htm

Activity Codes

Muddy Mountain Environmental Education Area

Location

18 miles south of Casper, Wyoming.

Description

Located within a lodgepole pine forest at an elevation of about 8,000 feet,

the 1,260-acre Muddy Mountain Environmental Education Area (EEA) also contains sagebrush and grassland habitat. An extensive network of trails can be used for hiking, biking or equestrian activities. The Muddy

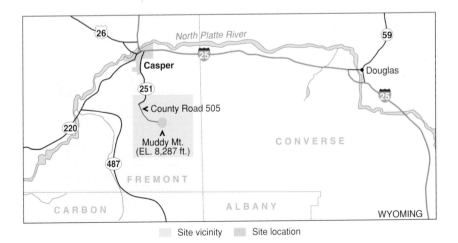

Site vicinity   Site location

Mountain National Recreation Trail is one of many that comprise the Muddy Mountain Environmental Education Area's 15-mile trail system. The trail has 28 interpretive sites.

Directions

From Casper, drive south approximately 9 miles on State Highway 251 to the top of Casper Mountain, where the State Highway ends and County Road 505 begins. Continue on this paved road for approximately 3 miles, where it turns into a maintained dirt road. Follow this road for 3 miles to its intersection with Circle Drive. A BLM gravel road begins here; a sign indicates that it is 4 more miles to the EEA.

Visitor Activities

Picnicking, hiking, mountain biking, interpretive trails, horseback riding, and snowmobiling.

Special Features

The diversity of terrain and vegetation provides habitat for small birds and mammals, such as blue grouse and foxes,

With its extensive system of hiking trails, Muddy Mountain is a popular recreational and educational retreat for local residents and tourists alike. *(Jerry Sintz, BLM Utah State Office (retired))*

as well as deer, antelope, and elk. The EEA contains a self-guided interpretive trail system.

Permits, Fees, Limitations

There is a day-use fee from June–September.

Accessibility

The area within the campground loop road at Lodgepole Campground contains approximately 2 miles of hard-surfaced, wheelchair-accessible interpretive trail for hiking. This trail was designated a national recreation trail in 2001 because of its wheelchair accessibility and interpretation; Lodgepole Campground has 14 sites that have been upgraded with accessible picnic tables and concrete pad fire pits. One of the two vault toilets at this campground is wheelchair-accessible.

Camping and Lodging

There are two campgrounds with a total of 20 campsites; fees are charged. Lodgepole Campground, at the south end of the area, is the more developed, with potable water and fully-accessible toilets and campsites. The Rim Campground, about 0.5 mile to the north, is more primitive. It has a vault toilet, six campsites and two day-use sites, for large groups or families. Both campgrounds are first come, first served; no reservations are taken. The nearest lodging is in Casper.

Food and Supplies

Food and supplies are available in Casper.

First Aid

There is no first aid available on site. The nearest hospital is in Casper.

Additional Information

Visitors should be prepared for all types of weather.

Contact Information
BLM - Casper Field Office
2987 Prospector Dr.
Casper, WY 82604
Tel: (307) 261-7600
Fax: (307) 261-7587
www.wy.blm.gov/cfo

Activity Codes

National Bighorn Sheep Interpretive Center and Whiskey Mountain Bighorn Sheep Area

Location
76 miles northwest of Lander.

Description
The Whiskey Mountain Bighorn Sheep Area is located in northwestern Wyoming, just off a main travel route to Yellowstone National Park. The area of-

fers spectacular views and unparalleled opportunities to see the largest wintering Rocky Mountain bighorn sheep herd in North America. The nearby Interpretive Center in Dubois provides an excellent educational experience that features bighorn sheep. The central exhibit, "Sheep Mountain," draws visitors

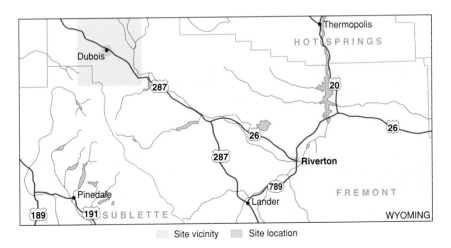

Site vicinity   Site location

The largest herd of wintering Rocky Mountain bighorn sheep in North America inhabits the mountains just outside the National Bighorn Sheep Center's front door. Here, two rams use those big horns to settle a dominance dispute. *(BLM)*

into the world of the bighorn sheep; the exhibit features naturally-posed, mounted bighorns and other animals, surrounded by native-plant replicas.

Directions

From Lander, take U.S. Highway 287 north 76 miles to the town of Dubois. The Center is located in the western part of the town on U.S. Highway 287. Whiskey Mountain is located 5 miles southwest of Dubois.

Visitor Activities

Interpretive center, wildlife viewing, birdwatching, and plant viewing.

Special Features

The largest herd of wintering Rocky Mountain bighorn sheep in North America inhabits the mountains just outside the center's front door. The elevation of Dubois is 6,917 feet; the Whiskey Mountain area is located at 8,000-9,000 feet above sea level. In addition to bighorns, the area supports elk, mule deer, and beavers. Moose, golden eagles, and migrating waterfowl are also sometimes seen.

Permits, Fees, Limitations

There is a small fee for admission to the Interpretive Center. Motor-vehicle travel is limited to a few roads through the bighorn sheep range.

Accessibility

The interpretive center has wheelchair-accessible parking, restrooms, and interpretive exhibits.

Camping and Lodging

Commercial campgrounds and motels are available in Dubois. Several private campground facilities are available at Ring Lake and Trail Lake, 8 miles southeast of Dubois. Forest Service campgrounds are located west of Dubois in the Shoshone National Forest.

Food and Supplies

Restaurants, groceries, and sporting goods stores are located in Dubois.

First Aid

There is a medical clinic in Dubois. Ambulance service and 911 emergency service are also available in the area.

Additional Information

To view bighorn sheep in the Whiskey Mountain area, please inquire at the center for suggested locations. The best time of year to view bighorn sheep is from mid-November–March. Warm days and cool nights are the norm for summer; thunderstorms are common. In the spring and fall, snowstorms may occur. Winter storms can be severe. Winds are common throughout the year. Privately-run tours to the Whiskey Mountain Bighorn Sheep Area are available from the center, P.O. Box 1435,

Dubois, WY 82513, (307) 455-3429. The center is a partnership amongst BLM, U.S. Forest Service, Wyoming Division of Game and Fish, and the City of Dubois.

Contact Information:

BLM - Lander Field Office
P.O. Box 589
1335 Main Street
Lander, WY 82520
Tel: (307) 332-8400
Fax: (307) 332-8447
www.wy.blm.gov/whatwedo/sheep/wy.sheep.1.html

Activity Codes

National Historic Trails Interpretive Center

Location

In the city of Casper, Wyoming.

Description

The BLM National Historic Trails Interpretive Center interprets the stories of the Oregon, Mormon Pioneer, California, and Pony Express National Historic Trails. This family-oriented facility appeals to history buffs and novices alike. The center features interactive exhibits, including a simulated river crossing aboard a covered wagon, lifelike dioramas, and an 18-minute multimedia presentation. Visitors not only learn the history of emigrant trails, but they are also provided information on public lands trail sites in the region.

The NHTIC is located in Casper, an area once criss-crossed by historic trails.
(Marlyn Black (used with permission))

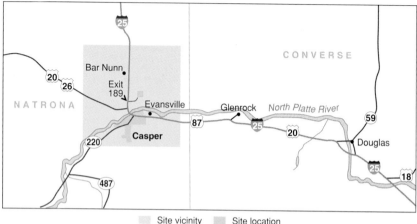

Site vicinity   Site location

Directions

The Interpretive Center is conveniently located off Interstate 25 at Exit 189 in Casper. Follow signs to the facility.

Visitor Activities

Historic site and interpretive site

Special Features

The state-of-the-art visitor center features a multi-media trails orientation presentation, a simulated river crossing aboard a covered wagon, a handcart-pulling simulation activity, a stagecoach replica, and lifelike dioramas. Within 0.25 mile of the center is the North Platte River greenway trail, which parallels the national historic trails corridor through Casper.

Permits, Fees, Limitations

Hours are: April 1–October 31, 8 a.m.–7 p.m., daily; November 1–March 31, 9 a.m.–4:30 p.m., Tuesday–Saturday. The center is closed on Thanksgiving Day, Christmas Day, New Year's Day, and Easter Sunday. An admission fee is charged. Tour and group rates are available by request. Contact the center for details.

Accessibility

The center is fully accessible.

Camping and Lodging

Camping and lodging are available in Casper, Glenrock, and Douglas. Glenrock is about 25 miles and Douglas is about 51 miles east of Casper on Interstate 25.

Food and Supplies

Gas and groceries are available in Casper.

First Aid

Emergency services are available through local law enforcement. A hospital is located in Casper.

Additional Information

BLM worked in partnership with The National Historic Trails Center Foundation and the City of Casper to develop the center.

Contact Information:
National Historic Trails
   Interpretive Center
1501 North Poplar St.
Casper, WY 82601
Tel: (307) 261-7700
Fax: (307) 261-7798
www.wy.blm.gov/nhtic

Activity Codes

North Platte River

Location

This BLM-managed portion of the river begins at the Wyoming/Colorado border, 27 miles southeast of Riverside/Encampment, Wyoming, and runs 122.5 miles north to the Seminoe Reservoir.

Description

The North Platte River crosses various types of terrain as it flows north from the Colorado border to the Seminoe Reservoir. The upper 20 miles run through rugged forest. The next 40 miles alternate between agricultural meadows and rugged sagebrush/juniper communities. The rest of the river to Seminoe Reservoir flows primarily through rolling sagebrush hills and juniper breaks.

The North Platte River is a "Blue Ribbon" wild trout fishery from the Colorado border to the Pick Bridge access north of Saratoga, about 65 river miles. Seminoe Reservoir, 57 river miles

The North Platte River, a "Blue Ribbon" wild trout fishery, crosses a variety of ecosystems as it flows north from Colorado. *(Mary Apple, BLM)*

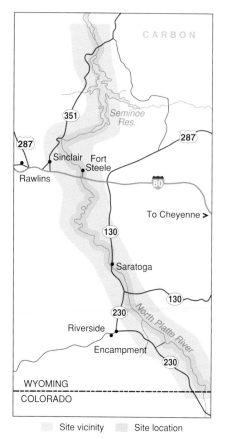

CARBON

351

Seminoe
Res.

287

287

Sinclair Fort
Steele

Rawlins

80

To Cheyenne >

130

Saratoga

130

230

Riverside

Encampment
230

North Platte River

WYOMING
COLORADO

Site vicinity   Site location

Riverside/Encampment. Then, go 23 miles southeast on State Highway 230 to the Six Mile Gap Access Road, which is close to the river.

Other river access points are marked by signs along the highways on the way to Six Mile Gap. As you head south on State Highway 130 from Interstate 80, look for access points at Pick Bridge, Foote, Saratoga, Treasure Island, and Bennett Peak.

River access is also available at Fort Steele, 13 miles east of Rawlins on Interstate 80. Take the Fort Steele exit south to the east frontage road. Follow this to the dirt road that runs south along the river.

To access Seminoe Reservoir and the North Platte River north of Interstate 80, take the west Sinclair exit and follow County Road 351 north. It's about 8 miles to BLM's Dugway Recreation Site on the river and about 23 miles to Seminoe Reservoir.

Visitor Activities
Fishing, floating, wildlife viewing, plant viewing, birdwatching, picnicking, and big-game hunting

Special Features
The North Platte River attracts numerous species of wildlife, including bighorn sheep, elk, bobcats, black bears, and mountain lions. Mule deer are often seen along the banks, and pronghorn antelope enjoy the open valleys and foothills that are visible from the river. Small mammals in the riparian areas include muskrats, coyotes, raccoons, and beavers. Birds range from blue and sage grouses to Canada geese, mallards, common mergansers, goldeneyes, great blue herons, kingfishers, and pelicans.

north of Pick Bridge, is popular for its trout and walleye fishing, as well as boating opportunities. The river is floatable but there are several rapids in the 13 miles just north of the state border. The first 5 miles of those 13 can be floated by raft or kayak only.

Directions
To reach Six Mile Gap, the uppermost access point, nearest the Wyoming/Colorado border (on U.S. Forest Service lands): From Interstate 80 between Rawlins and Cheyenne, Wyoming, take State Highways 130/230 south to

Raptor species along the river include golden and bald eagles; Swainson's, red-tailed, and ferruginous hawks; prairie falcons; and American kestrels.

Permits, Fees, Limitations
There are no day-use fees. State hunting and fishing licenses are required.

Accessibility
Bennett Peak Campground has wheelchair-accessible restrooms and campsites.

Camping and Lodging
No hookups are available at public campgrounds. Bennett Peak is a BLM river access point with a campground. There are camping fees at Bennett Peak Campground.

To get to camping facilities at Bennett Peak and Corral Creek, travel 4 miles east of Riverside on State Highway 230, then travel 12 miles east on graveled County Road 660, and take BLM Road #3404 for another 6 miles to the river and campgrounds. Camping is also available at Dugway Recreation Site and various Wyoming Game and Fish and U.S. Forest Service sites. Lodging is available in the towns of Rawlins, Saratoga, and Riverside/Encampment.

Food and Supplies
Grocery stores and sporting goods are available in Rawlins, Saratoga, and Riverside/Encampment.

First Aid
No first aid is available at the river access sites. There are hospitals in Rawlins and Casper. There is a clinic in Saratoga.

Additional Information
Camping is best from June–September. Weather may be extreme at any time of year. Roads may be muddy and rough. County Road 351 between Seminoe Reservoir and the Miracle Mile is gravel and very steep in places, so it is not recommended for RVs, motor homes, or trailers. The river itself is public, but it crosses both public and private lands. Where the river crosses private land, the river itself is considered private; visitors should not wade or anchor in these places. Red and blue 1-foot-square signs are placed along the river indicating where people are permitted to get out.

The Miracle Mile is a popular fishery managed by the Bureau of Reclamation and is located downstream from Seminoe Reservoir.

Contact Information:
Downstream from Pathfinder Reservoir:
BLM - Rawlins Field Office
P.O. Box 2407
Rawlins, WY 82301
Tel: (307) 328-4200
Fax: (307) 328-4224
www.wy.blm.gov/rfo/index.htm

From the Colorado border to Pathfinder Reservoir:
BLM - Casper Field Office
2987 Prospect Drive
Casper, WY 82604
Tel: (307) 261-7600
Fax: (307) 261-7587
www.wy.blm.gov/cfo

Activity Codes

Oregon, Mormon Pioneer, California, and Pony Express National Historic Trail Auto Tour

Location
Central and southwestern Wyoming.

Description
The Historic Trails Corridor includes the Oregon, Mormon Pioneer, California, and Pony Express National Historic Trails. These historic trails generally parallel highways throughout central and southwestern Wyoming. The trail corridor in Wyoming is marked and contains many important sites that are emblematic of the courage and hope of the people who traveled the trail. This scenic drive offers many interpretive sites right off the road, including Bessemer Bend, Devil's Gate, Split Rock, Ice Slough, South Pass, False Parting of the Ways, Simpson's Hollow, and Lombard Ferry. There are hiking, picnic and photography spots along the way.

Directions
Take State Highway 220 west out of Casper for about 74 miles to Muddy Gap. Take State Highway 287 north to Lander. From Lander, travel west along State Highway 28, which goes all the way to the Green River. These highways parallel the main trail corridor encompassing the four emigrant trails.

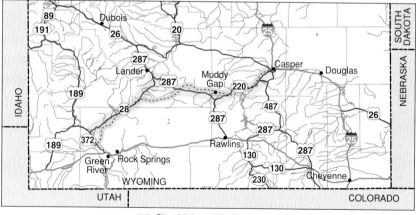

Site vicinity   Site location

Visitor Activities
Scenic drives, historic site, interpretive sites, picnicking, and hiking.

Special Features
This corridor of overland routes was utilized by more than 500,000 emigrants as they traveled west from 1840–1870. Of those who started the journey, one in 10 did not complete it. Thousands died along the way, mostly from accidents, cholera, and other diseases. The historic landscape that the trails traverse remains virtually unchanged from what it was during the emigration period. South Pass is the most important landmark on the historic trails and the geological feature that unlocked the Pacific Northwest to overland immigration. It has been designated a National Historic Landmark as a lasting tribute to its historical importance and significance to the settlement of the West. Devil's Gate, another important landmark along the trails, is a spectacular canyon cut through the Rattlesnake Mountains by the Sweetwater River.

Permits, Fees, Limitations
None.

Accessibility
Devil's Gate, Split Rock, and South Pass interpretive sites have wheelchair-accessible paths. Devil's Gate and Split Rock also have accessible vault toilets.

Camping and Lodging
BLM's Atlantic City and Big Atlantic Gulch Campgrounds are located near South Pass, 28 miles south of Lander. In addition, BLM campgrounds are located on the Sweetwater River and Fontenelle Reservoir. Camping and lodging are available in Casper, Lander, Rock Springs, and Green River. Most of these cities are located on Interstate 25 and Interstate 80.

Food and Supplies
Gas and groceries are available in Alcova, Muddy Gap, Lander, and Farson located on State Highways 220, 287 and 28.

First Aid
Emergency services are available through local law enforcement. Hospitals are located in Casper, Lander, and Rock Springs.

A trail marker designates one of the many miles of historic trails that cross Wyoming.
(Jerry Sintz, BLM Utah State Office (retired))

Additional Information

Federal, State, and private lands are intermingled along the various trail routes.
Wyoming's weather can affect highway
travel, particularly in the winter. The best
season of use is May–October. Visitors
are encouraged to contact BLM for detailed information prior to traveling the
historic trail corridor.

Contact Information

National Historic Trails
  Interpretive Center
1501 North Poplar St.
Casper, WY 82601
Tel: (307) 261-7700
Fax: (307) 261-7798
www.wy.blm.gov/nhtic

BLM - Casper Field Office
2987 Prospector Ave.
Casper, WY 82604
Tel: (307) 261-7600
Fax: (307) 234-1525
www.wy.blm.gov/cfo/index.htm

BLM - Lander Field Office
1335 Main Street
P.O. Box 589
Lander, WY 82520
Tel: (307) 332-8400
Fax: (307) 332-8447
www.wy.blm.gov/lfo/index.htm

BLM - Rock Springs Field Office
Highway 191 North
P.O. Box 1869
Rock Springs, WY 82903-1869
Tel: (307) 352-0256
Fax: (307) 352-0329
www.wy.blm.gov/rsfo/index.htm

Activity Codes

Red Gulch/Alkali National Back Country Byway and Red Gulch Dinosaur Tracksite

Location

8 miles east of Greybull, Wyoming.

Description

The 32-mile byway runs along the
western slopes of the majestic Bighorn
Mountains and offers spectacular views,

unique geologic features, abundant
wildlife, and a rich history as an early
transportation route. Along the route
is the Red Gulch Dinosaur Tracksite,
Wyoming's rare Middle Jurassic
discovery site of more than 1,000 dinosaur tracks and 125 dinosaur track-

Hundreds of dinosaur footprints have been found in Red Gulch in the area nicknamed "The Ballroom." *(Jerry Sintz, BLM Utah State Office (retired))*

ways. A developed recreation site near the tracksite includes restrooms, picnic shelters, and an interpretive boardwalk that leads to the rippled, track surface where these 167-million-year-old fossils can be closely examined.

Directions

From Greybull, travel 8 miles east on U.S. Highway 14 to the northern entrance of the byway. Five miles south from this entrance is the Red Gulch Dinosaur Tracksite. The byway continues south for another 27 miles and joins State Highway 31 just north of Hyattville.

Visitor Activities

Picnicking, scenic drives, geologic sightseeing, birdwatching, wildlife viewing, interpretation, and fossil viewing.

Special Features

This is the largest tracksite in Wyoming and one of only a few in the world from this time period. The Red Gulch Dinosaur Tracksite contains thousands of fossil tracks ranging in size from 3–8 inches which were made by two-legged dinosaurs, the most common of which were meat-eaters.

Permits, Fees, Limitations

None.

Accessibility

The Red Gulch Dinosaur Tracksite trail is fully accessible all the way to the tracksite. However, for those uncomfortable walking the sloped, uneven track surface, a flatter accessible track begins next to the main entrance road to the tracksite.

Camping and Lodging

The nearest campground is in Shell (4 miles east of the north byway entrance on U.S. Highway 14). Camping is also available at the Medicine Lodge State Historical Site at the southern end of the byway. The nearest motels are located in Greybull on U.S. Highway 16/20. Lodging is also available in Worland, 38 miles south of Greybull on U.S. Highway 16/20.

Food and Supplies

No services are available at the tracksite. Food and supplies can be found in Greybull or Worland, or in Hyattville, located near the southern end of the byway.

First Aid

No first aid is available at the tracksite. Worland and Cody have hospitals. Cody is 53 miles west of Greybull on U.S. Highway 14/16/20. There also is an emergency care facility approximately 4 miles south of Greybull on U.S. Highway 16/20.

Additional Information

High-clearance vehicles are required for visitors continuing south on the byway beyond the tracksite. The best time of year to visit is May–October. Travel is not recommended during wet weather. Some portions of the road south of the tracksite can accumulate several inches of dust, creating hazardous driving conditions.

Contact Information

BLM - Worland Field Office
101 South 23rd Street
P.O. Box 119
Worland, WY 82401-0119
Tel: (307) 347-5100
Fax: (307) 347-5228
www.wy.blm.gov/wfo/index.htm

Activity Codes

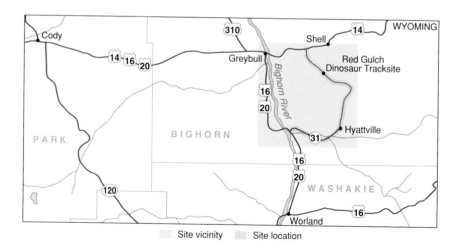

Site vicinity   Site location

South Pass
Historic Mining District

Location
28 miles south of Lander, Wyoming.

Description
The South Pass area is located in the foothills of the Wind River Mountains and is marked by steep hills, stream drainages, and broad slopes with patches of timber. This 30-square-mile area was a focal point for the discovery of gold in 1842 and the resultant 1867 Gold Rush that settled this part of Wyoming. By 1868, about 1,500 people lived in the mining towns of South Pass City, Atlantic City, and Miner's Delight, but by 1872 the boom was over and the area was all but abandoned. BLM maintains the ghost town of Miner's Delight in the area. Other major attractions in the vicinity include the South Pass City State Historic Site, the Wild Iris world-class rock climbing area, four National Historic Trails (Oregon, Mormon Pioneer, California, and Pony Express), the Continental Divide National Scenic Trail, and a Volksmarch Trail.

Directions
From Lander, take U.S. Highway 287 south for 9 miles. Continue south on U.S. Highway 28 for another 19 miles. Turn left on the Atlantic City Road (Fremont County Road 516) and proceed 2 miles to the town of Atlantic City. Other attractions within the district can be accessed from there.

Visitor Activities
Picnicking, hiking, historic site, fishing, big-game hunting, wildlife viewing, scenic drives, mountain biking, horseback riding, cross-country skiing, and snowmobiling.

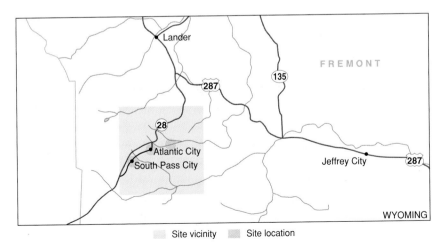

Site vicinity   Site location

Special Features

The best-preserved remnants of Wyoming's early Gold Rush era are found in the South Pass area. This site also is near four National Historic Trails and one National Scenic Trail. (See site description for the Oregon, Mormon Pioneer, California, and Pony Express National Historic Trail Auto Tour.) Visitors may see mule deer, moose, antelope, and elk, although elk are relatively difficult to spot here. Raptors are often seen in the sky.

Permits, Fees, Limitations

Licenses are required for hunting and fishing and are available from licensing agents in Lander. Please consult BLM for motor-vehicle use limitations.

Accessibility

BLM campgrounds have wheelchair-accessible sites and vault toilets.

Camping and Lodging

There are two campgrounds in the area, Big Atlantic Gulch and Atlantic City; both charge a nightly fee, are open from May 15–October 15, and will accommodate campers with tents as well as RVs. Water, picnic tables, fire pits, and vault toilets are provided. From Atlantic City, travel north on Atlantic City Road for 2 miles to signs for the campgrounds. Hotel and motel accommodations are available in Lander (28 miles away) and Atlantic City.

Food and Supplies

Groceries may be obtained in Lander. Restaurants are available in Lander and Atlantic City.

First Aid

Emergency first aid is available from local law enforcement. A hospital is located in Lander.

Additional Information

Elevations in the area average 8,000 feet. Weather conditions in the summer generally produce warm days and cool nights, with a chance of thunderstorms. Snow showers can occur in the spring, fall, and winter. Sustained winds are often present throughout the year. Winter storms can be severe. Visitors should avoid the numerous old hazardous mine shafts that are present in the vicinity.

Contact Information

BLM - Lander Field Office
P.O. Box 589
1335 Main Street
Lander, WY 82520
Tel: (307) 332-8400
Fax: (307) 332-8447
www.wy.blm.gov/lfo/index.htm

Activity Codes

Early miners made their homes in cabins such as this, many of which are still standing in the ghost town of Miner's Delight. *(Jerry Sintz, BLM Utah State Office (retired))*

The majestic South Fork of the Snake River flows for 66 miles across eastern Idaho through high mountain vallleys, rugged canyons, and broad floodplains to its confluence with Henry's Fork. *(BLM)*

Appendix A
Names and Addresses of BLM State and Headquarters Offices

WASHINGTON OFFICE
(National Headquarters)
Bureau of Land Management
Office of Public Affairs
1849 C Street, NW, LS-406
Washington, D.C. 20240
Tel: (202) 452-5125
Fax: (202) 452-5124
www.blm.gov

ALASKA STATE OFFICE
222 West 7th Avenue, #13
Anchorage, AK 99513-7599
Tel: (907) 271-5960
Fax: (907) 271-3684
www.ak.blm.gov

ARIZONA STATE OFFICE
222 North Central Avenue
Phoenix, AZ 85004-2203
Mailing Address:
P.O. Box 555
Phoenix, AZ 85001-0555
Tel: (602) 417-9504
Fax: (602) 417-9424
www.az.blm.gov

CALIFORNIA STATE OFFICE
2800 Cottage Way, Room W-1834
Sacramento, CA 95825
Tel: (916) 978-4610
Fax: (916) 978-4620
www.ca.blm.gov

COLORADO STATE OFFICE
2850 Youngfield Street
Lakewood, CO 80215-7093
Tel: (303) 239-3600
Fax: (303) 239-3934
www.co.blm.gov

EASTERN STATES
(includes FLORIDA, MARYLAND,
MINNESOTA, VIRGINIA, &
WISCONSIN)
7450 Boston Boulevard
Springfield, VA 22153
Tel: (703) 440-1713
Fax: (703) 440-1722
www.es.blm.gov

IDAHO STATE OFFICE
1387 South Vinnell Way
Boise, ID 83709-1657
Tel: (208) 373-4000
Fax: (208) 373-3899
www.id.blm.gov

MONTANA STATE OFFICE
(includes DAKOTAS)
5001 Southgate Drive
Billings, MT 59101
Tel: (406) 896-5004
Fax: (406) 896-5020
www.mt.blm.gov

NEVADA STATE OFFICE

1340 Financial Boulevard
Reno, NV 89502
Mailing Address:
P.O. Box 12000
Reno, NV 89520-0006
Tel: (775) 861-6586
Fax: (775) 861-6601
www.nv.blm.gov

NEW MEXICO STATE OFFICE
(includes OKLAHOMA)

1474 Rodeo Road
Santa Fe, NM 87505
Mailing Address:
P.O. Box 27115
Santa Fe, NM 87502-0115
Tel: (505) 438-7514
Fax: (505) 438-7684
www.nm.blm.gov

OREGON/ WASHINGTON
STATE OFFICE

333 S.W. 1st Avenue
Portland, OR 97201
Mailing Address:
P.O. Box 2965
Portland, OR 97208-2965
Tel: (503) 808-6027
Fax: (503) 808-6280
www.or.blm.gov

UTAH STATE OFFICE

324 South State Street, Suite 301
Salt Lake City, UT 84145
Mailing Address:
P.O. Box 45155
Salt Lake City, UT 84145-0155
Tel: (801) 539-4021
FAX: (801) 539-4013
www.ut.blm.gov

WYOMING STATE OFFICE

5353 Yellowstone Road
Cheyenne, WY 82009
Mailing Address:
P.O. Box 1828
Cheyenne, WY 82003
Tel: (307) 775-6256
Fax: (307) 775-6129
www.wy.blm.gov

Appendix B
Sources of Additional Information

BLM Offices: More information about individual sites and surrounding areas is available through the BLM field office listed with each site description. "Outdoors America," a detailed, interagency U.S. map that depicts recreational activities on Federal lands, is available from BLM Headquarters and State Offices. State recreation maps and selected site brochures are also available from BLM State Offices. (BLM Headquarters and State Office contact information is listed in Appendix A.)

Cooperating and Interpretive Associations: These non-profit organizations support recreational and educational activities on Federal lands by providing information and services to visitors. Information about the Public Lands Interpretive Association and participating information centers may be accessed online at *www.plia.org* or by telephone at 1-877-851-8946. The Association of Partners for the Public Lands supports member cooperating and interpretive associations in the western states, and may be reached online at *www.appl.org* or by telephone at (301) 946-9475.

Other Land Management Agencies: Public lands managed by BLM often are intermingled with lands managed by other Federal, State, or local government agencies. You may wish to check in advance with these other agencies for recreation information

about adjacent lands. Recreation.Gov, a Federal interagency website located at *www.recreation.gov*, permits detailed, online searching of recreation opportunities on Federal lands, and also provides links to State recreation websites.

Contact information for individual Federal land management agencies is:

- National Park Service
  1849 C Street, NW
  Washington, D.C. 20240
  Tel: (202) 208-6843
  www.nps.gov

- U.S. Fish & Wildlife Service
  1849 C Street, NW
  Washington, D.C. 20240
  Tel: (202) 208-4131
  www.fws.gov

- USDA Forest Service
  Recreation, Heritage & Wilderness Resources
  Mail Stop 1125
  1400 Independence Avenue, SW
  Washington, D.C. 20090
  Tel: (202) 205-1706
  www.fs.fed.us/recreation
  www.reserveusa.com

- Bureau of Indian Affairs
  1849 C Street, NW
  Washington, D.C. 20240
  Tel: (202) 219-4150
  www.doi.gov/bureau-indian-affairs.html
  (Note: website may be unavailable indefinitely)

- U.S. Army Corps of Engineers
  Natural Resources Management
  Branch (CECW-ON)
  U.S. Army Corps of Engineers
  Washington, D.C. 20314
  Mail and web inquiries only.
  www.usace.army.mil/public.html
      #Recreation
  www.reserveusa.com

- Bureau of Reclamation
  1849 C Street, NW
  Washington, D.C. 20240
  Tel: (202) 513-0600
  www.usbr.gov/main/programs/
  recreation.html

Index

Italics indicate photographs outside site descriptions.